Medieval Manuscripts in the Digital Age

Medieval Manuscripts in the Digital Age explores one major manuscript repository's digital presence and poses timely questions about studying books from a temporal and spatial distance via the online environment.

Through contributions from a large group of distinguished international scholars, the volume assesses the impact of being able to access and interpret these early manuscripts in new ways. The focus on Parker on the Web, a world-class digital repository of diverse medieval manuscripts, comes as that site made its contents Open Access. Exploring the uses of digital representations of medieval texts and their contexts, contributors consider manuscripts from multiple perspectives including production, materiality, and reception. In addition, the volume explicates new interdisciplinary frameworks of analysis for the study of the relationship between texts and their physical contexts, while centring on an appreciation of the opportunities and challenges effected by the digital representation of a tangible object. Approaches extend from the codicological, palaeographical, linguistic, and cultural to considerations of reader reception, image production, and the implications of new technologies for future discoveries.

Medieval Manuscripts in the Digital Age advances the debate in manuscript studies about the role of digital and computational sources and tools. As such, the book will appeal to scholars and students working in the disciplines of Digital Humanities, Medieval Studies, Literary Studies, Library and Information Science, and Book History.

Benjamin Albritton is the Rare Books Curator at Stanford Libraries. He is a medievalist and musicologist and spent nearly a decade managing digital projects including Parker on the Web, collaborations with the Vatican Library and others, and playing a key role in the inception and development of the International Image Interoperability Framework.

Georgia Henley is Assistant Professor of English at Saint Anselm College and a Junior Fellow in the Andrew W. Mellon Society of Fellows in Critical Bibliography. Previously she held a postdoctoral appointment at Stanford's Center for Spatial and Textual Analysis.

Elaine Treharne is Roberta Bowman Denning Professor of Humanities at Stanford University, and Director of Stanford Text Technologies. She is a medievalist and handmade book expert, currently completing *The Phenomenal Book*. She is a Fellow of the Society of Antiquaries, of the Royal Historical Society, and of the English Association.

Digital Research in the Arts and Humanities

Series Editors: Marilyn Deegan, Lorna Hughes, Andrew Prescott, Harold Short and Ray Siemens

Digital technologies are increasingly important to arts and humanities research, expanding the horizons of research methods in all aspects of data capture, investigation, analysis, modelling, presentation and dissemination. This important series covers a wide range of disciplines with each volume focusing on a particular area, identifying the ways in which technology impacts on specific subjects. The aim is to provide an authoritative reflection of the 'state of the art' in technology-enhanced research methods. The series is critical reading for those already engaged in the digital humanities, and of wider interest to all arts and humanities scholars.

Humans at Work in the Digital Age
Forms of Digital Textual Labor
Edited by Shawna Ross and Andrew Pilsch

Feminist War Games?
Mechanisms of War, Feminist Values, and Interventional Games
Jon Saklofske, Alyssa Arbuckle, and Jon Bath

The Power of Networks
Prospects of Historical Network Research
Edited by Florian Kerschbaumer, Linda von Keyserlingk, Martin Stark and Marten Düring

Transformative Digital Humanities
Challenges and Opportunities
Edited by Mary Balkun and Marta Deyrup

Medieval Manuscripts in the Digital Age
Edited by Benjamin Albritton, Georgia Henley and Elaine Treharne

To learn more about this series please visit: https://www.routledge.com/Digital-Research-in-the-Arts-and-Humanities/book-series/DRAH

Medieval Manuscripts in the Digital Age

Edited by
**Benjamin Albritton, Georgia Henley and
Elaine Treharne**

Routledge
Taylor & Francis Group

LONDON AND NEW YORK

First published 2021
by Routledge
2 Park Square, Milton Park, Abingdon, Oxon OX14 4RN

and by Routledge
52 Vanderbilt Avenue, New York, NY 10017

Routledge is an imprint of the Taylor & Francis Group, an informa business

British Library Cataloguing-in-Publication Data
A catalogue record for this book is available from the British Library

Library of Congress Cataloging-in-Publication Data
A catalog record has been requested for this book

ISBN: 978-0-367-42661-3 (hbk)
ISBN: 978-1-003-00344-1 (ebk)

Typeset in Times New Roman
by Taylor & Francis Books

Contents

List of illustrations   x
List of contributors   xii
Preface   xv
GEORGIA HENLEY

1 Introduction   1

PART 1
Theory and Practice   15

2 What it is to be a digitization specialist: Chasing medieval
   materials in a sea of pixels   17
   ASTRID J. SMITH

3 From the divine to the digital: Digitization as resurrection and
   reconstruction   25
   KERI THOMAS

4 A note on technology and functionality in digital manuscript
   studies   33
   ABIGAIL G. ROBERTSON

5 Ways of seeing manuscripts: Exploring Parker 2.0   37
   ANDREW PRESCOTT

PART 2
Materialities   55

6 A note on Cambridge, Corpus Christi College, 210   57
   ORIETTA DA ROLD

7   Cambridge, Corpus Christi College, 367 Part II: A study in (digital) codicology   64
PETER A. STOKES

8   Pocket change: Cambridge, Corpus Christi College, 383 and the value of the virtual object   74
ANYA ADAIR

9   Rolling with it: Navigating absence in the digital realm   82
SIÂN ECHARD

PART 3
Translation and Transmission   91

10   'Glocal' matters: The Gospels of St Augustine as a codex in translation   93
MATEUSZ FAFINSKI

11   Encyclopaedic notes in Cambridge, Corpus Christi College, 320   100
JOHN J. GALLAGHER

12   Cambridge, Corpus Christi College, 322: Tradition and transmission   112
DAVID F. JOHNSON

13   Cambridge, Corpus Christi College, 41 and 286: Digitization as translation   120
SHARON M. ROWLEY

PART 4
Of Multimedia and the Multilingual   129

14   Fragmentation and wholeness in Cambridge, Corpus Christi College, 16   131
A. JOSEPH McMULLEN

15   Cambridge, Corpus Christi College, 144 and 402: Mercian intellectual culture in pre-Conquest England (and beyond)   142
LINDY BRADY

16   *Philologia* and philology: Allegory, multilingualism, and the Corpus Martianus Capella   154
ELIZABETH BOYLE

17 Remediation and multilingualism in Corpus Christi College, 402 163
   CARLA MARÍA THOMAS

PART 5
Forms of Reading 171

18 Living with books in early medieval England: *Solomon and
   Saturn*, bibliophilia, and the globalist Red Book of Darley 173
   ERICA WEAVER

19 Severed heads and sutured skins 190
   CATHERINE E. KARKOV

20 Books consumed, books multiplied: Martianus Capella, Ælfric's
   Homilies, and the International Image Interoperability
   Framework 205
   ALEXANDRA BOLINTINEANU

21 Making a home for manuscripts on the Internet 216
   MICHELLE R. WARREN

   Index 228

Illustrations

Figures

6.1 The Parker Library, Corpus Christi College, Cambridge, MS
     210, p. 6   62
7.1 Diagram of changes in folio order in CCCC367 Section B   68
7.2 Extract of quire diagrams for current structure of MS 367
     (created with VisColl, using the original manuscript foliation) 68
7.3 Extract of the 'VisColl' visualization of MS 367 with its
     original structure   69
9.1 The Parker Library, Corpus Christi College, Cambridge, MS
     61, f. iv   89
10.1 The Parker Library, Corpus Christi College, Cambridge, MS
     286, f. 2v   98
14.1 The Parker Library, Corpus Christi College, Cambridge, MS
     16II, f. 53v   136
15.1 The Parker Library, Corpus Christi College, Cambridge, MS
     144, f. 1r   148
16.1 The Parker Library, Corpus Christi College, Cambridge, MS
     153, f. 79r   160
17.1 The Parker Library, Corpus Christi College, Cambridge, MS
     402, f. 1r   168
18.1a and b. The Parker Library, Corpus Christi College,
     Cambridge, MS 422, pp. 52–3   177
18.2 Screenshot of CCCC 422 and Parker annotations from
     M. R. James   185
19.1 Humility and Hope with the severed head of Superbia. CCCC
     MS 23, f. 16v   192
19.2 Initial to Psalm 1 (*Beatus vir*). CCCC MS 4, f. 14r   194
19.3 Incipit to the Gospel of Luke. CCCC MS 4, f. 193v   196
19.4 Discord/Heresy dismembered by the Virtues. CCCC MS 23,
     f. 35r   198

21.1   Parker 1.0 Home page, screen capture from archived page:
       https://swap.stanford.edu/20170124002144/https://parker.sta
       nford.edu/parker/actions/page.do?forward=home   217
21.2   Home page image identifications, screen captures from archived
       page: https://web.archive.org/web/20100621231457/http://pa
       rkerweb.stanford.edu/parker/actions/page.do?forward=home   218
21.3   Parker 1.0, screen capture of featured image and navigation   222
21.4   Parker 2.0, screen capture of navigation   224
21.5   The Parker Library, Corpus Christi College, Cambridge, MS
       575, p. 1   226

Tables

7.1   Overview of the contents and structure of MS 367   65
7.2   Contents and structure of MS 367, Section E   66
7.3   Structure of MS 367, Section B   66
11.1 Topics of encyclopaedic notes   108

Contributors

Anya Adair is Assistant Professor in Law and Humanities at the University of Hong Kong. Her present research includes medieval law and literature, the history of the English language, manuscript studies, and digital humanities.

Benjamin Albritton is the Rare Books Curator at Stanford Libraries. He is a medievalist and musicologist and spent nearly a decade managing digital projects including Parker on the Web, collaborations with the Vatican Library and others, and playing a key role in the inception and development of the International Image Interoperability Framework.

Alexandra Bolintineanu is an Assistant Professor in Medieval Digital Studies at the University of Toronto. She studies Old English wonders in digital environments. Her publications address *Beowulf*, *Andreas*, Old English homilies, and illegal typewriters in Eastern Europe.

Elizabeth Boyle is Head of the Department of Early Irish at Maynooth University, Ireland. She was a postdoctoral researcher on the Parker on the Web project at Corpus Christi College, Cambridge, from 2008–2009.

Lindy Brady teaches in the School of History at University College Dublin and studies the multilingual and transcultural early medieval northwest Atlantic region. She previously taught in the Department of English at the University of Mississippi and is the author of *Writing the Welsh Borderlands in Anglo-Saxon England* (Manchester University Press, 2017).

Orietta Da Rold is a University Lecturer and Fellow at St John's College, Cambridge University. She is a member of the Centre for Material Texts and has recently completed a book *From Pulp to Fictions: Paper in Medieval England* for Cambridge University Press.

Siân Echard is Professor in the Department of English Language and Literatures at the University of British Columbia. Her publications in book history include *Printing the Middle Ages* (University of Pennsylvania Press, 2008) and *The Book in Britain: A Historical Introduction*, with Daniel Allington, David A. Brewer, and Stephen Colclough, edited by Zachary Lesser (Wiley-Blackwell, 2019).

Mateusz Fafinski is a Postdoctoral Researcher at Université de Lausanne. Previously, he was a Stanford Text Technologies Postdoctoral Fellow. His PhD at Freie Universität Berlin focused on the uses of the past in early medieval Britain. He researches the nature of historical sources in the digital sphere, mapping medieval manuscripts, and the role of urban space in early medieval societies.

John J. Gallagher teaches English and Divinity at the University of St Andrews where he received a PhD in 2019 on versions of the Bible and biblical textual criticism in exegesis from early medieval England. John's research interests include biblical interpretation, early medieval science and cosmology, and digital humanities.

Georgia Henley is Assistant Professor of English at Saint Anselm College and a Junior Fellow in the Andrew W. Mellon Society of Fellows in Critical Bibliography. Previously she held a postdoctoral appointment at Stanford's Center for Spatial and Textual Analysis. Her current book project considers how interest in the Welsh past influenced book transmission in the Anglo-Welsh borderlands.

David F. Johnson is Professor of English at Florida State University. He specializes in medieval English, Latin, and Germanic literatures, with particular interest in Old English, manuscript studies, and Middle Dutch Arthurian romance. He is co-editor of the journal *Arthurian Literature.*

Catherine E. Karkov is Chair of Art History at the University of Leeds. She is the author or editor of numerous volumes on art, manuscripts, and the material culture of early medieval England.

A. Joseph McMullen is an Assistant Professor of English at Indiana University, Bloomington. He received his PhD in English and Celtic Literatures and Languages from Harvard University in 2015. His work is broadly concerned with medieval literary landscapes and connections between early medieval England and Ireland.

Andrew Prescott is Professor of Digital Humanities in the School of Critical Studies, University of Glasgow. He was a Curator of Manuscripts in the British Library from 1979–2000 and was the principal library contact for *Electronic Beowulf.* He was recently theme leader fellow for the AHRC Digital Transformations theme.

Abigail G. Robertson is an independent scholar who received her PhD from the University of New Mexico in 2018 and worked on digital manuscript projects at the Getty Research Institute from 2018 until 2020. Her current book project considers the art, architecture, and literature born out of the cult of St. Swithun.

Sharon M. Rowley is Professor of English at Christopher Newport University. She is currently working on a National Endowment for the Humanities-funded edition of the Old English version of Bede's *Historia ecclesiastica* with Greg Waite and has articles published in *The Chaucer Review* and *The Cambridge History of Early Medieval English Literature.*

Astrid J. Smith is the Rare Book and Special Collections Digitization Specialist with Stanford University Libraries' Digital Production Group. She is interested in how the materiality of objects is visually translated in pixel form, and has a background in fine art and the humanities.

Peter A. Stokes is *directeur d'études* (approximately 'research professor') in digital and computational humanities applied to historical writing at the École Pratique des Hautes Études—Université PSL, in Laboratoire AOROC, where his research and teaching focuses on combining the fields of palaeography, codicology, digital humanities, and informatics.

Carla María Thomas is Assistant Professor of English at Florida Atlantic University. Her current projects include a book on English and French devotional poetry in post-Conquest England, an essay on inclusivity in college curriculum for medieval studies, and a digital edition of all seven extant copies of *Poema Morale.*

Keri Thomas is an independent academic based in Mid Wales. Her PhD thesis, conducted at Aberystwyth University in partnership with KESS and the National Library of Wales, examined Bourdieu's theory of cultural capital and how this might affect digitization strategies. She is currently focused on the theoretical consequences of replication.

Elaine Treharne is Roberta Bowman Denning Professor of Humanities at Stanford University, and Director of Stanford Text Technologies. She is a medievalist and handmade book expert, currently completing *The Phenomenal Book*. She is a Fellow of the Society of Antiquaries, of the Royal Historical Society, and of the English Association.

Michelle R. Warren is Professor of Comparative Literature at Dartmouth College. She currently leads the collaborative digital research project *Remix the Manuscript: A Chronicle of Digital Experiments* (https://sites.dartmouth.edu/RemixBrut). Her book about Parker Library is forthcoming from Stanford University Press.

Erica Weaver is Assistant Professor of English at the University of California, Los Angeles. Her current book project traces the role of distraction in the development of early medieval literature and literary theory, with a related article—on attentive reading in Aldhelm's *Enigmata* and the 'hermeneutic style'—in *New Literary History.*

Preface

Georgia Henley

For any medieval manuscript researcher who has made the journey to Stanford to study manuscripts amidst sun-washed sandstone and citrus fruit, the juxtaposition between the glaring sunlight of the California coast and medieval Europe's distant remove can feel startling, perhaps even irreconcilable. And yet that is precisely what Parker on the Web has made possible: to illuminate, with bright entrepreneurial spirit, the words and images of the distant past, which can now be drawn up on computer screens anywhere in the world with an internet connection. In this era of increased connectivity, scholars have taken great interest in networks of exchange, influence, and the ideas that bring us together across distances of time and space. The Parker 2.0 conference, held at Stanford in March 2018 as the Stanford Text Technologies Fourth Annual Collegium, celebrated the connectivity that is made possible by technology and knowledge while also critiquing the gaps, problems, and perceptual changes that arise from digitization. Bringing together palaeography, digital humanities, and textual and art-historical methods, the Collegium sought an interdisciplinary framework for analysing the relationship between digital representation and physical object, for articulating the interaction between material and immaterial in manuscript studies. While the Collegium provided the impetus for the present volume, the concept has grown apace, with additional contributions from practitioners and researchers whose work continues to drive the field forward. We, the editors, are deeply grateful to Julia Crick, Suzanne Paul, Anne McLaughlin, and Cat Jarman for their participation in the conference and for giving papers; to Ranjeshni Sharma, Amanda Wilson Bergado, Celena Allen, and Amita Kumar for their tireless aid behind the scenes; to Jonathan Quick, Jeanie Abbott, and Peyton Lepp for their help during the conference; and to the generous funding of Stanford Text Technologies for making our collaboration possible.

1   Introduction

I: Investigating digital archives

Elaine Treharne

Thousands of medieval and early modern scholars have benefitted in the last 15 or so years from the digitization of manuscript materials held by major repositories around the world. While, at first, many of the images uploaded by libraries were not made easily available—paywalls, huge file sizes, and impenetrable catalogues kept all but the most assiduous expert researchers out—recently, we have seen the flourishing of Open Access as a principle guiding many institutions' efforts. Among those repositories that now practise Open Access are the British Library, the Walters Art Gallery, the Schoenberg Institute, the Pierpont Morgan Library, Trinity College, Cambridge, and, perhaps most completely, the Parker Library at Corpus Christi College, Cambridge. This last library has been at the forefront of digitization since the inception of the Parker on the Web project. It is to this project that this volume is dedicated, many of the chapters offered here having their initial instantiation as papers delivered to the Stanford Text Technologies Fourth Collegium in March of 2018, with the theme of Parker 2.0—a celebration of the launch of that digital repository's second 'edition', now in glorious Open Access.

Stanford Text Technologies, which hosted the Collegium, is directed by Elaine Treharne, and is in its seventh year of operation.[1] The project is invested in describing, evaluating, and investigating all information technologies from 70,000 BCE to the present day, but with a special focus on the handmade book. The project is supported by the Denning fund, Stanford's Dean of Research, the Stanford School of Engineering, and the Center for Spatial and Textual Analysis. It has held, to date (2019), five major Collegia, published a variety of books and articles,[2] and assisted the work of a range of graduate, postdoctoral, and faculty fellows from the USA and internationally. Four major funded projects have been run under Text Technologies' auspices: the NEH-funded 'Stanford Global Currents';[3] the CyberInitiative-funded 'CyberText Technologies';[4] the multi-funded East-West Text Technologies that brings Western Sinologists into conversation with Chinese and Japanese scholars (to date) in thinking through issues of the history of the global book in manuscript, print and digital forms; and the new 'Stanford Ordinary People Extraordinary Stories' (SOPES), which brings personal archives and ephemera under the scholarly spotlight.

This volume, *Medieval Manuscripts in the Digital Age*, is one of the first of its kind to focus on scholarship that has been completed, in almost all cases, on medieval manuscripts seen from a distance. Scholars at the Collegium were provided with a single manuscript to investigate, and participants were paired up for the respective sessions. In planning this gathering, we wanted all the scholars to work with the digital images online, and while we were not expecting technical investigation or commentary on the metadata or the potential of digital tools, we were keen to see what scholars from a range of disciplines could learn from looking at manuscripts provided to them. Disciplines represented include Archaeology, Archival and Library Studies, Art History, Book History, Celtic Languages and Literature, Digital Humanities, Manuscript Studies, Medieval English Language and Literature, History, Law, Musicology, and Textual Editing. Many of the chapters here examine the manuscripts through 'traditional' and disciplinary lenses; some, as will be discussed below, focus on general observations about the ways in which scholars perceive and interpret the virtual world of medieval manuscripts—the online dimension.

Interesting information on the Parker manuscripts emerged in every exploration, whether that was the status of marginal annotations; the tiny details hidden from the naked eye, but available through Parker on the Web's zoom tool; the surprising lack of attention paid to less well-known books; the results that could be uncovered through combining digital tools; the importance of textual detail for our understanding of literary transmission; and the significance of size and heft to the way in which we conceive of books' functions in the medieval and early modern periods. Every contribution here owes a debt to the imaginers and imagers of Parker on the Web, since the ability to view these unique materials—even to the necessarily fragmented form of the medieval book—is made possible through this platform. The digital environment makes accessible textual artefacts that are otherwise at a physical distance—too expensive or time-consuming to get to; or not available to researchers any more for a variety of reasons to do with conservation and preservation. The ways in which we interact with these material remains of earlier cultures of literacy are mediated by the affordances of the digital, and while we are conscious that not every reader can reliably access Parker on the Web, or the Internet more broadly, these chapters often showcase the manuscript in its new dimension—online and through the metadata provided by the Parker on the Web team for whom manuscript scholars are grateful, and with whom we are glad to collaborate.

Some of the chapters in this volume focus very much on the fundamental point of interest for the particular author. Lindy Brady's work on Cambridge,

Corpus Christi College, 144, for example, examines the detail of gloss and textual transmission. In this kind of investigative scholarship, the medium through which the manuscript is perceived is effectively elided, because the scholars' interest is entirely in the text, not the vessel of that text. Yet, the digital allows persistent and repetitive attention to detail that was not always possible in the medium of photography or other forms of facsimile. Moreover, access to the digital repository, for those with connectivity, is a 24-hours-a-day, 7-days-a-week privilege—quite unlike the restricted opening hours of major scholarly libraries; and one can examine tiny details alone in any room or environment, without scrutiny from a librarian. What difference does it make to future scholarship to be able to read a digital manuscript in bed or on the bus? What differences are created by the type of device upon which one accesses online manuscripts? These questions require detailed attention in the years to come, though they did not form the core of questions put to the authors in this volume. Having completed the editing of the volume, it has become clear that such new modes of research are always present in the thoughtfulness given to digital cultural heritage by interested browsers and these new modes do invite reflection and evaluation. Here, Keri Thomas, Catherine Karkov, and Michelle Warren, in particular, carefully address the digital platform of study. Elsewhere in the past few years, scholars such as Bridget Whearty, Dot Porter, Barbara Bordalejo, Dorothy Kim and Jesse Stommel[5] have initiated important conversations about digital scholarship with particular reference to the medieval era and its manuscripts. Their work is demonstrating that scholarship within the Digital Humanities has the ability to be both disruptive to, and reflective of, earlier periods in the long history of text technological transformation. Among publications and projects that have promoted the uses of digital and computational tools and methods in the pursuit of humanistic research in medieval manuscript studies are the journals *Digital Medievalist* and *Digital Philology: A Journal of Medieval Cultures*; the AHRC-funded *The Production and Use of English Manuscripts from 1060 to 1220*; the AHRC-funded project *Manuscripts of the West Midlands*, led by Wendy Scase; the ERC-funded *DigiPal*, by Peter Stokes with Stewart Brookes; *French Renaissance Paleography*; and *Late Medieval English Scribes* by Linne Mooney and Estelle Stubbs.[6] These projects, which are all fully functioning (unlike so many projects that have dead links, suggesting they were never finished or they have not been maintained), also produced print volumes of research that emanated from the digital scholarship undertaken. Still other projects are reviewed at the Medieval Academy of America site, though it is far from complete.[7] Ongoing work takes place in many institutions, as at Stanford Text Technologies, for example; or at the University of Toronto's 'Old Science New Books' Lab; or at the University of Cambridge's Manuscripts Lab, and each new round of centrally funded grants from agencies and foundations highlights new projects getting underway in all historical periods, and including all types of textual objects.[8]

Digital catalogues, establishing corpora of manuscripts (like *Manuscripts of the West Midlands*), online projects focused on palaeography and codicology, and other major projects promising innovation in textual critical work have tended to dominate the broad field of digital manuscript studies in the last 20 years. Millions in grants from major external funding bodies have facilitated the success, or often partial success, of scholars' research projects since the late 1990s. Having established online transcriptions or editions of key works in literature and history, researchers have also begun examining the ways in which new technologies, especially in the fields of multispectral imagery, DNA analyses, and image manipulation can lend themselves to furthering knowledge about the ways in which medieval books were produced.[9] In many respects, while these are interesting and lead to some valuable discoveries, there is also a tendency in this work (as there was at the beginnings of print in the fifteenth century and the beginnings of photography in the nineteenth century) to focus on those books and texts that are already among the best known. In literary terms, Early English poetic books, highly illuminated manuscripts, Chaucer texts, and *Piers Plowman*, have attracted by far the most attention, and there is a danger (if 'danger' it is) that with every new technological development, the same manuscripts get the new treatment.[10] Moreover, as digitization moves on apace, with whole collections being digitized and disseminated online (like Parker's at Corpus Christi College, Cambridge, or the French-English manuscripts from 700 to 1200),[11] more and more primary sources are available to scholars and the interested general reader, with dramatically varying frameworks of interpretation, though, happily, increasingly standardized imaging metadata.[12] Yet that which is online and openly accessible is usually from the larger repositories, and currently estimated to be only around 2%[13] of extant holdings in the public cultural heritage sector. Many other libraries of all types and sizes around the world with less well-known collections have no digital outlet and no likelihood of digitizing their materials in the coming years. Should funders prioritize support to libraries that are smaller, or whose holdings are in greater danger than, say, national libraries and archives, or major university libraries? Should the priority for administrators of libraries and archives, no matter where, be more imaging, more uploading of holdings into digital repositories?

A few years ago, Andrew Prescott sagely commented:

> We have assumed that digitisation is a service provided by information professionals for a wide community of users, including scholars, rather than that it is a tool by which scholars, curators, conservators, computer scientists and other disciplines can jointly explore the complexities of manuscripts and other cultural artefacts from the past. We have envisaged digitisation as a simple once and for all process, similar to photography or microfilming. As a result we haven't stopped to think about how we are approaching the way in which we undertake digitisation and considered whether our expensive digitisation projects are fulfilling their potential.[14]

Prescott made these comments almost six years ago, but they ring true at the beginning of 2020, too. There have been fascinating projects that employ new technologies to advance knowledge of texts or manuscripts. An example of exciting editorial and investigative research that involved the digital reconstruction of early English poetry from manuscript is Mary Rambaran-Olm's work on the tenth-century Exeter Book (Exeter Cathedral Library 3501);[15] the interactive apps that are in development for Chaucer's *Canterbury Tales* also have potential to engage students and the general public.[16] These are again focused on textual explication. Other large-scale projects aim to capitalize on the digital medium to provide texts, translations, and multimedia resources that bring to public attention the rich and diverse range of versions and adaptations available for study and teaching; most notable among these efforts for medievalists is Barrington and Hsy's *Global Chaucers*.[17] It is perhaps not surprising that this canonical author's most canonical work attracts substantial attention globally. These digital projects demonstrate the potential of the medium for bringing a wide range of medieval works and adaptations to broader attention, inspiring further scholarship.

The 20 chapters in this volume tackle both the canonical and the less well-known manuscript or author. Some of these manuscripts are among the best known in the Parker Collection; Cambridge, Corpus Christi College, 286, for example (in Mateusz Fafinski's chapter), is the Gospel-book reputed to have been brought by St Augustine in his conversion of the early English in AD 597; and Carla María Thomas evaluates Cambridge, Corpus Christi College, 402—the *Ancrene Wisse*. But most contributors have worked on manuscripts that are familiar only to scholars working on very specialist topics, and they bring to light, here, new findings derived from close examination of the digitized manuscripts. In the light of the discussion above about the current status of digital approaches to manuscript studies, all the chapters here represent fresh approaches to the manuscripts upon which authors have focused, but these approaches are bibliocentric, focused on the digital object of the medieval book, even as it is split into its individual folios through the process of digitization. Astrid Smith expounds in her chapter on the practice of digitizing textual objects, and the ways in which these practices can be intellectually conceived, so that readers can appreciate the time, patience, and artistry required to produce images many simply take for granted now. Complementing this, the three other chapters in the first part of the volume, 'Theory and practice', take us through theoretical explorations of the practices of the digital environment: what that means for a scholarly and more general understanding of how affective images are (Keri Thomas and Abigail Robertson); and through a set of careful reflections upon the history and reception of manuscript studies, manuscript collecting and recent research (Andrew Prescott). These four initial chapters set up the contexts of theory and practice for the following detailed explorations of individual manuscripts in the volume, which demonstrate the different disciplinary methods of approaching early textual materials in digital format.

The following chapters are divided into themed parts that reflect the scholarly methodology employed in working with the digital manuscript. In the second part, 'Materialities', the authors are particularly concerned with how the digitized book can be read for its physical attributes, utilizing the specialist skills of codicology (how to determine the physical make-up of the codex) and palaeography (how to identify, read, date, and localize ancient handwriting). Orietta Da Rold tackles the substrate of paper in her note on Cambridge, Corpus Christi College, 210, but her principal question is how the digital medium facilitates the work of the codicologist. In his thorough analysis of Cambridge, Corpus Christi College, 367 Part II, Peter Stokes not only minutely examines the materiality of the digital manuscript for codicological cues but he also employs VisColl—a newly developed visualization tool for codicologists.[18] Anya Adair's contribution focuses on the twelfth-century legal manuscript, Cambridge, Corpus Christi College, 383, and its part in the larger collection within a digital repository. She considers the physical attributes of the manuscript, as they are displayed in an online medium: colour, size, and heft. Her important observations highlight both that which is present virtually and that which is absent. The latter is the focus of the fourth chapter in 'Materialities', Siân Echard's investigation of Cambridge, Corpus Christi College, 61—a manuscript best known for its frontispiece depicting Geoffrey Chaucer, but which exemplifies multiple blank spaces within its body that are seldom the focus of intellectual study.

Filling in the blanks of medieval scholarship is often a case of detailed scrutiny of clues left within the manuscript text itself. What sources do texts seem to rely upon? Are those sources extant within other books? How do medieval texts get transmitted through rewriting or wholesale translation? In the third part, 'Translation and Transmission', the four contributions zoom in to the detail of how text and meaning is carried across manuscripts, or transferred from reader to reader ('transfer' and 'translate' are both ultimately derived from Latin 'transferre') and evinced through words, glosses, and readers' marks. In Mateusz Fafinski's chapter, he shows how two seemingly unrelated manuscripts in the Parker Collection (Cambridge, Corpus Christi College, 286 and 41) can be fruitfully read in unison and alongside other textual artefacts. This is what digital scholarship permits: a serendipity in the bringing together of manuscripts and written records where the discoveries can emerge as a view-between objects. Also highlighting the discoveries to be found from close examination of manuscripts that might not normally form the focus of a planned research agenda is John J. Gallagher, whose work centres on Cambridge, Corpus Christi College, 320. He notes that from scrupulous study so much can still be done when one cannot spend time with the physical object itself. This important observation and demonstration of close contextualized reading is reinforced by David F. Johnson's chapter on the eleventh-century version of Gregory the Great's *Dialogues* in Cambridge, Corpus Christi College, 322 and its signs of use. He discusses his own visits to the Parker Library and demonstrates how being able to study texts online permits easy access to more than one manuscript simultaneously—something usually not allowed within reading rooms. He also shows how other digital resources and tools aid in the scholarly effort to detect later readers' interventions. Later uses of manuscripts form the focus of Sharon M. Rowley's analysis that complements Fafinski's, particularly. Rowley thinks through the issue of 'digitization as translation', with special emphasis on Cambridge, Corpus Christi College, 41 and 286. Here, she considers the dissemination of key religious texts, their *mise-en-page* and function as repository of texts—a function that parallels the Parker 2.0 virtual repository itself.

Translation, carrying across and through media and language, is evaluated in the four chapters of the fourth part of the book, 'Of Multimedia and the Multilingual'. Rather than thinking of transmission per se—the movement and carrying across of texts through a long history of dissemination—these chapters evaluate whole manuscripts, and complete components of the book, as the digital object allows us to do at (relative) leisure; and they reflect on what it means to move between areas of the manuscript page that are usually treated separately by textual scholars. In A. Joseph McMullen's chapter on Matthew Paris's engaging corpus of work, he emphasizes (from the distance of his desk) the study of the whole by incorporating marginal and authorial evidence into his evaluation of how Cambridge, Corpus Christi College, 16 manifests Paris's vision of history and geography. Lingering on images as well as words, and on ideas of wholeness, McMullen offers an appreciation of the benefits of the digital to a holistic account of the extant record. The holistic also concerns Lindy Brady in her complex account of the glossing and literary traditions exemplified by Cambridge, Corpus Christi College, 144 and 402. Her point of contact becomes that of regional cultural legacy—the demonstration of learning and a specific linguistic tradition within the Mercian context, a surprise that emerges from putting two unrelated manuscripts together for examination—something that would rarely, if ever, happen in a reading room visit when scholars' time is pressured to complete particular tasks in the few days set aside for first-hand manuscript research. The linguistic and intellectual contexts of Martianus Capella in the ninth-century Cambridge, Corpus Christi College, 153 are Elizabeth Boyle's main foci. As a contributor to the original Parker on the Web team of describers, Boyle builds on her work there to offer a fuller description of the manuscript, demonstrating the living medium of the digital environment—that often, information is not static; it is dynamic. Such an expanded and updated description is also a reminder of the significance of good interpretative materials for digital repositories, which often rely upon catalogues that are now a century or more in age. Boyle's new work on Martianus Capella supports the view that allegorical literature was a means of promoting grammatical knowledge and expands scholarly understanding of the sophistication of early medieval reading practices, just as it expands understanding of the different ways in which scholars can approach manuscripts in digital form. 'Remediation and multilingualism in Corpus Christi College 402' by Carla María Thomas completes this part with a call for an understanding of the importance of remediation, seeing an analogy between the technological re-formation of knowledge in digital and physical modes and the linguistic reformulation of a text like *Ancrene Wisse*, which exists in Latin, French, and English. Placing these linguistic variants side-by-side as scholars are able to do with manuscripts from different repositories, using interfaces like Mirador, will yield new interpretative possibilities for the milieux of production and for the ways in which these texts and their manuscripts can be read.

'Forms of Reading' is the final part of the volume and it is opened with Erica Weaver's detailed and expansive discussion of how *Solomon and Saturn* in Cambridge, Corpus Christi College, 422 and its numerous analogues can be effectively read and understood in an age of efforts to open up early medieval studies to a much more inclusive audience—just as the best digital repositories and projects also seek to make information, knowledge, and participation open to all. Weaver reimagines readerly interactions with the manuscript to bring alive the ways in which those who encounter texts respond to the physical object they see before them (and, incidentally, I might add, reminding us that even an encounter with a digital text is mediated by a deskful of devices and tools; and that digital texts are themselves physical objects, even if their virtuality seems misleadingly immaterial). Conscious of the lenses by which one studies the manuscript, Catherine Karkov reads 'Severed heads and sutured skins' in her chapter on Cambridge, Corpus Christi College, 4 and 23. Again, finding commonalities is the serendipitous consequence of putting two manuscripts together that would rarely be combined outside scholarship through the digital medium; here, Karkov is made keenly aware of the physical manuscript substrate of skin—its damage, and its representation of damage through illustrations of dismemberment and wounding. Karkov's argument is reminiscent of the dismemberment of digitization itself, as manuscripts are displayed folio by folio, and, in the case of the Parker on the Web original project's work, manuscripts were sometimes disbound in order to be imaged and conserved. That images are displayed as individual files and that digital books are not simply videos of readers moving through the manuscripts, but separate static screens of one or two folios, is hardly suprising to scholars and browsers of the online realm. How these files can be encoded and made available across repositories has been the task of the International Image Interoperability Framework (IIIF), and this is one of the areas of investigation for Alexandra Bolintineanu in her chapter, the penultimate in the volume. Focusing on Cambridge, Corpus Christi College, 162 and (like Boyle earlier) 153, Bolintineanu is concerned to reflect upon the encounters that readers have with the technologies of text through the approaches of wonder, consumption, and community. Working outwards from Martianus Capella and Old English homilies, where nourishment and the miraculous form part of the discourse of creation, Bolintineanu finds these early medieval ideas of the consumption of words to be equally applicable to encountering manuscripts digitally in the Parker on the Web platform. The language of consumption engages designers of tools like IIIF, and reminds scholars of the nurturing of the intellect through the ingestion of learning. If books are cerebral nourishment, then for many readers books represent a sanctuary, a place of comfort, a home. In the final chapter in the volume by Michelle R. Warren, she discusses 'Making a home for manuscripts on the internet', a chapter that beautifully forms a coda to the chapters in the volume: final words, for now, on Parker on the Web. Warren provides a detailed reading of the first Parker on the Web site alongside the second—Parker 2.0—to demonstrate the fascinating ways in which these websites reflect the evolution of scholarship through the online medium. She considers what makes us feel at home on these sites—what is comfortable and known, what is disorientating. From the typeface to the layout of the Parker digital repository, Warren thinks through the language and framing of the digitized manuscript's home. She contemplates copyright, Open Access, and how to navigate the site, providing a context for her own work and the work of the 20 authors that have preceded her in this volume. Warren reminds us of the ecology of the digital, its history embedded in its physical manifestation and in its online instantiation, the site's use and usefulness, and this strange and yet familiar workspace we inhabit when we click into a manuscript.

Strange and yet familiar: the manuscripts discussed in *Medieval Manuscripts in the Digital Age* are among some of the best known and some of the least studied medieval books. That those with the resources might access them any time of day is one thing; that we can understand them better as a result of these chapters is undoubted. This volume offers a wide-ranging and cogent set of new readings of old textual objects that have been recast in virtual form. The editors hope that the chapters assembled here, the questions asked, and the provocations offered, will inspire further scholarship on medieval manuscripts and their contents and move the field forward in interesting and useful ways. The book's energizing blend of reflection, suggestion, criticism, investigation, theorization and demonstration of advanced scholarship should provide food for thought for every medievalist, and we look forward to new conversation and enhanced understanding of how the digital environment is changing scholarship—we hope—for the better.

II: Parker on the Web

Benjamin Albritton

When Corpus Christi College, Cambridge, and Stanford Libraries first began the collaborative effort that has become Parker on the Web, the goals were focused on providing access to the unique collection of manuscripts left to the college by Matthew Parker, Archbishop of Canterbury (1559–75), the result of a particular type of collecting at a particular period in history. Christopher de Hamel had recently taken the post of Donnelly Fellow Librarian at the

Parker and was eager to celebrate the collection when a fortuitous connection was made by Corpus alumnus Andrew M. Thompson between his former college and Stanford Librarian Michael Keller. At the time, Keller was eager to bring Stanford's digital expertise to the service of scholarship in a variety of cultural heritage projects and, in 2004, the idea of Parker on the Web was born. It would take five years, an additional partner in Cambridge University Library, and the generous support of the Andrew W. Mellon Foundation and the Gladys Krieble Delmas Foundation, to bring the initial project to fruition, but in October 2009 Parker on the Web 1.0 was launched with full digitization of 556 manuscripts, a comprehensive bibliography of available scholarship for each manuscript, links to the original manuscript descriptions from M. R. James's catalogue, and a TEI-encoded version of that catalogue with updates and summaries from a team of bibliographers who worked on the project.

The creation of metadata describing digital manuscript images, and the role it plays across platforms intended for multiple types of users, continues to be debated in a variety of venues. Parker on the Web 1.0 started with a catalogue that was a hundred years old and added enhancements that sat uneasily alongside M. R. James's descriptions, sometimes leading to puzzling factual discrepancies in a single catalogue record. In the initial site, distinctions between old and new data were highlighted by graphic interventions that allowed a user to see what originally derived from James and what had been layered on more recently. That graphic distinction, unfortunately, became difficult to sustain across platforms. It also imagined a static update tied to scholarly activity between 2006 and 2009, and did not take into account ongoing discoveries, updates, and corrections that would inevitable come as more people interacted with the Parker manuscripts. Parker 2.0 continues to search for ways to use the core James descriptions, but updated that with scholarly accretions that can expand over time. The first step in accomplishing this was to confront the differences between a web delivery platform and a published manuscript catalogue. This confrontation, played out again and again by digital manuscript repositories worldwide, raises critical questions: how much metadata is needed to find an object? Can we present differing amounts of information to different types of users? Can we find a balance between structured information that supports newer initiatives like linked data or modern web platforms and the more narrative, detailed descriptions that are familiar to scholars from print publication? These questions were not close to being settled at the time this volume was produced, and the mixed responses to metadata in Parker 2.0 reflect a larger issue across the digitized manuscript landscape. Fortunately, structured data can be reconfigured, rearranged, updated, and re-presented in new discovery frameworks without loss. In time, scholarly and library communities will determine new best practices that can be adopted and to which well-curated metadata stored in widely-used standards can be made to adhere, even if current practices are somewhat fluid.

The initial Parker 1.0 platform was a custom-built piece of software that supported searching of the bibliography, searching of the manuscript descriptions, and some curated browsing of various aspects of the catalogue (authors, titles, date ranges, incipits, etc.). It contained a bespoke image viewer that supported zoom and pan, as well as a simulated page-turning environment that allowed users to navigate the book as if they were turning the pages. This software was useful but expensive to maintain, was not used by any other projects, was fully understood by a small handful of software engineers at Stanford, and thus required a level of support that guaranteed that it could not be sustainable in the long term. This was accounted for in the initial project plan (most web applications have a limited currency, with a lifespan of 3–5 years before changing technologies and design patterns render them stale), with a commitment by the project to change platforms at least once within an initial ten-year timeframe.

At the time it launched, in 2009, Parker on the Web 1.0 compared favourably to similar projects of that vintage like *e-codices* or the *Roman de la Rose Digital Library*. It was unique in that Parker on the Web represented a complete library digitization project, where every manuscript in the library was digitized in full and offered on the web. These have become somewhat more common in the intervening decade, but Parker was one of the first projects to attempt to provide complete digital coverage of a library's holdings. However, when it launched, Parker on the Web was a two-tiered application. Because of funding commitments between the partners, an institutional subscription service was offered for full access to the high-resolution images and to some features of the website, like the bibliography for each manuscript. A free version of the site was also available that allowed access to lower-resolution images and a restricted suite of functions. This meant that, for many scholars, the full potential of the Parker digitization had not yet been unlocked.

In 2017, with the introduction of Parker 2.0, we were finally able to offer the rich Parker data to the world for no fee. This was accomplished by migrating from a tailor-made, non-sustainable, custom platform to a more generalized digital library framework. In addition, the International Image Interoperability Framework (IIIF), sparked in part by the initial scholarly desire to compare materials in Parker on the Web with materials in other digital sites, had reached a level of maturity which meant we could make that a core feature of Parker 2.0. This interoperability standard opens up some paradigm-changing possibilities for digital manuscript study: it makes each manuscript a portable digital object, one that can be displayed, analysed, enhanced, and annotated in any compatible environment. Users are no longer restricted to the Parker portal to access and work with these materials, though Parker 2.0 still maintains a function as a location for presenting comprehensive information about these manuscripts. In addition, IIIF allows the use of a suite of open source software tools for comparison across repositories, for annotation, and in the near future, for scholarly enhancement of these digital resources. We have already seen Parker materials integrated into European aggregation sites like Biblissima and DigiPal for comparative palaeographic study. Parker manuscripts have been included in From the Page and other transcription tools for crowd- and club-sourced transcription and have been subject to machine-learning feature extraction through the Global Currents project managed by Elaine Treharne. In more and more ways, the digitized Parker manuscripts have grown beyond just a Parker on the Web environment and are becoming dynamic objects used in a variety of ways across a variety of projects. This is the type of access that originally sparked the Parker on the Web project in 2003 and 2004, but it poses a challenge to a user base that operates in a period that is torn between new possibilities and an older notion that a manuscript website is analogous to a published catalogue, in the sense of being a resource one 'goes to' in order to reference a curated set of information about some set of objects.

This paradigm shift has not been fully absorbed by the scholarly communities who engage with Parker material. The chapters in this volume display an ongoing tension between newly available methodologies and a desire for a highly curated experience, between the role of scholar as explorer in uncharted territory and of Parker 2.0 as reliable or omniscient guide. One can read, in the subtext of some of these critical engagements, an anxiety about control of information and othering of responsibility for data navigation that highlights some of the challenges we face when familiar information-management borders begin to erode. These are challenges faced by institutions that hold cultural heritage materials, by those who study those materials and produce new knowledge, by those who engage with scholarly publication in general, and by the producers of sites like Parker 2.0, who cross all of those categories. These challenges pose new questions for us all. How do we curate new information about digital manuscripts as it begins to be produced in born-digital forms and integrated back into online platforms through a variety of sources? How do we credit contributors to a site like Parker 2.0 fairly as that new information becomes part of the graph of knowledge that orbits each manuscript? Do future iterations of Parker simply supply the raw data to be used by others, or is there a central role for a site like this to aggregate information and provide a curated experience of the materials? Is there an imagined other who is responsible for what appears on the site, or are we—as a community of scholars, librarians, technologists, casual viewers—engaged in a new model for managing a growing abundance digital information about these objects?

Many of these questions are raised here, fewer have been attempted to be answered. Parker 2.0 finds us at a critical juncture between web portal as a primary locus of activity and engagement, on the one hand, and web portal as one venue for accessing portable data that can be taken elsewhere and worked upon in the tool(s) of the scholar's choice. The digital objects have already become a primary source for scholarly research, providing a subset of information held in the richly encoded physical object, but a subset which can be queried in both traditional and non-traditional ways, as the chapters in this volume demonstrate. There remains a world of opportunity for critical inquiry into the ways the digital resources are used in research and, moreover, how the portability afforded by IIIF, new methods of engaging digital images, and new mechanisms for publishing scholarship linked to the digitized manuscripts, may slowly alter the ways we think about a project like Parker 2.0: from just a site we go to in order to learn more about a given manuscript, to a source for different kinds of data about a manuscript which can then be assembled, engaged with, distorted, manipulated, and represented elsewhere.

Notes

1 https://texttechnologies.stanford.edu/
2 Including, for example, Elaine Treharne and Claude Willan, *Text Technologies: A History*, Stanford Text Technologies (Stanford: Stanford University Press, 2019); and Elaine Treharne and Greg Walker, eds., *Textual Distortion* (Woodbridge: Boydell and Brewer, 2017).
3 https://globalcurrents.stanford.edu/
4 https://cybertext.stanford.edu/
5 Bridget Whearty, 'Adam Scriveyn in Cyberspace: Loss, Labor, Ideology, and Infrastructure in Interoperable Reuse of Digital Manuscript Metadata', in *Meeting the Medieval in a Digital World*, ed. Matthew Davis, Ece Turnator, and Tamsyn Mahoney-Steel (Leeds: Medieval Institute Publications/Arc Medieval Press, 2018), available at: https://orb.binghamton.edu/english_fac/5/; Dorothy Porter at www.dotporterdigital.org/; Barbara Bordalejo, 'Digital vs. Analogue Textual Scholarship or the Revolution is Just in the Title', in *Digital Philology: A Journal of Medieval Cultures* 7 (2018): 7–28: https://doi.org/10.1353/dph.2018.0001; and B. Bordalejo and P. Robinson, eds., Special section on *Social Digital Scholarly Editing* in *Digital Scholarship in the Humanities* (formerly *Literary and Linguistic Computing*) 31 (2016): 782–919; and Dorothy Kim and Jesse Stommel, eds., *Disrupting the Digital Humanities* (Earth: Punctum Books, 2018).
6 *Digital Medievalist*: https://journal.digitalmedievalist.org/ (2003—); *Digital Philology*: https://www.press.jhu.edu/journals/digital-philology-journal-medieval-cultures; Orietta Da Rold, Takako Kato, Mary Swan, and Elaine Treharne, *The Production and Use of English Manuscripts, 1060 to 1220* (Leicester, 2010; Stanford, 2018): https://em1060.stanford.edu/; Wendy Scase, *Manuscripts of the West Midlands*: https://www.dhi.ac.uk/mwm/; Peter Stokes, *DigiPal: Digital Resources and Database of Palaeography, Manuscript Studies and Diplomatic*: www.digipal.eu/; Carla Zecher, *French Renaissance Paleography*: https://paleography.library.utoronto.ca/; Linne Mooney, Simon Horobin, and Estelle Stubbs, *Late Medieval English Scribes*: https://www.medievalscribes.com. The focus in this footnote's references is to Western European manuscript projects, because those are predominantly the manuscripts collected by Archbishop Matthew Parker, upon which the Parker on the Web repository is based. For Parker's collecting, see R. I. Page, *Matthew Parker and his Books* (Kalamazoo, MI: Medieval Institute Publications, 1993). Many other digital projects and publications focus on manuscript traditions in countries and regions, such as Korea, China, North Africa, Israel, Turkey, Eastern Europe, India, and Bhutan. See, as an excellent and recent starting point, the essays in Bryan C. Keene, ed., *Toward a Global Middle Ages: Encountering the World through Illuminated Manuscripts* (Los Angeles: Getty Publications, 2019).
7 http://mdr-maa.org/
8 See above, footnote 1; Alexandra Gillespie, Old Science New Books Lab: https://oldbooksnewscience.com/; Orietta Da Rold, The Manuscripts Lab: https://www.english.cam.ac.uk/manuscriptslab/

 9 See, *inter alia*, Bill Endres, *Digitizing Medieval Manuscripts: The St Chad Gospels, Materiality, Recoveries, and Representation in 2D & 3D* (Amsterdam: ARC Press, 2019); and Myriah Williams, 'The Black Book of Carmarthen: Minding the Gaps', *National Library of Wales Journal* 36 (2017): 357–410: https://www.llyfrgell.cymru/fileadmin/fileadmin/docs_gwefan/amdanom_ni/cylchgrawn_llgc/cgr_erth_XXXVI_rhif_4_2017_1.pdf; Timothy L. Stinson, 'Knowledge of the Flesh: Using DNA Analysis to Unlock Bibliographical Secrets of Medieval Parchment', *Papers of the Bibliographical Society of America* 103 (2009): 435–53; Elaine Treharne, Mohamed Cheriet, Benjamin Albritton, Celena Allen *et al.*, *Stanford Global Currents* (2014—): https://globalcurrents.stanford.edu

10 For example, Kevin Kiernan, ed., and Emil Iacob, dev, *Electronic Beowulf*, 4th edition: https://ebeowulf.uky.edu/; Estelle Stubbs, Michael Pidd, Orietta Da Rold, Simon Horobin, and Claire Thomson with Linda Cross, eds., The *Norman Blake Editions* of Chaucer's *Canterbury Tales* (University of Sheffield, 2013—): https://www.chaucermss.org/; Hoyt Duggan, Timothy L. Stinson, and Thorlac Turville-Petre, *Piers Plowman Electronic Archive* (Society for Early English and Norse Electronic Texts, 1994–2019): http://piers.chass.ncsu.edu/. Thanks to Andrew Prescott for many conversations on these important points.

11 London, British Library, and Paris, Bibliothèque Nationale with the Polonsky Foundation: https://www.bl.uk/press-releases/2018/november/polonsky-project-medieval-manuscripts-website-launch

12 Thanks to the collaborative IIIF initiative—the International Image Interoperability Framework (https:iiif.io/) which allows images to be shared between repositories, and read alongside each other, or otherwise manipulated.

13 This is a best guess, communicated to me by Benjamin Albritton, and based on his extensive work with IIIF and digital libraries internationally.

14 Andrew Prescott, Keynote Lecture, 'From Glass Case to Cyber-space: Chaucerian Manuscripts across Time / Syrffio'r silff: hynt a helynt llawysgrifau Chaucer' at the National Library of Wales /Llyfrgell Genedlaethol Cymru, 14–16 April 2014, available at: https://medium.com/@Ajprescott/keynote-lecture-for-the-conference-from-glass-case-to-cyber-space-chaucerian-manuscripts-across-72fb56d25980. I should like to thank Professor Prescott for sending me a copy of this lecture.

15 M. R. Rambaran-Olm, *John the Baptist's Prayer or The Descent into Hell from the Exeter Book: Text, Translation and Critical Study*, Anglo-Saxon Studies 21 (Cambridge: D. S. Brewer, 2014).

16 See A. Harbin, T. O'Callaghan, A. Craig, and R. Rocha, 'Augmenting Chaucer: Augmented Reality and Medieval Texts', in *The Routledge Research Companion to Digital Medieval Literature*, ed. J. E. Boyle and H. J. Burgess (London: Routledge, 2017), pp. 63–81.

17 C. Barrington and J. Hsy, eds., *Global Chaucers*: https://globalchaucers.wordpress.com/ <accessed 13 January 2020>.

18 Freely available, and developed by Dot Porter, Alberto Campagnolo *et al.*, 'VisColl': https://github.com/leoba/VisColl

Part 1
Theory and Practice

2 What it is to be a digitization specialist
Chasing medieval materials in a sea of pixels

Astrid J. Smith

Digital images of medieval objects have a tremendous dualistic power to both represent and conceal. When working with digitized objects, it is important to consider not only how and why these pixels came to be arranged just so but also to recognize the many individuals who facilitated and contributed to their creation. As the rare book and special collections digitization specialist for Stanford Libraries' Digital Library Systems and Services, specifically within the Digital Production Group,[1] I have observed that while medievalists are often especially adept at working with digital objects, the work that happens while transmitting the physical object into its digital state is less visible. I hope that sharing insight into the process of digitization will offer readers and colleagues a heightened understanding of those who have dedicated our professional lives to digital preservation for the benefit of scholars, research, and cultural heritage. These ideas represent my own personal perspective and experiences in my role digitizing archival materials at Stanford for almost a decade. I bring my training in fine art, liberal arts, and the humanities, to my work. The majority of my technical training has been hands-on in the imaging lab, in conjunction with work completed alongside the Stanford Libraries' Conservation Department. This said, many of the most powerful things that I have learned over the years have been intuited through ingenuity and problem solving as each and every object offers a unique opportunity for the digitizer, with many possible solutions to the questions of how it can be processed and displayed.

At the core, the concept of digitization is the process of working with a physical object and using imaging technology to produce a digital object. However, there are many steps that happen before, during, and after that process, and countless factors and considerations involved. When viewing digital objects, viewers must acknowledge not only the physical object being represented but also the elements that have contributed to its creation, and must not make assumptions, but inquire about what is being viewed and what might not have been made readily apparent. When objects are presented in a viewing environment, we may be able to pick up additional information from descriptive metadata and image copyright, or use and reproduction statements, but most often we are viewing these images in isolation, without the context of how they were produced. It is up to users to help flesh out this missing context as well as to draw attention to the *importance* of context, and it is up to digitization specialists to help tell these missing stories. While the following examples are taken from the day-to-day work of the imaging labs at Stanford Libraries, cultural heritage imaging professionals strive to actively share best practices, knowledge, and ideas as they continually grow and refine the skills required for the work, and one would find much parity in any high-quality digital preservation lab.

Before digitization: Review and assessment

Prior to imaging, there is a review and assessment period in which the requester or curator will be consulted directly. In order to initiate the digitization, they will have already placed a ticket in a job-tracking system, providing much of the necessary information: the intended use or purpose driving the digitization, the object's shelf mark, barcode, dimensions, and a physical description of the material itself. During the consultation, however, it is important to me that I also make sure that I have a sense of not only the historical context of the object but the *story* and the *identity* of the object, because these are things that I am going to try to honour and convey through the digital images. Some requesters, such as rare book curators, are particularly involved in this information exchange, sharing bibliographic and provenance details, answering questions and listening to ideas. Keeping in mind these intangible aspects helps the digitization specialist to look for and feature visual clues that it is desirable for the end user to be able to observe.

In order to make decisions about what resolution would be ideal for the object, we take measurements to use a technique that is called 'Item Driven Image Fidelity' (IDIF)—a term first encountered on a visit to the Smithsonian Digitization Program labs.[2] Cultural heritage imaging professionals typically use some version of this technique, but IDIF offers a concise way to articulate the method in which one will identify the smallest visual detail in an object, measure it with a scientific loupe, and then meet or exceed the corresponding resolution that ensures every aspect will be clearly visible in the digital image. In addition to determining imaging resolution, we perform a physical assessment to identify particular areas of fragility or concern. I look carefully at the object from every angle to get a sense of how it was made and what materials and techniques were used— parchment, pigment, gilding, rag paper, paste-down, cords and thread, among countless others—thinking always about how these elements come together to create the whole. The materiality of the object will drive imaging methodologies; an autograph manuscript letter by Abraham Lincoln presents different considerations than a medieval codex. How will I protect and showcase these various elements during the imaging process? What details do I see that I want to make sure do not get overlooked? I pay attention to and remember all these things when making later decisions, and draw from previous experiences with similar objects.

The physical assessment allows me to determine what device will be appropriate to image a particular object. It is important that imaging staff have a good understanding of the driving force behind a digitization request so that the correct device can be selected, as it is not only an issue of safety but also of producing an optimal image for the intended use-case. A digital image that is requested with the intention of printing a large banner would be produced differently to one which will be used for a small reference image in a publication. The Digital Production Group's labs are equipped with a variety of devices, each optimized for different materials and purposes: a large sheet-feed scanner; flatbed scanners; an Atiz mass book scanner; a robotic book scanner for the most robust of volumes; versatile high-resolution digital cameras at copystands for imaging maps, oversized materials, loose archival materials, fragile medieval codices and documents; a custom-built piano roll scanner; and a number of 3D-imaging technologies. Along the far wall of our neutral-grey lab are a number of dual-monitor quality control stations, which are imperative for producing high-quality digital images.[3] Most days, there are between five and ten lab staff members working in shifts at the various devices and stations at any given hour between 7am and 7pm.

Planning and calibration

After the physical assessment and the device selection, an estimate for the end-to-end elapsed time needed for the digitization process is used to determine when the work can be scheduled, given current lab commitments, priorities, available staffing, and deadlines. Once those determinations have been made, and a unique identifier created to associate the files with metadata in the digital repository, the object will be brought to the lab and the chosen equipment will be calibrated. When beginning a shift or capture session at one of the high-end overhead camera stations, the first photograph taken will be of a rectangular grey object called the device-level 'GoldenThread Target', which features focus or resolution lines, neutral scale tones and colour patches, and other tools for generating qualitative image quality metrics.[4] It was designed by image colour scientist Don Williams, founder of Image Science Associates, who is well known for helping to 'keep honest' cultural heritage imaging practitioners by enabling a systematized way to evaluate accuracy.

Running the image of the target through accompanying GoldenThread software, we are able to use the resulting data to verify that the photographs we are producing will meet standards set by the Federal Agencies Digital Guidelines Initiative's (FADGI) Technical Guidelines for Digitizing Cultural Heritage Materials.[5] If the results summary page for the image shows the green 'pass' box, then checks of parameters such as the grayscale and colour response, resolution, sampling frequency, and spatial frequency response, white balance, lighting uniformity, noise, and colour channel registration, have all fallen within the accepted range and imaging can begin. This also means that if any portion of the object needs to be shot on a different photography rig, such as a fold-out that is too large for the capture area, the resulting images would be able to be integrated seamlessly into the file set. If the target evaluation were to 'fail', the photographer will continue to work on producing an optimal setup, and possibly use other tools such as a light meter to evaluate the light-cast on the copystand, until it has passed. Typically, the equipment calibration steps take only 10 to 15 minutes and a setup that has produced a passing target will not often require anything more than minor adjustments unless significant changes have been made. In the Digital Production Group, lead photographer and image quality assurance specialist, Wayne Vanderkuil, is also always available for help getting stubborn targets to cooperate.

During digitization: Imaging

After a perfect, beautifully passing target has been achieved, the photographer will move into the digitization phase. Many rare and fragile books may not be safely opened to the 180 degrees necessary to capture a full opening or spread, and the same is true of many medieval codices, which are often fragile or tightly bound. For this reason, a codex will typically be photographed one leaf at a time while open to approximately a 120-degree angle. Most often, foam cradles will be used to support the opened portion of the upright board and leaves while the portion that is laid on the copystand, perpendicular to the camera, is photographed. The codex's front board and then all of the recto leaves will be shot first, and then the object is gently turned over and the verso is photographed in the same manner. Image focus is ensured by checking the distance between the camera and the object-plane being photographed, in this case the surface of the leaf, after every few shots. I prefer to do this with a small stack of archival grey board set to the same height as the object, though many imaging specialists use a small length of chain set to descend to just slightly above the capture plane when verifying focus.

While codices have their considerations, so too do loose leaves, fragments, and unbound documents on parchment. One of the most noticeable issues with parchment objects is that they tend to be highly heat sensitive, curling up like a like a Shrinky Dink if exposed to even the radiant heat from one's hand.[6] While the lighting in our labs does not emit damaging levels of heat, handling the objects even momentarily can produce this curl and inhibit a clear, evenly lit surface. Furthermore, parchment documents and charters that have been folded tend to hold their creases extremely well, producing deep shadows and dramatic topography in the resulting digital images. Cultural heritage imaging best practices are ever-evolving, and, in most circumstances, it is not considered best practice to put glass onto parchment that has pigment applied, so I designed and created clear, adjustable holding aids, with the approval of the institution's Conservation Department, in order to keep fragile objects flat during the imaging process. These have come in very useful both for codices and loose medieval materials, and I'm working on refining them further based on some years of evaluation in production.[7] Other labs use bone folders, grey card, semi-transparent straps, or any number of myriad ways to hold down parchment that do not involve 'glassing', and this is just one signature among many that users might notice if looking for clues about imaging choices and differing lab policies.

There is a very tactile quality to the imaging, and despite constant hand-washing and well-maintained collections, digitization is still sometimes a messy job. In one memorable instance, I was assisted by conservation technician Deb Fox who was cleaning pages from Eadweard Muybridge's mounted-photograph album for *The Attitudes of Animals in Motion* so that we could reduce the dust and get the best possible image.[8] Sometimes I just need another set of hands; when working with objects that are so extremely fragile that they require undivided attention and focus, it is very helpful to have someone assisting at the computer while I am situated at the copy-stand. Most often in this scenario, I am joined by long-time lab staff member Micaela Go who will be looking at the tethered images that are being produced in real-time while I'm shooting so that she can make sure everything that we need to capture is indeed being captured, no leaves being missed. At other times I may need to take a particularly creative shot and might call for backup; in one noteworthy case involving the early musical score to *Cavalleria Rusticana*, composer Pietro Mascagni had chosen to omit a section by sealing the pages together with wax. When I came across this section during imaging, I stopped the process and checked in with Ray Heigemeir, librarian for music, to discuss our options. We wanted to be able to give researchers an understanding that there was information hidden within the pages without taking the wax off and altering the object permanently, and without going against the intentions of the composer. As a compromise, we got a handful of angled shots of that concealed area and integrated the object-shots into the larger set of images for access.[9] The decisions made in the dimly-lit curtained-off imaging stations, in consultation with conservators and library staff, have a direct and significant impact on the resulting digital objects.

Post-production and quality assurance

Following imaging at the capture rig, raw files will be processed out of the capture software as tiff files that are then uploaded to either a shared server, or directly into a workflow management tool called *Goobi*. Goobi was created by the German company Intranda in order to facilitate streamlined and systematized production across many users and projects, and it is used by many cultural heritage institutions of varying sizes. Once the files have been uploaded to the 'Image capture' step in Goobi, they will move into the post-production and quality assurance phases. Staff members will look through all the files to make sure everything physically present was captured, performing the highly important 'Completeness check' step. If all leaves, all fronts and backs, and all items are present, then the cropping step can begin.

Prior to cropping an image, we will have an in-depth conversation about the crop decisions for the object, as these can have tremendous visual and intellectual impacts. I am so deeply concerned about cropping that I have been known to send thank-you emails to our lab staff members, such as John Pearson, because his crops were stunning, illustrating perfect margins around all sides, and uniformity across a whole codex or collection. One notable topic is whether or not to retain the entirety of the gutter-region of the book, allowing for a small amount of facing page to be shown, which is an important decision we shall advise on, but ultimately leave up to the curator or subject specialist's discretion. Cropping can also be a very subjective exercise, especially in situations where the objects do not have square edges or uniform shapes; a good example of irregular edges was a series of medieval charters and wiggly-edged chirographs—legal documents dating from the early thirteenth to the fifteenth centuries, and originating from, or near, Cabourne in Lincolnshire.[10] One must decide what reference points to use for straightening, and how much breathing room to leave on all sides; much like an artist's framed work is highlighted by an elegantly proportioned mat, an over-tight crop can make an object appear choked and closed-in. During later stages, it is possible to review the objects and send them back for changes to any crops that do not look appropriate or precise.

Lastly, once post-production is complete, lab staff will perform a series of quality assurance checks on the images to make sure that there are not any focus issues; no dust or other organics on the object, such as a smidgeon of fuzz or a hair; that there are no digital artefacts or anomalies created at any point during the process; that the cropping and straightening meet the project's needs; and that everything looks correct before approving them for publication. Each evaluative step will receive a rating between poor, fair, and good, but if any step receives a 'poor' rating, it is likely that the image will be deemed unacceptable, a 'fail'. These ratings might receive further review; for instance, an item that received a 'poor' rating for organics could be found to have a small hair physically embedded in the rag paper, in which case it would be noted that this was indeed a characteristic of the object and allowed to 'pass'. These careful quality assurance methodologies are established to ensure high standards among the digital images that our lab produces, and the process is an ongoing opportunity for conversation, training, growth, and refinement.

Special cases: Composite images

In some special cases, particular objects may necessitate additional non-routine work such as compositing multiple images to produce representations that visually depict the qualities of the physical materials. One example was the case of a safe conduct document featuring a wax seal, housed in a small circular box and attached by a vellum strip, with detailed dimensionality to the relief design.[11] After producing a FADGI-compliant standard photograph of the object under normal lighting, it was clear that the deep shadows of the box and the light bouncing off the shiny wax produced an effect which all but eliminated the very attributes that made the object so remarkable. By creating a composite image of the wooden box and wax seal using elements from a variety of different lighting techniques, we were able to get a much better sense of the three-dimensionality of the shape. This is the same technique that we might use when brilliantly glinting gold does not render visually under one lighting scenario. Using raking light, reflective boards, and angling the softboxes as needed, additional shots of the gold are captured and used for the compositing in such a way that the image reflects the visual truth of objects under more befitting viewing lighting circumstances.[12] These methods are used sparingly and with caution, most often for images that will be used for exhibits.

After digitization: Digital preservation and access

As a digitization specialist, it is highly rewarding to see how the fruits of our labours are used, as in many cases they are delivered to stakeholders, accessioned into the Stanford Digital Repository, and made available through our searchable library catalogue. Working with medieval and early modern manuscripts, it is especially gratifying to attend lunchtime palaeography group workshops, where students gather to enjoy a meal (which they would never be able to do with the actual physical object), as they view digital images on a widescreen and work on their interpretative skills together. The images are used in Library initiatives such as the Ancient, Medieval, and Early Modern Manuscripts Spotlight exhibit, and in countless publications.[13] We have many requests by library staff supporting the work of international researchers who need access to special collections objects for their projects. Stanford is actively involved in furthering and supporting the International Image Interoperability Framework (IIIF), which allows images to be served up in rich viewing and comparison environments such as the recently released Mirador 3.[14] Ultimately, an awareness and understanding of the sort of project, exhibits, and research that are made possible by digitization have the reciprocal benefit of informing the conscious decisions that are made throughout the imaging process. These images are intended to embody and render visually the physicality and materiality of the object in a way that is meaningful for users. Digitized objects carry their own authenticity, complementary to the physical object.

I feel as though digitization work is a calling in many respects, and it is important that users have an awareness of the hours of work and all the considerations that have gone into the creation of digital objects. There is work that happens before, during, and after digitization, which becomes an intrinsic part of the digital objects users research and view, infused in the images but largely invisible. I did not realize that the work I do now as a rare book and special collections digitization specialist was a profession when I was considering my career path some time ago, but in retrospect my experiences have informed and aided what feels like the perfect fit for my skills and passions. Like many cultural heritage imaging professionals, I have an equal love, or at least a vacillating love, of the physical and the digital, and I find that successfully and accurately bridging the gap from material to pixel is both the core responsibility and motivation for my work.

Notes

1 Stanford Libraries Digitization Services: http://digitization.stanford.edu
2 IDIF: http://dpo.si.edu/resource/item-driven-image-fidelity-hitting-digital-capture-sweet-spot
3 Lab spaces are all painted GTI Munsell neutral grey ISO 3664:2000 or 3664:2009: https://www.iso.org/standard/43234.html and https://www.rpimaging.com/munsell-neutral-gray-paint.html
4 Image Science Associates: www.imagescienceassociates.com
5 Federal Agencies Digital Guidelines Initiative's (FADGI) Technical Guidelines for Digitizing Cultural Heritage Materials: www.digitizationguidelines.gov/guidelines/digitize-technical.html and International Organization for Standardization: https://www.iso.org/standard/64220.html
6 *Shrinky Dinks* are an arts and crafts project for children, invented in 1973, in which sheets of polystyrene are decorated and cut out and then baked in an oven. During the baking process, the sheets crinkle and curl before finally lying flat to form tiny artistic creations. https://www.alexbrands.com/pa_brand/shrinky-dinks
7 The clear holders that I created were first used to hold down the parchment leaves of the codex *Septistellium Meditationis*: https://searchworks.stanford.edu/view/11371697
8 *The Attitudes of Animals in Motion*: https://searchworks.stanford.edu/view/1251795
9 *Cavalleria Rusticana*: https://searchworks.stanford.edu/view/10734734
10 Cabourne (Lincolnshire) legal documents: https://searchworks.stanford.edu/view/4082897
11 Safe conduct document for German Jew, 1802 July 29: https://searchworks.stanford.edu/view/4083968
12 The production process employed for *Horae Beatae Mariae Virginis*: https://searchworks.stanford.edu/view/4082816 in November 2014 is explored in much depth in Bridget Whearty, *Digital Codicology: Medieval Books and Modern Labor* (forthcoming, 2020).
13 Ancient, Medieval, and Early Modern Manuscripts at Stanford: https://exhibits.stanford.edu/mss/
14 IIIF: https://iiif.io and Mirador 3: https://projectmirador.org/

3 From the divine to the digital

Digitization as resurrection and reconstruction

Keri Thomas

The digitization of cultural artefacts seems, at first glance, to be far removed from the process of creation as enacted by medieval scribes. In their blog for the British Library in 2014, Kathleen Doyle and Patricia Lovett described the meticulous processes by which manuscripts were created.[1] From the construction of quills and oak gall ink, to the stretching of skins for the production of parchment and vellum; the preparation of the page through to the concoction of pigments and paints used to illustrate those blank folios, the gilding and binding that was enacted thereafter. For these early religious manuscripts, we see the devotional experience performed through the ritual of creation. Indeed, Henrike Lähnemann, in her inaugural lecture as Professor in German Medieval Literature and Linguistics at the University of Oxford, welcomed a Medingen Psalter to the Bodleian by declaring: 'It is God himself, ambidextrously writing the world, who is the exemplar for manuscript production. When the nun puts pen to parchment, she emulates the creative act of God.'[2]

The Rule of St Benedict sets out the importance of reading to the daily routine of monastic life, a rule to live by in order to regulate the lives of those who obey it and to free the mind to the contemplation of higher things. A life in Christ, for Benedict, meant engaging in the ordinary, and this allowed the medieval monk to understand that God did not require magnificent feats to show faithfulness, but everyday accomplishments such as reading and writing. Further, it was also the physical act of copying that allowed for the continued fight against Satan's wiles; as Cassiodorus put it, 'the antiquary copies the works of Christ, so many wounds does he inflict upon Satan'.[3] Reading and writing were ritualistic, allowing for the contemplation of a greater truth and for the continued battle against the forces of the Devil. In this work, a certain discomfort should be expected and, indeed, it was also part of the sacrament. Lähnemann describes the first lines of Dombibliothek Hildesheim MS. J27, which were a commonplace defence of scribal work: writing requires total commitment from heart, hand, and body; *Explicit expliciunt, que cordis intima promunt. Scriptando manu, totoque corporis usu,* 'Here comes to an end what flows from my innermost heart.'[4] And the whole body suffered during the act of creation: Corinthians tells us 'the more we suffer for Christ, the more God will shower us with his comfort through Christ'.[5] The physical suffering of the scribes was therefore part and parcel of piety—the physicality of a hard-fought battle against the wiles of Satan, manifested in the long hours putting quill to paper. Florentius of Valeranica described it thus:

> Because one who does not know how to write thinks it no labour, I will describe it to you, if you want to know how great is the burden of writing; it mists the eyes, it curves the back; it breaks the belly and the ribs; it fills the kidneys with pain, and the body with all kinds of suffering. Therefore, turn the pages slowly, reader, and keep your fingers well away from the pages, for just as a hailstorm ruins the fecundity of the soil, so the sloppy reader destroys both the book and the writing. For as the last port is sweet to the sailor, so the last line to the scribe.[6]

The work of the scribes was also isolated and uncomfortable. In London, British Library, Royal 10 A. xiii,[7] we see St Dunstan, dressed in his full bishop's garb, perched on a rigid-looking chair, which is not exactly the sort of outfit or seating one would expect for someone writing for hours at a time. Stephen Greenblatt, in his typically negative view of the medieval, described the monks working in those conditions as suffering from a form of clinical depression; acedia, a 'foul darkness' that caused hopelessness, apathy, and anxiety.[8] These difficulties were part of the continual proof of faith required from the monastic scribes. Jesus revealed that pain and suffering would be part of all humans' lives, and that only in the Kingdom of God would we be free of such torments. The pain in writing is not purposeless; its reason was to remind scribes of a better age to come.

In Emma Hardiman's essay on medieval materiality, she mentions Thomas Aquinas's explanation that God 'placed within material objects the potential for divinity, and that it was through a process of refinement that they were able to become divine'.[9] The manuscript's relationship to a living animal, a life given to it by God, meant that once it went through the ritual of preparation, it was imbued with divinity. There was no object, therefore, that was created from a material that had once been living, which did not carry His spirit. Moreover, Bill Endres tells us that the use of gold in illuminated manuscripts was meant to emulate 'a sense of divine light', which was 'believed necessary to illuminate the more difficult passages of the Bible, that is, make them clear and inspire insight into their sacred truth'.[10] Illuminated manuscripts in particular, then, are 'sacred artefact[s] that … generat[e] a force far greater than most historical artefacts';[11] strongholds of spirituality painted in 'fair colours',[12] where the myths and legends of the world are made real by dint of tint and faith.

The physical labour, the materials chosen, the illustration, and the content, are all therefore part of a process whereby a creator reinforces their relationship with the Almighty. The routines of whittling, soaking and scraping, writing and illustrating are meditative and, almost like the Holy Rosary, each round knot of action is a component prayer that allows for contemplation of a greater truth. The personal relationship with God that would inevitably develop in the spaces within the ritual can be seen in the unique technique each scribe developed to hold their pen. As each person's method of worship is personal to them and develops over years of devotion, so too the scribal hand developed similarly. The Devil, however, is in the detail. In addition to the many perils suffered by scribes in the creation of manuscripts, the slightly more unexpected peril was the potential for their work and their actions to attract the attention of a demon. Readers might be familiar with the work of the demon Titivillus, who worked for Satan to introduce errors into the work of scribes. He was certainly responsible for the famous mistake in the Wicked Bible[13] that encouraged all readers to commit adultery, as we shall see.

The purpose in relating these familiar processes is to reinforce the labour involved in the creation of a medieval manuscript. Copying texts was not simply a task to be undertaken to enforce routine; it was a weapon against Satan, the means by which the word of God could be taken to a wider audience. Manuscripts were objects of reverence in their own right, as well as containing the power of the words, because of the beauty of their illustrations and the luxuriousness of their component parts. The myths of the world are represented to us in the pages of such manuscripts, religious tomes within which scribes painted blood-red flames to represent to the congregation the fires of Hell. The *Apocalypsis cum figuris*[14] is filled with vividly painted angels and apostles and, memorably on folio 79r, a leering demon sinking his teeth into a hound amidst a squirming mass of animals. The *Smithfield Decretals*[15] are rich with bizarre and affecting images and tales: armed apes, the Devil pushing a nun off a bridge and folio 61v, where a rabbit beheads a man. A scene in the Apostle prayer-book written by a nun, Barbara Viskule, for St Bartholomew, which now resides in the Victoria & Albert Museum in London, contains an image on folio 45v which shows the saint 'stretched on the bench with his skin hanging down and being nibbled by a dog',[16] which cannot have been the most edifying experience. Rather brilliantly, the nun in question has used a flaw in the parchment, which she has surrounded in red ink, to create a peephole that allows the viewer to keep watching the saint as they proceed on their journey through the text, *Saluta vivum excoriatum apostolum* ('the skinned-alive apostle'). The nun 'relates the materiality of parchment to her personal devotion to the martyred patron saint'.[17] Perhaps it is also supposed to represent that the eye of God sees all, even if one should attempt to turn the page.

Nothing, perhaps, conveys the weight of God's wrath quite like the *Stavelot Bible*,[18] which is enormous, with each of its two volumes weighing 40lbs. Completed during the First Crusade, when the necessity to lay out the word of God on the page would have seemed even more imperative, it contains a full-page miniature of Christ in Majesty and historiated initials throughout the text. Such manuscripts on a lectern in a house of worship, written in a language perhaps unknown to anyone outside the clergy, would represent to the mind of man the literal word of the Lord. In their very physicality, they embodied Christ. Indeed, the image of Christ in the Stavelot Bible would have been as close as anyone could come to gazing upon and perhaps touching the face of God:

> First we lay the foundation in history, then by following a symbolical sense we erect an intellectual edifice to be a stronghold of faith and lastly by grace of moral instruction we, as it were, paint the fabric in fair colours.[19]

In the manuscript to which Treharne refers, she explains that in Cambridge, Trinity College, R. 17. 1 (Eadwine's *Psalterium triplex*, datable to *c*. 1160), the *mise-en-page* parallels the architecture of nave, clerestory and triforium of Christ Church in Canterbury. Here, then, even the way in which the manuscript is laid out is meant to convey religiosity; a vessel for divinity down to the very design of the page.

In terms of design, in the present-day era, one might ask where does the digital lie in the never-ending battle against the seductions of the Devil? It seems to lie on the dark side, beyond the illuminating light of the rich gold illustrations of our physical objects. In the digital domain we worship by the electronic light of a false god. A digital artefact is burdened with an uncanny otherness; Willard McCarty described it as 'anomalous existential ambiguity'.[20] And with the lack of physicality comes an assault on the strongholds of faith. The scribe, to Malcolm Parkes, was a warrior fighting with pen and ink against the fraudulent wiles of the Devil.[21] The digital has no such scribe, and lacks the corporeal elements that carry the Lord's grace: the inks and parchment that were once living things. Perhaps Titivillus, sent by the Devil himself to plague modern readers in our devotions, is the demonic presence that we so fear within the digital.

Is this why many scholars seem so afraid of the digital, because it removes the physical from which we derive comfort? Digitization represents the destruction of man and the death of myth. It represents the application of science and logic to the mystical and arcane. It relocates the storytelling of the world to a flat space. When we repackage our faith and transport it into such a place, we cannot expect it to perform in the same way. And in our desire to access these manuscripts digitally we are replicating the Faustian pact, perhaps—selling our souls for unlimited knowledge and worldly gratification. Mihai Nadin explains that '[we are] willing to give up a better Judgment for the Calculation that will make the future the present of all [our] wishes and desires fulfilled'.[22] Indeed, our desire to engage with the digital more generally is 'a continuous wager on the most primitive instincts ... sexually explicit messages and invitations to mob activity ... trade in gossip and selling illusions'.[23] Looking at it this way, we are not likely to attain entry to the Kingdom of Heaven through this method; more likely is that we succeed in eternally damning our souls.

In the Book of Psalms we are told about those who worship false gods: 'Their idols are silver and gold, the work of human hands. They have mouths, but do not speak; eyes, but do not see. They have ears, but do not hear; noses, but do not smell. They have hands, but do not feel; feet, but do not walk.'[24] These are the false gods of the digital landscape, the ones that we have created in silver and gold with our own hands; they do not react and interact with us in the same way as the physical does. We turn the page that isn't a page; search for a scent that does not come. The book-lickers amongst us cannot taste it on our tongue. This, then, is how the digital is often viewed— as a usurper. To torture the biblical analogies still further, the digital is the Absalom to the David of the physical; Absalom sets himself up to be a viable alternative to the authority of the latter. Of course, his fate is already laid out to us: trapped by his neck in the branches of a tree, he is killed with three darts to the heart, as shown in the Huntingfield Psalter.[25]

On a deeper level, the fear of the digital is perhaps a result of the fetishization of the written word, but it is more likely because the encroachment of the machine robs us of a relationship developed between signs, structures, and materials. We are less likely to anthropomorphize a laptop, or an algorithm. Furthermore, we see the physical manuscript as representational of individuality, and variance: it could also be argued that there is no serendipity in the use of a digital artefact, because all the secrets have been discovered in advance in order to replicate it. The word of God has been converted into 0s and 1s. The implication is that the digitization process is undermined by a need for the physical, but the physical works upon which we base so much importance have arguably no stable meaning in themselves: there are a multitude of significations between their presentation and their reception; the physical manuscripts are as amorphous as the digital domain over which they claim superiority.

What digitization also does is elicit discomfort in those who see it as a breaking up into pieces, as a form of destruction. Manuscripts 'are now metaphorically dismembered ... literally broken up for digitization by expert scholarly teams'.[26] eBay can be seen as a charnel house for medieval manuscripts broken up by book dealers, where the once-living parts of a text can be appropriated by anyone with the means to do so. It is disconcerting in the extreme to see these 'fleshy and intimate links to peoples and cultures from centuries past'[27] disinterred and dismembered.

What does this mean for our digitized manuscripts? If they were created to spread the word of God and are loci to the divine, what happens when they are replicated in the digital domain? The digitization process represents something more than the simple replication of medieval manuscripts (though indeed, the process is not always technically simple). For, as we engage with newer technologies and delve ever deeper into them, the digital is neither more nor less than the realization of the medieval clergy's ideas of bodily resurrection. Manuscripts have not simply transitioned 'to the Zuckerberg galaxy of fast-paced, high-volume, networked flows',[28] they are allowing us the means of attaining the spiritual salvation the medieval scribes were trying to reach.

If the digital is the mortal reconstruction of the body,[29] as Baudrillard described it, then perhaps digitization is the body of a manuscript resurrected into eternal life on the digital plain. Put even more simply, if the body itself is a construct, so too is the physical manuscript, and therefore perhaps even its divinity can be replicated. At death, depending on how you've lived your life, you either enter the calm, ordered ranks of Heaven or are condemned to the chaos of Hell, a place where, Caroline Walker Bynum told us, 'the wicked are divided, digested and eaten forever'.[30] Fortunately, at the end of time we will all be resurrected in readiness for the Last Judgement (or perhaps only the worthy amongst us!).

The body now becomes even more important—so important 'that the soul itself appeared somatomorphic', as Caroline Walker Bynum suggests. Medieval ideas of bodily resurrection were taken up in endless discussion as to the difficulties involved in such an endeavour, given that some believed bodies would not be resurrected intact, but if we can piece together broken books, why not broken bodies? *Broken Books*[31] is one such example: it is a project at St Louis University, which endeavours to create a central portal for the virtual reconstruction of dismembered manuscripts uses the International Image Interoperability Framework [IIIF].[32] If we can acknowledge the *deus ex machina* of 'God will fix it', can we not accommodate the similar thought that the digitizer can encode it, and piece together those bits of manuscript eaten up by greed and consumerism?

The digital lacks either soul or real body, however; and while the physical manuscript is a locus to the divine, according to Caroline Walker Bynum, the sense remains that the digital one is a heresy. How, then, can digitization recreate God in the machine? A religious manuscript is, arguably, the word of God, a weapon in the armoury for the good fight, and it is fair to say then that they are relics in themselves and are treated as such. When they are pieced together in the digital domain as part of projects like *Broken Books*, whilst it might be a touch hyperbolic to compare the efforts of digitizers to early Christians, reassembling and burying the bits of their martyred heroes and heroines, there are comparisons to be made. Caroline Walker Bynum comments that 'Theologians agreed that the body is crucial. What is and must be redeemed is a psychosomatic unity, a person, fully individual both in its physicality and its consciousness.'[33] The suggestion, then, is that if a manuscript is put back together in the digital domain, it will not be fully resurrected in the theological sense, as there is not unity between physicality and the soul of the manuscript. But if technology implies a transcendence of the materials used to comprise it, we can push this statement further and say technology *allows* a transcendence of the materials used to comprise the experience. Goldthwaite claimed that, 'Christianity was ... a religion oriented around things [and] it was accepted that these things could mediate a dialogue between the mortal and divine.'[34] Why can't those things be keyboard and screen, the software and hardware?

The postmodern orthodoxy is that the body is a linguistic and discursive construct. 'The body's materiality is secondary to the logical or semiotic structures it encodes', and 'although the bodies of the disciplined do not disappear ... the specificities of the corporealities fade into the technology'.[35] There is an ongoing fascination with technology as an extension of the human body. Technology allows for mediation with the divine, a transformation of the human condition. In *The Age of Spiritual Machines*, Kurzweil prophesied that twenty-first-century humanity will be in a position to change the nature of mortality in a post-biological future.[36] We would be able to resurrect our minds into the computer network and live forever. This is radical technological philosophy, and such transhumanism has a following. Elon Musk counts himself as a believer; so too Peter Thiel. They eschew the religious ideology behind transhumanism and embed it in projects at Google, Space X and Tesla.[37] This, then, would be a digital resurrection; the problem we have is the flesh. Eric Steinhart suggested that uploading to the digital domain 'does not leave the flesh behind ... it aims at *the intensification of the flesh*'.[38] By the same token, then, why can't a digitized manuscript be considered an intensification of the physical, a *requies aeterna*? It can certainly turn a broken-up manuscript into a whole one again. If access to those medieval manuscripts allowed 'proximity to the divine through the creation of an experience',[39] digitization in this view is resurrection through technology and a continuation of the scribal devotion to faith.

Notes

1 Kathleen Doyle and Patricia Lovett, 'How to Make a Medieval Manuscript', *The British Library*: https://www.bl.uk/medieval-english-french-manuscripts/articles/how-to-make-a-medieval-manuscript <accessed 1 July 2019>.

2 Henrike Lähnemann, 'The Materiality of Medieval Manuscripts' (Inaugural Lecture, University of Oxford, 2016): https://doi.org/10.1080/00787191.2016.1156853

3 George Haven Putnam, *Books & their Makers during the Middle Ages* (Ann Arbor: University of Michigan Library, 2009), pp. 24–5.

4 Lähnemann, 'The Materiality of Medieval Manuscripts'.

5 2 Corinthians 1:5–6.

6 Florentius of Valeranica in Madrid, Biblioteca Nacional, Cod. 80, folio 500v, translated in André Grabar and Carl Adam Johan Nordenfalk, *Early Medieval Painting* (New York: Skira, 1957).

7 *Expositio in Regulam S. Benedicti*, London, British Library, Royal 10 A. xiii.

8 Stephen Greenblatt, *The Swerve* (New York: W. W. Norton & Company, 2011), p. 26.

9 Emma K. Hardiman, 'Medieval Materiality: The Multisensory Performance in Late-Medieval Manuscripts', *Reinvention: An International Journal of Undergraduate Research*, BCUR Special Edition (2014): https://warwick.ac.uk/fac/cross_fac/iatl/reinvention/archive/ur2014specialissue/hardiman/ <accessed 1 July, 2019>.

10 Elaine Treharne, 'Fleshing out the Text: The Transcendent Manuscript in the Digital Age', *postmedieval: a journal of medieval cultural studies* 4 (2013): 465–78: http://dx.doi.org/10.1057/pmed.2013.36

11 Bill Endres, 'Research', *billendres.com*, 2013: http://billendres.com/research.html <accessed 1 July 2019>.

12 Treharne, 'Fleshing out the Text'.

13 Royal printers Robert Barker and Martin Lucas published the Wicked Bible, also known as the Sinner's or Adulterous Bible, in 1631. It famously omitted the word 'not' from the exhortation not to commit adultery within the Ten Commandments (Exodus 20:14).

14 *Apocalypsis cum Figuris*, Abbaye de Saint-Victor de Paris, Bibliotheque Nationale Francais, MS Latin 11440, folio 79.

15 Decretals of Gregory IX with gloss of Bernard of Parma, in London, British Library, Royal 10 E. iv, *c.* 1300–1340.

16 Lähnemann, 'The Materiality of Medieval Manuscripts'.

17 Lähnemann, 'The Materiality of Medieval Manuscripts'.

18 Stavelot Bible, Netherlands, S. (Stavelot), 1094–1097; London, British Library, Additional 28106 and Additional 28107.

19 Treharne, 'Fleshing out the Text', quoting Gregory the Great.

20 Willard McCarty, 'Getting There from Here: Remembering the Future of Digital Humanities', *Literary & Linguistic Computing / The Journal of Digital Scholarship in the Humanities* 29.3 (2014): 283–306.

21 M. B. Parkes, *Their Hands before our Eyes: A Closer Look at Scribes* (Aldershot: Ashgate, 2008), p. 13.

22 Mihai Nadin, '*Antecapere Ergo Sum*: What Price Knowledge?' *AI and SOCIETY* 28.1 (2012): 39–50: doi:10.1007/s00146–012–0400–8 <accessed 1 July 2019>.

23 Mihai Nadin, 'Enslaved by digital technology', in *Digital Humanities and Digital Media: Conversations on Politics, Culture, Aesthetics and Literacy*, ed. Robert Simanowski (London: Open Humanities Press, 2016), pp. 184–205. https://doi.org/10.25969/mediarep/11917

24 Psalm 115:4–5.

25 Psalter New York, Pierpont Morgan Library, M. 43, folio 17v.

26 Treharne, 'Fleshing out the Text'.

27 Treharne, 'Fleshing out the Text'.

28 Janneke Adema and Gary Hall, 'Posthumanities: The Dark Side of "The Dark Side of the Digital"', *The Journal of Electronic Publishing* 19.2 (2016): doi:10.3998/3336451.0019.201 <accessed 1 July 2019>.

29 Jean Baudrillard and Sheila Faria Glaser, *Simulacra and Simulation* (Ann Arbor: University of Michigan Press, 2014).

30 Caroline Walker Bynum, 'Death and Resurrection in the Middle Ages: Some Modern Implications', *Proceedings of the American Philosophical Society*, 142.4 (1998): 589–96: https://www.jstor.org/stable/3152283?seq=1 <accessed 1 July 2019>.

31 'Broken Books', *Brokenbooks.Org*: http://brokenbooks.org/brokenBooks/home.html?demo=1 <accessed 1 July 2019>.

32 IIIF | International Image Interoperability Framework, *Iiif.Io*: https://iiif.io <accessed 1 July 2019>.

33 Bynum, 'Death and Resurrection in the Middle Ages'.

34 R. A. Goldthwaite, *Wealth and Demand for Art in Italy 1300–1600* (Baltimore, MD: Johns Hopkins University Press, 1993).

35 Nancy Katherine Hayles, *How We Became Posthuman* (Chicago: University of Chicago Press, 2010).

36 Ray Kurzweil, *The Age of Spiritual Machines: When Computers Exceed Human Intelligence* (New York: Penguin, 2000).

37 Meghan O'Gieblyn, 'God in the Machine: My Strange Journey into Transhumanism', *The Guardian*, 2017: https://www.theguardian.com/technology/2017/apr/18/god-in-the-machine-my-strange-journey-into-transhumanism <accessed 1 July 2019>.

38 Eric Steinhart, *Your Digital Afterlives* (London: Palgrave Macmillan, 2016), p. 60.

39 Hardiman, 'Medieval Materiality'.

4 A note on technology and functionality in digital manuscript studies

Abigail G. Robertson

When we think about the uses of manuscripts in a digital setting, the need for greater accessibility[1] is often considered a primary benefit of the online object. Creating opportunities to make access to ancient texts more widely available is a worthwhile and fundamentally important endeavour, given that the physical objects have often been behind institutional lock and key or inaccessible because they're in a repository thousands of miles from the researcher. These digitized manuscripts and documents have gone by many names in the academic discourse that has taken place in the advent of mass manuscript digitization—digital surrogate, digital facsimile, or avatar, to name a few in recent years—and even these names relegate the digital object to a position of a replacement, copy, or replica of the original material object.[2] The implication thus seems to be that the original is primary or alpha and the digital is secondary or beta. While working with the physical manuscript allows for the study of features that the digitized version certainly cannot facilitate—determining the type of skin used for the writing support, examining the binding, or the study of any number of codicological attributes of the manuscript—the relegation of digital manuscripts to secondary status diminishes the technological advantages they facilitate for certain kinds of study as well as the advantage of accessibility that the digital realm facilitates.

In reality, so much of what scholars do with digitized manuscripts challenges this primary/secondary dichotomy. The implied hierarchy in the scholarly consciousness where the original manuscript surpasses all other forms of the manuscript and its contents (whether digital or physical facsimile) does not take into account the way that we use each of these manifestations of the textual artefact differently on a case-by-case basis. While using the physical object itself is often necessary for scholarship, the digitized manuscript would almost certainly be preferred in other circumstances, such as in a teaching context; after all, what better way would there be to showcase a ligature, rare letter form, or hard-to-read gloss than zooming in on it?

Digitized manuscripts undoubtedly democratize and aid in the disassembly of power structures related to the privilege of institutional access; only "*bona fide*" scholars can see most manuscripts, and only a tiny number of curators have access to the 'treasures' in a collection. From a practical point of view, though, digital manuscripts allow us to do even more. They are manufactured based on the way that people work, study, and share data and scholarship; in some ways, they allow scholars and interested citizens to interact with a manuscript in ways that can be even 'better' than interacting with the material object itself. The digital images are often are made in accordance with best practices for the web and metadata creation that allow researchers to identify and utilize objects, sometimes serendipitously, that they might have never known could be useful for their research. Of course, there are situations where the digital manuscript cannot fulfil the needs of a researcher; for example, as Elaine Treharne has noted, digital manuscripts obscure features such as the size of the actual objects they exist to represent.[3] This alone should not distract from the vast advantages their functionality presents that cannot be facilitated by the physical objects themselves. It is reductive to view the digital manuscript as 'less than' or even as a replacement or understudy for the physical object; instead, the digital manuscript ought to be conceived of as a complement to the physical object. This digital complement can certainly 'replace' the physical one for those without interest in or access to visiting the material object itself, but the digital complement allows us to study the manuscript in ways that augment the investigation of the physical object. For this reason, it is unhelpful to think about any digital manuscript as a substitute or an absolute replacement for the physical object. While it may function as a substitute for individual researchers, it is instead part of its own new genre of virtual object and thus resists a direct comparison to the original in any way other than its use. The digital manuscript is a translation of the original into a new form that is entirely different in terms of medium, identical in content, and complementary to the physical object for those who work with it.

It does not take more than a few minutes to understand the differences between working with a physical object and a digital one; a quick glance around the Parker Library's new reading room at Corpus Christi College, Cambridge, finds scholars standing over oversized codices or hunched over smaller books with magnifiers as they transcribe. This is not how researchers interact with digitized manuscripts because the objects are not meant to merely replicate or stand in for the physical objects themselves or the experience of working with them. Researchers can be anywhere in the world and access these textual materials; they can work on digital images on any device—from a smart phone to a large monitor. The physical interaction of the researcher with the digital must alter the ways in which information is examined and evaluated, and there is clearly an opportunity for scholarly research into these uses. Equally, there is often a conflation of the digital and physical object in terms of how we use them, when in reality these objects are not used in the same way and the unique functional attributes of the digital version of the object mean that a direct comparison misses the point. To think of the digital image itself as anything other than a unique way to study an object is to reduce the digital and physical to what they have in common, rather than to acknowledge the ways that they inherently change how scholars are able to interact with and study ancient texts.

Furthermore, referring to digitized manuscripts as facsimiles or surrogates erases decades of technological research related to imaging and usability that span not only digitization in libraries, but efforts to digitize and preserve documents, books, and other text-based objects across genre, period, and form. We can see the transformation and evolution of such technologies clearly in the functionality of digital manuscripts. Gone are the days of magnifying sections of an image with a digital magnifying glass and almost obsolete are remnants of technology that remind us of the book itself (such as animation showing the turning of pages, for example). Rather than mimicking the way that scholars work in libraries and archives and the tools that they employ when working with objects *in situ*, the functionality of digital manuscripts is entirely based on the way that scholars aspire to work with manuscripts insofar as technology allows. The limitations of physical objects—their inaccessibility, the fastidiousness with which they must be handled, the limits of the time one can spend studying them first-hand—are replaced by technology that allows scholars to do work more efficiently, creating an entirely new workspace through the digital complement. In this way, the only thing that a digital manuscript 'replaces' is the way that we as scholars work—rather than being limited to the tools in our physical workspace, a manuscript's availability, and the hours of operation for a library, the digital offers an entirely new set of tools to aid in research that are limited only by technological innovation and the cost of its implementation. This means that the success of digital manuscripts comes from the tools working with them produces. As Crostini, Iverson, and Jensen put it:

> In itself access to manuscript images changes nothing fundamental in textual scholarship, other than thousands of manuscripts and books online are immediately available ... Unless scholars combine this access with radically new digital tools and use them to make new editions, in a manner never seen before, we cannot yet talk about a digital revolution.[4]

Modern readers of physical and digital medieval manuscripts, and their utilization of technology to improve the usability of manuscripts, mirror the ways that medieval scribes developed systems of technology. Varying scripts, colour, capitalization, and rubrication were used to create a visual hierarchy which helped readers navigate within the manuscript and aided their understanding of particular sections. Corrections, glosses, and annotations served as metatextual elements, offering information outside the body of the text itself that was still connected to the volume as a kind of metadata. If we agree that one of the basic tenets of technology is the application of something for a practical purpose, the metatextual elements like underlining and bracketing that were marked onto the writing surfaces of medieval manuscripts serve much the same purpose as digitized manuscripts that feature links to different sections of the digital object itself. This means that we should be considering the way we use objects as a baseline in discussions of digital manuscripts and reframe our thinking around this idea of 'use' as the fundamental component of how we understand the role of digital manuscripts in academic study.

With this in mind, the notion of the digitized manuscript as a complement to the physical manuscript allows us to think about the digital object as a tool to aid in the fulfilment of research goals; it is complementary insofar as it addresses some of the most basic concerns of those working with medieval manuscripts, yet does not aim to replace the object itself. When we consider digitized manuscripts in this light, we are thus able to shift our collective focus away from the hierarchy of physical above digital and instead move toward the way that we interact with objects and their digital presences. Digital manuscripts are an innovation of the original medium, a riff that forever gestures to the original yet builds upon it and opens doors for further study. In this way, digital manuscripts are in a symbiotic relationship with their referent, each allowing scholars to investigate their contents and learn more about their makings based on the way that we as humans work best.

Notes

1 It is important to note that accessibility is still an issue even when manuscripts and other digital objects are made freely available online. For more on the challenges associated with manuscript digitization and accessibility standards, see Kathyrn Wymer, 'Why Universal Accessibility Should Matter to the Digital Medievalist', *Digital Medievalist*, 1: http://doi.org/10.16995/dm.9
2 For more on names for digital manuscript as well as an in-depth overview of how these terms determine our perception of digitized manuscripts, see Dot Porter, 'Is This Your Book? What We Call Digitized Manuscripts and Why it Matters', *Dot Porter Digital*, 16 July 2019: www.dotporterdigital.org/is-this-your-book-what-digitization-does-to-manuscripts-and-what-we-can-do-about-it/
3 Elaine Treharne, 'Fleshing out the Text: The Transcendent Manuscript in the Digital Age', *postmedieval* 4 (2013): 465–78, at p. 465. https://doi.org/10.1057/pmed.2013.36
4 Barbara Crostini, Guinilla Iverson, and Brian M. Jensen, 'Introduction', *Studia Latina Stockholmiensia LXII*, Ars Edendi Lecture Series 5 (2016): xi.

5 Ways of seeing manuscripts

Exploring Parker 2.0

Andrew Prescott

A technicolour Middle Ages

When I joined the British Library as a junior curator in 1979, the publications describing the Library's illuminated manuscripts contained a handful of illustrations, mostly in black and white. Even the postcard stock was quite restricted. For many years, the chief means of access to illustrations of the British Library's illuminated manuscripts was through the series of *Reproductions from Illuminated Manuscripts*, published from 1907 to 1965, which consisted of portfolios containing 50 loose black and white pictures of pages from illuminated manuscripts.[1] The *Faber Library of Illuminated Manuscripts* published between 1959 and 1962 was eagerly anticipated because it promised eight coloured plates, but reviewers bewailed the poor quality of Faber's colour and asked for more.[2] The book published by the British Library to accompany its exhibition of *The Benedictines in Britain* in 1980 was considered at the time to be handsomely illustrated, but contained just four colour plates, with the other illustrations being black and white.[3] The first book to include a large number of colour illustrations of the British Library's illuminated manuscripts was Janet Backhouse's *The Illuminated Manuscript*, published in 1979 just after I joined the library.[4] Janet's book caused controversy in the British Library because it was undertaken for an external publisher, Phaidon Press, and it was only afterwards that the British Library began to produce its own highly illustrated volumes such as Janet Backhouse's own *Books of Hours* in 1985.[5]

During the past 30 years, we have moved from a monochrome text-dominated view of the Middle Ages to one suffused with colour and vibrant imagery, thanks to the growth of digital imaging. Parker 2.0 illustrates how digital imaging has revolutionized access to manuscripts. Parker 2.0 makes freely available high-quality colour images of the vast majority of the manuscripts in the library of Corpus Christi College, Cambridge, which notoriously was until recently one of the most difficult major collections of manuscripts to access. Now anybody with an Internet connection can explore the Parker Library freely at any time of the day or night, no matter where they are or what they are doing. And they can do it in colour. That is truly revolutionary, and I feel privileged to have witnessed such a remarkable transformation during my career as a scholar. The generosity of Corpus Christi College, Stanford University, and the Mellon Foundation in making Parker 2.0 freely available can only be applauded.

As soon as we photograph a work of art, we transform the way we see it. It is 80 years since Walter Benjamin explored this theme in his celebrated essay *On The Work of Art in Age of Mechanical Reproduction*,[6] but it is only now with the explosion of digital images that the implications of Benjamin's study for the way we perceive medieval manuscripts are becoming clearer. In order to view art works, it is no longer necessary to go to an art gallery or library or archive. Parker 2.0 is an emblem of a world in which art is available everywhere at any time. We can take images of medieval manuscripts home, make giant posters of them, pin them to a wall, turn them into cushions or curtains, use them in films or television programmes. We can deform and disfigure them, maybe turning them into Instagram memes. Images of manuscripts can even inspire interior decor, as in Exeter where images of the Exeter Book are incorporated in the carpets, bars, and shower screens of a local hotel.[7] Instead of being something that we approach reverentially in a hushed atmosphere, the art work has now become part of everyday life, accompanying us in work and leisure. This inevitably changes its meaning.

We are in the midst of an astonishing remediation of culture as we transfer vast swathes of our museums, libraries, and archives to digital form. Each printed volume or manuscript is a complex social, cultural, and economic artefact. By digitizing a manuscript or printed book, we reinvent its form and give it a new cultural context. As John Berger put it in his book *Ways of Seeing*, inspired by Benjamin, 'When the camera reproduces a painting, it destroys the uniqueness of its image. As a result the meaning changes. Or, more exactly, its meaning changes. Or, more exactly, its meaning multiplies and fragments into many meanings.'[8] This chapter will use Parker 2.0 to explore how digital images are changing the ways in which we see medieval manuscripts. How does the availability of Parker 2.0 change our understanding of the Parker Library? Is digitization more than simply a tool making it easier and more convenient to research the Middle Ages? How far does digitization change our cultural understanding of medieval manuscripts?

Many of the tools offered by digital imaging are now familiar and established weapons in the armoury of the manuscript scholar. We can magnify images to examine details more closely. We can manipulate an image by inverting colours or altering the contrast to make faded text or other details more visible. We can compare different parts of the manuscript or different manuscripts. The tools provided by the new generation of image browsers such as Mirador make such manipulation easier than ever before. Twenty-five years after Kevin Kiernan first elicited 'oohs' and 'aahs' from academic audiences by showing how digital imaging could record letters hidden by conservation work in the *Beowulf* manuscript, the use of multi-spectral imaging to reveal details of a manuscript not visible with the naked eye still elicits cries of astonishment.

These advantages of digital images of manuscripts are well known and do not need further elaboration. Instead, I will follow the lead of Benjamin and his disciples like John Berger and think about the way in which digital imaging is changing the way we see manuscripts. Digitization is more than just a study aid. It transforms our engagement with manuscripts as cultural, social, and economic objects. As manuscripts become more accessible, so a host of social and institutional vested interests swing into action to maintain the cultural exclusivity of the original manuscript by insisting on its aura. This aura is of course Benjamin's most well-known formulation and it describes a process whereby wealth and privilege counteract the democratic possibilities of the mass reproduction of art. This process of cultural mystification is evident in the work of scholars such as Christopher de Hamel who deprecate digital images and insist on an elitist connoisseur approach to manuscripts.

A digital facsimile of a manuscript can never replace the manuscript, but using a digital collection like Parker 2.0 gives us many fresh perspectives. Parker 2.0 offers a wonderful bird's eye view of the Parker Library that would be difficult to achieve in any other way, even if we were sitting in Cambridge. Using Parker 2.0, we can think about the overall shape of the library and this gives us insights into Parker's intellectual strategies. We can more readily contrast the characteristics of the Parker Library with other collections like that of Sir Robert Cotton. Using Parker 2.0, it is easier to explore neglected byways of the Parker Library and to linger with more obscure items. Browsing digitally through the Parker Library, fresh cultural contexts for the collection emerge. When using digital images instead of the printed mediation of editions, our view of text fundamentally shifts, and we begin to appreciate anew how text forms one element of the complex craft production that is the medieval manuscript. We can compare Parker manuscripts side by side with those in other collections and fresh insights into their context quickly emerge.

The aura of the connoisseur

Galleries find that allowing visitors to take selfies with famous art works dramatically increases visitor numbers. The demand to take selfies with Mona Lisa causes huge queues at the Louvre and during the summer of 2019 visitors were restricted to just one minute with Leonardo's painting.[9] What is the point of spending just one minute with Mona Lisa in order to take a digital image which is readily available elsewhere? The reason is the public fixation with the aura. Benjamin described the aura as the presence of the original artwork in time and space, its unique character which cannot be captured even in the most perfect reproduction. Taking an image showing how you shared time and space with the artwork is a way of invoking that aura.

As a work is more widely reproduced, so the aura of the original is enhanced. The selfie with the original artwork becomes the most desirable form of reproduction. Financial, political, and social interests support this process. Collectors and art dealers are anxious to maintain the value of their investment. Galleries and museums seek to increase visitor numbers to ensure future grants and donations. Governments welcome a healthy tourist industry. Scholarship is complicit in this process by focusing on attribution, provenance, conservation history, and all the other details necessary to ensure that the object maintains its aura, thereby supporting the inflated financial value of art works.[10]

By focusing on increasingly minute details of art works, scholars promote a process of cultural mystification. Even though any of us can own a reproduction of a painting or a medieval manuscript, we are told that we cannot fully understand the original object and that expert elucidation is required. When great works of art were shown on colour television for the first time in Britain, it was felt essential that Kenneth Clark should explain how they represented civilization. As Clark put it: 'I am pleased that the responsibility for understanding works of art, and interpreting them to the average man, must rest with a small minority.'[11] The digitization of manuscripts and other art objects democratizes access to them, but a process of cultural interlocution insists that the uninitiated cannot understand these objects, thereby reinforcing elite cultural narratives and power structures.

Just as Kenneth Clark mediated television's view of civilization, likewise some manuscript scholars are anxious to persuade us that digital resources like Parker 2.0 are cheap and untrustworthy and that we require expert help to use them. The fundamental message of Christopher de Hamel's best-selling book, *Meetings with Remarkable Manuscripts*, is that 'No one can properly know or write about a manuscript without having seen it and held it in their hands.'[12] Although digitized manuscripts promote a wider public appreciation of medieval manuscripts, they are nevertheless for de Hamel ultimately 'rootless and untied to any place'.[13] De Hamel's insistence on consulting the original manuscript is, in the context of the celebrity manuscripts featured in his book, absurd, since virtually nobody can have any hope of handling any of the manuscripts de Hamel discusses. Every manuscript scholar will agree that it is hazardous to rely on digital images alone, but there are few scholars who could follow in de Hamel's footsteps by obtaining permission to handle the Gospels of St Augustine, the Codex Amiatinus, and the Book of Kells. They have to use whatever digital surrogates are available.

De Hamel makes it clear that to have a conversation with these manuscripts we need an experienced and knowledgeable interlocutor, namely Christopher de Hamel. De Hamel uses every imaginable rhetorical trick to emphasize the aura of the original manuscript. He describes at length his long journeys to the libraries to see the manuscripts. He emphasizes the difficulty of getting the manuscripts and the need to pull strings with senior librarians to secure the necessary permissions to see the manuscripts. He describes with glee the excitement caused by the appearance in the library of the celebrity manuscript: 'As you sit in the reading-room of a library turning the pages of some dazzling illuminated volume, you can sense a certain respect from your fellow students on neighbouring tables consulting more modest books or archives.'[14] De Hamel goes out of his way to stress physical aspects of the manuscript such as the collation which his readers will never see for themselves.

De Hamel uses his celebrity manuscripts to illustrate a well-worn narrative of medieval culture running from St Augustine to the deluxe Renaissance opulence of the Spinola Hours. In De Hamel's words, this is 'a story of intellectual culture and art from the final moments of the Roman Empire right through the high Renaissance and then on again'.[15] For De Hamel, the frisson of these manuscripts lies in the way they seem to bring us directly in touch with the stereotypical moments of European history: the arrival of Augustine in England, Bede at Jarrow, or the Normans breathing 'new vigour and life into the declining monastic standards of Anglo-Saxon England'.[16] In De Hamel's hands, these manuscripts become a means of preserving a backward-looking elitist view of medieval culture, rather than rich cultural productions which can unsettle our preconceptions about the past. De Hamel portrays manuscript studies as an agreeable fraternity of like-minded enthusiasts who exchange collations and make new attributions, rather like stamp collectors. De Hamel's world is that of the connoisseur: 'Read a Book of Hours in bed and you are transported back 500 years.'[17]

For Walter Benjamin, the value of mechanical reproductions of works of art was the way they undermined such concepts as creativity, genius, and everlasting value—the very values that de Hamel invokes in celebrating his meetings with celebrity manuscripts. Just as the mechanical reproduction was for Benjamin a means of escape from the smug verities of art world, so likewise digitized manuscripts can undermine the complacent ethos of the manuscript connoisseur which has hitherto dominated the field of manuscript studies. Using and sharing images of digital manuscripts encourages us to engage with manuscripts which are marginal, forgotten, and challenging rather than constantly returning to the same celebrity items. A digital collection such as Parker 2.0 subverts the connoisseur mindset by offering new macro and micro views of the Parker manuscripts which are not possible even if you are sitting beneath the mullioned windows and oak bookcases of Corpus Christi College, Cambridge, lovingly described by Christopher de Hamel.

Parker's concept of his library

Far from distancing us from the physical characteristics Parker's library, the bird's eye view of the Parker Library offered by Parker 2.0 encourages us to think about the library's shape. Browsing through the Parker Library on Parker 2.0, one is immediately struck by the Parker Library's consistency of form. The Parker Library consists overwhelmingly of codices. Only one genealogical roll can be firmly identified in Parker's bequest (CCCC 98). It is not clear if the fifteenth-century chronicle roll which is now CCCC 98A was ever owned by Parker. The Parker Certificates describing the state of church benefices dating from 1560 and 1561 in CCCC 97 and CCCC 122 originally contained some rolls but these were cut up and mounted in volumes.[18] CCCC

97 also contains from folios 3-28 a rental of Merton College, Oxford, which was also cut up. Other rolls in the Parker Library were acquired or transferred to the Library long after Parker's bequest.[19]

Rolls are anomalies in the Parker Library, whose shape is that of a series of codices. In this respect, the Parker Library contrasts strongly with Sir Robert Cotton's collection. The Cotton Library comprised not simply manuscript volumes but also hundreds of rolls, charters, portfolios of maps, coins, and even such objects as a plate used to make tonsures.[20] It seems that for Parker, a library consisted of a series of volumes, whereas for Cotton it was more wide-ranging in character. Cotton's conception of a library, with rolls and charters forming major components, was more characteristic of the early modern period. The overall shape of Parker's library, as revealed by Parker 2.0, suggests that Parker had distinctive personal views on the nature of libraries and the way in which knowledge should be organized.

Anthony Grafton has recently illustrated Parker's profound interest in archival procedure and practice.[21] As Master of Corpus Christi College, Parker ordered the compilation of a 'Black Book' of documents relating to the college. He deposited a notarized description of his consecration in the college archives and was familiar with archival procedures for preparing certified copies of documents. Grafton argues that Parker saw his library as a form of archive which embodied the official history of medieval England. He suggests that Parker sought to gather those monastic chronicles embodying the history of medieval England which English kings such as Edward I had used to support dynastic and other claims. In Grafton's view, Parker blurred the distinction between archival documents in the form of charters or rolls and the interpretative narratives of chronicles.

It seems, however, that Parker was keenly aware of these distinctions, and had strong views on what was appropriate to an archive and what belonged in a library. In his preface to Asser, Parker talks fulsomely of *'quoniam diplomata multa, & vetustioris aetatis monumenta, tum regiae quae in archiuis custodiuntur chartae, tam ante, quam post Normannorum in Angliam aduentum'* ('many diplomas and monuments of olden times, both before and after the Normans arrived in England, and the royal charters that are kept in the archives').[22] He also refers elsewhere to charters 'ut in Archivis patet' ('as appears in the archives').[23] It seems that broadly Parker considered charters, diplomas and rolls as suitable for the archives, and books as appropriate for a library. The shape of the Parker Library at Cambridge reflects his view of what was appropriate for a college library. Rolls, diplomas, and charters were consigned to the archives, either in Lambeth Palace Library or at Corpus Christi College. Parker's stress on format is in many ways very forward-looking and anticipates aspects of the modern distinctions between different types of collection which were to emerge much later. The digitized Parker Library helps us understand how Parker's categorization of his library is a significant stage in the gradual emergence of modern ideas about the shape, structure, and content of libraries in the sixteenth and seventeenth century, which has been memorably described by David McKitterick.[24]

The joys of browsing

It is a common lament that e-books deprive us of the pleasure of browsing along the shelf. This may be true of printed books, but manuscript scholars rarely have the opportunity to browse along the shelves of a manuscript collection. A major advantage of having a collection like the Parker Library available in digital form is that it gives us the opportunity to browse and dip into unfamiliar manuscripts. With a digital manuscript library, we can browse through manuscripts in a way that security and conservation considerations otherwise make impossible.

With Parker 2.0, we can indulge ourselves by lingering and exploring manuscripts that are unfamiliar and outside our own range of expertise. We can wander off the well-beaten Parkerian tracks of Old English texts and medieval chronicles. We can probe other areas of Parker's interests. When making a special research trip to Cambridge, time and money mean that we focus on items relating to our own research priorities and we stay on familiar ground. It would be a waste of time to order an Arabic or Armenian manuscript out of curiosity. But Parker 2.0 encourages us to treat ourselves and wander.

The conventional view of collections such as those of Archbishop Parker and Sir Robert Cotton is that they are primarily repositories of English literary and cultural origins. It is partly because this perception of these foundational archives is so deeply entrenched that colonial narratives of 'Anglo-Saxon'[25] exceptionalism remain embedded in much British and North American medieval scholarship. But as we start to browse collections like the Parker and Cotton libraries, we can appreciate how these great manuscript libraries do not, as Christopher de Hamel would have us believe, simply document well-worn narratives of European progress and civilization. Using digital libraries like Parker 2.0 to browse the marginal and overlooked elements of these collections generates fresh cultural perspectives and takes us in unexpected directions.

Robert Cotton was not simply a collector of medieval manuscripts and state papers documenting the English Reformation. He was keenly interested in Elizabethan colonial ventures and acquired manuscripts relating to distant countries.[26] Elizabethan contact with Russia is reflected in Cotton's acquisition of a copy of the Russian Primary Chronicle, London, British Library, Cotton Vitellius F. x. Cotton preserved documents relating to the negotiations between the East India Company and the shogun in Japan for trading privileges, London, British Library, Cotton Charter iii. 13.[27] Concealed in London, British Library, Cotton Vespasian F. xvii, folios 62v-111v, under the vague catalogue description 'Merchant's Account Book' is an account book of the East India Company Factory at Hirado in Japan from September 1615 to January 1617,[28] which contains an intriguing detail that among the gifts distributed to the Japanese by the English merchants was a painting 'of Saxon kinges'.[29]

Cotton's library contained 14 manuscripts in Asian and Afroasiatic languages including Arabic, Persian, Turkish, Hebrew, and Chinese. These are among the forgotten and abandoned components of the Cotton Library. Transferred to the British Museum's Department of Oriental Manuscripts on its creation in 1867, they have only sketchy catalogue descriptions and have not been digitized. London, British Library, Cotton Claudius B. viii is a Samaritan Pentateuch presented to Cotton by Archbishop Ussher of Armagh. Cotton Cleopatra A. ix is a volume of Persian poems. Cotton Caligula A. v contains *Nazm al-Jauhar*, a chronicle in Arabic by Eutychius, Patriarch of Alexandria, while Cotton Titus C. xiv contains a work by the sixteenth-century Egyptian scholar and mystic Abd al-Wahhab al-Sha'rani. Cotton Vitellius A. iv is a life of Mohammed, and Vitellius F. xviii and Vitellius F. xix are compilations on Islamic law, dated 1447. Cotton owned a number of copies of the Koran. Cotton Tiberius A. i is a fifteenth-century Koran. Cotton Galba A. ix and Galba A. x were Arabic manuscripts of the Koran and a book of prayers and were both badly damaged in the fire of 1731. Cotton Galba A. xvi was, according to Thomas Smith, another manuscript of the Koran, but was missing by 1802. Cotton Titus D. xvii was a Chinese printed book.

Cotton was far more culturally and geographically adventurous in his collecting than Parker. Although Parker remained focused on seeking historical and linguistic justifications for the Elizabethan church settlement, his search for the roots of the Anglican Church nevertheless opened up global perspectives. Parker's collection contains one Arabic and one Armenian manuscript. And Parker 2.0 encourages us to linger and contemplate these neglected aspects of Parker's library.

Parker's Arabic manuscript, CCCC 401, is a sixteenth-century copy of Abd Allah Baydawi (d. A.H. 716), *Tawali' al-Anwar min Matali' al-Anzar* and the commentary on it by Mahmud Isfahani (d. A.H. 749/750), *Matali' al-Anzar, Sharh Tawali' al-Anwar*, commentaries on Islamic theology that had been widely used in Islamic seminaries for centuries. It seems to have been the only Arabic manuscript possessed by Parker; there are other Arabic manuscripts at Corpus Christi College but these were acquired later, such as CCCC 249, a seventeenth-century Koran donated by James Hitchcock of Grantchester, and CCCC 384, a sixteenth-century translation of the First Epistle of John into Arabic, presented by one Thomas Dag (or Day).

The reason for Parker's interest in CCCC 401 is evident from folio 8, where he states that the manuscript had belonged to the seventh-century Archbishop of Canterbury, Theodore of Tarsus. This is clearly preposterous since the manuscript dates from about seven hundred years after Theodore's death, and the claim to an association with Theodore prompted M. R. James to three exasperated exclamation marks. CCCC 401 is one of a number of manuscripts which Parker thought (equally erroneously) had belonged to Theodore. CCCC 81, a copy of Homer, has a gold cartouche with the name 'Theodore' on p. 1 and Parker was convinced that this was Archbishop Theodore, but the manuscript dates from the fifteenth century and the cartouche is probably an ownership mark of Theodore Geza. Likewise, CCCC 401, a copy of Euripides, dates from the fifteenth century, and CCCC 480, a Greek Psalter, is twelfth century. They are all far too late to be associated with Theodore of Tarsus, but Parker still fondly believed that they were relics of this important early Archbishop of Canterbury. He showed these precious volumes to William Lambarde, who recorded how Parker was convinced 'being therto reasonably led by great shewe of antiquitie' that these were remnants of the library of Archbshop Theodore.[30] Parker's Arabic manuscript may nowadays seem a strange curio, but for Parker it was a relic of the early English church comparable in antiquity and significance to the Gospels of St Augustine.

The Armenian Psalter in the Parker Library, CCCC 478, opens up even more unexpected perspectives. The colophons in CCCC 478 (folios 27r, 188r, 219r, 247v) tell us that it was written in the year of the Armenian calendar 805 (= 1355 CE) by the scribe Xač'eres for Grigores of the city of Karin (now Erzurum in Eastern Anatolia), as a memorial for Grigores, his parents, his progenitor called Sosik, his mother T'ager and his brothers Šaher and Awetik'. It might be tempting to see Parker's acquisition of this manuscript as part of the European interest in building trade and cultural links with Armenia in the late sixteenth and seventeenth centuries, but Parker had no idea what this strange manuscript was. Baffled by its 'strange charect', Parker asked his friend Richard Davies, the Bishop of St Davids, known for his Welsh translation of the Book of Common Prayer, to look at the manuscript, and dispatched it to Abergwili.[31] Bishop Davies was likewise puzzled by the manuscript, and consulted his collaborator William Salesbury, who translated the Bible into Welsh and was reputed to be not only the most learned scholar of the Welsh language in Britain 'but also in Hebrew, Greek, Latin, English, French, German, and other languages'.[32]

In a fascinating letter, Salesbury describes how he attempted to decode the language of Parker's Armenian manuscript. He took certain capital letters and tried to match them against the Book of Psalms. He tried to identify proper names such as Sion or Israel. Salesbury concluded that the text read left to right in the Latin fashion, but 'cold not make of it neither Walsh Englysh Dutche Hebrew Greke nor Latin'.[33] In April 1570, the erstwhile exchequer official and biblical scholar William Patten in a remarkable act of linguistic decoding managed to decipher Parker's Armenian Psalter and used it to compile the first English-Armenian wordlist.[34] Patten was the first person in England to study Armenian and his work was a major landmark in the early modern European encounter with Armenian language and culture.

The way in which Parker 2.0 enables us to browse Archbishop Parker's manuscripts opens up unexpected cultural narratives which disrupt the traditional view of Parker as a fount of Old English studies. We do not readily imagine Parker acting as the source of early Armenian studies in Britain. Nor do we expect the indigenous languages of Britain such as Welsh to feature in this story. The triangulation between Canterbury, Abergwili, and Armenia represented by CCCC 478 gives us fresh vistas in our appreciation of Parker.

Text as image

In the monochrome pre-digital world, our engagement with medieval texts was mediated through print. Printed editions are disconnected from the way in which scribes conceived and presented their texts. I first encountered Matthew Paris as an ocean of print in Henry Luard's edition of the *Chronica Maiora* for the Rolls Series. Yet Paris, in compiling his chronicle, created an immersive experience in which text was fused with marginal drawings, heraldry, and maps. Paris's autograph manuscripts in the Parker Library, CCCC 16 and 26, epitomize the holistic character of the medieval manuscript. Although sumptuously illustrated volumes of Matthew Paris's art have been published,[35] it is only with the availability of a full digital version of these manuscripts in Parker 2.0 that we can appreciate for the first time the scale, complexity, and virtuosity of Paris's achievement in integrating image and text. It is not the digital image which is rootless but rather the printed editions on which we have previously relied. Digitization enables scholars to reintegrate text and manuscript.

Medieval manuscripts fuse text and image in ways that challenge our logocentric ways of thinking. Digitization enables us to once again view text as image. Digital images enhance our appreciation of the ways in which the manuscript as a craft object intersects with and shapes the text. Matthew Paris was not unique in his multi-media vision; others saw visual imagery as an integral to their textual vision. For example, CCCC 76, folios 1–24v, comprises extracts from the *Abbreviationes Chronicorum* by Ralph de Diceto, Dean of St Paul's London from 1188 until his death in 1199 or 1200, perhaps made by Ralph for presentation to Archbishop Hubert Walter. Ralph used marginal symbols such as a crown or sword to categorize events in his chronicles. These marginal symbols were integral to Ralph's conception of his text and he conceived of his chronicle as much visually as verbally.[36]

Digital images are the perfect vehicle for conveying the fusion of the visual and verbal which characterizes the medieval text. Matthew Paris's work was perhaps an inspiration for the Book of Benefactors of St Albans Abbey, compiled in 1380 by the chronicler and precentor of St Albans, Thomas Walsingham, written by William Wyllum and decorated by Alan Strayler, which is now London, British Library, Cotton Nero D. vii. Each record of a gift to the abbey is accompanied by a portrait of the benefactor. These include not only kings, nobles, bishops and higher clergy but also many people of lower status such as merchants, craftsmen, and lawyers. While the portraits are not realistic, they comprise a remarkable visual directory of medieval society.

The way in which these portraits were regarded as integral to the Book of Benefactors is evident from CCCC 7, a copy of the St Albans Book of Benefactors made in the early fifteenth century found in the cell of William Wintershill of St Albans on his death in about 1435. The copy of this text in CCCC 7 also includes portraits. These are mostly in pen and wash and much less opulent than Strayler's miniatures, but nevertheless it is evident that the copyist thought it essential that portraits were included. James Clark suggests that the Parker copy was a working document made to provide information about the abbey's confraternity while the Cotton manuscript was kept on the high altar.[37] Perhaps the portraits enabled the social status of the benefactor to be quickly established. Whatever their function, the portraits were more than a decorative feature.

The way in which digital images reunite us with the scribal vision of a text is particularly evident from Parker's chronicle manuscripts. CCCC 197A is a chronicle compiled as a continuation of the *Polychronicon* at Westminster Abbey during Richard II's reign. It is a major source for political history from 1381 to 1394. It was first edited by J. R. Lumby for the Rolls Series in 1886 and is now available in a superb detailed edition by L. C. Hector and Barbara Harvey published by Oxford Medieval Texts in 1982.[38] It might seem that Parker 2.0 can add little to our understanding of a text edited to such high standards, but working with the digital images gives us a strong sense of how the chronicler grappled with piecing together the text. The Westminster Chronicle in CCCC 197A is the work of a single scribe. Estelle Stubbs has suggested that the scribe's hand shows similarities to that of Richard Frampton, a commercial scribe who worked for the Duchy of Lancaster and the London Guildhall.[39] Although the Westminster Chronicle is not in Frampton's hand, it is, in Stubbs's words, 'from the same hay field'[40] and perhaps the scribe worked with Frampton at some point. The chronicle begins in 1327 with Higden's own continuation of the *Polychronicon* to 1344, followed by an anonymous continuation from 1346 to 1348, and John of Malvern's continuation from 1348 to 1381. The digital version in Parker 2.0 is the first time these earlier sections of the chronicle have been made available; the printed editions only begin in 1381. The Westminster Chronicle from 1381 to 1394 was probably the work of two authors, with the change in authorship occurring in the account of events in late 1383 and early 1384.

The manuscript of the Westminster Chronicle is full of visual features showing the compilers grappling with the chronological structure of the narrative. Visual cues are also used to pick out particular events. These visual elements can be noted in a printed edition and in the case of the Westminster Chronicle are assiduously recorded by Hector and Harvey. But digital images provide a more holistic view of the manuscript which bring out the complex visual and textual cross-currents in the manuscript.

The digital images bring home strongly how the margins of the Westminster Chronicle were fields of lively scribal intervention. The scribe carefully noted the years being described in Arabic numerals in the margin, sometimes annotating years with 'A' and 'B' to make it clear when particular events occurred.[41] There are frequent marginal annotations noting references to particular people or events such as the first appearance of Wyclif in 1376 or departure of Bishop Despenser's crusade and an outbreak of plague in 1383.[42] Variations in ink colour show that these marginal notes were made over a period of time. The scribe also used small marginal sketches of human faces to highlight particular events, such as the launch of a crusade by Peter I of Cyprus in 1364, an outbreak of plague in 1375, the death of Wyclif in 1384 and the murder of Ralph Stafford in 1385.[43] These sketches were apparently an integral part of the scribe's scheme of annotation.

By using the digital images, we obtain a much stronger sense of the process by which the text was assembled than can easily conveyed in a printed edition. After he had copied John of Malvern's account of the death of Edward III in 1377, the scribe decided to add an encomium by Thomas Walsingham.[44] He had trouble finding space on the page for Walsingham's text. He squeezed as much as he could in after Malvern's text, then had to add the rest in the bottom margin. This in turn precipitated a change of plan for the whole manuscript. Up to this point, it was intended that the capital letters in the manuscript should be decorated and the scribe had provided guide letters for the decorator. This plan was abandoned. The scribe also started from page 127 systematically writing the regnal year and year of grace on the top right-hand corner of each recto leaf.[45]

The way in which the compilers of the Westminster Chronicle grappled with their documentary materials comes home powerfully in the digital images, as in the way a large section of the report of Bishop Henry Despenser's crusade against supporters of the anti-pope in Flanders in 1383 was cancelled by being struck through with a large cross.[46] As the chronicler increasingly uses documentary sources for his narrative, he uses the margins of the manuscript to insert commentaries on them, as in the case of the accusations of treason brought by a Carmelite friar against John of Gaunt in 1384.[47] The dynamic between the margin and the central text frame in the Westminster Chronicle is a lively one.

Far from being 'rootless', digital images enable us to tether to a text back to its manuscript origins. They enhance our awareness of how a text was put together and how different components of the text function. For too long, we have suffered from monochrome views of medieval texts as abstract deracinated entities in printed editions. Digital images enable us to escape the limitations of print and develop more holistic and multi-faceted views of the manuscript contexts of medieval texts.

Annotating and comparing

Not only do digital images offer the prospect of medieval studies becoming more deeply grounded in manuscript and other material remains, but digital images also increasingly facilitate innovative ways of recording and sharing commentary on these manuscripts, creating the possibility of different types of scholarly communication. Parker 2.0 is a flagship for the International Image Interoperability Framework (IIIF). The latest generation of IIIF compatible image browsers such as Mirador, developed at Stanford University and used in Parker in the Web, promote new ways of viewing and discussing manuscripts by enabling comparison of images and annotation of those images.

The ability of IIIF to support annotations of images of manuscripts in an open standard so that they can readily be shared and downloaded is particularly exciting. In Parker 2.0 at present, the annotation facility is currently used in a limited way to provide summary details of manuscript contents and to identify illustrations. But there is the potential to use annotations more extensively and adventurously. Different scholars can use annotations to discuss particular features of a manuscript and this commentary can be linked directly to the image. At present, scholarly discussion takes place in one venue such as an academic journal, while the images are available elsewhere. The annotation facility in IIIF offers the prospect of embedding scholarly discussion in the digital representation of the manuscript. I hope that IIIF might usher in a world where we write fewer articles and books, and instead use annotation to collectively discuss manuscripts.

IIIF also makes comparison of digital images from different libraries and archives much easier. We can place images from such IIIF-complaint repositories as the Bodleian Library, National Library of Wales, Durham University, and Vatican Library side by side with images from the Parker Library. By facilitating easier comparison of manuscripts, IIIF allows new relationships between manuscripts to be traced. Hitherto, it has often been difficult to compare manuscripts side by side. Even if two manuscripts are in the same library, many libraries are wary of allowing readers to consult more than one volume at a time, and special permission may be needed to compare manuscripts. In the sixteenth century, there were fewer inhibitions about sharing and lending manuscripts. When Parker consulted Bishop Davies and William Salesbury about his Armenian Psalter, he sent the manuscript to Wales. William Patten probably also borrowed the manuscript when he deciphered it. In modern times, opportunities for comparing manuscripts kept in different libraries are rare and unusual. One possibility occurs when manuscripts are borrowed for exhibition, but the rigorous restriction on handling such loans make detailed comparison difficult. The evacuation of manuscript collections because of risk of damage can also present opportunities for comparison. The most dramatic illustration of this was during the Second World War. Manuscripts from the British Museum, the Parker Library, and many other institutions were sent for safekeeping to the recently completed National Library of Wales in Aberystwyth. Many of the most precious manuscripts of the National Library and British Museum were stored in a specially built air-conditioned tunnel in the hillside beneath the library.[48]

An Assistant Keeper from the British Museum was sent to Aberystwyth to look after the manuscripts. For much of the war, this was Robin Flower, known for his work on the antiquary Laurence Nowell and on Irish literature and manuscripts. Flower was in a fortunate situation at Aberystwyth because he had at his disposal three great collections of manuscripts from the Parker Library, the British Museum, and the National Library of Wales. In fascinating articles published in the recently established journal of the National Library of Wales, Flower enthusiastically explored this opportunity for comparative study.

Flower's growing interest in the intersections between the British Museum collections, the Parker Library, and the National Library of Wales was illustrated by his publication of the correspondence between William Salesbury, Richard Davies, and Parker concerning Parker's Armenian Psalter.[49] Flower emphasizes the parallels between Davies and Salesbury's investigations of the ancient practices of the church in Wales and Parker's own searches for historical precedents for Anglican practice. He notes how London, British Library, Additional 18160, is a copy of Parker and Joscelin's translation of Ælfric's Easter homily, published in 1566–7 as *A Testimonie of Antiquitie*, containing annotations by Parker and Joscelin himself. Flower points out that a Welsh pamphlet by Salesbury is bound up with a fifteenth-century copy of the Laws of Hywel Dda in CCCC 454 in the Parker Library, and suggested that Parker acquired the manuscript from Salesbury's circle. Flower's excitement at the extraordinary opportunity to explore these manuscripts side by side is almost palpable.

These discoveries led Flower to investigate how Lord Cecil, another great collector of the period, was also acquiring manuscripts from Wales and particularly St Davids, resulting in Flower making a major identification.[50] Cecil acquired a manuscript of Gerald of Wales from St Davids. Flower showed that this was Aberystwyth, National Library of Wales, 3024C. He also showed that this manuscript is the only medieval witness to Gerald's final corrections to his *Journey through Wales* and *Description of Wales*. The third edition of the *Journey* and the second edition of the *Description* had previously been known from a thirteenth-century manuscript, London, British Library, Cotton Domitian A. i, but this lacked the final corrections, which were otherwise only known from a sixteenth-century copy, London, Royal 13 B. xii.

With the Parker Library and an increasing number of manuscripts from the National Library of Wales and the British Library available in IIIF format, we can all repeat Flower's experience at Aberystwyth in wartime and compare manuscripts which have not been seen side by side for hundreds of years. There can be little doubt that the potential offered by IIIF for comparing digital images of manuscripts now held in separate repositories will lead, as it did in Robin Flower's case, to major new textual and codicological discoveries.

Which new ways of seeing?

Far from being rootless, digital images of manuscripts offer a chance for medieval studies to reengage with its roots. Instead of the colourless representation of texts in printed editions, we can engage more strongly with the vibrancy, variety, and complexity of the way in which text interacts with the craft construction of the manuscript. By working directly with images of text, we can gain a deeper and more subtle understanding of the structure and shape of the text than will ever possible from working with printed texts. We move from a monochrome Middle Ages to one suffused with colour and light.

But there are dangers. In the early days of digitization, there was something of a land grab, as scholars rushed to be the first to digitize the canonical texts: *Beowulf*, the Exeter Book, the *Canterbury Tales*, *Piers Plowman*, and so on. This stress on the digitization of treasures continues, as libraries and museums are anxious to make their most precious items more widely available. There is a danger in this activity, as it can result in digitization simply reinforcing traditional narratives and canonicities. The risk that the web will more strongly embed traditional and outmoded cultural values in medieval studies is immense.

One benefit of digitization should be that it gives unfamiliar and non-canonical materials greater prominence, but unfortunately in the rush to digitize treasures, this does not always happen. By giving us access to the vast majority of the manuscripts in the Parker Library, Parker 2.0 offers the potential of disrupting traditional perspectives of Parker's collections. We can linger with unexpected items, such as Parker's Armenian or Arabic manuscripts, and see how these can be just as informative an artefact as the more celebrated Old English manuscripts. Parker 2.0 gives us a chance to root out the obscure, forgotten, and overlooked in Parker's library. This is much more valuable than focusing on the aura of the treasure, wonderful though it is to have the treasures in digital form. It is by encouraging us to look beyond the celebrities and to have conversations with more humble and reticent manuscripts that Parker 2.0 makes its most important contribution towards creating new ways of seeing the Middle Ages.

Notes

1 George F. Warner, ed., *British Museum: Reproductions from Illuminated Manuscripts*, Series I–III, 3 vols. (London: Trustees of the British Museum, 1907–8); Eric Millar, *British Museum: Reproductions from Illuminated Manuscripts*, Series IV (London: Trustees of the British Museum, 1928); D. H. Turner, *Reproductions from Illuminated Manuscripts*, Series V (London: Trustees of the British Museum, 1965).

2 Phyllis Giles, review of *The Parisian Miniaturist Honoré* by Eric Millar, *The Library*, Series 5, 15.1 (1960): 75–6; Adelheid Heimann, review of *The Douce Apocalypse* by A. G. Hassall and W. O. Hassall and *The York Psalter in the Library of the Hunterian Museum, Glasgow* by T. S. R. Boase, *Burlington Magazine*, 105.722 (May 1963), p. 222.

3 D. H. Turner, Rachel Stockdale, Philip Jebb, and David M. Rogers, *The Benedictines in Britain* (London: The British Library, 1980).

4 Janet Backhouse, *The Illuminated Manuscript* (Oxford: Phaidon, 1979).

5 Janet Backhouse, *Books of Hours* (London: The British Library, 1985).

6 Walter Benjamin, *The Work of Art in an Age of Mechanical Reproduction*, trans. J. A. Underwood (London: Penguin, 2008).

7 'Mercure Flagship a Tribute to Exeter History': https://www.hotelfandb.co.uk/news/2015-10-02-mercure-flagship-a-tribute-to-exeter-history <accessed 21 September 2019>.

8 John Berger, *Ways of Seeing* (London: Penguin, 2008), p. 12.

9 Rhiannon Lucy Cosslett, 'Art, Aura and the Doomed Search for the Perfect Selfie', *The Guardian*, 22 August 2019: https://www.theguardian.com/commentisfree/2019/aug/22/art-aura-doomed-search-perfect-selfie <accessed 21 September 2019>.

10 These points are succinctly explained by Berger, *Ways of Seeing*, chapter 1.

11 James Stourton, *Kenneth Clark: Life, Art and Civilisation* (London: William Collins, 2016), p. 213.

12 Christopher de Hamel, *Meetings with Remarkable Manuscripts* (London: Allen Lane, 2016), p. 2.

13 De Hamel, *Meetings*, p. 2.

14 De Hamel, *Meetings*, p. 4.

15 De Hamel, *Meetings*, p. 6.

16 De Hamel, *Meetings*, p. 256.

17 De Hamel, *Meetings*, p. 571.

18 The remaining Parker Certificates from 1560–1 are described in the Parker Register as being 'in rotulis longioribus' but were marked as missing. They were identified in the College Archives in 1959 and are now CCCC 580A, 580B and 580C: Richard Vaughan and John Fines, 'A Handlist of Manuscripts in the Library of Corpus Christi College, Cambridge, Not Described by M. R. James', *Transactions of the Cambridge Bibliographical Society* 3.2 (1960): 119.

19 CCCC 545, a sixteenth- or seventeenth-century Old Testament Chronology, was transferred from the College Archives in 1959 and a Parker connection cannot be established; CCCC 546, a genealogical chronicle written in 1527 by Ambrose Middleton, was presented to Corpus Christi College in 1692 by Thomas Whincop; CCCC 583 is a vellum roll containing autobiographical notes by Parker was probably given to the College by Archbishop Tenison: Vaughan and Fines, 'Handlist', pp. 115, 120.

20 Andrew Prescott, 'What's in a Number? The Physical Organization of the Manuscript Collections of the British Library', in *Beatus Vir: Studies in Early English and Norse Manuscripts*, ed. A. N. Doane and Kirsten Wolf, Medieval and Renaissance Texts and Studies, 319 (Tempe, AZ: ACMRS, 2006), pp. 515–7; Colin G. C. Tite, *The Early Records of Sir Robert Cotton's Library: Formation, Cataloguing, Use* (London: The British Library, 2003), pp. 100–2; Peter Barber, 'Monarchs, Ministers and Maps, 1550–1625', in *Monarchs, Ministers and Maps: The Emergence of Cartography as a Tool of Government in Early Modern Europe*, ed. David Buisseret (Chicago: University of Chicago Press, 1992), p. 83; G. Meer, 'An Early Seventeenth-Century Catalogue of Cotton's Anglo-Saxon Coins', in *Sir Robert Cotton as Collector*, ed. C. J. Wright (London: The British Library, 1997), pp. 168–82; Marion M. Archibald, 'Cotton's Anglo-Saxon Coins in the Light of the Peiresc Inventory of 1606', *British Numismatic Journal* 76 (2006): 171–203; Colin Tite, 'Sir Robert Cotton and the Gold Mancus of Pendraed', *Numismatic Chronicle* 152 (1992): 177–81. The tonsure plate is British Museum, Department of Britain, Europe and Prehistory, 1916, 1106.1. This was Cotton Charter xvi. 73 and was transferred from the Department of Manuscripts to the British and Medieval Antiquities Department on 13 March 1916. See further: www.britishmuseum.org/research/collection_online/collection_object_details.aspx?objectId=51380&partId=1&searchText=manuscript+disc&page=1 <accessed 21 October 2018>, and W. Sparrow Simpson, 'The Tonsure-Plate in Use in St. Paul's Cathedral during the Thirteenth Century', *Journal of the British Archaeological Association* 38 (1882): 278–90.

21 Anthony Grafton, 'Matthew Parker: The Book as Archive', *History of Humanities* 2.1 (2017): 15–50.

22 *Ælfredi Regis Res Gestæ* (London: John Day, 1576), sig. Aiiij (verso); Grafton, 'Matthew Parker', p. 35.

23 Grafton, 'Matthew Parker', p. 35.

24 David McKitterick, *Print, Manuscript and the Search for Order* (Cambridge: Cambridge University Press, 2003), pp. 11–21.

25 Now widely accepted as a term that perpetuates structures of white power.

26 A point emphasized in E. Boehmer, R. Kunstmann, P. Mukhopadhyay, and A. Rogers, eds., *The Global Histories of Books: Methods and Practices* (Basingstoke: Palgrave Macmillan, 2017), pp. 1–2.

27 Anthony Farrington, *The English Factory in Japan 1613–1623*, 2 vols. (London: The British Library, 1991), vol. 1, pp. 83–4, 622–23, 626–32, 719, 725–7, 747–9, 766–9; vol. 2, pp. 869–73, 942–3; 953–7.

28 Anthony Farrington, *English Factory*, vol. 2, pp. 1289–1471. In the list of documents, vol. 1, p. 47, this manuscript is wrongly listed as London, British Library, Cotton Vespasian F. xviii. It was not included in Smith's 1696 catalogue. Planta described it as a merchant's account book and this description is still current in the online manuscript catalogue at the time of writing (September 2019).

29 Farrington, *English Factory*, vol. 2, p. 1363.

30 Grafton, 'Matthew Parker', pp. 16–17.

31 Robin Flower, 'William Salesbury, Richard Davies, and Archbishop Parker', *National Library of Wales Journal* 2 (1941): 9–11.

32 R. Brinley Jones, 'Salesbury [Salisbury], William (*b.* before 1520, *d. c.* 1580)', *Oxford Dictionary of National Biography*.

33 Flower, 'William Salesbury, Richard Davies and Archbishop Parker', p. 10.

34 Betty Hill, 'Trinity College Cambridge MS. B. 14. 52, and William Patten', *Transactions of the Cambridge Bibliographical Society* 4.3 (1966): 195–200; S. Peter Cowe, 'An Elizabethan Armeno-Latin Wordlist and the Inception of Armenian Studies in England', *Le Muséon: Revue d'Études Orientales* 104.2 (1991): 277–333.

35 Suzanne Lewis, *The Art of Matthew Paris in the Chronica Majora* (Berkeley and Los Angeles: University of California Press with Corpus Christi College Cambridge, 1987).

36 On Ralph's use of marginal images in his historical writing, see further Laura Cleaver, *Illuminated History Books in the Anglo-Norman World, 1066–1272* (Oxford: Oxford University Press, 2018), pp. 87–95, and Michael Staunton, *The Historians of Angevin England* (Oxford: Oxford University Press, 2017), pp. 75–9.

37 James G. Clark, 'Monastic Confraternity in Medieval England: The Evidence from the St Albans Abbey *Liber Benefactorum*', in *Religious and Laity in Western Europe, 1000–1400: Interaction, Negotiation, and Power*, ed. Emilia Jamroziak and Janet E. Burton (Turnhout: Brepols, 2007), p. 316 n. 2.

38 L. C. Hector and Barbara Harvey, eds., *The Westminster Chronicle 1381–1394* (Oxford: Clarendon Press, 1982).

39 Estelle Stubbs, 'Richard Frampton and Two Manuscripts in the Parker Library', *Digital Philology* 4.2 (2015): 225–62.

40 Stubbs, 'Richard Frampton', p. 231. Lawrence Warner, *Chaucer's Scribes: London Textual Production, 1384–1432*, (Cambridge: Cambridge University Press, 2018) p. 186 n. 54 confirms that it is unlikely that the hand of the Westminster Chronicle is Frampton's, but notes that Stubbs is chiefly interested in mapping scribal networks and contacts.

41 For example, in allocating events to 1364 and 1365: CCCC 197A, p. 116.

42 CCCC 197A, pp. 123, 139, 140. These marginal headings are incorporated into the main text by Hector and Harvey, *Westminster Chronicle*, pp. 48–56.

43 CCCC 197A, pp. 116, 122, 147, 149. These marginal sketches are not noted by Hector and Harvey.

44 CCCC 197A, p. 126; Hector and Harvey, *Westminster Chronicle*, pp. xviii–xix.

45 Hector and Harvey, *Westminster Chronicle*, pp. xviii–xix.

46 CCCC 197A, p. 138.

47 MS 197A, pp. 142–3; Hector and Harvey, *Westminster Chronicle*, pp. 70–1.

48 David Jenkins, *A Refuge in Peace and War: The National Library of Wales to 1952* (Aberystwyth: Llyfrgell Genedlaethol Cymru, 2002), pp. 266–70; N. J. McCamley, *Saving Britain's Art Treasures* (Barnsley, South Yorks.: Leo Cooper, 2003), pp. 29–38, which includes illustrations of the tunnel at Aberystwyth showing British Museum

material in store, on pp. 30–1; W. Ll. Davies, 'War-Time Evacuation to the National Library of Wales', *Transactions of the Honourable Society of Cymmrodorion*, 1945 [1946]: 171–8; J. Leveen, 'The British Museum Collections in Aberystwyth', *Transactions of the Honourable Society of Cymmrodorion*, 1945 [1946]: 194–200; A. Prescott, 'Robin Flower and Laurence Nowell', in *Old English Scholarship and Bibliography: Essays in Honor of Carl T. Berkhout*, ed. Jonathan Wilcox, Old English Newsletter Subsidia 32 (Kalamazoo, MI: Medieval Institute Publications), pp. 48–9.

49 Flower, 'William Salesbury, Richard Davies, and Archbishop Parker'.
50 Robin Flower, 'Richard Davies, William Cecil, and Giraldus Cambrensis', *National Library of Wales Journal* 3.1–2 (1943): 11–14.

Part 2
Materialities

6 A note on Cambridge, Corpus Christi College, 210

Orietta Da Rold

As the Parker on the Web description of Cambridge, Corpus Christi College, 210 states, the manuscript 'contains the unique copy of William Worcester's *Itineraria*. William Worcester (1415–1480/85), a servant of Sir John Fastolf, wrote the *Itineraria* in note form during a series of journeys he undertook throughout southern and western England between 1478 and 1480, and the manuscript must date from this period. The text's eclectic mixture of local history, biography, and geography reflect a lively and curious mind.'

In what follows, I shall briefly consider how technology can serve to answer, but also to formulate, new research questions. The perspective is very much that of a codicologist approaching the book in its digital dimension. By 'codicologist', I do not simply mean someone who is looking to analyse the structure of the book, but I mean the more expansive definition, which defines codicology as that branch of scholarship focused on studying the manuscript book in its material realization and, more broadly, in all its cultural and historical interrelationships.[1] I conclude with a desideratum.

My first question for the Parker on the Web site is to ask how it can help a scholar to think codicologically. The answer is that it assists in quite satisfactory ways. Most obviously, high resolution images are always helpful, but the interoperability between technologies is the highlight of what Parker on the Web has got to offer at present. The inclusion of IIIF images with the outstanding ability to display numerous images from multiple repositories simultaneously, and of pulling the manuscripts together in Mirador, is a new and outstanding feature in this project.[2] This is remarkable because it enables a variety of close comparisons and stimulates fascinating questions prompted by the juxtaposition of images of folios in front of us. From the simple question that is 'What am I looking at?' to 'How can we begin to describe the effects of this juxtaposition?' to 'To what cultures of the book do these images belong?' to 'Why are these images so different?'— such possibilities open up a range of opportunities and challenges for manuscript scholars to work upon.

By juxtaposing Cambridge, Corpus Christi College, 26 and 210, notable observations emerge. In the former case, we have the impressive thirteenth-century hand of the St Albans monk and historian Matthew Paris, who wrote in a monumental Gothic script, and composed a chronicle framed with double columns and penned on parchment. In CCCC 210, as Wakelin puts it, we have a sample of Worcester's 'atrocious handwriting, with its jagged and irregular sized anglicana letter form and its disjointed flow'.[3] In terms of the material of the manuscripts, Worcester writes on paper and this paper is of an oblong size, rather different from CCCC 26, which is written, of course, on membrane. This compare and contrast technique could take a number of approaches: we could go down the line of the pauper versus the prince (which one is which?) or we could consider low grade versus high grade production; expensive production costs versus cheap; professional scribe and production team versus amateur, and so on. Most scholars know, however, how unhelpful it is to use binary descriptors in codicological evaluation. This is particularly true whether we apply this technique diachronically, as in this case, or synchronically. Numerous examples of fifteenth-century manuscripts on membrane could provide similar observations; for instance, putting Cambridge, Corpus Christi College, 61, a copy of Geoffrey Chaucer's *Troilus and Criseyde* side by side with CCCC 210 would be equally hazardous.[4] Too much of this still appears in current literature on medieval manuscript studies and even though we should acknowledge differences, I should like very much to propose that we reject binaries.

Binary descriptions are unnuanced, and do not help scholars to understand scribal practices; such descriptions tend toward the subjective and can easily be misinterpreted in the pursuit of grand narratives that are not attested in the evidence. For instance, I could easily say that CCCC 26 shows the constraints of the handwritten culture of the thirteenth century, while CCCC 210 represents the great freedom that cursive scripts brought about during the last three centuries of the medieval period. Obviously, these differing material realizations of text are symptomatic of book cultures that are themselves chronologically sensitive, but also reflect a continuously evolving relationship between those who wrote and what they needed to write. This evolving relationship had implications for the number of choices people had to take: from the material to the type of script, to the format of the book, and, significantly, these varied over time, so that to talk of 'medieval manuscripts' or a monolithic 'book history' is to do a disservice to the long medieval period, which included tremendous regional variation, too. These choices facing scribes and others involved in the manufacture of manuscripts are what interest me, because they have stories to tell about book production practices and keep us out of the binary mischief. Let me briefly illustrate what I mean using CCCC 210.

I would like to go back to what I said about 'freedom to write'. It is well known that the economic and social changes during the twelfth and thirteenth century intensified the need for written communication. Letter writing as a practice, for example, grew and developed because of the increase in the variety of official and personal interactions. People either looked for or communicated information about political, economic, and financial events more assiduously than before. Petrucci declares: 'L'Europa reimpara a scriversi', 'Europe re-learns to write itself'.[5] This does not mean that in earlier centuries people did not write to each other—personal and official communications abounds—but it means that the nature of the correspondence intensifies, becomes more frequent and carries clearer news or simple instructions; the mercantile community, in particular, conduct their business in this way.[6] The need for more information spreads into all walks of life, and, in particular, the need to keep accurate records intensifies at all levels of society. This, Petrucci suggests, is the environment in which 'I liberi di scrivere', those who are free to write, thrive. And indeed, within this freedom, people chose to write cursive rather than set scripts.

We know that cursive scripts are not confined to the later part of the medieval period: as Parkes reminds us 'cursive handwriting is a way of writing rather than a particular style or tradition of script, and is not confined to any period', but he also suggests that there is a close link between readership and cursivity.[7] As we know cursive scripts speed up writing in relation to their currency, and I contend that it is not the reader who is uppermost in the mind as the script is being selected, but the writer; that is, cursivity is for the writer not the reader. Trained writers needed to be free to write quickly and, more importantly, in their own hand. One might recall Chaucer's oath to keep in his own hand the record of the Petty Custom, and indeed the same advice is given by Benedetto Cotrugni Raguso to merchants. He tells readers to mistrust those who 'fanno scrivere de mano d'altri', 'those who ask others to write'.[8] The ability to write for oneself is seen as a sign of being trustworthy. Worcester is the exemplification of this freedom. For William Worcester, a pointy cursive anglicana script is the ideal choice for his text, which notes expenses on his journey around Bristol including the halfpenny spent on paper (Figure 6.1). Worcester's hand defies the reader, because it is about remembrance; it is about keeping a journal of his journey rather than legibility for others' eyes. This is also the beginning of a process that will lead to reading and writing becoming a conjoint set of skills rather than separated by their function.

A similar freedom is evinced in the choice of the format of Worcester's records. This format can be achieved in two ways. The basic characteristics of the handmade paper sheet in the later Middle Ages are laid lines, formed with thinly spaced wires across the mould, the chainlines, wires running at interval and perpendicularly to the laid lines, and the watermark. Paper arrives with the buyer folded lengthwise in half, with chainlines running vertically, and nested in quires of 25 sheets. This packaging would create the folio shape of paper which could be readily employed for writing on single sheets or in quires, depending on the purpose for which the paper was purchased. Then the paper can be further folded as many times and in as many ways as the original size of the sheet of paper allows. For example, folding the folio one more time from the shorter side to the shorter side would create the quarto (with the chainlines running horizontally). However, if the folio is folded one more time from the longer side to the longer side, the chainlines would still go vertically and form a sort of vertical quarto. Cambridge, University Library, Dd.1.1 is a classic example of these two ways of folding paper in one book. If users of the Parker on the Web zoom into an image of CCCC 210, they can see the laid lines, rather than chainlines, going across the sheet of paper, which means that the paper is folded lengthwise twice. Both Harvey and Wakelin comment on the shape of CCCC 210 as an ideal format for immediate jottings and for portability.[9] This is a shape of book that Worcester uses in four of his other manuscripts.[10]

Wakelin comments on the 'unusual format' of these books, and while it is certainly true that statistically it is more common to find books shaped in a more proportional rectangular fashion such as CCCC 26, after spending many years looking at paper books and records, it is clear that this way of folding paper, and sometimes parchment, is more common than previously thought. Worcester himself does not confine this format to precarious jottings; he finds it a convenient shape for keeping much of what he wishes to commit to written memory, in particular, when he is using paper. Worcester, as Wakelin notes, takes great care in what he records, even though the resultant books from the assembly of loose quires may seem heterogeneous.[11] How did this book-making practice come into being and how portable does such a practice make the book itself? This format is very common amongst the records preserved at The National Archives in Kew and is extensively used in ports records, but also in an account of medicine for Edward II.[12] If the reader zooms into some of the sheets of CCCC 210, there is also a clear fold in the middle, which probably indicates that the oblong-shaped paper was folded one more time across. This makes the paper portable and easy to handle, but would this be more pocket-sized than holster-sized?

Manuscript scholars usually refer to the shape of this type of book as 'holster books', and printed book historians as 'agenda format'.[13] On the one hand, scholars have argued that this shape was used to be carried in a saddlebag or holster, and others argued for accounting practices. Foxton suggested that this format may be related to the way in which people needed to handle the book itself: 'Turning the pages of a quarto with one hand while endeavouring to hold it with the other is only too likely to end in catastrophe; with a long quarto each hand supports one of the covers and the fingers can reach round the spine while the thumbs control the pages.'[14] If Ivy commented that 'We sometimes find account-books of this shape, but "literary" holster-books are rare',[15] Robinson has offered an excellent overview of how this type of books, often deemed unusual, came to be named 'holster books', and notes this format in computistical texts, Apocalypses, Latin verse, Books of Hours, and *cantatoria*, remarking on the ease of holding the book with one hand and performing another task with the other.[16] I find this explanation persuasive. It is striking that many examples of paper documents and also paper books have this format. However, I am not convinced that this format is exclusively about portability, even though the case of CCCC 210 may support this claim.[17]

There is so much more to say about how Parker on the Web can facilitate the close consideration of a single manuscript, bringing evidence to bear on wider issues that currently form the focus for new research, such as the shape of books produced for particular kinds of text. Other issues that emerged as a result of this examination of CCCC 210 included the question of how many other manuscripts on Parker on the Web are written in cursive script and whether any other manuscripts are produced in an oblong shape. It was not possible to ascertain this information from current search functionality within the platform; thus a desideratum would be that if any future development and implementation is scheduled, might scholars be provided with a way of carrying out quantitative analysis of the data through nuanced relational data? These kinds of investigations are served well by the digital medium and it would be useful to develop this fuller exploitation of the affordances of the digital object. By 'affordance', I mean a greater use of what the digital environment offers in relation to how the data is structured and tagged, and possibly expanding the data to permit an expansion of the properties of the digital object to create an environment which cannot yet be anticipated.

Thus, can we now go beyond user-friendly interfaces, which do not try to *anticipate* what a user might like to find, but instead to offer boundless possibilities which will push the technology as far as possible, leaving options open for users to engage serendipitously with the data and its accompanying tools? I am advocating that software designers go beyond usability as it is currently defined and think about the digital environment from the data outwards rather than from looking into the data. As a quantitative codicologist, I want to be able to gather data and search for patterns; this is not just about distant or close reading, it is about a critical mass of knowledge that can be used for comparative purposes. 'Dimension', for example, is tagged in the XML file and available in the first iteration of Parker on the Web. The file can in turn be usefully downloaded onto my computer, but I cannot query the XML files across Parker on the Web. I could resort to manually downloading each and every file and then search through them all together, but it would be wonderful to be able to do it from the portal itself. And while there might be technical reasons for not being able to do this at present, because more indexing or subsequent software development is required, so much information has already been tagged that thinking about how to move forward in new directions would be ideal. Scholars might then be able to use this wonderful resource in very different ways: if, as developers, we do not simply anticipate needs, then we also do not constrain; and if we do not constrain, then we dramatically increase opportunities for what can be done with what has been created. Of course, this is not just about the reuse of data and metadata, this is about working with the very affordance of the intrinsic characteristics of what technology provides. This is how paper became a success story and there can be no doubt that Parker on the Web has every chance to follow suit.

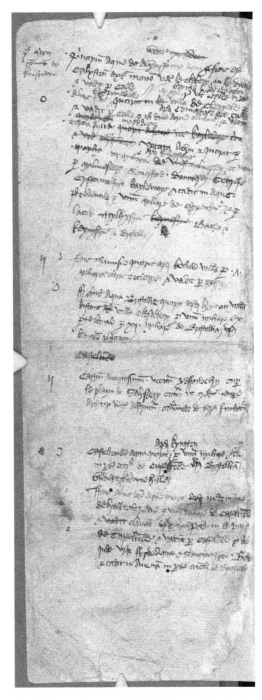

Figure 6.1 The Parker Library, Corpus Christi College, Cambridge, MS 210, p. 6.

Notes

1 For a brief overview, see Orietta Da Rold, 'Codicology', in *The Encyclopaedia of Medieval British Literature*, ed. Siân Echard and Robert Rouse (Oxford: Wiley-Blackwell, 2017), pp. 531–38.

2 See Andrew Prescott's chapter and Benjamin Albritton's introduction in this volume for more on the International Image Interoperability Framework and Mirador.

3 Daniel Wakelin, 'William Worcester Writes a History of His Reading', *New Medieval Literatures* 7 (2005): 53–71, at p. 56.

4 See Cambridge, Corpus Christi College, 61 at: https://parker.stanford.edu/parker/catalog/dh967mz5785; and see Siân Echard, Chapter 9 in this volume.

5 Armando Petrucci, *Scrivere Lettere: Una Storia Plurimillenaria* (Roma: Laterza, 2008), p. 49.

6 Petrucci, *Scrivere Lettere*, pp. 49–51.

7 M. B. Parkes, *Their Hands before Our Eyes: A Closer Look at Scribes* (Aldershot: Ashgate, 2008), p. 85.

8 Benedetto Cotrugli, *Libro e l'arte de la mercatura*, ed. Vera Ribaudo (Venice: Edizioni Ca'Foscari, 2016), p. 66.

9 See John Harvey, ed., *Itineraries [of] William Worcestre* (Oxford: Clarendon Press, 1969); Wakelin, 'William Worcester', p. 56

10 The manuscripts are London, British Library, Additional 28208 which includes estate records; London, British Library, Cotton Julius F. vii, which contains texts on classicism and history; London, British Library, Sloane 4 which includes medical texts. For an excellent overview see Wakelin, 'William Worcester', p. 56.

11 Wakelin, 'William Worcester', p. 57.

12 There are numerous records in The National Archives relating to the customs of Bordeaux, but also later Calais and other affairs on the territories in France; all these documents are on paper and can be found by perusing the King's Remembrancer section, E 101. Some of this material dates to as early as 1302. On the Bordeaux records, see, for example, E 101/158/10, Book of Customs at Bordeaux. 31 and 32 Edw I; E 101/158/2, Book of Customs at Bordeaux. 31 Edw I, E 101/160/3, Book of Customs at Bordeaux. 33 Edw I, Unbound; E 101/160/8, Part of a book of John Guiciardi, controller of Bordeaux; E 101/161/2, Account of Customs at Bordeaux. 34 and 35 Edw I; E 101/161/3, Book of Customs at Bordeaux. Richard de Havering and Jordan Morant, Constables. On some of these books, see Edward Heawood, 'The Position on the Sheet of Early Watermarks', *The Library* 38 (1928): 38–47. On the apothecary's account for Edward II, see The National Archives, E 101/127/10.

13 D. F. Foxton, 'Some Notes on Agenda Format', *The Library* 5-VIII (1953): 163–73.

14 Foxton, 'Some Notes', p. 173.

15 G. S. Ivy, 'The Bibliography of the Manuscript-Book', in *The English Library before 1700: Studies in its History*, ed. Francis Wormald and C. E. Wright (London: Athlone Press, 1958), p. 64, n. 71.

16 Pamela Robinson, 'The Format of Books: Books, Booklets and Rolls', in *The Cambridge History of the Book in Britain, Volume II 1100–1400*, ed. Nigel Morgan and Rodney M. Thomson (Cambridge: Cambridge University Press, 2008), p. 54. This conclusion was also reached by Erik Kwakkel, 'Decoding the Material Book: Cultural Residue in Medieval Manuscripts', in *The Medieval Manuscript Book: Cultural Approaches*, ed. Michael Johnston and Michael Van Dussen (Cambridge: Cambridge University Press, 2015), p. 71.

17 I further discuss this issue in O. Da Rold, *Paper in Medieval England: From Pulp to Fictions* (Cambridge University Press, forthcoming).

7 Cambridge, Corpus Christi College, 367 Part II

A study in (digital) codicology

Peter A. Stokes

Cambridge, Corpus Christi College, 367 is a relatively small manuscript. In its current form it measures approximately 220 mm in height and 145 mm in width—almost exactly the size of an A4 paper folded in half, but slightly taller—and a little over a hundred folios in length.[1] The book was described by M. R. James as being in two parts, the first comprising 53 leaves of paper and the second 52 leaves of parchment. However, this division is somewhat arbitrary since, as James himself noticed, the book as it stands today comes from at least five and indeed almost certainly six if not seven different manuscripts, ranging from the eleventh through to the fifteenth centuries. The structure of the book and its five 'main' manuscripts are listed in Table 7.1, below; these manuscripts have no apparent relation to each other, with texts comprising historical chronicles, homilies in Old English, logic tracts, an anti-Goliardic poem, and a saint's life and some other texts loosely related to this. References to the manuscript are complicated further by the fact that the manuscript was foliated in two separate sequences: first the paper, from folio 1 to folio 53, then the parchment starting again with folio 1 and extending to folio 52. However, as part of the cataloguing and digitization work for Parker on the Web, the manuscript was refoliated into a single continuous sequence. Table 7.1 therefore gives both new and old foliations, partly to aid the reader when consulting earlier publications which of course use the older foliation, but the new foliation will be used throughout the rest of this chapter.

Although already relatively complex, Table 7.1 in fact simplifies further details. Section E includes several texts which were written at different times from the late eleventh century through to the second half of the twelfth century; details of this are given in Table 7.2.

Significantly more complex is Section B. Rather than being from a single manuscript, this section is in fact made up of materials most likely from two different manuscripts, or at least certainly written by different people at different times.[2] The parts of this section are shown in Table 7.3, with Bi indicating material originally from the earlier manuscript and Bii that of the later one.

Table 7.1 Overview of the contents and structure of MS 367

		Quire	Num. Leaves	Folios (new)	Folios (old)
Part I: 53 leaves of paper.					
A	Epitomæ chronicæ Cestrensis	1	10	1–10	1–10
		2	10	11–20	11–20
		3	12 (wants 10–12)	21–29	21–29
	Breuiarium historiae Anglicae	4	14	30–43	30–43
		5	10	44–53	44–53
Part II: 52 leaves of parchment.					
B	Old English De Temporibus	a	2 singletons	54–55	1–2
	Old English Homilies	b	2	56–57	3–4
		c	2	58–59	5–6
	Old English De Temporibus (ctd.)	d	4	60–63	7–10
	Old English Homilies (ctd.)	e	2 (wants 2)	64	11
		f	6 (wants 6)	65–69	12–16
		g	14 (10 cancelled)	70–82	17–29
C	Logic Tracts	A	12	83–94	30–41
D	Apocalypsis Goliae pontificis	B	4 (wants 4)	95–97	42–44
E	Vita breuior of St Kenelm	I	8 (wants 1, 7, 8)	98–101	45–49
	and additions (see below)	II	2 + 1	101–105	49–52

Regarding content, the simpler and chronologically earlier is Bii which contains the remains of ten vernacular homilies, seven of which are from Ælfric's *Sermones Catholici* and one of which is from his *Lives of Saints*. The text is written by a single scribe dated to the first half of the twelfth century. There are two later additions, both medieval: the first appears to be a pen-trial in a cursive script on folio 81r, and a document in the outer margin of folio 56r from 53 Henry III (A.D. 1268/9).[3] Section Bi contains Ælfric's translation of Bede's *De temporibus*, dated by both Ker and Treharne to the second half of the twelfth century; Treharne has identified the scribe as that of Cambridge, University Library, Ii.1.33.[4] A brown ink was used throughout, with a large green initial at the start of the text, and with occasional undecorated majuscule initials in the margins in the same ink as the main text. The only additions to the text are Latin marginalia on

Table 7.2 Contents and structure of MS 367, Section E

	Date	*Quire*	*Folios*
Vita breuior of St Kenelm (incomplete at beginning)	Saec. xi ex.	I	98r–101r
Additions to the Vita, from Vita et miracula	Saec. xii[1]	I	101r
Booklist	Saec. xi ex.	I	101v1–3
'Vision of Leofric'	Saec. xi/xii	I–II	101v4–103v15
Note on 'vesper'	Saec. xii[1]	II	103v17–20
Latin neumed sequence	Saec. xi[2]	II	104r
Letter to the prior, cantor, and monks of Worcester	Saec. xii[1]	II	105r1–5
Charm	Saec. xii[1]	II	105r16–17
Monastic constitutions (incomplete at beginning)	Saec. xii[2]	II	105v

This table is reproduced from Stokes, 'Vision of Leofric', p. 531, updated for the current foliation.

Table 7.3 Structure of MS 367, Section B

Section	*Text*	*Quire*	*Num. Leaves*	*Folios*
Bi	Old English *De Temporibus*	a	2 singletons	54–55
Bii	Old English Homilies	b	2	56–57
		c	2	58–59
Bi	Old English *De Temporibus* (ctd.)	d	4	60–63
Bii	Old English Homilies (ctd.)	e	2 (wants 2)	64
		f	6 (wants 6)	65–69
		g	14 (10 canc.)	70–82

folios 54v–55v which relate to the text, and which Ker dated to the four-teenth century.[5] Although the first section of the text is missing, it is otherwise complete, and in fact this omission is apparently by design, since the text begins neatly with a large green initial at the top of folio 1r. Similarly, the last 16 lines of folio 63r (lines 21–36), and all of folio 63v, are blank. Interestingly, the rulings on the page do not match the prickings which remain in the outer margin. The text runs continuously across all six folios, in the order in which they are currently bound, thereby lending support to Ker's statement that they constitute 'a quire probably of 8, [which] wants 7, 8'.[6] However, the text has been crowded into the margins on folio 55v (lines 24–39), which is difficult to explain if indeed these leaves did once form a single quire.

Table 7.3 shows clearly that Section B interleaves material from the two original manuscripts, but what is less clear is that the leaves in this section have also been jumbled significantly from their original order, even with two cases of a bifolium folded back on itself so that what was the first recto is now the last verso and so on. Indeed, to convey this it is helpful to quote in full the collation description by Elaine Treharne, who has followed those of M. R. James and Neil Ker:

> Collation appears to be as James 1912 suggests: Paper 1^{10}, 2^{10}, 3^{12} (wants 10–12), 4^{14}, 5^{10}. Parchment is as Ker suggests: 1^{8}, wants 7 and 8 (now forms fols 1, 2, 7–10), 2^{3} (a singleton and bifolium originally leaves 3, 4, 5 of a quire of eight, now fols 21, 20, 26), 3^{2} (a middle bifolium, now fols 17, 29), 4^{8} wants 2, 7 (now fols 23, 6, 3–5, 24), 5^{8} wants 7 and 8 (now fols 11–16), 6^{4} (two bifolia, leaves 2 and 3 of a quire of 8, now fols 28, 19, 27, 18), 7^{2} (a bifolium, perhaps leaf 2 of a quire, now fols 22, 25). Ker suggests that Quires 5 and 6 were adjacent, as were 4 and 5. Furthermore, a quire is missing between 3 and 4, leaves are missing after 1 and 2, and an indeterminate number of leaves are missing at the beginning and end; 8^{12} (*Logica Quaedam*), 9^{3}, 10^{8} wants 1, 7, 8 (fols 48–49), 11^{2} (fols 50–51).[7]

Figure 7.1 attempts to show this information in diagrammatic form. The row of numbers across the top indicates the folios in the original manuscript, with X for those that are now lost; the rectangles around these numbers show the original quires. The row across the bottom shows the folios in the current manuscript. The lines between them therefore show the change in order from the original to the new structure. The first two folios in the current manuscript therefore remain in their original place. Blocks of parallel lines indicate groups of folios that remain together and in the same order as they once were, namely the seventh through tenth and the eleventh through sixteenth in the current order. Lines that cross indicate those that are reversed in order, so the seventh and eighth in the original order are reversed in the current one.

The description of the manuscript so far in this discussion has been accurate and follows the standards for cataloguing. It is also essential for understanding the manuscript and its texts, since the relationship between and even the dates of the texts and perhaps their composition depend at least in part on this codicological structure.[8] However, it also seems clear that descriptions in this form are very difficult to understand even for experts, let alone for others who are less versed in the intricacies of codicology but who may well need access to this information. The question therefore arises whether we might be able to present this same information in more accessible ways, particularly with current developments in modelling and visualizing manuscripts in digital form and especially in the context of Parker on the Web. One approach to this is to use the VisColl software developed by Dot Porter, Alberto Campagnolo, and team at the

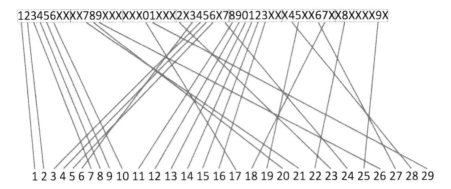

Figure 7.1 Diagram of changes in folio order in CCCC367 Section B

Schoenberg Centre for Manuscript Studies in the University of Pennsylvania.[9] This software is designed to create interactive visualizations of the codicological structure of books, with two visualizations in particular. The first is a quire diagram of the entire manuscript. The second takes this diagram and, for each bifolium in the original manuscript, it provides a virtual representation of that bifolium as it would appear if removed from the manuscript book and laid out flat on a table. For example, whereas a conventional facsimile image might show an image of folio 1v alongside that of folio 2r to give a representation of the opening, VisColl would instead give an image of folio 1v alongside the recto of the conjugate leaf, so folio 7r in a quire of eight. Two extracts of the results are given in Figure 7.2 and Figure 7.3 below; the complete diagrams and the source that produced them are freely available online.[10]

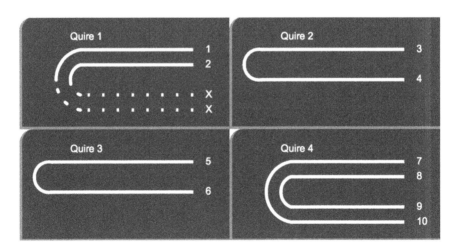

Figure 7.2 Extract of quire diagrams for current structure of MS 367 (created with VisColl, using the original manuscript foliation).[11]

Figure 7.3 Extract of the 'VisColl' visualization of MS 367 with its original structure.[12]

These visualizations show some interesting points. First, the collation diagrams make clear the highly irregular structure of the current binding, with two quires comprising single bifolia, one comprising two singletons, a quire of four, one of eight but lacking two folios, and one enormous quire of fourteen folios. Second, the VisColl visualizations also show the variation in parchment quality and state. For instance, it is clear that folio 60 (7 in the old numbering) is of poor quality, most probably because it came from the edge of the original piece of animal skin, and that, whatever the case, the curved edge of the page was that way before the time of writing.[13] What is not at all evident from the original manuscript, however, is that the conjoint folio 63 (10 in the old numbering) is also of poor quality, with several holes that appear to pre-date the writing of the manuscript. Folio 79 shows similar signs of being an edge piece, and the conjoint folio 73 clearly shows the same shape impressed on it, confirming that the bifolium was once in the middle of a quire without intervening pages, a point consistent with the reconstructed original ordering but by no means obvious from the manuscript in its current state. Original holes are also visible on folio 66 and the conjoint folio 69 (*olim* fols. 13 and 16), as well as the edges of 54, 57 and 80 (*olim* fols. 1, 4, and 27). Several bifolia from Section Bii also show evidence of damage along the fold forming the spine of the book. This damage appears to be confined to the final very large quire of this section, particularly the outermost and innermost leaves, and it seems to have affected leaves from across different quires in the original ordering. Furthermore, it becomes evident from the VisColl view that the parchment in this current quire seems to be significantly darker and more brown than that of the rest of the section. These points all seem very strongly to suggest that this quire of 14 that currently ends the section incurred damage after the leaves were arranged as they are now, in a way that the other leaves of this section did not. This information can be taken further as well. Looking carefully at Figure 7.1, it becomes clear that the first 16 folios of Section B are relatively undisturbed in the reordering from the original to the current state. That which remains of Bi, for instance, makes up exactly one quire of eight except for the last two leaves which are lacking or cancelled, and the leaves are still in their correct order except for the insertion of two bifolia from what was the fourth quire of Section B as a whole and the third that survives from Bii. Similarly, the original fifth quire is preserved essentially undisturbed except for the loss of the two final leaves. However, what is now the last quire of 14 comprises a jumble of leaves from throughout the original manuscript, with no apparent rationale or correspondence between the original and current orderings except for the fact that all the leaves come from Bii. In other words, the manuscript as it survives today can be described as the following:

1   A quire from Bi, in order but lacking the last two leaves and with two bifolia inserted from the middle of the third surviving quire of Bii.
2   The fourth surviving quire from Bii, in order but lacking the last two leaves.
3   A jumble of six bifolia and a singleton from five quires of Bii, including from the quire which also 'provided' the two bifolia in (1).

At this point, the question arises how one might use this information to reconstruct the 'biography' of Section B. Any such reconstruction is necessarily speculative, but at least some details seem relatively clear. The arrangement of text in Bi is such that it may never necessarily have comprised anything more than the existing six leaves, perhaps loosely bound in a booklet rather than as part of a larger manuscript.[14] Our Bi might once have been a regular quire of eight, with the last two leaves left blank and subsequently removed for use elsewhere. However, folio 54 is pricked for 30 lines to the page and folio 55 with 35 lines, and indeed the arrangement of pricks is different;[15] this and the cramming of text on folio 55v suggests that these two leaves may always have been singletons or at least were not originally prepared for use in the same quire. The fact that the next folio in the original Bi, namely the current folio 60, is the edge piece may further suggest that the person who put this together was using any pieces of parchment that could be found and this could also be consistent with the use of singletons for the first two leaves. In contrast, Section Bii seems more likely to have once been a complete manuscript, most likely in more or less regular quires of eights. At some point this manuscript was disbound (assuming it was ever bound at all), with one quire staying essentially intact but the other quires becoming entirely loose bifolia and many of these sheets being lost. At some point, the two largely intact quires from Bi and Bii were put together, followed by most of the remaining loose leaves from Bii which were simply gathered together into a single large gathering. Two bifolia from Bii, perhaps accidently left out from this large gathering, were also inserted near the start after the first two singletons in Bi. The damage in what is now the large final quire suggests that this new arrangement still was not bound for some time, and perhaps this quire was even once kept separately from the other two largely intact quires. This would mean that folio 70r was once the outermost page, and it does indeed show clear signs of wear, with more stains than other pages and with portions of the text showing clear signs of abrasion. Even if this large quire was kept separately, though, it still seems likely that the respective parts were all kept in the same institution and probably in more or less the same place, since otherwise it would be unlikely that they all ended up together in Matthew Parker's library.

The obvious question that remains in this account is when this postulated rearranging and rebinding took place. As hinted above, it is by no means necessary that the original manuscripts were ever bound, and even if they were, bindings from this period almost never survive and so these bindings could well have broken and been removed or even reused. Whatever the case, it seems very likely that the leaves were in this unbound state at the time when they reached the hands of Matthew Parker. It seems feasible that both Bi and Bii came to Parker from the same place, but it may also be that the two set of fragments were not united until Parker's time or even later. Neil Ker suggested that the different sections were 'bound together for Archbishop Parker ... in or before 1575' presumably because they are found as a single volume in the Parker Register of that date.[16] However, it seems significant that CCCC 367 is listed in the Register as one of the 'bookes in parchment closures as the[y] lye on heapes'.[17] The exact meaning of this phrase is unclear: Mildred Budny has suggested that it may refer to limp vellum covers or wrappers,[18] but it could refer to a range of possibilities including a parchment folder of some sort, or a loose attachment such as ticketing. Whatever the case, it does seem to raise the possibility that the pages were not bound into a volume of the sort that exists today at the time that the Register was produced. The Register itself does suggest that the texts were much as they are today, as it lists the Epitome, 'homilie quedam saxonice' and *A tauro torrida*, along with incipits that refer unambigiously to Sections A, B, and D above. The description by Thomas James of 1600 lists Sections A–D but not E, and William Stanley's more detailed description of 1722 finally lists the five sections that exist today.[19] The omission of Sections C and E in the earlier descriptions might be taken to suggest that these texts were added at later stages, with Section C between 1575 and 1600 and Section E between 1600 and 1722, but a much simpler explanation is that the earlier descriptions are very brief and so may well have omitted these short texts.

In conclusion, then, CCCC 367 has received relatively little attention compared to many other manuscripts in the Parker Library, but its modest form contains a great deal of codicological, palaeographical, and other interest. The focus here has been on the codicology of only one section, in an attempt to show how a close examination of the material structure can allow one to construct a relatively detailed 'biography of the object'. This 'biography' can no doubt be elaborated with further examination of the palaeography, the makeup of the parchment, more detailed study of the pricking and ruling, and so on, but that would require a much longer discussion than is possible here. However, what this also shows is how technological developments can also help in visualizing, experimenting with, and otherwise studying the book's structure. In particular, the combination of VisColl and the International Image Interoperability Framework (IIIF) allows one to create such visualizations very quickly and easily. As we have already seen, VisColl generates quire diagrams and representations of the book when it is 'virtually disbound'; although the XML model of the quire structure was generated by hand for this article, there is also an online form which can be used to create the model for those who wish to use it. IIIF, on the other hand, is an international standard for finding and accessing digital images online, particularly (but by no means necessarily) those in cultural heritage such as images of manuscript pages.[20] The fact that the digitized images of the Parker Library are available through IIIF and with an appropriate licence that allows largely free reuse means that any software including VisColl can automatically access images of any page of the manuscript at the resolution that is desired. In this case, all that was required was to create a spreadsheet with the list of pages (recto and verso of each folio) in one column and the corresponding URL to a low-resolution image in the second column. This then allows VisColl to find the image for each page, and to then create the visualization from there. In other words, the point of IIIF is not simply that one can see high quality images online, as in general this has been possible since the 1990s, if not before, but rather that one has a standard method by which one can find and access these images, and it therefore becomes very much easier than ever before for us to produce our own scripts, visualizations, interactions, and so on, according to our own needs and interests, and to communicate our arguments and conclusions more effectively than ever. This is the real potential of Parker on the Web: not to give the illusion of seeing what we would find in the library today, but rather to allow us *also* to see in new ways that we have never seen before.

Notes

1 The physical descriptions in this chapter come from a combination of existing printed descriptions, my own examination of the manuscript, and further checks by Dr Anne McLaughlin, whom I thank for her assistance. Important descriptions of the book are given by M. R. James, *A Descriptive Catalogue of the Manuscripts in the Library of Corpus Christi College, Cambridge*, 2 vols. (Cambridge: Cambridge University Press, 1912), 2, pp. 199–204; N. R. Ker, *Catalogue of Manuscripts Containing Anglo-Saxon* (Oxford: Clarendon Press, 1957), no. 63; Elaine Treharne,

'Cambridge, Corpus Christi College 367', in Orietta da Rold, Takako Kato, Mary Swan, and Elaine Treharne, *The Production and Use of English Manuscripts 1060–1220*, (Leicester: University of Leicester, 2010–13): https://www.le.ac.uk/english/em1060to1220/mss/EM.CCCC.367.htm; and 'Cambridge, Corpus Christi College, MS 367', *Parker Library on the Web* (Stanford: Stanford University, [2018]): https://parker.stanford.edu/parker/catalog/hp566jq8781; as well as Peter A. Stokes, 'The Vision of Leofric: Manuscript, Text and Context', *Review of English Studies* 63 (2012): 529–50: doi:10.1093/res/hgr052.

2 The scribes of this section have been discussed in detail by Elaine Treharne, 'The Dates and Origins of Three Twelfth-Century Manuscripts', in *Anglo-Saxon Manuscripts and their Heritage*, ed. P. Pulsiano and E. Treharne (Aldershot: Ashgate, 1998), especially pp. 234–5 (Section Bii) and pp. 238–40 (Section Bi).

3 The document has been described and printed by James, *A Descriptive Catalogue*, 2, p. 201.

4 Ker, *Catalogue of Manuscripts*, p. 108; Treharne, 'The Dates', pp. 240–1.

5 Ker, *Catalogue of Manuscripts*, p. 108.

6 Ker, *Catalogue of Manuscripts*, p. 108.

7 Treharne, 'Cambridge, Corpus Christi College 367', following James, *A Descriptive Catalogue* 2, pp. 199–204; and Ker, *Catalogue of Manuscripts*, no. 63.

8 Stokes, 'Vision'.

9 Dot Porter, Alberto Campagnolo *et al.*, 'VisColl': https://github.com/leoba/VisColl. This discussion uses VisColl Version 1. At the time of writing Version 2 is in an advanced stage of development but is not yet available and so has not been used here.

10 Peter A. Stokes, 'Collation Visualisation: Cambridge, Corpus Christi College 367': https://pastokes.github.io/CCCC-367/. Note, however, that at the time of writing these visualizations still use the old foliation.

11 The full diagram including its source is available at: https://pastokes.github.io/CCCC-367/Output (current order)/CCCC 367 Diagrams-current.html

12 The full diagram including its source is available at: https://pastokes.github.io/CCCC-367/Output (original order)/CCCC367.html

13 For discussion of these edge pieces see E. Kwakkel, 'Discarded Parchment as Writing Support in English Manuscript Culture', *English Manuscripts Studies 1100–1700* 17 (2012): 239–61.

14 The best-known discussions of booklets are those by P. R. Robinson, 'Self-Contained Units in Composite Manuscripts of the Anglo-Saxon Period', *Anglo-Saxon England* 7 (1978): 231–38, and '"The 'Booklet': A Self-Contained Unit in Composite Manuscripts', *Codicologica* 3 (1980): 46–69.

15 I again thank Anne McLaughlin for these observations about the pricking.

16 Ker, *Catalogue of Manuscripts*, pp. 108–110 (nos. 62–64).

17 Cambridge, Corpus Christi College, 575, 76 (no. 19.9).

18 Mildred Budny, *Insular, Anglo-Saxon, and Early Anglo-Norman Manuscript Art at Corpus Christi College, Cambridge: An Illustrated Catalogue*, 2 vols. (Kalamazoo, MI: Medieval Institute Publications), vol. 1, p. 50.

19 Thomas James, *Ecloga Oxonio-Cantabrigiensis, tributa in libros duos, quorum prior continet catalogum confusum librorum manuscriptorum in illustrissimis bibliothecis, duarum florentissimarum Acdemiarum, Oxoniae et Catabrigiae* (London: G. Bishop and J. Norton, 1600), no. 19.9; William Stanley, *Catalogus librorum manuscriptorum in Bibliotheca Collegii Corporis Christi in Cantabrigia, quos legavit Mattaeus Parkerus Archiepiscopus Cantuariensis* (London: G. & J. Innys, 1722), no. 19.9.

20 For further discussion see *IIIF: The International Image Interoperability Framework*: http://iiif.io.

8   Pocket change

Cambridge, Corpus Christi College, 383 and the value of the virtual object

Anya Adair

In 1681, Jean Mabillon's *De Re Diplomatica* was published: a commanding account of the scripts and material features of medieval charters that crystallized paleography as a scholarly endeavour.[1] Mabillon sought in *De Re Diplomatica* both to provide scholars with the tools for discriminating between authentic charters and clever fakes, and to assemble in his reproduced script-samples evidentiary support for his own numerous judgements on authenticity. His masterwork was revolutionary not only for its *ex nihilo* breadth in the description of medieval charters, but for its fundamental methodological promise: that collecting representations of the physical and visual details of medieval documents would allow the modern scholar to arrive at a secure judgement about their authenticity and status. Simply see enough manuscript examples, Mabillon's manual seemed to promise, and secure knowledge about them would follow. This approach was transformational: what Mabillon had done for continental charters was immediately desired for early English documents. A *De Re Anglorum Diplomatica* never materialized, but was enthusiastically planned in the late 1600s; Bodleian Library assistant Humfrey Wanley was one of the liveliest supporters of the project. It was taken for granted that new and profound insights into Anglo-Saxon legal and cultural history would be a direct result, 'When', in the words of Wanley in 1697, 'I have the whole Treasure of England in that kind, by me, to be seen at one view.'[2]

Present approaches to manuscript studies continue to privilege the reproduction, description, and collection of manuscripts as a way to knowledge; that this approach seems now to be an obvious, even an inevitable one demonstrates how fundamentally the method inaugurated by Mabillon continues to be of influence. And the digital humanities offers powerful tools to manuscript scholars engaged in the project of collection: online platforms allow for the precise visual reproduction of manuscripts, which are suddenly available on computer screens across the world 'to be seen at one view'—with the same startling effect of revelation that Mabillon's collection of scripts in *De Re Diplomatica* had in the seventeenth century. But projects of digitization and digital curation offer more than the capacity to see more manuscripts: they provide new lenses through which the methods and approaches of manuscript studies may themselves be challenged or reconfigured. Parker on the Web and digital manuscript collections like it make good on the commitment of Mabillon to collection and viewing as a way to knowing. But they also fulfil an energizing promise of the digital humanities: that the process of building things is a way to re-evaluate, as well as to extend, that which we think we know.[3] In projects like Parker on the Web lies the potential for a new scholarly confederation in which the approaches of digital humanities and the methods of palaeography and codicology combine.

The coalition of codicological interpretation and digital user experience design in Parker on the Web creates a platform of medieval manuscripts that has been radically refocused. In the process of digital collection, some aspects of the manuscript object are necessarily lost or destabilized. On screen, for example, the colours of the manuscript are relative, its size becomes variable, and its weight vanishes entirely. New hierarchies of information are created by the translation of meanings taken to be implicit in the manuscript artefact into information made explicit to the machine and searchable by the user. The very temporality of the manuscript object—its existence within linear time—is challenged by its new instantiation as an artefact digitally frozen at a single moment of its post-medieval existence, to be both preserved and perpetually renewed as computers across the world simultaneously render it on screen. The physical and temporal existence of the manuscript is changed utterly; in the recognition of this transformation comes the potential radically to reconsider our assumptions about the meaning of the manuscript's original existence within both space and time. Perhaps most significantly, the intangibility of the manuscripts in their digital form prompts the scholarly user to reconsider all that is tangible about the manuscript objects themselves.

In what follows, I take Cambridge, Corpus Christi College, 383 as a case study in the attempt to appreciate manuscripts as physical objects (with uses and values in their own time) from the position of our modernity and through the lens of the digital collection. I consider the significance of just one of the physical elements of this manuscript: its size. CCCC 383 was produced in the early twelfth century.[4] It principally contains Anglo-Saxon laws in Old English, augmented by a small number of texts dating from the early 1100s; its production may have been associated with St Paul's Cathedral, London. Thom Gobbitt summarizes its creation as follows:

> The manuscript is copied throughout in a late vernacular minuscule by a single scribal hand, with limning and rubrics added later, and emendations and alterations made by a separate scribal hand of the first half of the twelfth century, and another set of additions ... by a third hand dating to the second quarter of the twelfth century.[5]

There appears thus to have been a sustained interest in (or at least a fitful series of returns to) this manuscript over the course of the first half of the twelfth century. But why this post-Conquest attention? What might CCCC 383 have meant to its producers and presumed readers in this period? And how can its size help to answer this question?

'Size' on the computer screen is an ambiguous phenomenon. In Parker on the Web, in common with most digital manuscript collections, manuscript size is standardized, with codices of widely varying dimensions displaying on screen as though they are of equal size. The precise size of the manuscript image on screen is determined by the computer of the scholar, not the size of the represented manuscript; this image zooms between magnifications under the viewer's slightest scrolling touch. The catalogued dimensions of the manuscript—its height and width—are, in fact, not immediately apparent even upon selecting a single manuscript to view: the user clicks through to a page beyond this level to find (under 'More details') the measurements. Even if the viewer is adept at accurately imagining millimeter dimensions, it is clear that in the building of this digital collection, 'true' size is a codicological feature that has been (relatively speaking) marginalized, sacrificed to new priorities of display and interface. It is also clear that this is an aspect of the manuscript rendered radically mutable and unstable by the nature of the digital platform itself.

But in an interrogation of the meaning of the physical features of the manuscript, this instability becomes the crucial point: for the truth of manuscript size is an unstable one even with the manuscript solidly in the scholar's hands. The frequency with which manuscripts were trimmed in the centuries after their production means that an entirely different measure of size—the dimensions of the text block, rather than the manuscript dimensions overall—is often a more useful indicator of original size; but taking the text block as the central measure obscures the width of the margin, and so elides or obscures the size of the whole as a substantial object.[6] CCCC 383 poses just such a problem of size interpretation. The manuscript is not in its original binding; it was almost certainly trimmed at some point between its twelfth-century creation and its twenty-first-century digitization. The resulting reduction in its size may have been slight, but certainly weakens the foundation of any arguments based on the 'fact' of its size in the hands of its medieval users. And what of the putative original(s) from which this manuscript was copied? We can know little of size here, and so cannot guess at any deliberate choice to increase or reduce its size for a new audience at the moment of copying. The more securely we seek to pin down the truth of this fundamental and apparently obvious physical feature, the more elusive it becomes.

Manuscript size nevertheless attracts definite statements of meaning. Massive liturgical manuscripts, like the vaulting spaces of the churches in which they lay, are understood to have suggested the great spiritual importance of their contents; these manuscripts seem to have been intended to play a prominent ceremonial role as objects. Large and luxurious manuscripts are spoken of as conspicuous witnesses to the wealth and status of their owners, as much as to their own precious contents. And small manuscripts suggest to the modern eye deliberate portability, and so imply the quotidian utility of the texts they contain. The size of the book, in other words, seems to speak directly to the meaning and utility of its contents. As Erik Kwakkel has it, insofar as 'the recipient of the manuscript had an opportunity to voice his [*sic*] preferences', this material feature of the book may allow us to 'read the reader'.[7] This logic has been applied to legal manuscripts: across the medieval period, small size in law books (and books of statutes are often small) suggests to scholars their active use as reference books in courts both royal and legal, and in the everyday attempts of their users to understand and establish legal rights.

CCCC 383 principally collects Anglo-Saxon laws written in Old English. Many of the laws it contains were centuries out of date, relics of kings long dead in disparate kingdoms long ago brought under new legal administration. The laws of English kings from Ine of Wessex (*c.* 694) to Æthelred II and Cnut are found among its 62 folios, as well as (on its final folios) lists of 'scipmen' and of kings, saints, and bishops. Some of its legal texts are found in no other surviving manuscript. Its compendious nature has led Patrick Wormald to label it (along with other similar collections like the *Textus Roffensis*) a legal 'encyclopedia'.[8] Its apparently synoptic nature has been coupled with the fact of its relatively small size to produce claims that hint at its practical use. Gobbitt writes that the manuscript is 'quite portable in size and, although this does not prove that it actually was carried, evokes the image of a pocket-sized legal reference book, to say the least'.[9] CCCC 383 is recorded in Parker on the Web as being 190 x 119 mm, or about half as large again as a current iPhone, and with an extent of folios 9 + 62, considerably thicker. Does this relatively small size suggest that it was intended to be as mobile a reference as the modern device, or was it intended to remain in one place (possibly St Paul's), to be archived but little used; that is, as an object of perhaps antiquarian or political interest but little active legal relevance?

The question of size and its relation to manuscript meaning and use has been little studied, despite the frequency of scholars' passing pronouncements. In fact, critical accounts of manuscript size are rare.[10] Witness size is occasionally noted in analyses of particular medieval texts, and there exist some quantitative surveys of continental manuscripts, but taken as a whole, scholarly explorations of medieval book size are few. The fundamental issue, however, is not merely one of measurement uncertainty and scanty scholarship: the question to be asked is what size really means in terms of the production and use of manuscripts; what can it signify?

A modern smartphone, wildly anachronistic through it is, is in many ways a useful starting place in the reconsideration of the meaning of size, and in particular the problem of a frequently used size classification purporting to describe small medieval manuscripts: the pocket-book. The smartphone is certainly an object intended to be carried in the pocket, but it is at the same time an object whose size is constantly in flux. With each new generation or brand, the size of 'pocket-size' changes, and so does the meaning of size as a signifier of value and prestige: in the recent history of mobile technology, there have been trends in which the cost-value and cultural status of the device increased as the object decreased in size; at other times, the more expensive and desirable devices are those that are larger than their predecessors. Our own experience teaches us that the relation between size and meaning, both in terms of value and in terms of use, is difficult to determine: what size means is mutable, and alters as it finds alteration in a complex array of cultural influences and technological constraints.

In terms of practical use, of course, size is not the only consideration. At least two related concerns must also be addressed: those of the manuscript's total original weight, and of what we might call the text's consultative convenience: the mechanics of the individual book in its original binding. Did its stitching and covers allow it to fall open and lie obediently flat on the surface upon which it was placed, or was a reader's hand needed to keep its folios from springing stiffly closed? These are data of the medieval manuscript that remain almost entirely uncollected and unstudied, as well as being experiential realities totally erased from the digital surrogate. Neither is easy to adduce from the evidence of size alone: Daniel Sawyer, by taking a scale to the Bodleian and tallying the weight of a number of late medieval codices in their original bindings, was able to demonstrate the surprising lack of correlation between manuscript dimensions and total codex weight.[11] Larger did not always mean heavier—an important consideration if portability is a central concern. In the case of the mechanics of holding the manuscript open, size and submission to the reader's physical needs may correlate inversely: it is often the smallest books that are the most stubborn, snapping obstinately closed unless held open with both hands. Such manuscripts may be small enough to be kept close at hand, but if they are intended to guide their user through the work of writing legal text, or of consulting multiple laws, they are likely to frustrate, rather than facilitate, their reader's efforts. Of course, weight and the mechanical effects of original stitching and binding as features of the manuscript at the point of its creation are even harder to discover than original size. But these features have the potential to contradict or corroborate claims about the convenience of use so often taken to be implied by small size; they are significant complicating factors in any quest to link size with use.

The relation between purpose and size has in fact troubled the denotation of the word 'pocketbook' for its entire history. In the sense 'small bag or pouch worn on the person' and later 'a pouch sewn into or on clothing', the word 'pocket' is attested only from *c*.1450. (The earlier sense of the word, 'sack or bag', is far more variable in size, changing according to the commodity contained: a pocket of hops still weighs 90 kg; a pocket of South African onions might weigh 5 kg.) The word 'pocketbook' occurs much later, appearing in the early 1600s. Portability is certainly at the heart of that term's first attested use: an advertisement for Jean Barbier's *Janua Linguarum quadrilinguis*, printed in 1617, claims that the author 'sought … to render the volume yet as portable as might be, and, if not as a manuall or pocket-booke, yet a pectorall or bosome-booke, to be carried twixt jerkin and doublet'. But the term pocket-book seems even in this early use to mean as much a collection constructed for easy reference as 'a book small enough to fit in a pocket'—the former sense can be readily discerned in many early uses. (In this sense, the word 'pocket-book' follows a similar trajectory to the word 'manual': the sense 'of a size to fit the hand' coexists with the sense 'intended to be kept at hand for reference'.) There is here a slippage between the size of the object and the intended use of the text it contains. It is perhaps this duality of sense that has influenced the language of scholars who reach for the term to describe manuscripts of laws.

Finally, and crucially, the overwhelming anachronism of the modern portable device serves to remind us of the fundamental and finally misleading anachronism of the pocket-book classification itself. The relationship between size and status, between size and use, is not a stable or straightforward one for the pocket-sized information devices of today; nor was it, I would suggest, for the codex in the twelfth century, and certainly not across all medieval times and textual genres. When we come to grapple with the image of a truly portable medieval reference codex—with all the implications of storage during travel, the risk of damage or loss, the carry-bag or cloth folds to keep it in, the convenience of the layout of the text itself, and the mechanics of its being opened and held open in readiness for consultation—the connection between intended use and manuscript size becomes less and less direct. Within the broader economy of medieval book production, with its economic and environmental constraints, was the single issue of portability a primary determinant of manuscript size? And how accurate is this conflation of portability with (relatively) small size? Physical size is certainly a factor significant enough to warrant real thinking about how the material substance of the manuscript should be represented in future digital collections; but what this information tells us about use in the medieval pasts of the manuscript objects we collect and seek to represent remains, finally, ambiguous.

Given the fact that scribes continued to work on CCCC 383 after its initial creation, and the fact that it was bound, trimmed, and rebound over the course of its life as a codex, its physical existence was (even in the century that produced it) under constant construction, and subject to the changing realities of its own fluid development. In order that the significance of its physicality might be fully explored, still more gathering must be undertaken: further information is needed relating to size and the genre of the legal book or legal text collection for the centuries after the Conquest. But this gathering, this building of new digital tools with which to collect and present the realities of physical form, is only the beginning. The inability of the digital database to represent the physical realities at the centre of the question of manuscript use reminds us of the limitations of the act of collection as a way to knowing.

As a physical record of the lived experience of medieval readers and producers of text, codicological and palaeographic evidence is tantalizingly solid. Manuscripts themselves are tangible envoys of a past time, and the data that is gleaned from them as they are measured, photographed and described offers a reassuringly scientific approach to the reconstruction of their production and use—and so to the discovery of the meaning they held to those who produced and used them. But this solidity has proved illusory. The very nature of digital data brings with it a corollary, which is both cautionary and bright with promise: what is lost in the departure from the physical domain is compensated for by the questions that the resulting digital abstraction makes possible. Two questions have animated this brief exploration of the limitation and advantage of the digital archive. In broad terms, can the method inaugurated by Mabillon—gathering together reproductions as a way to attain a secure knowledge of the things they represent—achieve its intended aim? And with regard to one particular, does the small size of a manuscript imply a portability and ease of use, as has so often been claimed? My reading of CCCC 383 in Parker on the Web suggests that the answer to both questions may be *no*; and it urges above all the imperative for thoughtful interpretation and sceptical appraisal of even the most apparently straightforward of the manuscript data that Parker on the Web so brilliantly supplies.

Notes

1   Jean Mabillon, *De Re Diplomatica*, Libri VI (Paris: Charles Robustel, 1681).
2   Wanley to Hickes, May 23 [?], 1697 [dated 28 May 1697]: *Letters of Humfrey Wanley, Palaeographer, Anglo-Saxonist, Librarian, 1672–1726: With an Appendix of Documents*, ed. P. L. Heyworth (Oxford: Clarendon Press, 1989), nos. 31, 54. See also Alfred Hiatt, 'Diplomatic Arts: Hickes against Mabillon in the Republic of Letters', *Journal of the History of Ideas* 70 (2009): 351–73, at p. 361.
3   In these formulations I am influenced by the phrasing of Matthew K. Gold, who writes that 'What sets the digital humanities apart from the other humanities disciplines is its methodological commitment to building things as a way of knowing': Matthew K. Gold, quoted in 'Day of DH: Defining the Digital Humanities', in *Debates in the Digital Humanities*, ed. Matthew K. Gold (Minneapolis: University of Minnesota Press, 2012), pp. 67–74, at p. 69.
4   For a detailed account of this manuscript, see Thom Gobbitt, 'Cambridge, Corpus Christi College 383', in Elaine Treharne, Orietta Da Rold, Mary Swan, and Takako Kato, *The Production and Use of English Manuscripts 1060–1220* (Leicester: University of Leicester, 2010): www.le.ac.uk/english/em1060to1220.htm <accessed 30 June 2018>.
5   Thom Gobbitt, 'Treaty of Alfred and Guthrum (AGu)', *Early English Laws Online*: www.earlyenglishlaws.ac.uk <accessed 30 June 2018>.
6   On the gulf between such catalogue data and the manuscript as an experienced object, see further Joseph A. Dane, *Abstractions of Evidence in the Study of Manuscripts and Early Printed Books* (London: Routledge, 2009), pp. 4–7.
7   Erik Kwakkel, 'Decoding the Material Book: Cultural Residue in Medieval Manuscripts', in *The Medieval Manuscript Book: Cultural Approaches*, ed. Michael Johnston and Michael Van Dussen (Cambridge: Cambridge University Press, 2015), pp. 60–76, at 67.

8 Patrick Wormald, *The Making of English Law: King Alfred to the Twelfth Century*, vol. 1 (Oxford: Blackwell, 1999), p. 224.

9 Thom Gobbitt, 'Audience and Amendment of Cambridge, Corpus Christi College 383 in the First Half of the Twelfth Century', *Skepsi* 2 (2009): 9 at: www.blogs. kent.ac.uk/skepsi <accessed 30 June 2018>.

10 But see, for example, Elaine Treharne, 'Fleshing out the Text: The Transcendent Manuscript in the Digital Age', *postmedieval: a journal of medieval cultural studies* 4 (2013): 465–78, at pp. 470 and 475–6.

11 Daniel Sawyer, *Reading English Verse in Manuscript c.1350-c.1500* (Oxford: Oxford University Press, 2020). The relevant chapter is "4. Handling."

9   Rolling with it

Navigating absence in the digital realm

Siân Echard

Cambridge, Corpus Christi College, 61 is one of the Parker Library's more famous manuscripts, a copy of Chaucer's *Troilus and Criseyde* that opens with a much-reproduced frontispiece, commonly described as the poet reciting his poem to the court.[1] The frontispiece's ubiquity means that people who have not seen the manuscript in person or consulted a complete facsimile—either the 1978 photographic facsimile by Malcolm Parkes and Elizabeth Salter,[2] or the Parker digitization—are often unaware that, after this splendid opening, the manuscript is characterized by absence, by the spaces left for a programme of illustration and illumination that was barely started. Cambridge, Corpus Christi College, 98 is far less famous, but it, too, is characterized by absence, by blanks of different kinds. The massive roll has an unusual amount of blank space, but the direction for this chapter was suggested by another, quite accidental, absence. The only scholar who has written about CCCC 98 at length calls it the Adam and Eve roll, because it begins with an image of Eve with a distaff, followed by one of Adam delving.[3] However, until recently the Parker digitization offered, as its first image, the top of the dorse of the roll. One could make out the outline of Eve through this image, but a visitor would look in vain for anything more, as neither Eve nor Adam appeared at all in the online digitization. While the roll was fully imaged at the time of the original Parker project, an incomplete jumble of images made its way to the online presentation. This was a temporary situation, now corrected, but it points to the issue I shall explore here; that is, to the intersection of absence with digital presence. CCCC 61 and 98 are material objects that many scholars can access only through surrogates, and digital surrogates create unique barriers and opportunities, sometimes by accident and sometimes as a result of deliberate choice. The digital has the potential both to obscure and to reveal, not only the objects it delivers to us but also the process of manuscript scholarship itself, in the past and the present.

The Corpus *Troilus* is characterized by absences, by spaces ranging from whole folios, to three-stanza gaps, to large initials. Apart from the frontispiece, none of what would have been a lavish programme of decoration has been completed. While Matthew Parker and his circle often filled in gaps in his manuscripts, there is very little added material, from any source, in this manuscript. Three of the planned initial letters—at the beginning of Books I, II, and IV—are sketched in roughly. M. R. James's 1912 catalogue of the Corpus manuscripts does not mention these additions.[4] Malcolm Parkes, in the 1978 facsimile, attributes them to a sixteenth-century owner, made before the manuscript entered Parker's collection (which was by 1575).[5] Parker and his circle were chiefly interested in histories and related texts; the persistent blankness of the Corpus *Troilus* may indicate a lack of interest in vernacular literary manuscripts.[6] However, even earlier owners seem to have been oddly reticent. On the whole, additions to the Corpus *Troilus* are limited to writing on its end leaves and, in a very few instances, to small marginal additions. Yet, to quote *Troilus and Criseyde*, just 'as an ook cometh of a litel spyr' (II.1335), stories can be told about these small additions. And when we cannot make mighty oaks out of those little acorns, even that failure has something to tell us about our scholarly past and our digital present.

One early owner of the manuscript is Edward Franton, who writes his name backwards, as *Notnarf Drawde*, in a fifteenth-century hand, enclosed in a scroll, on the front flyleaf of the book. He also writes it on what would then have been a blank leaf at the end of the manuscript, where it now appears along with a great jumble of names, scribbles, and a recipe for an enema. The scroll around his name on the front suggests he is not shy about writing in the book; however, he appears only once in the text proper, where he fits his name neatly in between the ruling at the end of Book V, line 1678, a section of the poem where Troilus laments Criseyde's change of heart. Why write his name here? Had he been recently betrayed by a lover? Was Troilus speaking for his poor, confused, backwards heart?

This is of course complete speculation, but that is the point. No one who has written about the manuscript has been able to identify Edward Franton, and as a chief interest in the formal description of manuscripts has to do with identifying possible owners, then someone with a name but no historical biography drops out of the discussion, becomes notionally absent even when he is visually present. Far more ink has been spilled, for example, on Anne Nevill, who writes on folio 101v, in a late-fifteenth-century hand, 'ne*uer* Foryeteth Anne neuill'. Scholars have been faithful to the admonition, attempting to determine which Anne Nevill this might be. The two best candidates are Anne Beauchamp Neville, the daughter of Richard Beauchamp, Earl of Warwick, and Anne Neville Stafford, daughter of Ralph Neville, Duke of Westmoreland. Anne's possible possession of the book has been embedded in scholarly discussions of the circumstances in which the manuscript was commissioned and circulated. Margaret Connolly has suggested that the inscription might reflect Anne Beauchamp Neville's concern for what would happen to her estates as a result of her husband's death in 1471, and Amy Vines has written about the intersection between female ownership and readership, and the textual and material features of

CCCC 61.[7] What no one has asked, as far as I know, is, why here? Why, in this mostly blank manuscript, is *this* the spot where Anne writes her plea? This is the section of Book IV where Troilus, in despair, laments to Pandarus the plan to trade Criseyde to the Greeks. Criseyde has not yet gone, nor has she yet forgotten him, but it is an ominous moment in the narrative, the anticipation of the lovers' parting. And can we make any inferences about Dorote Pennell, who writes her name and 'Iesu mercy lady helpe me' in a very faint, early sixteenth-century hand on folio 63r, next to the Proem to Book III? There is no obvious reason that Dorothy would write a prayer to Jesus and Mary next to the poet's appeal to various pagan deities: these traces of an unidentifiable former reader are all but impossible to read, both literally and interpretively, today.

None of the names discussed thus far is a new discovery; detailed descriptions of the *Troilus* manuscript include as much about them as may be soberly concluded. What is different is the ease with which the Parker project brings aspects of the manuscript that have in the past been divided up between different specialties together, into one, accessible package. The facility offered by a digital facsimile—the ability to zoom in, to alter, to peer down almost to the pixel level—seems to encourage curiosity from any scholar, regardless of discipline, about these ghosts of the past. Still, the names that we can bring swimming back up to the parchment's surface, the names we can blow up on our computer screens, remain embedded in a larger network of scholarly practice and assumption, through which our encounters are still inevitably mediated.

Part of that practice has to do with what is described, and where. The verso of the first flyleaf in the manuscript includes the title, 'Thys ys the Booke of Troilus and Criseyde'. This same leaf features Edward Franton's backwards name, the phrase 'daye of may ffor my solas 1546', and apparently random numbers below the title and above the dated phrase. Of all of these bits and pieces, M. R. James mentions only the date, as part of the general category of material 'on flyleaves'. The next item in that category in James's list appears on fol. iir, but he does not mention either a second instance of the title, or the phrase 'good Fortune in hevyn to Abyde', that appears directly below that, nor 'Jesu mercy helpe mary' and 'For my Right', both of which are at the bottom of the same flyleaf. The final item in his category of material on flyleaves is not on a flyleaf at all, properly speaking, but rather, on the recto of folio 1, featuring the famous frontispiece. The couplet is in the hand of John Shirley. Below it, 'added', as James has it, presumably because it is of slightly later date, is a book curse. Next in the James entry is a detailed description of the frontispiece, and then a contents list, which includes references to some, but not all, of the added names I have been discussing. That is, the James description lands on some additions and not others, and is only sometimes concerned to locate those items it does describe in their original material space.

Part of what is happening here has to do with what can be firmly identified: with people for whom a history can be provided, with hands for which a secure date seems obvious, with additions whose purpose seems clear. These habits persist in later interactions with the manuscript. The description of the frontispiece in Richard Marks and Nigel Morgan's *Golden Age of English Manuscript Painting* mentions only the first couplet on its recto, perhaps because the point of the book is to describe manuscript painting, and the short account lists Shirley as the manuscript's earliest known owner; there is no need for a full provenance or a full description in this particular context.[8] But as my dissection of the James description suggests, this tendency to focus on some additions while overlooking others is common in a range of approaches to the manuscript. The very thorough account of the manuscript by Parkes in the 1978 facsimile, for example, does record both couplets on the recto of the frontispiece, but then consigns much of the other material from the flyleaves to the category of 'scribbles and pen trials'. Some of this material is discussed later in the very thorough account of the manuscript, but the flyleaves and margins are, organizationally speaking, cut apart and redistributed into separate sections of the description titled 'Contents', 'Correction and Supervision', and 'History'.

Parkes's 'Contents' list, like James's, starts with the poem itself (as does the online table of contents sidebar in Parker on the Web 2.0), and also includes the recipe for an enema on folio 151r, the Shirley couplet, and the book curse. 'Correction and Supervision' includes the few marginal references to missing stanzas. 'History' considers Ann Neuill, Dorote Pennell, Edward Franton, and Stephen Batman, whose ownership note appears on folio 150v. This note is transcribed in a pop-up window that appears in the Parker 2.0 digitization; a description, but not a transcription, appears on the enema recipe. In these cases, the digital presentation facilitates the reading of at least some of the 'scribbles' in the manuscript. Absence prompted by the passage of time, the fading of ink, and the challenges of certain hands, becomes presence again, through the medium of the computer interface. This is, however, just as the written descriptions are, a partial view, at least for the moment.

At issue in general, then, is how scholars approach the pages of CCCC 61. Divisions of labour in the scholarly approach to medieval manuscripts can carve any codex up between different specialists. Even as it has become more common for modern manuscript scholars to work across disciplinary boundaries, codicologists, palaeographers, art historians, textual scholars and the like still have their own foci, often rooted in the histories of their disciplines. The contrast between the manuscript's splendid frontispiece and the spaces left throughout risks exacerbating such tendencies, so that the frontispiece appears, often, on its own. But there have been attempts to think through what might have gone into the spaces, and thanks to the ready availability of digital images, both from Parker 2.0 and elsewhere, it is possible literally to visualize some of these, as image manipulation allows the creation of pages that do not exist, but that might reflect what could have been. These visual experiments also allow us to combine the insights of different disciplines on the virtual page. For example, Kathleen Scott has worked to find the Corpus Master in other manuscripts.[9] She identifies his hand in borders, such as in Paris, Bibliothèque national de France, Latin MS 1196, folio 81r. We can superimpose that border on folio 3v of CCCC 61, which is currently completely blank. Within the border, one can place the Orosius Master's split picture of the building and destruction of Troy, from Philadelphia, Museum of Art, MS 1945-65-1, folio 66v: Phillipa Hardman, one of two literary scholars who has considered at length what images might belong in the gaps, suggests that here, in the full-page blank opposite the opening of Book I of Troilus, an image of Troy would be appropriate, and that the Orosius Master's linking of the city's beginning and its ending would be particularly suitable.[10] Hardman also points out that the three-stanza gaps in the middle of the manuscript are quite mechanical in placement, suggesting not a specific reading of the text, but rather, 'a purely formal concern for the appearance of the manuscript: a desire to produce a "picture-book" layout'. She argues that the images would be formulaic, pointing to London, British Library, Royal 20. D.i, a *Roman de Troie*, as a possible analogue.[11] We can imagine inserting one of its many scenes featuring Troilus in battle into a space on folio 30v, a section in Book II in which Pandarus is describing Troilus's prowess to Criseyde. The generic quality of the many possible scenes that could be chosen from the Royal manuscript (for my experiment, I used folio 139r) is a good match for the generically hyperbolic praise of the romantic hero.

These confected images represent, for me, an attempt to capture visually the fact that scholars of medieval texts and manuscripts inevitably have many contexts and points of reference, formed from years of reading and looking (or overlooking), whenever we approach a medieval object. These will include, as they did for Scott and Hardman, many other medieval touchstones. They might also include all manner of later material as well. One of the scenes chosen by Eric Gill to illustrate for the 1927 Golden Cockerel *Troilus* is the parting of the lovers, which I can imagine in the blank on folio 119v, the opening of Book V in the Corpus manuscript. Gill's striking and frankly erotic images, once seen, are never forgotten, and the blanks of CCCC 61 create screens upon which I can project them. Warwick Goble provided illustrations in rather a different character to the 1912 *Modern Reader's Chaucer*, and his fairy-tale inspired rendition of the first encounter is another visual that might float across one of Corpus's blank spaces, perhaps the full blank at folio 8v.

Thus far this chapter has considered some of the opportunities offered by the manuscript and its blanks, as they are presented through Parker 2.0. A digital presentation that allows immediate access, zoomability, and the possibility for side-by-side comparison of folios encourages us to read and reassemble—to rehome—the scribbles and other fugitive traces left by previous readers of the book. More fancifully, these digital canvases invite a kind of play, allowing a visual realization of the jumbled hybrids potentially produced in the overstocked, bookish junk-room that is part of many a scholarly brain. But as with previous attempts to deliver the material object to a later audience, Parker 2.0 is also about containment, classification, and control. I noted at the outset how the frontispiece has dominated earlier discussions of the manuscript. The first published colour plate dates to 1949, when it appeared in Margaret Galway's article in *Modern Language Review*.[12] In this piece, Galway offered precise historical identifications for the figures in the scene. While many of these have been dismissed, in some ways the facsimile gave the article extra longevity. Galway noted that the frontispiece had never been reproduced in colour before, and indeed, the plate came to be referenced in later scholarly discussions long after Galway's arguments had been rejected. The 1978 photographic facsimile also presented the frontispiece in colour, in this case printed on glossy paper and tipped in to the front of the book. The rest of the manuscript is reproduced in grayscale, on matte paper. The frontispiece, in other words, has been the defining aspect of CCCC 61, repeatedly singled out for attention that the rest of the manuscript does not receive. Both the photographic and digital facsimiles allow us to see beyond the frontispiece, while also potentially directing our stance towards the whole. The 1978 printed book elevates part of the manuscript through colour reproduction on glossy paper; by contrast, there is a flattening in Parker 2.0 that has nothing to do with colour, and everything to do with size.

In my university library, the 1978 facsimile is shelved on its spine, because it is too tall to fit into the range. Next to it and a few books along are two more *Troilus* facsimiles, of the St John's and Morgan manuscripts, and they, too, are obdurately wrong-sized, compared to other items on the shelf. Their failure to conform to the standard octavo size typical of a scholarly monograph derives from the fact that these facsimiles are the size of their originals. These life-sized objects are unruly, resisting normal (modern) institutional containment strategies. They also reflect the variability in size of manuscript objects, a fact which is all the more clear when we consider CCCC 98 and its institutional presence, both physical and digital. CCCC 61 is a substantial book that would need a reading desk for consultation, a situation that is still possible (indeed, required) in the Parker Library today. At almost 12 meters in length, CCCC 98 cannot easily be viewed at all. In order to grasp the sheer size of the roll, it is necessary to unroll it, and in its current home, the only space large enough is the floor of the upper library as noted by Anne McLaughlin in the 'Parker on the Web' collegium. But both roll and manuscript are the same size in Parker 2.0—the scalable size of the screen upon which they appear. And those screens can be almost anywhere.

This fact reminds us of a final constraint in our encounters with the material survivals of the past. Before projects like Parker 2.0, modern scholars met their medieval originals in the highly controlled environments of libraries and rare book rooms. There is no such thing as a neutral space—even if we were sitting in Parker's own library, we would not be encountering his books as he did. Digitization imposes an interface, and it also imposes its own space, because we need to be somewhere with a device and an Internet connection to access Parker 2.0. Still, as our devices shift and as subscription-based models give way to open access, the space of the digital expands, and perhaps even offers a version, or at least an interesting variant, of that original intimacy. While an iPad is not the right size, or smell, or texture for a medieval manuscript, it is possible to curl up with it in one's den. If we cannot unroll CCCC 98 on our own floor, we can blow up its images, no matter where we are, to puzzle over their details. If we cannot carry CCCC 61 around with us, we can carry its simulacrum, and view it on the dining room table next to a cup of coffee or scroll through it on the balcony.

In this chapter I have considered some of the problems in both old and new ways of delivering medieval manuscripts. The point has not been to focus on complaining about what a description or an interface can and cannot do; rather, the point is that the gaps and fissures between material object and print or digital realization open a productive space where we can think through how we relate to these objects. *Horror vacui*, the fear of emptiness, is the way art historians describe the impulse to fill all available space on a manuscript page. But if we agree to sit with absence, and play with gaps, might *delectatio*, delight, or *illuminatio*, enlightenment, step in?

Notes

1 There have been many discussions of the frontispiece, dividing themselves broadly, as Matthew Boyd Goldie puts it, into 'as specific as stating that the foreground shows Chaucer reciting the poem to an audience of identifiable nobles and the background as a particular scene ... [while] other explications point to the generic and non-specific aspects of the oral performance in the foreground and probably a fifteenth-century interpretation of the poem in the background': *Middle English Literature: A Historical Sourcebook* (Oxford: Blackwell, 2003), p. 143. For two recent assessments, both of which address the larger reading/performance context, see Joyce Coleman, 'Where Chaucer Got His Pulpit: Audience and Intervisuality in the *Troilus and Criseyde* Frontispiece', *Studies in the Age of Chaucer* 32 (2010): 103–28; and Mary Carruthers, 'The Sociable Text of the "Troilus Frontispiece": A Different Mode of Textuality', *English Literary History* 81 (2014): 423–41.

2 Malcolm Parkes and Elizabeth Salter, eds., *Troilus and Criseyde: A Facsimile of Corpus Christi College Cambridge 61* (Cambridge: D.S. Brewer, 1978).

3 Diana B. Tyson, 'The Adam and Eve Roll: Corpus Christi College Cambridge MS 98', *Scriptorium* 52 (1998): 301–16.

4 The quite brief description is M. R. James, *A Descriptive Catalogue of the Manuscripts in the Library of Corpus Christi College Cambridge* (Cambridge: Cambridge University Press, 1912), pp. 126–7; most of James's attention is given to the frontispiece, which he calls 'a full-page painting of the most beautiful quality', p. 126.

5 Parkes and Salter, *A Facsimile*, p. 8.

6 Bruce Dickins, 'The Making of the Parker Library', *Transactions of the Cambridge Bibliographical Society* 6,1 (1972), p. 33, remarks in passing, 'I do not think that [Parker] had any deep interest in arts or in letters', and notes that CCCC 61 was Parker's only Chaucer, whether in manuscript or print.

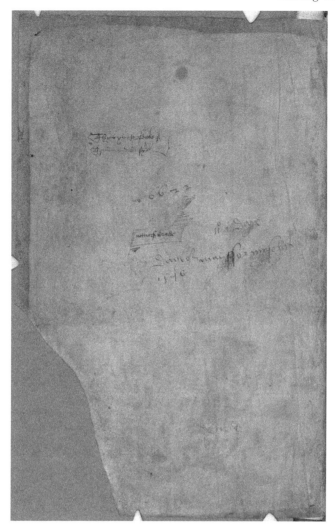

Figure 9.1 The Parker Library, Corpus Christi College, Cambridge, MS 61, f. i v.

7 Margaret Connolly, *John Shirley: Book Production and the Noble Household in Fifteenth-Century England* (Aldershot: Ashgate, 1998), 110; Amy Vines, *Women's Power in Late Medieval Romance* (Cambridge: D. S. Brewer, 2011), p. 22.
8 Richard Marks and Nigel Morgan, *The Golden Age of English Manuscript Painting 1200–1500* (New York: George Braziller, 1981), p. 113.
9 Kathleen Scott, 'Limner-Power: A Book Artist in England *c.* 1420', in *Prestige, Authority and Power in Late-Medieval Manuscripts and Texts*, ed. Felicity Riddy (York: York Medieval Press), pp. 55–75.
10 Phillipa Hardman, 'Interpreting the Incomplete Scheme of Illustration in Cambridge, Corpus Christi College MS 61', *English Manuscript Studies 1100–1700* 6 (1997): 60. An earlier attempt to fill the gaps is John H. Fisher, 'The Intended

Illustrations in MS Corpus Christi 61 of Chaucer's *Troilus and Criseyde*', in *Medieval Studies in Honor of Lillian Herlands Hornstein*, ed. Jess B. Bessinger, Jr., and Robert R. Raymo (New York: New York University Press, 1976), pp. 111–21.

11 Hardman, 'Interpreting', pp. 55–56 and 61.

12 Margaret Galway, 'The *Troilus* Frontispiece', *Modern Language Review* 44 (1949): 161–77.

Part 3
Translation and Transmission

10 'Glocal' matters

The Gospels of St Augustine as a codex in translation

Mateusz Fafinski

Translation can build bridges: it can transform not only books and texts but societies as well. François Jullien writes in *Il n'y a pas d'identité culturelle*:

> Only translation can be the language of the world ... The world of the future has to be a world of in-betweenlingualism: not of one dominant language (whichever it would be), but of Translation, which would activate the resources of languages ... Having one language might be easier, but it would mean from the beginning a forced standardization. The exchange might well be easier, but soon there would be nothing to exchange, or at least nothing really unique.[1]

CCCC 41, the Old English Bede, and CCCC 286, the Gospels of St Augustine, two manuscripts from the Parker Library, seem to be the very embodiment of the idea of 'in-betweenlingualism'.

We first need to ask: what is translation? After all, it is not only a transfer between languages. Roman Jakobson has included in his tripartite definition of translation the possibility of transmutation of verbal signs by means of non-verbal ones: 'translation involves two equivalent messages in two different codes'.[2] Yves Gambier, on the basis of his work in film, has proposed a term for such transmutation, a translation between media: 'a tradaptation'.[3] Both CCCC 41 and CCCC 286 are ripe in such examples of exchange between the media. But there is one more kind of translation, especially important when talking about books as physical objects, as tactile objects to be engaged with not only mentally but also spatially and tangibly: the Latin *translatio*, which can be seen both as a physical transfer of an object and as a transfer of power and culture—*translatio studii et imperii*.[4] All three types of translation are present in CCCC 41 and CCCC 286.

By examining the codices, it is clear that this is where the two manuscripts are linked to one another in the most visible way. It is, after all, the case that CCCC 41 contains the story of *translatio* of CCCC 286 from Rome to England—on page 62 we find the famous passage describing the books brought to England by the Augustinian Mission in 597 CE.[5] In a way, CCCC 41 contains, to use a digital term, the metadata of CCCC 286—it provides the encoding necessary for us to understand how the Gospels of St Augustine found their way to Britain. As anybody working with large sets of information, in fact anybody working with digital repositories, will be able to tell, without metadata scholars cannot access the true potential of information. Those two manuscripts are therefore linked on a structural level and this connection is crucial.[6]

CCCC 286 was brought to England either together with Augustine himself or with a second group of missionaries shortly afterwards. It came with the Gregorian mission, a mission that can be seen not only as an endeavour to bring Roman Christianity to Britain but also as a very imperial endeavour to reclaim the island as part of the Roman world. In this understanding, CCCC 286 is a postcolonial object *par excellence*, a product of the metropole brought into the periphery. The subsequent engagement with it (also in the history of its arrival in England, translated into Old English on the pages of CCCC 41) can be seen as a history of a postcolonial engagement.

CCCC 286 contains the complete Latin texts of the four gospels, written in all probability in the sixth century in a provincial centre in Italy. It attracted a great deal of early scholarly attention because of its two splendid, full-page illuminations, one of the most stunning late antique illuminated pages that have survived to the present day. Their quality and beauty made many later researchers ignore or even criticize other drawings and aspects of this book. Francis Wormald, for example, described the drawing of the symbol of Mark as being 'not a very competent work of art', as if such evaluation was even possible, let alone desirable.[7]

Now, with the manuscript digitized, scholars can focus on those other aspects of the manuscript's production and functionality. Scholars can try to look at CCCC 41 and CCCC 286 as texts in perpetual translation— translation in its broadest sense. We can try to see CCCC 286 as a multi-lingual manuscript, which aspect now, with the ability to explore its digitized form, can be brought to the fore. This trope can be explored by following two paths that are to a certain degree intertwined: those of 'tradaptation' and of translation.

The first path can be taken in multiple ways through the codex, but perhaps the most rewarding one leads through the four evangelists' symbols. As Francis Wormald assumed, full-page miniatures originally preceded probably all four gospels, each likely featuring evangelists' symbols and their seated portraits.[8] Only the celebrated miniature of Luke has survived. When we begin with Matthew, we are immediately confronted with an excellent example of a tradaptation, a translation from one medium to another. Instead of the missing miniature, we are presented with two words written in square capitals: *Matteus Hominem* at folio 2v. This is where the human, the symbol of Matthew, should be—but the figure is absent. The empty space where the miniature should be could be seen as an example of the 'post-colonial void'—the empty space left by Rome.[9] The image, not only produced in Italy but also referencing Rome, has been lost, and is filled instead with an inscription, which translates this non-existent illumination into a scriptural description. A non-verbal object mutates into language. Is the human or angel of Matthew therefore completely absent It is not: not if we look at the ignored, the marginalized. One can argue that we are able to see his face in a marginal scribble of a human head on folio 1—this is he, his face the face of the early medieval translator or tradaptator, a medieval face filling the void created by the lack of a late antique one. The marginal drawing is difficult to date; the style might place it around the eighth century, contemporary with the glosses correcting some passages of the text. It is small, a little over 4 cm.

After this comes the evangelist Mark, who has a little sketch, a caricature almost. This sketch is also a translation of a miniature that does not exist anymore into a different medium. It has been suggested that the sketch was copied at a time when the full-page, late antique illumination still existed.[10] It might well have been, but we need to entertain a different hypothesis, that it was drawn into the page to make up for the lack of the illumination at a very early date. While it is most definitely a lion of Mark, I believe it can also be seen as a tetramorph—it has the face of a human, the horns of an ox, the mane of a lion, the talons of an eagle. It is composite; it draws from Irish tradition; it exists in between the cultural languages of Late Antiquity and the Early Middle Ages, in between the provincial Italian workshop and early medieval Britain.

Moving on, we see Luke, extant in his full late antique glory at folio 129v. This miniature has attracted possibly the most attention. Even though this illumination is extant, it does not mean that it cannot be seen as an adaptation of a different sort. It is a translation of a different time, done by the original illuminator. Luke (and, we can presume, the other, missing original evangelists) is also Vergil (perhaps Vergil from Vergilius Romanus, Cod. Vat. lat. 3867). Luke is an evangelist, but he is also a rhetor, an ancient author translated to a new milieu. We will never know why his miniature survived (and perhaps it does not matter), but the annotations on the scenes from the life of Jesus surrounding him are also crucial to our understanding of CCCC 286 as a book in permanent translation.

John is perhaps the most poignant: there is just the ghost and the word left, which might have been a guide-word left by the scribe for the artist. On folio 206r, there is a faint ghost of the miniature that preceded the Gospel, which was simply impossible to see on any earlier reproduction of the manuscript. In order to be able to notice it, one had to engage with the actual object, with the light just right. Now, in the digitized form, we can finally, although just barely, see the ghost of this miniature. But it is on the next page that we can witness readers' engagement with it. Miniatures of each of the evangelists were in all probability accompanied by verses from Sedulius, a fifth-century Christian poet, but only the verse on Luke's miniature is still extant. On the top of folio 207v is the following inscription from Sedulius, copied probably from the volume of the original miniature of John: *More volans aquilae* [*verbo*] *petit astra Iohannes*, 'Flying like an eagle, John reaches for the stars with his word'.[11] John is the different Gospel, non-synoptic, late; it starts by putting the Word at the beginning. Is it not poignant that in CCCC 286 the word and a ghost of the past introduce his Gospel?

CCCC 286 is not only a book of translation between mediums, it is also a book of many languages, an in-betweenlingual object, and it is, just like CCCC 41, a translation to begin with. This second path might help us also to explore CCCC 286 as a performative object. The Latin Gospels are a translation, which, for the late antique scribe who copied CCCC 286 (probably in the middle of the sixth century), would still be their language, a higher register of their vernacular. The Gospels of St Augustine are therefore a translated book *par excellence*, just like Old English Bede. Their earliest users would be essentially very close to each other in their *mentalité* and in the way they might perceive the texts.

What about the new, post-conversion English users of the Gospels? The anonymous eighth-century scribe went as far as to correct the translation at folio 14v; indeed, the codex includes multiple such corrections, belonging also to later scribes. Perhaps we should not be surprised—such agency, not only on the basis of scriptural knowledge but also linguistically, can again be explained through CCCC 41, the 'metadata' of CCCC 286. Bede writes that after the explosion of learning brought by Theodore, there were, on the island of Britain, still in his day, people who could read and write Latin and Greek as if they were native speakers.[12] This internalization of language is very important—the Gospels of St Augustine are a kind of 'postcolonial bridge', a translation of Rome onto early medieval England. People of eighth-century Britain could engage linguistically with the texts in these manuscripts just as closely as their scribes.

Translation could also create new meanings—the best example is the case of the 'foxes miniature' from folio 129v. Here, the early English scribe adorned a miniature lacking any distinct features with a caption referring to a Biblical parable from Luke 9:58.[13] Various models have been brought up to explain this, the most convincing being Henderson's idea that this caption—a translation of the visual into the scriptural—is a reaction to the very eighth-century preoccupations with the possession of land by the Church that were spurred on by Bede.[14] A semantically malleable space of a miniature exhibiting very limited defining features was therefore used to convey a contemporary meaning— CCCC 286 was becoming more and more reflective of the context in which it was used and, at the same time, more and more performative.

Gospels became performative and also bilingual. Folios 74v and 77v contain copies of two charters, S1198 from *c.* 850 and S1455 from *c.* 990, respectively.[15] Those are both Old English documents, both containing provisions of liturgical commemoration. Although we lack such information from early England, we know that on the Continent the practice of

charter writing and charter validation was deeply connected to perfor-
mances with the altar of the saint and often the Gospel-book itself.[16]

The grant of S1455 is particularly interesting. It is one of the very few
surviving vernacular wills in pre-Conquest manuscripts[17] and it contains a
provision for the soul of Siferth:

> þis sy gedon for Siferð. 7 for his ofsprincg to hyra sawle ðearfe a butan ende;
> Amen[18]

We can, without an overly large leap of faith, imagine CCCC 286 being involved
in those commemorations, activating the codex as a performative object. We
encounter Siferth in a short gloss on folio 2v. We do not know who he was, but
his life was bound with this object in front of our eyes—a local man, linked
through an Old English document to a late antique Gospel-book.

Both CCCC 41 and CCCC 286 are glocal artefacts, objects existing in the
global and local context at the same time,[19] simultaneously exerting their pull
in an English and a pan-Christian context. The Old English Bede is a translation of a locally produced text, written originally in Latin, into the vernacular.
This text became in its original form, Latin, almost a staple in European
libraries, with copies in such important centres as Fulda, Lorsch, Reichenau, St
Gall, Würzburg, Murbach, and Trier.[20] It is perhaps its translation into Old
English that makes it into a glocal text. The case of the glocality of CCCC 286
is, possibly, more complicated. It is a universal text *par excellence* in its context
that through a slow process of corrections, glosses, and tradaptations becomes
a local object. The peak of that process we see perhaps in the person of Siferth,
whose liturgical commemoration in charter S1455 and folio 77v incorporates
the codex tangibly into the community. It completes the *translatio* by integrating it in the local context. The very inclusion of charters in CCCC 286, repur-
posing it as an archive, as an ark of memory (both of land, of economical
renders as well as of people and their souls), is an expression of that glocality as
well. By the virtue of it, the codex becomes in-betweenlingual, begins to exist in
the *écart*, the gap, that allows it to be reinterpreted.

We could conclude by asking about the place of digital versions of CCCC
286 and CCCC 41 in relation to those paths. Are they tradaptations or
translations, or perhaps neither of those phenomena? The very way we use
their digital versions is functionally very similar to the way a medieval
manuscript would be used—with an important role being given to annotation,
side-by-side comparison, magnification, and experiencing parts of the codex
that are omitted or treated in passing in editions. Digital form helps us to
understand the codices as non-static objects that were not 'completed' at the
dates given to them in their metadata, but continued to be worked on for
centuries. At the same time, they are facsimiles, reflections, maps. We may
add that (apart from obvious wide dissemination), in the case of manuscripts, the usefulness of digitization is further enhanced by similar 'user
experience'. Some scholars worry about the spread of the use of digital

facsimiles, that their employment in research will remove us from the experience of actual codices. This might be, but at the same time those digitizations are not only digital reproductions of manuscripts; they are also a (possible) digital reproduction of a method, and, indeed 'translations' in and of themselves. We are, as researchers, allowed to interact with them in a simulation of the original user experiences. The very existence of those manuscripts in this different medium opens new avenues of research, but it also redefines our engagement with them.

In their digital forms, they are therefore next steps on those paths, allowing us to more fully experience aspects that were, until now, treated in passing or completely overlooked: their postcoloniality, their multi- and in-betweenlingualism, their performative character. As codices in perpetual translation—here in Parker on the Web—they are now entering another phase.

Figure 10.1 The Parker Library, Corpus Christi College, Cambridge, MS 286, f. 2v.

Notes

1 François Jullien, *Es gibt keine kulturelle Identität: wir verteidigen die Ressourcen einer Kultur*, trans. Erwin Landrichter, 1. Auflage, deutsche Erstausgabe, edition suhrkamp 2718 (Berlin: Suhrkamp, 2017), p. 58. Translated by the author.

2 Roman Jakobson, 'On Linguistic Aspects of Translation', in *On Translation*, ed. R. A. Brower, Harvard Studies in Comparative Literature (Cambridge, MA: Harvard University Press, 1959), p. 233.

3 Yves Gambier, 'Tradaptation Cinématographique', 2004, pp. 169–81: https://doi.org/10.1075/btl.56.18gam

4 Emma Campbell and Robert Mills, 'Introduction: Rethinking Medieval Translation', in *Rethinking Medieval Translation, Ethics, Politics, Theory* (Woodbridge: Boydell and Brewer, 2012), p. 1.

5 Bede, *Bede's Ecclesiastical History of the English People*, ed. Bertram Colgrave and R. A. B. Mynors, Oxford Medieval Texts (Oxford: Clarendon Press, 1969), I.29.

6 Metadata is a term we should, as medievalists, use, problematize and theoretize more often. The theory of linked information, developing now in informational technologies, will be in the future crucial for our research as well.

7 Francis Wormald, *The Miniatures in the Gospels of St Augustine* (Cambridge: Cambridge University Press, 1954), p. 4.

8 Wormald, *Gospels of St Augustine*, p. 3.

9 Nicholas Howe, 'Anglo-Saxon England and the Postcolonial Void', in *Postcolonial Approaches to the European Middle Ages: Translating Cultures*, ed. J. Kabir and D. Williams, Cambridge Studies in Medieval Literature (Cambridge: Cambridge University Press, 2005), pp. 25–47.

10 Wormald, *The Miniatures in the Gospels of St Augustine*, p. 4.

11 Sedulius, *The Paschal Song and Hymns*, trans. Carl P. E. Springer, Writings from the Greco-Roman World 35 (Atlanta: Society of Biblical Literature, 2013), p. 21.

12 Bede, *Bede's Ecclesiastical History of the English People*, IV.2.

13 Carol F. Lewine, '*Vulpes Fossa Habent* or the Miracle of the Bent Woman in the Gospels of St. Augustine, Corpus Christi College, Cambridge, Ms 286', *The Art Bulletin* 56.4 (1974): 492.

14 George Henderson, '"The Foxes Have Holes", Once Again', *Wiener Jahrbuch Für Kunstgeschichte* 46–47.1 (January 1994): 252–53.

15 See E-Sawyer: https://esawyer.lib.cam.ac.uk/about/index.html

16 Rosamond McKitterick, *The Carolingians and the Written Word* (Cambridge and New York: Cambridge University Press, 1989), pp. 68–72.

17 Linda Tollerton, *Wills and Will-Making in Anglo-Saxon England* (Woodbridge and Rochester, NY: Boydell Press and York Medieval Press, 2011), pp. 258–59.

18 S. E. Kelly, ed., *The Charters of St Augustine's Abbey, Canterbury, and Minster-in-Thanet*, Anglo-Saxon Charters 4 (Oxford: Oxford University Press, 1995), no. 31.

19 On 'glocality', see Victor Roudometof, 'The Glocal and Global Studies', *Globalizations* 12.5 (2015): 774–87.

20 Joshua Allan Westgard, 'Dissemination and Reception of Bede's *Historia Ecclesiastica Gentis Anglorum* in Germany, c. 731–1500: The Manuscript Evidence' (unpub. PhD dissertation, University of North Carolina, 2005), p. 128.

11 Encyclopaedic notes in Cambridge, Corpus Christi College, 320

John J. Gallagher

This chapter examines the sources and authorship of the encyclopaedic notes in Cambridge, Corpus Christi College, 320 that foregrounds the richness and complexity of seemingly prosaic and dully factual, anonymous material. I argue that these notes bear close resemblances to the digested oral exposition extant in the encyclopaedic Canterbury and Leiden *glossae collectae*. Encyclopaedic texts are frequently overlooked, as they often form later additions to codices, and are commonly described as 'miscellaneous' and therefore unexceptional. This chapter shows their central and long-lived position in early medieval intellectual culture. In addition to making some of the greatest treasures of early medieval manuscript culture readily available online, the digital and readily accessible website, Parker 2.0, encourages a re-evaluation of lesser-studied texts such as 'miscellaneous' encyclopaedic notes. By way of conclusion, a reflection on the role of Parker 2.0 in contemporary research is offered.

Encyclopaedic notes and the Canterbury School

A relatively consistent batch of encyclopaedic notes appears in five early English manuscripts, which exemplify a more widespread genre of 'micro-texts' found throughout the extant corpus. Such notes are generally of a numerical, biblical-Christian, or encyclopaedic nature. Table 11.1 below outlines the topics addressed in the series and the manuscripts in which the notes appear.[1] Kees Dekker and Birte Walbers use CCCC 183, the second-oldest manuscript witness to the notes, as the basis for their editions, rather than London, British Library, Cotton Vespasian B. vi, the oldest manuscript containing the notes, as CCCC 183 contains the oldest textual recension.[2] There are only minor lexical differences between CCCC 183 and 320. Dekker's study in particular establishes the importance of analysing the 'changing manuscript context' and the 'textual and contextual differences' between witnesses of the texts.[3]

Note 1 concerns the threefold Incarnation of Christ (Conception, Nativity, and Resurrection) and the precise dates for these three moments in the hypostatic union.[4] Dionysius Exiguus, a well-known sixth-century computistical writer, is the main source for this note's calendrical information.[5] The reference to *secundum legem Moysi xiiii die lune passus*, 'according to Moses's Law the fourteenth day of the moon' is, as Dekker notes, a deviation from Dionysius Exiguus and a reference to Quartodeciman observance of Easter.[6] Some early Christians followed Jewish practice and continued to observe Passover with a distinctly Christian understanding.[7] The Torah instructs that the Passover is to be observed on the fourteenth day of Nisan when the Paschal lamb is to be sacrificed in order to be consumed that night; that is, the fifteenth of Nisan, since days begin at sunset in Jewish time.[8] For the Quartodecimans, the Passover at which the Eucharist was instituted and the sacrifice of Calvary occurred on the same day. The typological correspondence between the Paschal sacrifice and liberation from Egypt and the sacrifice of Christ and the salvation it achieved was not lost on these Jewish Christians who saw the death of the Lord as the event most worthy of commemoration in their religious calendar.[9] It is unclear if the Quartodecimans actually celebrated Easter (the *anastasis* or Resurrection) on this day, on the third day after the Passover, or even at all; all we know is that they celebrated a Christian Passover presumably commemorating Christ's saving and life-giving death.

Today, relatively little is known for certain about Quartodeciman practices or theology. Most of what we know comes from Eusebius's *Historia ecclesiastica*.[10] How much could our English author have known about such customs? Dekker suggests that the note could indicate that the author was familiar with the divergent customs of Asia Minor and Antioch.[11] Quartodecimanism was most commonly practised in the first and second centuries; Victor I, Bishop of Rome, attempted to suppress it at the end of the second century and the question was addressed at the Council of Nicaea in 325, after which it receded.[12] The note does not refer to contemporary custom, but to historic practice, which is likely to have been garnered from sources such as Eusebius's *Historia* or Rufinus's Latin translation of Eusebius, which was more influential in the West. Theodore of Tarsus and Canterbury, a Byzantine Greek educated in Asia Minor, surely would have learned about the historical controversies concerning the Great Sabbath in his own cultural milieu.[13] The pivotal role he played in settling the Easter dispute at the Council of Hertford in 672 indicates that he was intimately familiar with divergent computational practices.[14] Excerpts from Rufinus's translation of Eusebius's *Historia* are contained in the Leiden Glossary, showing that this text was known at the Canterbury School.[15]

Note 1 in fact goes beyond mere passing familiarity with Quartodecimanism. Dekker has shown how 'the author of the note is anxious to have the Annunciation on a Friday, the same day as Christ's Crucifixion'.[16] I propose that this detail could suggest an author or teacher who was familiar with a tradition that places the Annunciation on a Friday and saw the significance that could be drawn from conflating the day of the Quartodeciman Passover and the Crucifixion. Theodore, who was familiar with the customs of the early church in Asia Minor, may well be behind this divergent date for the

Annunciation and this explanation of Quartodecimanism. However, most early medieval computists confused Quartodecimanism with the discordance between Alexandrian (Roman) or Dionysiac (a variation) Easter reckoning and the Victorian (Irish) method. The *Vita S. Wilfrithi*, for example, refers to Irish reckoning as Quartodeciman in opposition to the correct method of reckoning espoused by the Apostolic See.[17] I would suggest that the correct use of the term Quartodecimanism indicates an author, teacher, or scholarly environment that is entirely *au fait* with the intricacies of the divergent and historical methods of *computus*. I would posit that Theodore, the students who attended his school, and those working with the sources that remained at Canterbury after his day are the most likely seventh- or eighth-century candidates in early medieval England to have had such facility and knowledge at their disposal.

Note 6 details the length and breadth of the earth. The concern with the size of the earth, or geodesy, was a notable preoccupation in the encyclopaedic genre as well as in biblical commentaries, which are one of the primary loci for scientific, numerical, and encyclopaedic knowledge. The source of this note betrays its possible link to the Canterbury School and has been outlined by Dekker.[18] For the purposes of the present argument, these sources are worth laying out again in brief before exploring the connection with the Canterbury School more fully. An almost identical note on the dimensions of the earth can be found in a batch of excerpts from patristic and ecclesiastical authors following the Leiden Glossary in Leiden, Bibliotheek der Rijksuniversiteit, Voss. Lat. Q.69, at folio 38v, which gives the proportions of the earth using the unit *mansiones* 'day's march' rather than *milia* 'miles'.[19] This is certainly the same note as the ones found in our series of encyclopaedic notes and in the Canterbury Commentaries, but it employs a different unit of measurement. Rolf Bremmer sees the Canterbury School of Theodore and Hadrian as the origin of this text based on Cosmas, since, 'After all, these two men were well at home in the Greek patristic and theological literature.'[20] Old English glosses accompany this batch in the Leiden Glossary, and the texts strongly resemble the Second Commentary on the Gospels, *EvII*, in the Canterbury Commentaries, as well as the notes under discussion here. Although we cannot be certain, it seems likely that the excerpts in Voss. Lat. Q.69 are a Canterbury product, given the hypothesized presence of a copy of the *Topographia* in this context.[21] Note 6, the Canterbury Commentaries, and the excerpts in Vos. Lat. Q.69 all refer to one 'Christian historian' and relate rarefied information from the *Topographia*, strongly suggesting a common origin at the Canterbury School.

Simon Keynes acknowledges that the *Topographia* was cited in the Canterbury Commentaries, and, concludes that 'we need not doubt that [the *Topographia Christiana*] was available in Southumbria in the early ninth century'.[22] I would argue, essentially, that it is more likely that knowledge of this fairly obscure Greek cosmographer came from a Greek copy in Theodore's Canterbury School or that the note itself is a product of the School. No

Latin translation of this Greek work is known to have existed in the early medieval Latin West, suggesting that it was Theodore who related details of the *Topographia* to his students from a Greek copy of the work or *ex corde*. Bede's *Historia abbatum* refers to a certain cosmographical work (... *cosmographiorum codice* ...) acquired by Benedict Biscop in Rome and sold to King Aldfrith, but it is unclear if this was the same work by Cosmas.[23] It seems unlikely to have been, given that no Latin versions appear to have been in circulation during this period. Benedict could have brought back a Greek copy, but it is not likely that it would have been read by an Anglo-Saxon, given that knowledge of Greek in this context, aside from Theodore and Bede, was limited. To my knowledge, no other mention of Cosmas Indicopleustes by name or pseudonym, nor any citation from his work, occurs in the surviving Anglo-Saxon corpus.[24] Dekker writes that 'every indication points, therefore, to the Canterbury School as the place of origin for this note'.[25] Additionally, Keynes argues convincingly for the possibility of a Canterbury provenance for the separate booklet containing the encyclopaedic notes in Vespasian B. vi, folios 104–9, which is usually designated as Mercian.[26] This adds further strength to the possibility that all these notes were a product of the seventh-century Canterbury School. Given the highly rarefied nature of its source, the *Topographia Christiana*, which is used with certainty in the other texts associated with the Canterbury School, it seems highly likely that this note originated at the Canterbury School in Theodore's lifetime, and was the work of a student of the School or a scholar at Canterbury working with an inherited seventh-century library that might have contained either the *Topographia* or works from the School that cited that source.

Note 9 on St Peter's Basilica appears in all five manuscripts; and variations appear in London, British Library, Cotton Tiberius A. iii and London, British Library, Cotton Julius A. ii. No source can be readily identified.[27] Although it is not a biblical site or one directly associated with the life of Christ, it is related to the other notes on the Tabernacle, the Temple, and the Holy Sepulchre. Note 9 demonstrates encyclopaedic curiosity about far-away structures on the part of those who copied and transmitted it, and it informs exegesis and geographic learning. It is quite likely that such a text was produced or copied at a school expressly dedicated to biblical exegesis, such as the Canterbury School. The information in this note could have come from any of the numerous English pilgrims who travelled to Rome, or from a text that records such knowledge.

Note 15 on Jerusalem and the Church of the Holy Sepulchre is unique to CCCC 320 and does not appear in any of the other four manuscripts that contain this series of notes.[28] The note describes the location of the Holy City, but it is primarily concerned with the Church of the Holy Sepulchre. It is rubricated in the same style as the other rubrics to the notes in Corpus 320 and, therefore, an integral part of the series. The rubric to this note near the bottom of folio 169r and the entirety of its title, *De hierosolima et rubus in ea gestis*, is decorated in the same fashion as the initials that rubricate most of preceding other notes on folios 166v–168v. The rubric of *De annis Domini* on folio 166v is of a comparable length to the rubric of *De Hierosolima* and shares the same hand and decoration. Today, the two differ in that the ink of the rubric *De Hierosolima* has bled quite badly, thereby making it more prominent. While it is additional to the series, as it is not preserved in the other four manuscripts, its similar hand and decoration suggest that it is integral to the series as it was copied into CCCC 320. As Note 15 is literal in its interests in and concerns for the architecture and furnishings of this sacred site, it is certainly of a piece with other literal notes in this series concerning sacred locations and structures, particularly Note 9 on St Peter's Basilica. Note 15 strongly resembles the *interpretamenta* in the Canterbury Commentaries that are concerned with Holy Land sites, particularly the city of Jerusalem. I propose that while Vespasian B. vi is the oldest manuscript containing these encyclopaedic notes, the appearance of this additional note might suggest that CCCC 320 bears witness to a more complete recension of notes than the other four manuscripts, a complete recension that potentially goes back to the Canterbury School.

Notes on the biblical Tabernacle, the Temple, St Peter's Basilica, and the Church of the Holy Sepulchre reflect the literal-Antiochene interest of the Canterbury Commentaries in biblical and Christian sites and structures of religious significance. The measurements for the Temple and the Ark given in Notes 8 and 10 can probably be traced to Josephus's *Antiquitates Iudaicae*.[29] Bede, who cites the same details in his *Commentarius in Genesim*, drew extensively on the *Antiquitates Iudaicae* throughout his exegetical oeuvre, citing it in eight of his major biblical commentaries as well as in his reworking of Isidore's scientific and encyclopaedic work, *De natura rerum*, and in his topographical treatise based on Jerome and Josephus.[30] We know that a copy of the *Antiquitates Iudaicae* or at least knowledge of this text had an earlier entry point in Anglo-Saxon England, at the Canterbury School of Theodore and Hadrian: this work is cited (erroneously by name) in one comment and seems to underlie a number of *interpretamenta* in the Canterbury Commentaries.[31] Lapidge writes, 'The Canterbury Commentator was arguably familiar with both these works [*Bellum Iudaicum* and *Antiquitates Iudaicae*], though he may not have had them in front of him while lecturing, and may have been quoting inaccurately from memory.'[32] The oral circulation of classical and patristic texts as a means by which sources were known to Anglo-Saxon authors bears emphasizing. Rather than showing comprehensive knowledge of a text such as the *Antiquitates Iudaicae*, I argue that these encyclopaedic notes strongly resemble the digested oral exposition attested in the encyclopaedic Canterbury and Leiden *glossae collectae*. It is plausible that these encyclopaedic notes were, originally, the product of similar oral, classroom exposition, if not, in some instances, the product of the same Canterbury School or sources associated with it.

Note 11 deals with the typology and symbolism of the biblical number 72, which is, as the note explains, the number of biblical books, languages in the world, and of Christ's disciples. The number 72 or sometimes 70 is a commonly-employed *topos* in late antique and early medieval exegesis.[33] It is associated with the table of nations in Genesis 10 and the scattering of languages following the destruction of the Tower of Babel.[34] Dekker writes that while the number of disciples is scripturally based, it was only fully worked out in either a third-century Greek or sixth-century Byzantine work.[35] A list corresponding to this inventory is preserved in both CCCC 183 and Vespasian B. vi; the list could, as Dekker suggests, 'be of eastern origin'.[36] The appearance of an uncommon eastern source that displays an interest in the biblical-numerological significance of 72 in two manuscripts witnesses of the notes could further link the encyclopaedic notes to the Canterbury School, since it seems to have been the primary conduit for obscure Greek and Syriac sources in early medieval England: in reference to the use of Cosmas Indicopleustes and the eastern list, Keynes writes that the compiler of Vespasian B. vi was able to draw on 'obscure material, some of which would appear to have been brought to England in the late seventh century by Archbishop Theodore'.[37] The significance of 72 or 70 is explored in the opening of the Canterbury Commentaries where it holds additional weight as the number of translators who miraculously produced 72 identical translations of the Hebrew Bible or Old Testament into Greek, showing divine sanction for the Septuagint as the first vernacularisation of the Hebrew Scriptures.[38]

Dekker traces the details in Note 11 to Isidore's *De ecclesiasticis officiis*, where the 72 biblical books are linked to Christ's disciples and to the number of nations and languages.[39] Isidore also points out the correspondence with the number of elders and prophets chosen by Moses in Numbers 11:24–25.[40] This work did not enjoy a notable career in Anglo-Saxon England,[41] though it is cited in the scholarship of the Canterbury School, Aldhelm, and Bede. The use of this work seems to be second-hand and from intermediary sources, rather than from first-hand knowledge of the text. Although four manuscripts survive, this work seems to have been comparatively rare in the early medieval world. *De ecclesiasticis officiis* was known in the early period of scholarly activity at the Canterbury School where it was used with certainty in the Leiden Glossary.[42] It is also cited by Aldhelm, an alumnus of the Canterbury School.[43] Given the nature of how the *glossae collectae* were compiled, it is entirely possible that the usage in the Leiden Glossary represents a later addition to the Glossary. For a work that does not seem to have been commonly known first-hand in this period, the Canterbury School seems like a likely avenue for the transmission of the details from *De ecclesiasticis officiis* contained in Note 11.

Attempts to clarify biblical, Roman, and English systems of measurement in Note 13 resemble the strong metrological interest displayed in the material associated with the Canterbury School.[44] Dekker calls our attention to metrological excerpts from Eucherius of Lyons that accompany the notes in Vespasian B. vi.[45] These seem to have been selected as a complement to the thematically-similar notes with which they possibly share a common origin. Eucherius may also have been used as a source in the Canterbury Commentaries and the Leiden Glossary.[46] I argue that it is possible that an intermediate version of Eucherius was brought from the Continent to Anglo-Saxon England by Theodore. The evidence is far too limited to draw any firmer conclusions concerning the relationship between the ancillary material in Vespasian B. vi and the Canterbury School. The presence of Eucherius in these bodies of texts, however, suggests that there may be a relationship between the sources and the origins of this material. Such highly technical scholarship on contemporary and historical measurements seems highly likely to have been produced and utilized in an intellectual environment primarily devoted to biblical exposition such as Theodore's School.

While this evidence does not conclusively prove a link between the notes and the Canterbury School, the use of works by Cosmas Indicopleustes, Josephus, Isidore, and Eucherius in the notes and the similarities between the notes and the Canterbury Commentaries and related texts suggest that a connection is probable. It must be conceded that there is a striking similarity between the form of these notes and the Antiochene exegesis practised at Canterbury. None of the notes constitutes complete excerpts or word-for-word quotations of passages from other sources, but seem to be synthetized and remediated explanations of various scholarly and Christian topics, much like the Canterbury Commentaries.

Beyond the sources, the manuscript context of the notes is telling. Online access via Parker 2.0 encourages us to appreciate these texts in their manuscript context. The notes are transmitted in CCCC 320 with the *Paenitentiale Theodori*, the *Libellus responsionum* of Augustine and Gregory, and the *Paenitentiale Sangermanense*, which is rubricated by an autographic poem of Archbishop Theodore addressed to Bishop Hæddi. The *Paenitentiale Theodori* is a later compilation of Theodoran pronouncements and insular penitential material assembled in its primary version by the unknown Eoda Christianus. The *Paenitentiale Theodori* was copied into CCCC 320 from a continental exemplar alongside related material from St Augustine's, some of which is connected to Theodore. Additionally, the contents list of CCCC 320 on folio 117v, written by the thirteenth-century Tremulous Hand, indicates that the encyclopaedic notes were thought of as an integral component of the manuscript.[47]

It may well be that CCCC 320, inadvertently or by design, is a compendium of Theodorian material. The relationship of these notes to the Canterbury School is strengthened by the appearance of texts in this collection that are associated with Theodore. There is no obvious connection between the penitential judgements intended for use by confessors and the encyclopaedic notes, except their tenth-century Canterbury provenance. Nevertheless, the penitential material associated with Theodore provides an apposite comparison in examining the texts' possible authorship. The numerous recensions of the *Paenitentiale Theodori* constitute a complex body of literature with various layers of accretions, but an original kernel of Theodorian penitential teaching. Similarly, with the Canterbury Commentaries and Leiden Glossary, it is difficult to be confident about what forms are Theodore's original teaching and what constitutes additions by the commentator or later transmitters. We cannot know precisely if or how the notes relate to Theodore's scholarly exposition, to texts produced at the Canterbury School, or to sources used and taught in this milieu. However, the sources deployed in the notes suggest that there may well be an original Theodorian core within these texts. Understanding the relationships between these texts and the influence the Canterbury School had on their development provides us with a fuller insight into the incomplete picture of this foundational period in Anglo-Saxon intellectual history and its afterlife.

Conclusions

I hope this chapter has underscored the fruitfulness of examining anonymous texts within a major manuscript, a methodology encouraged by Parker 2.0. The ability to easily consult digital facsimiles of Parker manuscripts encourages a comparative approach more strongly than is invited by editions or transcription of short, supplementary, or marginal texts in disparate editions and studies from the past three centuries. The online repository calls us to return to the manuscripts and to re-evaluate sources and authorship. The digital repository prompts us to view texts in their complete manuscript context and to look for networks of relationships within and without the Parker collection, which can transform our appreciation of a text such as the notes in CCCC 320. It is tempting to see these shorter 'micro-texts' as manuscript fillers. Codicological arrangement does not, however, absolutely define importance, interest, or function. Although the digital cannot replace the physical manuscript, digital facsimiles are more than serviceable for editorial purposes. In examining variation between textual witnesses, there is very little distance between physical consultation and digital surrogate. Indeed, the convenience of digital access expedites this process. It is easy to lose sight of the ease with which material can now be consulted: Parker 2.0 makes many early medieval manuscripts instantly accessible whereas it is still necessary to rely on physical consultation, photographic reproductions, microfiche, or even photocopies of the hardcopy edition of microfiche facsimiles through interlibrary loan for medieval manuscripts that have not yet been digitized, such as Oxford, Bodleian Library, Hatton 113. If physical consultation is necessary for the purposes of codicological investigation, then it is possible to familiarize oneself with the manuscript beforehand, thus utilizing limited time in the archive. Most scholars agree that nothing can replace the physical manuscript; however, what we find in an online repository such as Parker 2.0 are excellent substitutes for the physical manuscript when we cannot always be present with it.

Table 11.1 Topics of encyclopaedic notes

Encyclopaedic notes (position in Corpus 320)	CCCC MS 320	CCCC MS 183	London, BL, Cotton Vespasian B.vi [in a different order]	London, BL, Royal 2 B.v	Paris, BN lat. 2825
1. On the threefold Incarnation (folio 166r)	•	•		•	Fragmentary
2. On the age of the Lord (folios 166v–167r)	•	•		•	Fragmentary
3. On the Six Ages of the World (folios 167r–168r)	•	•	Substituted with a thematically similar but different note	•	•
4. On the Six Ages of Man (folio 168r)	•	•	•	•	•
5. On the number of bones, teeth, and veins in the human body (folio 168r)	•	•	•	•	•
6. Measurements of the world (folio 168v)	•	•	•	•	•
7. Measurements the Temple (folio 168v)	•	•	•	•	•
8. Measurements of the Tabernacle (folio 168v)	•	•	•	•	•
9. Measurements of St Peter's Basilica (folio 168v)	•	•	•	•	•
10. Measurements of the Ark (folio 168v)	•	•	•	•	•
11. Number of Biblical books (folio 168v)	•	•	•	•	•
12. Number of Psalm verses (folio 168v)	•	•	•	•	•
13. Units of measurement (folios 168v–169r)	•	•	•	•	•
14. Hexameron (folio 169r)	•	•			•
15. Jerusalem and the Holy Sepulchre (folios 169r–169v)	•			•	•

Notes

1 Thank you to Kees Dekker, Tristan Major, and Christine Rauer for providing many helpful comments, and for making material available to me. The production of this table is indebted to Dekker's study and edition of the notes. For the text of the notes as edited from CCCC 183, see Kees Dekker, 'Anglo-Saxon Encyclopaedic Notes: Tradition and Function', in *Foundations of Learning: The Transfer of Encyclopaedic Knowledge in the Early Middle Ages*, ed. R. H. Bremmer and K. Dekker, Mediaevalia Groningana New Series 9 (Leuven: Peeters, 2007), pp. 279–315, at pp. 281–4 and 313–15. For the text of the notes as they appear in CCCC 320, see Parker 2.0, folios 166r–169v.

2 Birte Walbers, 'Number and Measurement in Anglo-Saxon Christian Culture: Editions and Studies of Numerical Notes in Eight Anglo-Saxon Manuscripts, *c.* 800–*c.* 1150' (unpub. PhD dissertation, University of York, 2012), pp. 123–32.

3 Dekker, 'Anglo-Saxon Encyclopaedic Notes', pp. 280, 300.

4 For the place of this note and others in CCCC 320, see Table 11.1.

5 Dekker, 'Anglo-Saxon Encyclopaedic Notes', p. 285.

6 Dekker, 'Anglo-Saxon Encyclopaedic Notes', pp. 281, 313; 284.

7 For further background on the Quartodecimans, see William L. Petersen, 'Eusebius and the Paschal Controversy', in *Patristic and Text-Critical Studies: The Collected Essays of William L. Petersen*, ed. Jan Krans and Joseph Verheyden, New Testament Tools, Studies and Documents, vol. 40 (Leiden: Brill, 2011), pp. 204–18.

8 Exodus 12:14, 13:3; Leviticus 23:5–6.

9 See 1 Corinthians 5:7.

10 See Petersen, 'Eusebius and the Paschal Controversy', pp. 204–18.

11 Dekker, 'Anglo-Saxon Encyclopaedic Notes', p. 285.

12 Petersen, 'Eusebius and the Paschal Controversy', pp. 209–13.

13 On Theodore's background, see Michael Lapidge, 'The Career of Archbishop Theodore', in *Archbishop Theodore: Commemorative Studies on his Life and Influence*, ed. Michael Lapidge, Cambridge Studies in Anglo-Saxon England 11 (Cambridge: Cambridge University Press, 1995), pp. 1–29.

14 See Catherine Cubitt, *Anglo-Saxon Church Councils c.650–c.850* (Leicester: Leicester University Press, 1995).

15 Jan Hessels, *A Late-Eighth-Century Anglo-Saxon Glossary Preserved in the Library of the Leiden University* (Cambridge: Cambridge University Press, 1906), pp. iv, v, xxxv, 8–10, 10, 33–38; and Michael Lapidge, *The Anglo-Saxon Library* (Oxford: Oxford University Press, 2005), p. 176.

16 Dekker, 'Anglo-Saxon Encyclopaedic Notes', p. 285.

17 Stephen of Ripon, *Eddius Stephanus Life of Wilfrid. Edited and Translated by Bertram Colgrave* (Cambridge: Cambridge University Press, 1927), pp. 12–15, 24–32.

18 Dekker, 'Anglo-Saxon Encyclopaedic Notes', pp. 290–1.

19 The text of this note can be found in Rolf Bremmer, 'Leiden, Vossianus Lat. Q. 69 (Part 2): Schoolbook or Proto-Encyclopaedic Miscellany?', in *Practice in Learning: The Transfer of Encyclopaedic Knowledge in the Early Middle Ages*, ed. Rolf Bremmer and Kees Dekker, Mediaevalia Groningana New Series 16 (Leuven: Peeters, 2010), pp. 19–54, at 46–47.

20 Bremmer, 'Leiden, Vossianus Lat. Q. 69 (Part 2)', p. 47.

21 Bischoff and Lapidge, *Biblical Commentaries*, pp. 210, 545–6.

22 Simon Keynes, 'Between Bede and the *Chronicle*: London, BL, Cotton Vespasian B.vi, fols. 104–9', in *Latin Learning and English Lore*, ed. K. O'Brien O'Keefe and A. Orchard (Toronto: University of Toronto Press, 2005), vol. 1, pp. 47–67.

23 Bede, *Historia abbatum*, 15. Christopher Grocock and Ian Wood, *Abbots of Wearmouth and Jarrow* (Oxford: Oxford University Press, 2013), p. 58.

24 Lapidge, *The Anglo-Saxon Library*, p. 177.

25 Dekker, 'Anglo-Saxon Encyclopaedic Notes', p. 290.

26 Keynes, 'Between Bede and the *Chronicle*', pp. 47, 61.

27 Dekker, 'Anglo-Saxon Encyclopaedic Notes', p. 292.

28 Dekker, 'Anglo-Saxon Encyclopaedic Notes', has edited the Latin text of the note in his study and edition of the notes. Dekker, p. 307, n. 106. My translation reads: 'On Jerusalem and the things in it. It is positioned on an elevated mountain. And in the middle of that city there is a basilica in honour of St. Constantin [the church of the Holy Sepulchre]. And in the basilica is the treasure of King Solomon. And there is an altar made from gold and that altar is supported by nine gilded columns and in the right-hand part of that basilica is a half cubicle (edicule). In this edicule the cross of Christ was concealed on which the Lord suffered and was suspended for the salvation of the world. And there are nails from which the Jews fixed the hands of the Lord. And there is that lance with which Longinus pierced the side of the Lord. That cross and that lance shine radiantly in this place at night just as the sun in daytime. And from that place one comes to the chancel screen where the Lord hung on the cross, and that chancel is made from gold and silver, and beneath this chancel the body of Adam is buried. And the cross stood above the breast of Adam, and that drop which flowed from the side of the Lord, and by that blood the ground was purged and sanctified and Adam was redeemed from Hell.'

29 Dekker, 'Anglo-Saxon Encyclopaedic Notes', p. 291.

30 Lapidge, *The Anglo-Saxon Library*, p. 218. Bede cites this work in his commentaries on Genesis, Samuel, Ezra, Mark, Luke, *De Tabernaculo, De Templo, De natura rerum, In Regum librum xxx quaestiones*, and in his topographical work, *Nomina locorum ex beati Hieronomi presbiteri et Flavi Iosephi collecta opusculis*.

31 *PentI*, pp. 260, 301, 311, 327, and 391. On the use of Josephus in the Commentaries, see Bischoff and Lapidge, *Biblical Commentaries*, pp. 216–17.

32 Bischoff and Lapidge, *Biblical Commentaries*, p. 216.

33 See Tristan Major, 'The Number Seventy-Two: Biblical and Hellenistic Beginnings to the Early Middle Ages', *Sacris Eruditi* 53 (2013): 7–45.

34 On this biblical episode and its early medieval interpretation and adaptation, see Tristan Major's *Undoing Babel: The Tower of Babel in Anglo-Saxon Literature* (Toronto: University of Toronto Press, 2018).

35 Dekker, 'Anglo-Saxon Encyclopaedic Notes', p. 293.

36 Dekker, 'Anglo-Saxon Encyclopaedic Notes', p. 293.

37 Keynes, 'Between Bede and the *Chronicle*', p. 60.

38 *PentI* 1, Bischoff and Lapidge, *Biblical Commentaries*, pp. 298–9.

39 Dekker, 'Anglo-Saxon Encyclopaedic Notes', pp. 293–4. This is not to be confused with Book 6 of the same title in the *Etymologiae*.

40 Isidore of Seville, *De ecclesiasticis officiis*, 11.7. *Isidore of Seville: De ecclesiasticis officiis*, trans. Thomas Knoebel (New York: The Newman Press, 2008), p. 33.

41 Four manuscripts survive from Early England. Gneuss and Lapidge, pp. 263, 391, 713, and 845. Only 845 is old enough to be a physical source here. See Lapidge, *Anglo-Saxon Library*, p. 310.

42 Claudia Di Sciacca, *Finding the Right Words: Isidore's* Synonyma *in Anglo-Saxon England* (Toronto: University of Toronto Press, 2008), pp. 47–8; Hessels, pp. xxvi, 22; Lapidge, *The Anglo-Saxon Library*, p. 176.

43 Lapidge, *The Anglo-Saxon Library*, p. 181.

44 Walbers, 'Number and Measurement in Anglo-Saxon Christian Culture', pp. 235–76.

45 Kees Dekker, 'Eucherius of Lyon in Anglo-Saxon England: The Continental Connections', in *Practice in Learning*, ed. Bremmer and Dekker, pp. 147–73.

46 Dekker, 'Eucherius of Lyon in Anglo-Saxon England,' pp. 153–6.

47 M. R. James, *A Descriptive Catalogue of the Manuscripts in the Library of Corpus Christi College, Cambridge*, vol. 1 (Cambridge: Cambridge University Press, 2012), p. 60.

12 Cambridge, Corpus Christi College, 322
Tradition and transmission

David F. Johnson

Cambridge, Corpus Christi College, 322 contains a nearly complete text (one leaf is missing) of the Old English translation of Pope Gregory the Great's *Dialogues*, a translation attributed to Bishop Wærferth of Worcester, who, according to Alfred's biographer, Bishop Asser of Sherborne, translated it at the behest of the king as part of his famous programme of translation and education.[1] There are three other witnesses to the Old English text, none of which comes closer than to within a hundred years of Wærferth's original translation. It is as an editor of this text that I approach CCCC 322, and I shall explore how digital surrogates influence our understanding of material objects, book history, and textual transmission. A fair amount has been written about the transmission of the Old English *Dialogues* and the manuscripts in which this text is preserved— as is witnessed by the extensive bibliography appearing on the front page of the entry dealing with this manuscript in Parker 2.0. In fact, there is so much previous research that an editor might be forgiven for simply citing and summarizing the relevant studies by specialist codicologists and palaeographers when it comes to such things as date and place of origin, provenance, and textual transmission. But to do so would be to pass up an opportunity to test this new iteration of Parker on the Web as a tool for editing.

In this chapter, I first outline some of the benefits of digital surrogates like Parker 2.0 for editors of texts. The bulk of the chapter consists of one focused case study of such a benefit: how the resources available in Parker 2.0 might help us come closer to the answer to two of the most pressing questions surrounding CCCC 322 and indeed Wærferth's translation of Gregory's *Dialogues*: where and when was the manuscript written? At the end of the chapter, I shall broaden the conversation to consider some ways in which Parker 2.0 can help us think through manuscript design and use more broadly, through a comparison of CCCC 322 and CCCC 161, a compilation of Latin saints' lives which has thematic parallels to the *Dialogues*' collection of hagiographical vignettes. As Parker 2.0 opens up the resources of the Parker collection to a larger group of scholars than ever before, this resource allows us to learn more about the lives and afterlives of medieval manuscripts by virtue of the primary and secondary information it assembles in one place.

Other chapters in this volume discuss some of the philosophical differences between consulting the physical object and working from a digital surrogate, but simply having easy and regular access to the manuscripts containing the text one is editing is a great deal more than half the battle when preparing an edition. While working with Gill Cannell, the sub-librarian, in the reading room of the Parker Library in Cambridge was a true delight, in the four or five multi-week stints I spent in that library I was able to focus on one manuscript and one manuscript only: CCCC 322. I did get to know this manuscript, or thought I did, as a physical object, and I will always be grateful for that opportunity. But looking back at that experience, especially through the rose-coloured lens of Parker 2.0, I realize that I have made a great deal more substantial progress on the edition since my university subscribed to the first iteration of Parker on the Web. In this age of dwindling research travel budgets, it has helped compensate for my inability to make further expensive trips to Cambridge. And as all the contributions in this book suggest, one can do things with Parker 2.0 that one could not otherwise do with the physical manuscript, even in an environment as user-friendly as the Parker Library in the last two decades, such as looking at two manuscripts side by side. This arrangement would be unheard of, of course, as readers are seldom allowed to look at two select manuscripts side by side in a reading room. Comparing readings in multiple manuscripts using image viewers such as Mirador brings a level of immediacy and zoomability unattainable in an archival reading room. If this was all that Parker 2.0 made possible, it would already be an editor's dream come true. But Parker 2.0, like the library of manuscripts for which it is a surrogate, is itself an extremely important archive of materials necessary for decoding the context in which CCCC 322 must be understood. The digital repository contains a large number of vernacular manuscripts written in the eleventh and twelfth centuries, many of them attributed to Worcester, and so is of inestimable importance when considering the kinds of questions we traditionally ask of the texts we edit, such as when, where, by whom, for whom, and why was this manuscript produced?

I do not have the space to offer more than a single illustration of this, so I shall touch on how the resources available in Parker 2.0 might help us come closer to the answer to two of these questions: when and where was the manuscript written?[2] The story of the *Dialogues* in English—and its manuscript transmission—is one of opposite temporal poles on a spectrum inhabited by very few hard data points. Wærferth and the Alfredian programme of translation and education are at one end, with the Tremulous Hand at the other. When it comes to trying to determine what Wærferth's *ur*-text looked like, extracting information from the extant manuscript transmission is akin to trying to wring water from a stone. As I mention above, of the four extant manuscript witnesses to the Old English translation, none comes closer to Wærferth's original than a hundred years, at best. On the other hand, two of our manuscripts, London, British Library, Cotton Otho C. i, Part 2 (Manuscript O) and Oxford, Bodleian Library, Hatton

76 (Manuscript H), thanks to the interventions of the Tremulous Hand, provide us with a wealth of information about how and for what purpose such Old English manuscripts were used in the thirteenth century. More or less right in the middle of that spectrum, in the eleventh century, is CCCC 322, a perhaps not altogether reliable witness to Wærferth's ninth-century text, but potentially more eloquent when it comes to the situation in the late eleventh century, despite initial appearances.

As far as the date of composition of CCCC 322 is concerned, it has most recently been situated in the second half of the eleventh century, though the fact that Parker 2.0 gives an approximate date of (*c.*1000–1099) is perhaps a measure of how uncertain we are about our dating criteria. Still, no modern authority on pre-Conquest palaeography and codicology has to my knowledge put the date of this manuscript anywhere other than the second half of the eleventh century, including Neil Ker, Mildred Budny, Richard Gameson, Elaine Treharne, and Peter Stokes. Of course, Parker 2.0 now makes it much easier to verify the dates given by the experts, if one were so inclined to do so. There are no owner's marks or other internal information, such as other Worcester documents copied in with the main text, to help with the dating of the manuscript, so really the only more or less concrete evidence we have for dating it is the script itself. The nature of the script of CCCC 322 leads us to the second question I mentioned a moment ago, namely *where* the manuscript was made, to which I now turn.

In her 1997 *Illustrated Catalogue* of manuscripts in the Parker Library, Mildred Budny remarks of CCCC 322 that 'The presumed place of origin rests partly on the subsequent provenance, partly on the origin of the textual exemplar, which must have been associated with Wærferth's Worcester, and partly on the character of the script.'[3] Let me take that last point first. In support of her claim, Budny notes how the hand of the CCCC 322 scribe bears a resemblance to scripts in 'other' Worcester products, in particular the Old English texts in CCCC 391, the so-called *Portiforium of Wulfstan*. And indeed, a comparison of letter forms from a random folio of CCCC 322 with the Old English in Corpus 391 suggests that this is in fact the case. While CCCC 391 has other internal evidence linking it pretty firmly to Worcester, the only sure thing a comparison of the script with CCCC 322 tells us is that whoever wrote the text had learned the script either at Worcester or in one of the other houses associated with it. The manuscript could just as easily have been written elsewhere by a scribe trained at or in the style of Worcester. The glosses on folio 20, taken demonstrably from another book we know was at Worcester at the time (Oxford, Bodleian Library, Tanner 3), establish a twelfth-century Worcester provenance for the manuscript, but it need not follow that the book was actually made there. A full examination of all the hands in vernacular manuscripts attributed to Worcester from this period might bring us closer to a definitive answer to this question. To that end, it would be interesting and beneficial to see greater harmony between Parker 2.0 and DigiPal;[4] linking these two brilliant resources would take end-user utility to an entirely different level.

The other evidence adduced by Budny for localizing CCCC 322 is suggestive but equally inconclusive and circumstantial. Yes, it seems more than likely that the textual exemplar for the translation was ultimately associated with Worcester, and it is certain that the manuscript was in Worcester at some point in the twelfth century, when those glosses were added. But the sum of these for the most part circumstantial bits of evidence does not necessarily add up to a Worcester origin.

There is one more piece of relevant evidence to the question of localization, found also in the Parker archive. This is the booklist in CCCC 367, folio 101v, which lists, among the books in the priory library, two copies of the *Dialogues* in English.[5] Peter Stokes has recently and convincingly demonstrated that the booklist should be dated to the late eleventh century, rather than *c.*1050, as Ker and Lapidge have it.[6] What this means for a reading of the booklist in CCCC 367 is that we may now add CCCC 322 to the possible manuscripts being referred to there. Previous discussions of the list had always rather easily identified Oxford, Bodleian Library, Hatton 76 and London, British Library, Cotton Otho C. i, volume 2, as the books meant by the list, presumably due to their date of production and later Worcester provenance.[7] While this new dating of the booklist opens up possibilities for localizing CCCC 322, it is by no means conclusive evidence. There are, in fact, significant difficulties in linking *any* of the extant manuscripts of the Old English *Dialogues* definitively with the two *dialogas* recorded in this booklist. But working in the digital age, using tools like these, with so much data so readily available, has brought home to me the truth in Treharne's answer to the possibility of a Worcester origin for CCCC 322: as she notes in the relevant entry to *English Manuscripts, 1060 to 1220*, 'while [a Worcester origin] is quite probable, it is not certain, with much of the evidence adduced being circular'. It *is* circular, and no amount of repetition of seemingly accepted (and increasingly untested) hypotheses can change that. If anything, this exercise has taught me, as editor of the Old English *Dialogues*, how important it is to be critical of accepted opinion when it comes to such questions. Parker 2.0 can be a prophylactic against the unthinking propagation of potentially misleading information.[8]

It seems clear to me that more information helps us know more about a manuscript: more data, even as it may seem to complicate, can clarify a picture in the end. To that end, I conclude this chapter by discussing some fruitful points of comparison between CCCC 322 and CCCC 161, and what we can learn about them both by placing them in parallel and thinking through their similarities and differences.

The only text contained in CCCC 322 is, of course, the Old English translation of Gregory's *Dialogues*. This is perhaps one of the few points of similarity with CCCC 161. Whereas CCCC 161 contains the lives of predominately British and English saints, Gregory's original was intended to highlight the miraculous deeds of Italian holy men, who, according to

Gregory's interlocutor Peter, were not well known in his day. The contents of both of these manuscripts therefore cater to what one might regard as an originally 'localized' context or need. But the two manuscripts differ greatly in other particulars, namely, their putative localization, date of origin, and language.[9] And while they were certainly not produced in the same scriptorium, they do have in common a debate about their place of origin. At least three locations have been proposed for the origin of CCCC 161: Rochester Cathedral priory; the Cluniac house of Faversham in the diocese of Rochester, due to the inclusion of four lives of Cluniac saints; and St Augustine's, Canterbury, where Michael Lapidge seems certain it must have been written based on rubrics added to the Life of St Swithun.[10]

The decoration schemes in these manuscripts comprise another obvious contrast between the two, and this was discussed by Abigail Robertson in the 'Parker on the Web' collegium. The contrast is striking: there are no illustrations in CCCC 322, and decoration, such as it is, is limited to coloured initials of several different styles throughout the text. These are in blue or red (some of them now oxidized), and they are most frequently used to demarcate the shift in speaker, with Peter asking his question and Gregory responding. But there are more fancifully executed initials with foliate decoration, as well as rustic capitals at the beginning of lesser sections, some of them filled in with colour, usually red. One wonders whether the style of these coloured initials may provide some clue as to where or when the manuscript was made. So far as I know, no one has tried to connect them stylistically to known practice in a particular scriptorium (Worcester, for example), as has been done with the first half of Cotton Otho C. i.[11] This might be an avenue for further exploration, something that Parker 2.0 would now make a great deal easier.

I turn now to two final aspects of the manuscripts under consideration that I think are worth pausing over in this context. The first has to do with the relative absence of signs of use in CCCC 322, the traces left behind by later readers of a manuscript who annotated, corrected, and added text and other markings to their pages. CCCC 322 is exceptionally clean in this respect, remarkably so, in fact, for a vernacular manuscript associated with Worcester. There are only a very few such signs added by one later reader; that is, nine Latin glosses in a twelfth-century hand appearing on folio 20.[12] Apart from these, the only other significant additions are the rubricated Latin incipits in a thirteenth-century hand (folios 1r, 33v, 67r, 110r, 57v).

Related to signs of use, I argue, is the concept of accessibility; that is, the ways in which a manuscript aids or hinders a reader's attempts to navigate its contents. One of the biggest and most obvious impacts of Parker 2.0 is in this very area of accessibility. Potentially millions of people now have access to this library's collection of early medieval manuscripts, and the creators of this database have done a superb job in building an interface that makes it very easy to find one's way around the entire collection, from manuscript to manuscript, but also within each book, via thumbnails, annotations, links, and other tools of navigation. These are all in a way technologically-driven advancements of some features already observable in both of these manuscripts, features which were designed to aid the reader in navigating the texts they contain.

In the case of CCCC 322, *incipits* and *explicits* were added in the thirteenth century to let the reader know where they were in the book. In CCCC 161, the user interface, if we can call it that, is much more sophisticated, and there are even more advanced attempts to orient the reader.[13] Thus the original design and structure of CCCC 161 is more explicitly user-friendly, necessitated, perhaps, by the variety of materials it contained (18 separate items). The lack of such features in CCCC 322 may have been obviated by the fact that it contained just one text, and we can assume that it was a text its owners knew well.[14] The relative dearth of visual 'sign-posting' in CCCC 322 may indicate not so much a lack of sophistication in manuscript design, as a sign of how well the Old English text was known in the eleventh century. It may also provide us with a clue as to how this particular manuscript was used. Michael Lapidge has observed that, when the *Dialogues* appear in pre-conquest booklists, it usually indicates a copy of Gregory's work that would have been read out loud during refectory. Given the well-established facts that Worcester 'preserved Anglo-Saxon traditions and skills' after the Conquest,[15] and that the time and region were fertile grounds for the production of texts dealing with Gregory, especially the *Dialogues*, a manuscript like CCCC 322 might have served as a clean copy for refectory reading.[16]

In conclusion, I would argue that whereas in the past volumes without annotations might be thought of as 'unread', and signs of use themselves were quickly relegated to the realm of invisible ephemera in our editions of these texts, thanks to Parker 2.0, such traces left by later readers may now be collected and catalogued with relative ease, and may find a more prominent place in future histories of these manuscripts. As such, thanks in large part to Parker 2.0, all features of manuscripts can be taken into account for the fullest interpretation of the book.

Notes

1 Wærferth's work will obviously have taken place at some time during his episcopate, so *c*. 870 – *c*. 915.
2 Mildred Budny, *Insular, Anglo-Saxon, and Early Anglo-Norman Manuscript Art at Corpus Christi College, Cambridge: An Illustrated Catalogue* (Kalamazoo, MI: Medieval Institute Publications, 1997), p. 625: 'Made in England, probably at Worcester; second half of the eleventh century. The presumed place of origin rests partly on the subsequent provenance, partly on the origin of the textual exemplar, which must have been associated with Wærferth's Worcester, and partly on the character of the script.' As David Yerkes observed, 'the revised version of the translation in MS "H"—a version probably made at Worcester—agrees more closely with the text of the original version in MS 322 than with that in MS "O". Moreover, the script in 322 closely resembles script in some Worcester products of the second half of the eleventh century. Among them are the Old English portions

of the prayers and fragmentary prognostics, in both Old English and Latin (pp. 613–17 and 713–21), written by a single scribe, in the *Portiforium* of St. Wulfstan (no. 43)'. Elaine Treharne notes that while it may be probable that the manuscript was written at Worcester, 'it is not certain, with much of the evidence adduced being circular'. Elaine Treharne, with the assistance of Hollie Morgan and Johanna Green, 'Cambridge, Corpus Christi College, 322', in *The Production and Use of English Manuscripts 1060 to 1220*, ed. Orietta Da Rold, Takako Kato, Mary Swan, and Elaine Treharne (Leicester: University of Leicester, 2010): https://www.le.ac.uk/english/em1060to1220/mss/EM.CORPUS.322.htm#bud189 <accessed October 3 2018>.

3 Budny, *Insular, Anglo-Saxon, and Early Anglo-Norman Manuscript Art*, p. 625.

4 Peter Stokes *et al.*, 'DigiPal': http://www.digipal.eu/

5 See Peter Stokes, Chapter 7 in this volume, for discussion of this manuscript.

6 Peter Stokes, 'The Vision of Leofric—Manuscript, Text and Context', *Review of English Studies* 63 (2011): 529–50. But this in itself is a questionable conclusion, for a number of reasons, not least of which is the fact that one of the manuscripts is a composite consisting of parts of the *Dialogues* written at different times and in completely different places. Which one of these was at Worcester at the time when the booklist was written? So the argumentation for assigning O and H as the books referred to in this list seems more and more circular. This particular list notes two copies of the *Dialogues* in English *c*. 1050, when it was drawn up. O comprises two parts produced 40 years apart, according to Ker, so may well represent two halves of two separate copies of the book. The list might refer to these, but we have no way of knowing. Hatton 76 itself is a composite manuscript consisting of the first two books of the Dialogues, heavily revised, and a copy of an Old English translation of the enlarged *Herbarius Ps.-Apuleii* and *Medicina de quadrupedibus*. Physical evidence in the manuscript proves that they were at one point bound separately (see N. R. Ker, *Catalogue of Manuscripts Containing Anglo-Saxon* [Oxford: Clarendon Press, 1957; repr. 1991], p. 360: 'rustmarks and stains on f[olio] 67 show that part A was once bound separately.'). Both of these were annotated by the Tremulous Hand in Worcester, hence the assumption that the book must have been in Worcester in the middle of the eleventh century. This is possible, of course, but hardly a certainty. The dating of the scripts would seem to be the basis for Ker's attribution; Ker dates Part B, the *Herbarium*, to the middle of the eleventh century, and part A to the first quarter of that century. It seems likely that the *Dialogues* and *Herbarium* would have been bound together only at a fairly late date, when it must have seemed certain that the second half of the *Dialogues* was lost or would never be completed, and so there is no really good reason to believe that the manuscript *had* to be in Worcester very much prior to when the Tremulous Hand was able to access it. It is noteworthy that neither of the two booklists that reputedly report the status of the priory library in the middle of the eleventh century mentions an English *Herbarius Apuleii*. CCCC 322, moreover, probably postdates these lists by several decades, and so it seems that we cannot discount a Worcester origin just because we already have two other candidates for the *dialogas* mentioned in the booklists.

7 See, for example, Budny, *Insular, Anglo-Saxon, and Early Anglo-Norman Manuscript Art*, p. 625.

8 An important essay is Mary Swan's 'Mobile Libraries: Old English Manuscript Production in Worcester and the West Midlands, 1090–1215', in *Essays in Manuscript Geography: Vernacular Manuscripts of the English West Midlands from the Conquest to the Sixteenth Century*, ed. W. Scase (Turnhout: Brepols, 2007), pp. 29–42. Swan notes how Wulfstan II established a number of links with other houses and entered into a confraternity agreement with at least one, Ramsey. She notes what she calls the 'centripetal force' exerted by Worcester on scholars, who tend to

attribute a Worcester provenance as a kind of default. See especially pp. 31–2 on the likelihood of books being swapped in this confraternity network.

9 CCCC 322 is dated by most to the second half of the eleventh century, CCCC 161 to the late twelfth; CCCC 322 was written in the vernacular, and CCCC 161 in Latin.

10 Lapidge, p. lxxxi, in Dumville and Keynes, *The Anglo-Saxon Chronicle*, p. 17. See also: www.lancaster.ac.uk/staff/haywardp/hist424/seminars/Corpus161.htm: *De diuitis podagriti curatione quam beatus Augustinus sancto Swithuno reseruauit*, 'About the cure of a rich gout-sufferer whom the blessed Augustine reserved to St Swithun'. Michael Lapidge thinks that a rubric of this kind would have been problematic at Winchester Cathedral where St Swithun was venerated, but was the association implicit in the miracle really a humiliation? Partnership miracles of this sort are often celebrated in miracle collections, the hagiographers being anxious to show that their subjects enjoyed the recognition of other high-status saints. There are, unfortunately, no medieval ownership inscriptions, nor has the book been identified in the St Augustine's library catalogue. Also, CCCC 322 has been assigned to Bury St Edmunds, an attribution vigorously denied by Neil Ker, but as we just saw, it has most frequently been assigned to Worcester.

11 What does make a script a Worcester hand in the late eleventh century? Ker's features are recognizable, and Treharne's description is even more refined. For manuscripts localized to Worcester for other reasons than script, but that share a common style according to N. R. Ker, see *Medieval Libraries of Great Britain: A List of Surviving Books*, 2nd ed. (London: Royal Historical Society, 1964), p. xxi, n. 9.

12 Ker, *Catalogue of Manuscripts*, p. 107. Glosses dated to the twelfth century appear on folio 20, and Latin *incipits* and *explicits* were added in the thirteenth century.

13 Including a Table of Contents, and extensive rubrication, as well as running headers at the top of each folio page indicating the title of the life in question.

14 The reviser of the Old English *Dialogues* in Hatton 76, for example, took great pains to insert Old English translations of the Latin chapter headings that appear in some redactions of Gregory's *Dialogi*, which may reflect a need to access particular parts of the text for specific purposes.

15 Budny, *Insular, Anglo-Saxon, and Early Anglo-Norman Manuscript Art*, p. 625.

16 On the use of the *Dialogues* in refectory reading, Michael Lapidge says this in a footnote: 'Some idea of what books were read at mealtimes in the refectory may be gleaned from a twelfth-century list from Durham: "Hii sunt libri qui leguntur ad collationem: Vitae patrum; Diadema monachorum; Effrem cum vitis Egiptiorum; Paradisus; Speculum; Dialogus; Pastoralis eximius liber; Ysidorus de summo bono; Prosper de contemplatiua uita; liber Odonis; Iohannes Cassianus decem Collationes"' (*Catalogi Bibliothecarum Antiqui*, ed. G. Becker (Bonn, 1885), p. 24). When we encounter some of these titles in pre-Conquest booklists—especially the *Vitas patrum*, Gregory the Great's *Dialogi* and *Regula pastoralis*, Julianus Pomerius's *De vita contemplatiua*, Isidore's *Sententie* and Cassian's *Collationes*—there is some presumption that they may have been used for refectory reading.

13 Cambridge, Corpus Christi College, 41 and 286

Digitization as translation

Sharon M. Rowley

In the first chapter of *Rhetoric, Hermeneutics and Translation in the Middle Ages*, Rita Copeland describes Roman theories of translation, concluding that 'the essential paradox of the enterprise of translation as replication through a difference, through displacement, substitution, and cultural or canonical appropriation will gain new importance in the Middle Ages'.[1] In celebration of the launch of Parker on the Web 2.0, it seems productive to suggest that this 'essential paradox' will gain even greater importance in the age of digitization. Digitization, like translation, has been treated as secondary and inauthentic, as threatening to the truth and, potentially, reality.[2] From François Jullien's perspective, however, the future belongs to translation: '*Le monde à venir doit être celui de l'entre-langues: non pas d'une langue dominante, quelle qu'elle soit, mais de la traduction activant les ressources des langues les unes par rapport aux autres*' ('The world of the future will have to be a world of in-between-lingualism: not of one dominant language, whichever it might be, but of translation that activates the resources of languages with respect to each other').[3] If we read digitization as a form of translation, which is the central trope that Mateusz Fafinski and I explore in our chapters, then digitization can also be read as 'activating the resources', not just of languages but of vision, screenic sensoria, and knowledge. Using these tropes to deepen our understanding of CCCC 41 and 286 as powerfully transformative and performative texts, we can see how digitization activates new forms of presence, visibility, and meaning that echo and extend the ways in which these books were received, transmitted, and appropriated as manuscripts in medieval Britain.

On some genuinely basic level, CCCC 41 can be read as telling the story of the arrival of CCCC 286, the 'Augustine Gospels', in England. But CCCC 41 does not merely tell, it also shows and performs the effects of what CCCC 286 did there: convert reigning kings and their peoples to Christianity. This also brought about all the attendant social, political, and economic transformations, especially—for the purposes this chapter—conversion to Christianity, the return of Latin literacy, the development of written English, and the establishment of a multilingual ecclesiastical culture in England. The lived experience of these cultural transformations occupies the centre and the margins of CCCC 41, now in a way that every-one with a computer and Internet connection can see more clearly than ever.

The main text of CCCC 41 is the most complete surviving copy of the Old English translation of Bede's *Historia ecclesiastica gentis anglorum*, known as the B-text. It was copied by two scribes around the beginning of the eleventh century, with short stints written by at least two other scribes.[4] CCCC 41 has been described in detail by Ker, Gneuss, and Budny; it is a large-format book containing 244 leaves measuring 340 x 205 mm, with a writing space of *c.* 261 x 143 for the main text, and *c.* 334 x 199 for the largest secondary text.[5] Raymond Grant suggested that the manuscript was 'a working copy' of the Old English Bede, and concluded that it was 'not the best work of a leading monastic house' based on the incomplete decoration and the quality of the vellum.[6] Budny, however, describes the scribes as 'competent and clearly legible', concluding that the book was made at a 'disciplined center capable of rather good-quality book production'.[7] Peter Stokes has recently argued on the basis of the script—an English Vernacular minuscule retaining some characteristics of Square minuscule—that 'production in a house like Cred-iton seems entirely plausible'.[8] Given the form of the script, Stokes also notes that the manuscript may have been produced in Canterbury.[9] As is well known, Canterbury was an archiepiscopal seat; Crediton was an episcopal seat from *c.* 909 to 1050, when Bishop Leofric moved the seat to Exeter.[10] We know from a bilingual inscription that Leofric gave the manuscript to the library of the cathedral at Exeter sometime between 1069 and 1072. It remains possible that Leofric found CCCC 41 in Crediton and brought it with him to Exeter, but one cannot be certain. Given that both of these locations were important in the early eleventh century, the idea that it was a 'working copy' or 'made for a smaller center with a minimal library' should be set aside.[11]

Sometime in the middle of the eleventh century, another scribe (or scribes) added almost all of the now famous marginal materials, which include *for-mulae* in Old English and Latin, part of the Old English *Martyrology*, an Old English verse *Dialogue between Solomon and Saturn*, six anonymous Old English homilies, and extensive liturgical materials in Latin.[12] The manuscript also contains runic inscriptions, scribbles, names, and musical notations, the last of which were probably added in Exeter.[13] CCCC 41 came into the hands of Archbishop Matthew Parker in the sixteenth century and shows signs of use by Parker, Abraham Wheloc, and John Joscelyn (1529–1603). As the extensive bibliography for CCCC 41 on the Parker on the Web site indicates, this manuscript has been the subject of extensive study, which prompts the question: what could possibly be left to do? How can digitization help foster new insight into a book that has been so studied? I believe that comparative analysis fostered by the Parker interface and Mirador will lead to new insights concerning CCCC 41 as a whole book.

Looking at CCCC 41 together with CCCC 286 on screen animates what Nigel Thrift calls a whole new 'register' of understanding, one 'involv[ing] the active mediation of machines … in sending new kinds of life to us, changing the nature of "us" as a result'.[14] Through this lens, he explores the proliferation of screens not as distractions from the real, but as 'a new set of surfaces gradually covering the world, a kind of second skin of new forms of attention, of new body parts calling forth new counterparts—of something, to quote Wordsworth, "far more deeply interfused"'. He reminds us, 'after all', that:

> skin is in itself a multilayered, multipurpose organ that 'shifts from thick to thin, tight to loose, lubricated to dry, across the landscape of the body. Skin, a knowledge-gathering device responds to heat and cold, pleasure and pain. It lacks definitive boundaries, flowing continuously from the exposed surface of the body to its internal cavities. It is both living and dead, a self-repairing, self-replacing material whose exterior is senseless and inert while its inner layers are flush with nerves, glands and capillaries'.[15]

Skin forms a crucial part of the human ability to translate external sensoria into experience, thought, and knowledge; it always already replicates, displaces, substitutes, and transforms.

If skin already does all that, then mediation is more natural than new; after all, it is not as if screens have come into and changed a traditional world 'in which the social did not work through and with objects'.[16]

Manuscript books are also objects (made of skins and reanimated by the work of scribes and illuminators), and it is probably worth remembering that Æðelbert of Kent initially treated Augustine, his companions, their cross, songs, and their image of Christ as threats. Rather famously, when he meets them, Æðelbert:

> het hi(m) úte seldan gewyrcean 7 het agustinus mid his geferum þider to his spræce cuman. Warnode he hine ðy læs hi in hwylc hús to him ineodon breac he ealdre hælsunge gif hi hwylcne drýcræft hæfdon þ(æt) hine oferswiðan 7 beswican sceoldon.
>
> commanded them to make a seat outside, and commanded Augustine and his companions to come there to speak with him. He took heed, lest they go into any house with them, practiced a countercharm of old, if they had any magical craft by which they should overcome and deceive him.[17]

But Bede's translator assures his readers *Ac hi nales deoflescræfte, ac mid godcundum mægne gewelegode cómon: bæran cristes rodetacn sylefren, cristes mæl mid him hæfdon 7 andlicnesse on bréde hælendes cristes awritene*, 'But not at all with devilcraft, but enriched with holy power they came: they bore with them a token of Christ's cross, a silver crucifix of Christ, and image of the holy lord drawn and painted on a panel] and they were recounting holy names and singing prayers.'[18] After this meeting, Æðelbert gives Augustine a dwelling in Canterbury, to which he and his men proceed with their cross and image, singing *ðisne letaniam 7 antefn*, 'this litany and antiphon': *Deprecamur te, Domine, in omni misericordia tua ut auferatur furor tuus, et ira tua a ciui-tate ista et de domo sancta tua quoniam peccauimus. Alleluia*, 'We beseech Thee, O Lord, in Thy great mercy that Thy wrath and anger may be turned away from this city and from Thy holy house, for we have sinned. Alleluia.'[19] While this litany is neither accurately nor fully recorded in CCCC 41, the scribe nevertheless attempts to include a bilingual account of Augustine's first encounter with Æðelbert—although (as I have discussed elsewhere) the role of the translators Augustine brought with him from Gaul to help in just this kind of encounter has been erased.[20]

I have lingered on this episode for a few key reasons, especially the role of objects and the performance of liturgical Latin, even in the Old English translation of Bede's history. Bede tells us little about the lifestyle, prayers, vigils, and fastings of Augustine and his fellows—other than that they did these things, that they accepted only necessities, and that they 'despised all worldly things'.[21] As the story goes, all of this impressed the king and began the process of conversion, which in turn led to the request for more mis-sionaries and more things, including vessels, ornaments, altar covers, relics, and *manige bec* ('many books').[22] 'This', to borrow a line from A. J. Ford, 'immediately presents a paradox of a spiritual or transcendent realm reached *through* the material world'.[23] Whether CCCC 286 arrived with Augustine, in the second wave, or with another missionary prior to 700 is uncertain. As Fafinski points out, CCCC 286 was annotated and corrected in England shortly after 700, and it contains two early Old English charters. It seems clear that, as an illuminated book containing the Gospels, it fea-tured prominently in the process of conversion, as an object of impressive display, and as the story of the life of Christ. Or, to be more precise, four stories of the life of Christ, along with initially something like 72 narrative scenes (see folio 125r).[24]

Despite the longstanding emphasis of patristic thought on the singularity of the truth, the Gospels recount four versions of the life of Christ, which scho-lars today recognize as having different emphases and interests. Add then, that the Latin antiphon sung by Augustine and his followers as they entered Canterbury was not used in Rome at the time; rather, it was a Gallican anti-phon used during Rogation Day processions (which were also apparently practised in Jarrow).[25] Colgrave and Mynors suggest that Augustine learned this antiphon in Gaul on his way to Kent, but we have no way of knowing if that was the case. Although the question of divergent Easter practices has long been a topic for students of Bede's *Historia*, differing liturgical practices have been harder to track, primarily because of lack of evidence. Bede tells us of John the arch-cantor's arrival in Jarrow around 678, along with John's teaching of the celebration of all the festal days throughout the year. Bede claims this was all written down and copied by many, but very little written evidence survives from before the tenth century.[26]

This brings me back to the marginalia of CCCC 41, which includes a substantial portion of the liturgy, along with a range of bilingual materials regarding the kinds of rituals, masses, and prayers like the ones that Augustine and his followers performed for Æðelbert and his people, many of which reflect the idea that Christianity could (and did) have a tangible, or even transformative, impact on this world. Part of the marginal material in CCCC 41 has also been described as a 'copy' of an Anglo-Saxon service book, though there seems to be universal agreement it cannot have been *used* as a service book. As Richard Pfaff puts it, 'Though the liturgical material copied out [in CCCC 41] does not amount to anything like a complete service book, it is so extensive that something can be inferred about the liturgical text(s) from which it was copied.' He goes on to observe, however, that 'We are left wistful for the massbook from which the scribe copied.'[27] Pfaff's wistfulness is highly reminiscent of much scholarship on CCCC 41 and the Old English Bede, filled with nostalgic longing for the lost exemplar.[28] But, as Bruce Holsinger points out, only nine other '"massbooks" surviv[e] from Anglo-Saxon England; only five or six of them are considered at all complete', so the importance and possible usefulness of the texts in the margins of CCCC 41 should not be underestimated.[29]

Sarah Larratt Keefer's 'Margin as Archive' asserts the importance of the liturgical materials in CCCC 41, if not their usefulness. She analyses the first 17 pages with careful attention to the liturgical contents. She concludes that these represent an archive of texts that 'fit … neither a missal nor a pontifical or a benedictional', but rather 'a first step toward the production of' a 'compendium' like a 'portiforium' resembling CCCC 391.[30] Larratt Keefer asserts that CCCC 41 does not represent a haphazard copy of a text in the same tradition as the Missal of Robert of Jumièges and the Leofric Missal (which is Raymond Grant's assessment), but 'important evidence of the eleventh-century impulse … towards collecting diverse liturgical texts into single volumes'.[31] With this insight, Larratt Keefer emphasizes the living and changing nature of early medieval textual and liturgical practices, which in turn highlights the mediated nature of human knowledge; it also manifests a 'world of in-between-lingualism' that resonates with the complex linguistic milieu of Leofric's Exeter (Leofric came to Crediton from a monastery in Lotharingia), as well as the pastoral needs of the secular canons.

While these ideas are admittedly speculative, it seems to me that the question of the usefulness of this book and its marginalia can be productively revisited using the high-quality digital images that are available for close analysis. Larratt Keefer's important analysis examines only a small section of the marginalia and much remains to be done. Looking at some of the marginal materials, such as the charm to recover cattle (folio 206), we can see that some of the texts are somewhat cramped and difficult to read; others, however, are clear and widely spaced, like part of the Old English *Martyrology* (folio 124). While some of the early pages of the manuscript are very worn, some of the homilies, such as the one on the Last Judgement (folios 254ff.) are not; in fact, some of them follow the spacious ruling of the main text, so they are quite easy to read. Others, like the Homily for Easter (folios 298ff.), are ruled on narrower lines, but some of these have decorated initials, are punctuated, accented, and have been corrected (fol. 254). The liturgical Latin sometimes has Old English or Latin rubrics, visible starting on page two, along with punctuation, annotations, and corrections (fol. 9), and even musical annotations and directions (folio 22). Some are also rubricated (folios 370ff.). The *Responses on Job* are neumed (folio 475), which suggests the possibility that the text—like parts of the Old English Bede—may have been used for oral performance.

Given the large format of this book, and the ability of a priest or canon to prepare readings in advance, it seems to me that many of the marginal materials would have been useful as more than a temporary archive. Looking more closely at the first quarter of the eleventh century also suggests that CCCC 41 was an important book. After all, the late tenth century and the early eleventh century were periods of devastating and 'sustained Viking pressure'.[32] Exeter was overrun in 1003. Svein Forkbeard was on the throne by 1013, then Cnut in 1016. Severe famine also struck England in 1005.[33] We do not know how many books were destroyed in southwestern England and Cornwall during the raids, and famine would have negatively affected the quality and availability of vellum. In these contexts, the 244 large leaves of vellum used to make CCCC 41 represent a significant dedication of resources. Ker lists just over 50 surviving manuscripts made in England and dated to this period (first half of the eleventh century) in his *Catalogue*, only five of which measure greater than *c.* 300 x 200 mm. In addition to CCCC 41 (Ker 32), these include: CCCC MS 140, the Gospels in Old English; London, British Library, Cotton Claudius B. iv, the illustrated Old English Hexateuch (Ker 142); Oxford, Bodleian Library, Bodley 340, a homiliary (Ker 309); and Oxford, Bodleian Library, Junius 11, which famously contains Old English biblical verses and illustrations (Ker 334). The Hexateuch and Junius 11 are the largest next to CCCC 41, measuring 325 x 215 mm and 323 x 196 mm, respectively. This survey cannot be precise, given the many manuscripts burned in the Cotton fire of 1731, the imprecision of dating, and the trimming of manuscripts, but even with these caveats, CCCC 41 appears to be the largest surviving vernacular manuscript copied in the first quarter of the eleventh century in England. It was a major investment of time and resources.

The spaces left for illuminated initials also indicate an ambitious initial plan. A vernacular copy of Bede's *Historia* with spacious margins (whether they were filled already or not) must have been a major prize for Bishop Leofric, who dedicated significant funds and energy during his episcopacy to rebuilding the library at Exeter when he moved his see there. According to Frank Barlow, King Edward 'sanctioned the transfer of the see because of the vulnerability of the Cornish and Crediton churches to piratical devastations', and the choice of the walled city of Exeter 'was obvious', Barlow asserts, even if Exeter was 'not in a flourishing condition in the mid-eleventh century'.[34] It is unsurprising, then, as L. J. Lloyd puts it, that:

there were no books of any consequence ... in the little convent of St Peter when Leofric arrived from Crediton in 1050 to become Exeter's first bishop. All he could find, to quote the later list of his donations were: 'One capitulary, and one very old *Nocturnale,* and one epistle book, and two very old reading-books, very much decayed'.[35]

In such a situation, it seems likely that Leofric and his followers would have used all the books and texts at his disposal. Elaine Treharne has shown that during his time in Exeter, Leofric expanded his episcopal library in two ways: 'through his own careful acquisitions policy and a coherent plan of verna-cular copying'; she also demonstrates that Leofric's efforts resulted in the collection and production of an 'unparalleled number of Old English manu-scripts ... for his own use and at his direction', for preaching and pastoral care.[36] (One of these, of course, is the famous 'Leofric Missal', which Robert Deshman argues Leofric acquired sometime in the middle of the eleventh century, probably from Glastonbury).[37] Reconsidering CCCC 41 as a whole book in such contexts, especially in the light of the paucity of books available to Leofric when he arrived in Exeter, suggests that it must have been a useful and important part of his collection. As I have discussed elsewhere, early English signs of use pertaining to the main text suggest the book was used and marked by a range of readers, possibly for preaching to the laity or as a reading for a vernacular office.[38]

Arguably, then, it is because of, rather than despite, CCCC 41's linguistic and liturgical in-between-ness that it has been used and studied since it was first written. Although Bede and his translator play down the role of transla-tion in the conversion of Æðelbert of Kent, this book, as a whole, serves as a reminder of the crucial roles played by translation and bilingualism in the conversion of the English to Christianity, the development of pre-Conquest England, and the transmission of English history. As the most late-West Saxon of the surviving copies of the Old English Bede, it can even be read as a translation of itself. It provided an important resource for Leofric in the mid-eleventh century, and its useful in-betweenness enabled Parker and his circle with what Tim Graham calls the 'recovery of Old English'.[39] This list goes on, so I think it is safe to say that CCCC 41's latest translation from sequestered manuscript into a free, digital resource will activate new forms of knowledge and understanding in ways that are ever more 'deeply interfused'.

Notes

1 Rita Copeland, *Rhetoric, Hermeneutics and Translation in the Middle Ages: Academic Traditions and Vernacular Texts* (Cambridge: Cambridge University Press, 1991), p. 36.
2 'As Bill Brown has recently maintained, "no matter how variously the term may be deployed, materiality has come to matter with new urgency" because of the "threat" that digital media pose in a wide range of disciplines from film to the history of science.' Michael Ann Holly *et al.*, 'Notes from the Field: Materiality', *The Art Bulletin* 95 (2013): 10–37, at p. 16.

3 François Jullien, *Il n'y a pas d'identité culturelle* (Paris: L'Herne, 2016), pp. 88–9.

4 The additional hands are a new discovery, courtesy of Parker on the Web 2.0; details to appear in the edition of the Old English Bede I am working on with Greg Waite.

5 N. R. Ker, *Catalogue of Manuscripts Containing Anglo-Saxon* (Oxford: Clarendon Press, 1957; repr. 1991), no. 32; Helmut Gneuss, *Handlist of Anglo-Saxon Manuscripts: A List of Manuscripts and Manuscript Fragments Written or Owned in England up to 1100*, Medieval and Renaissance Texts and Studies 241 (Tempe, AZ: CMRS, 2001), no. 39; M. Budny, *Insular, Anglo-Saxon and Early Anglo-Norman Manuscript Art at Corpus Christi College, Cambridge: An Illustrated Catalogue* (Kalamazoo, MI: Medieval Institute Publications, 1997), no. 32. See also Timothy Graham *et al.*, eds., 'Corpus Christi College, Cambridge I: MSS 41, 57, 191, 302, 303, 367, 383, 422', *Anglo-Saxon Manuscripts in Microfiche Facsimile* 11 (Tempe, AZ: CMRS, 2003). See Parker on the Web: https://parker.stanford.edu/parker/cata log/qd527zm3425 and Budny for the measurements.

6 Raymond Grant, *CCCC 41: The Loricas and the Missal* (Amsterdam: Rodopi, 1978), pp. 1–2.

7 Budny, *Insular, Anglo-Saxon and Early Anglo-Norman Manuscript Art*, p. 507.

8 Peter A. Stokes, *English Vernacular Minuscule from Æthelred to Cnut C. 990–C. 1035* (Cambridge: D. S. Brewer, 2014), p. 142.

9 Stokes, *English Vernacular Minuscule*, p. 142, n. 106.

10 N. J. Higham and Martin J. Ryan, *Place-names, Language and the Anglo-Saxon Landscape* (Woodbridge: Boydell Press, 2011), p. 177. See also Charles Insley, 'Charters and Episcopal Scriptoria in the Anglo-Saxon South-West', *Early Medieval Europe* 7 (1998): 173–97.

11 Sarah Larratt Keefer, 'Margin as Archive: The Liturgical Marginalia of a Manuscript of the Old English Bede', *Traditio* 51 (1996): 147–77, at p. 147.

12 Editions and studies of the marginal texts are all listed on Parker on the Web 2.0.

13 Sharon M. Rowley, *The Old English Version of Bede's Historia ecclesiastica*, Anglo-Saxon Studies 16 (Woodbridge: D. S. Brewer, 2011), p. 165.

14 Nigel Thrift, 'Three New Material Registers', in *Materiality*, ed. Daniel Miller (Durham, NC and London: Duke University Press, 2005), pp. 231–255, at 232.

15 Thrift, 'New Material Registers', p. 232, is quoting E. Lupton, *Skin: Surface, Substance and Design* (New York: Princeton Architectural Press, 2002).

16 Thrift, 'New Material Registers', p. 235.

17 CCCC 41, 56–7. Punctuation added; translation mine. See also Thomas Miller, ed., *The Old English Version of Bede's Ecclesiastical History of the English People*, EETS, os 95, 96, 110, 111 (Rochester, NY and London, 1890–8; rpt. Woodbridge, 2003), pp. 58–9.

18 CCCC 41, 57.

19 CCCC 41 58; *Bede's Ecclesiastical History of the English People*, ed. and trans. Bertram Colgrave and R. A. B. Mynors (Oxford: The Clarendon Press, 1969; rpt. 1992), pp. 76–7.

20 See Rowley, *Old English Version*, pp. 98–113.

21 CCCC 41, 59.

22 CCCC 41, 62.

23 A. J. Ford, *Marvel and Artefact: The 'Wonders of the East' in its Manuscript Contexts*, Library of the Written Word 45 (Leiden: Brill, 2016), p. 62.

24 See Richard Gameson, 'The Earliest Books of Christian Kent', in *St. Augustine and the Conversion of England*, ed. by Richard Gameson (Stroud: Sutton, 1999), pp. 313–73, at 320.

25 Colgrave and Mynors, *Bede's Ecclesiastical History*, p. 76, n. 1. According to Colgrave and Mynors, we know that the processions were practised in Jarrow from the story of Bede's death recorded by Cuthbert.

26 *Bede's Ecclesiastical History*, IV.18, p. 388. On the dearth of evidence, see Richard Pfaff, *The Liturgy in Medieval England* (Cambridge: Cambridge University Press, 2009), p. 38.

27 Richard Pfaff, *The Liturgical Books of Anglo-Saxon England* (Kalamazoo, MI: Medieval Institute Publications, 1995), p. 25; also qtd. in Bruce Holsinger, 'The Parable of Cædmon's Hymn,' *Journal of English and Germanic Philology* 106 (2007): 163.

28 See Sharon M. Rowley, 'Nostalgia and the Rhetoric of Lack', in *Old English Literature in its Manuscript Context*, ed. Joyce Tally Lionarons (Morgantown: West Virginia University Press), pp. 11–35.

29 Holsinger, 'The Parable, p. 163.

30 Larratt Keefer, 'Margin as Archive', p. 152.

31 Larratt Keefer, 'Margin as Archive', pp. 150–1.

32 Simon Keynes, 'An Abbot, and Archbishop and the Viking Raids of 1006–7 and 1009–12', *Anglo-Saxon England* 36 (2007): 151–220, at p. 151.

33 Keynes, 'An Abbot...', p. 155. See also Ian Howard, *Swein Forkbeard's Invasions and the Danish Conquest of England, 991–1017* (Woodbridge: The Boydell Press, 2003), pp. 63–4.

34 Frank Barlow, 'Leofric and his Times', in *Leofric of Exeter: Essays in Commemoration of the Foundation of Exeter Cathedral in A.D.1072*, ed. Frank Barlow *et al.* (Exeter: University of Exeter Press, 1972), pp. 8–9.

35 L. J. Lloyd, 'Leofric as Bibliophile', in *Leofric of Exeter*, p. 34.

36 Elaine M. Treharne, 'Producing a Library in Late Anglo-Saxon England: Exeter 1050–1072', *Review of English Studies* 54 (2003): 155–72, at pp. 159 and 171.

37 Robert Deshman, 'The Leofric Missal and Tenth-century English Art', *Anglo-Saxon England* 6 (1977): 145–73, at p. 148.

38 See *The Old English Version*, pp. 156–73.

39 Timothy Graham, ed., *The Recovery of Old English: Anglo-Saxon Studies in the Sixteenth and Seventeenth Centuries*, Publications of the Rawlinson Center 1 (Kalamazoo, MI: Medieval Institute Publications, 2000).

Part 4

Of Multimedia and the Multilingual

14 Fragmentation and wholeness in Cambridge, Corpus Christi College, 16

A. Joseph McMullen

In 1235, Benedictine monk Matthew Paris took over Roger Wendover's *Flores historiarum*, a universal chronicle stretching from Creation to the present day. Matthew appears to have been Roger's natural successor at St Albans and would take over the chronicle for some 24 years (until his death in 1259). While others might have been content simply to continue the work Roger started, Matthew sought to make the text his own—copiously revising and updating Roger's work with marginal additions and inserted leaves.[1] He would also, with significantly expanded scope, painstakingly record the events of his own day. Indeed, the entries from the 24 years he was active (1235–1259) were roughly as long as the entire preceding history. This text would, in time, become the *Chronica majora*, which is today known for its ambitiously wide range of reporting (Matthew's focus is always England, but he comments on events stretching from Ireland to Armenia and Norway to Egypt). His scope is even more noticeable when compared to Roger's chronicle. As Björn Weiler notes, Roger's reporting is 'more limited in its geographical range' and events outside England 'barely merited recording'—'throughout the *Flores*, Roger rarely gazed beyond Britain, unless the matter at hand was directly relevant to English matters [e.g., a truce with Louis IX or events in the Holy Land] … In fact, it is striking just how much of Matthew's rewriting of Roger consisted of adding information about European affairs.'[2] This brief chapter will consider how Matthew's expanded geographical purview contributes to the *Chronica majora*'s world view and, further, how CCCC 16 as a holistic object is itself reflective of Matthew's cosmopolitan chronicle. I will argue that, when combining a study of the text of the chronicle with the manuscript's prefatory material, emendations, and marginal illustrations, a neglected but striking image of England appears. In his conception of England, Matthew Paris seems to imagine neither an isolated, insular bastion nor a 'Britannia' seizing on the same type of 'Matter of Britain' island mythologies as other, somewhat contemporaneous, propagandistic chronicles; instead, Matthew paints the picture of an England within the multilingual zone of cultural exchange that is Europe. England is never not the focus of his chronicle, but it also is not necessarily the epicentre of a new empire. Much like the different components of this digitized manuscript—which come together to form a greater whole than the sum of its parts—Matthew's Christian Europe was more than the number of fragmented peoples and polities that made it up.

It is a fortunate occurrence for palaeographers, codicologists, and literary scholars to have surviving three manuscripts—CCCC 26, CCCC 16, and British Library, Royal 14 C. vii—that form the autograph copy of the *Chronica majora*.[3] While these manuscripts present the *Chronica* in succession—CCCC 26 contains entries from Creation to 1188, CCCC 16 contains the annals from 1189 to 1253, and CCCC 14 completes the work from 1254 to 1259—they may never have been bound together, and surely were not when Parker acquired the former two manuscripts.[4] The two volumes in the Parker collection are large (roughly 355 mm x 240 mm; CCCC 16 has 284 manuscript leaves) and 'contain over 130 tinted drawings, 92 painted coats of arms, and numerous pictographic symbols in the margins of 422 parchment folios'.[5] Melvin Jefferson explains that CCCC 26 was 'probably bound shortly after it was written' and CCCC 16 was a 'working copy which was assembled over a period of time and bound for the first time at a much later date'.[6] It is this 'working copy' quality which makes CCCC 16 so fascinating from a codicological perspective: Matthew's hand can be seen at work in emendations and, of course, his well-known drawings and figures (both prefatory and marginal). As Suzanne Lewis has described it:

> With its wide margins often filled with additional texts, narrative sketches, heraldic shields, and other emblematic images, the Corpus Christi manuscripts of the *Chronica Majora* give the visual impression of a disorderly and rambling clutter, the result of a digressive, associative process of amplification that transpired over a period of many years. Even after Matthew began to compose the annals himself, he continued to expand the text with marginal addenda, sometimes written out in a disciplined script carefully enclosed with elegant borders, at other times hurriedly dashed off in a careless hand.[7]

This assessment is, on the one hand, a slightly exaggerated state-of-play (the manuscript is readable and the images generally complement the text), but, on the other, not entirely false (the manuscript surely does not seem like a final product). By pausing to consider how some of these marginalia relate to the worldview Matthew presents in the *Chronica* and, further, how the manuscript as a whole might reflect his cosmopolitanism, the reasons for which this manuscript is so well-known—the drawings, the revisions, and the prefatory material, alongside his experimentation with the codex itself—may, perhaps, look less like a 'rambling clutter' and more like a cohesive, coherent whole.

Before walking through how the more personal aspects of CCCC 16 contribute to the chronicle's vision, it is necessary first to place the *Chronica* contextually in its thirteenth-century milieu. In Weiler's recent work on Matthew Paris, he has stressed the *Chronica*'s greater European context while also noting that scholarship has generally ignored the connections and networks revealed in the text (with more attention instead placed on historical verisimilitude).[8] Random cross-sections of the *Chronica* display an author interested in these wider European political, ecclesiastical, and cultural currents. Take, for instance, his summary of the last 50 years at the originally intended end of his chronicle (1250, or 25 half-centuries). Matthew comments on events in England, Wales, Denmark, Norway, Germany, Iberia, France, and Italy, as well as Egypt, Russia, and the Holy Land, among others, over the course of about two full manuscript pages (folios 245r–246r). The events range from civil wars to crusades, the translation of saints to the indiscretions of popes, and eclipses to earthquakes. Weiler groups these events into geographic/thematic clusters—Britain, Scandinavia, Germany, Iberia, saints, the church, Christian and non-Christian relations, and portents—ultimately arguing that Matthew perceived England to be part of a greater Christian whole.[9] While the events curated by Matthew frequently were relevant to concerns related to his English audience, they showcase an author who clearly believed that England's affairs were inextricably linked to those of Christendom at large. This was perhaps most true with regard to the success of the crusades: after discussing how the failure of the Seventh Crusade led the pope and Roman Curia to absolve from their vows, for example, he notes that *Tota Christianitas ex odio et discordia inter ipsum Papam et Frethericum exortis guerris suscitatis perturbatur, et ecclesia universalis periclitatur*, 'The whole of Christianity was troubled and the universal Church endangered by the wars which arose from the hatred and discord between the pope and Frederick.'[10] Matthew's perception of the (Christian) West was one of cooperation as much as conflict, generally showing a genuine respect for other peoples and cultures, so long as they were Christian. Granted, there are moments of xenophobia and cultural stereotypes, but the worst of his vitriol is reserved for those in power (kings, popes, emperors, etc.) and their inability or unwillingness to support their people.

Unlike the *Flores historiarum* or other more objective chronicles, the *Chronica* is strongly opinionated and Matthew's personal annotations and emendations in CCCC 16 provide a glimpse into his developing thought process and widened focus. As the *Chronica*'s geographical orbit is wide, Matthew gives much attention to powerful figures outside England, particularly those who incite conflict within the broader European Christian community. Among the entries from 1249, for instance, he offers a letter by Cardinal Reiner of Viterbo to the pope with regard to the *nequitia … multiformi* ('manifold villainies') committed by Frederick II, the Holy Roman Emperor, against different continental bishops.[11] At various points throughout the letter, Matthew calls particular attention (with mounting disapprobation) to some of these crimes with marginal annotations (see folio 226v). Matthew first writes *Nota scelus et impietatem inhumanam*, 'Note this inhuman and impious crime' beside a description of how a bishop from Arezzo was bound with his head near the rear-end of the animal dragging him to the gallows.[12] After being hanged, the bishop was left on the gallows for three days before brothers took the body down and buried it without permission. On Frederick's orders, the executioners disinterred the body and put it back on the gallows after dragging it through the mud, leading Matthew to write, *Nota sævitiam in adhuc defunctum factam*, 'Note the ferocity against the already defunct.'[13] At the mention of Frederick's propensity for these kind of offences and further elaboration on the matter (he had a bishop from Gerace drowned and another from Cefalù put to the sword), Matthew adds *Nota aliud flagitium consimile*, 'Note another similar crime' and *Nota aliud facinus non minus prioribus*, 'Note another crime as bad as the others', respectively.[14] Lastly, when the letter mentions how Frederick had previously hired assassins to murder the pope, Matthew gives his last comment in this sequence: *Nota aliud majus prioribus*, 'Note another crime worse than the others.'[15] Though none of these annotations are particularly surprising—and are likely what many contemporaneous monks would have thought while reading the letter—they do showcase the attention Matthew pays both to continental matters and the health of the larger European Christian community. In CCCC 16, he is not solely reporting events or quoting a letter, he is offering a rubric for readers. This happens with great regularity elsewhere in the *Chronica*, as Matthew also frequently criticizes those in power closer to home (though these critiques were tempered with time). Among various examples (Vaughan counts some 61 edited passages),[16] I will briefly discuss two heading erasures in relatively close proximity that deal with Henry III which originally read *Promisso domini regis umbratilis*, 'The Lord King's Shady Promise' and *Item de cavillatione argumentosa domini regis ad extorquendam pecuniam*, 'An Ingenious Trick for the Lord King for Extorting Money'.[17] Both of these relate to Henry's profligacy: according to Matthew Paris, he was always seeking aid for dubious personal reasons, which led to the impoverishment of bishoprics and abbeys. In the first example, the king was responding to a 1248 Parliament and promised to find a solution. Unfortunately, as the second heading from 1249 makes clear, the situation instead worsened and the king continued to beg his people for money, to the point that he came up with a fictitious reason for his debt: that he was going to make war on the king of the French. Matthew would return to these headings, erasing *umbratilis* from the first and completely erasing the second later in life when he revised the *Chronica* to take out some of his most barbed comments against the king (see folios. 218v and 224v, respectively). Though he may have softened toward the king over time (possibly to 'try to correct some of his extravagances, many of which he must have realized were unjust and undeserved'),[18] he does not change the course of events, only some of his more outspoken critiques. Additionally, while these erasures show a changing attitude over time, they also reveal Matthew's initial priority did not seem to be to curry favour or participate in the

Plantagenet propaganda machine—his focus clearly seems to be on the well-being of the people.

Arguably of even more interest than Matthew's annotations and emendations is his extensive body of illustrations which accompany CCCC 26 and 16.[19] These range in variety: from a number of prefatory materials (such as a diagram of the winds, king lists, and maps) to marginal heraldic shields and drawings of all types. While more scholarly attention has been paid to these illustrations than the text of the *Chronica* itself, re-reading two of the most well-known images—the Veronica (folio 53v) (Figure 14.1) and the Wandering Jew (folio 74v)—will show them to be further instructive examples of Matthew's world view, especially since, following Ralph of Diceto, Matthew likely used his illustrations as a system of *signa*, indexing the work and making it both more accessible and memorable for the reader.[20] The first example, the Veronica image (folio 53v), can be found within a story that Matthew added to a section of Roger's chronicle for the year 1216, sandwiched between a two-part account of the siege of Berkhampstead Castle by Louis of France. In this section of the *Chronica*, Matthew tells of Pope Innocent who, as was his custom, carried the Veronica (that is, a cloth relic which bears the likeness of Christ) in a procession but, when the procession was finished, the image *se per se girabat, ut verso staret ordine; ita scilicet, ut frons inferius, barba superius locaretur*, 'turned around upon itself and was reversed in such a way that the forehead was below and the beard above'.[21] This was, naturally, taken as a foreboding sign and led the pope to compose a prayer. After this account, Matthew pasted in a painted image of Christ's face (not upside down). This is one of the only illustrations that has been framed and inserted and, as Lewis discusses, it creates a dramatic effect since the reader has become used to smaller scale, marginal sketches but now, all at once, is treated to a large, staring, hypnotic face which, in many ways 'ingeniously suggests the supernatural aura of the miracle without actually depicting the grotesque reversal of features described in the text'.[22] Much like how the inserted image in this digressive addition creates a dramatic effect, the context of the account is important too: Matthew transitions from England to Rome—*Dum vero fortunalis alea statum regni Angliæ talibus turbinibus exagitaret*, 'While the fortunes of the English king were in such a state of turmoil)'—and by so doing draws a parallel between the turmoil in England and that of the *ecclesiæ cura* ('administration of the Church') which was being *sollicitabat* ('upset') by the pope's *vacillantis* ('vacillating'; Lewis offers 'unsteady hand').[23] This may have been a way for Matthew to emphasize the importance of strong leaders (the castle would eventually surrender), but it may also have been an attempt to bring a deeper perspective to English events—forcing the reader not to lose focus of the larger Christian community while also suggesting some kind of interconnection between these geographically-distanced events. The second example, the image of the Wandering Jew (folio 74v), can also be found in a section of the *Chronica* (1228) first written by Roger. The general legend

Figure 14.1 The Parker Library, Corpus Christi College, Cambridge, MS 16II, f. 53v.

is that, while Christ was carrying the cross, a man yelled at him to walk faster while he was resting. Jesus purportedly responded that he was going, but that the man would have to walk until he came again (which then led to this man wandering the earth). When an Armenian archbishop comes to visit St Albans, the brothers eagerly ask if he knows anything about this man. The archbishop's interpreter responds that not only was this man alive, he had been baptized, took the name Joseph, and even ate at the archbishop's table recently. Matthew seems to have been rather interested in this story, drawing a sizeable image of Christ (carrying the cross) and the men speaking to one another at the bottom of the page, adding in more details for credibility (the name of the archbishop; another eyewitness), and mentioning it again elsewhere in the *Chronica* when the Armenian delegation returned in 1252 (Joseph was still living as usual). While this image has been read as a point of entry into Matthew's moralism, apocalypticism, or even anti-Semitism,[24] it also calls the reader's attention to oral transmission history and an unexpected connection between St Albans and the church in Armenia. It seems clear, from this account, that legends like this one could be circulated and perpetuated within an interconnected Christian community. Matthew does not seem surprised that the Armenian delegation returned in 1252—indeed, he states it very matter-of-factly, as though this were not too unique an occurrence.[25] As Matthew also would travel to Norway himself to settle an ecclesiastical (and perhaps financial) dispute,[26] these networks within Latin Christendom were fluid and open, especially given the increase in trade routes. Certain images in CCCC 16 can remind the modern reader of Europe as a multilingual zone of cultural exchange, even if that interplay was mediated through Latin.

These routes of travel (and the way they connected medieval Europe) are also on view in the prefatory material that accompanies the *Chronica* in CCCC 16, particularly the maps. Matthew crafted a handful of maps, with each volume of the *Chronica* originally containing an itinerary map (produced as a 'strip map' with stops along the way from London to Apulia to Jerusalem), a map of the Holy Land, and a map of Britain (the first surviving map of its kind). Much of the geographical material in CCCC 16— the Italy section of an itinerary map, a partial map of the Holy Land with a close-up on Jerusalem, and half of a map of Britain—is damaged and fragmentary, incomparable to the fuller, denser maps in CCCC 26. Nevertheless, these materials must be read alongside this section of the *Chronica*, as they preface it and, presumably, were meant to influence the way a reader would approach the text within. Recent scholarship has pursued this line of thought, with both Daniel K. Connolly and Katherine Breen reading the itinerary maps as imaginative journeys meant to lead the viewer/reader into the space of the map as a spiritual, or even perhaps devotional, exercise.[27] As such, before even beginning the *Chronica* itself, a reader could have traced an imaginary pilgrimage along the many stops on the way to the Holy Land and back,[28] marvelling at the travel network of the interconnected Christian West. As this geographical scope would be reflected in the content of the *Chronica* itself, the maps reinforce a sense of cultural exchange (perhaps even further emphasized by the tract on and image of the elephant Louis IX sent across the channel to Henry III in 1255, despite Matthew's heavy criticism of the political relationship between England and France). Indeed, even the CCCC 16 map of Britain speaks to this world view: it is immediately striking that Wales and Scotland appear to be partitioned by the natural and human-created features (inlets and rivers, but also walls), rather than subsumed into the growing English empire. Matthew seems to eschew the Matter of Britain propaganda used by other contemporaneous chroniclers, such as Geoffrey of Monmouth, Henry of Huntingdon, William of Malmesbury, and even adds this description of Wales to the map which reinforces the descent of the Britons from Brutus: *Terra montuosa & palustris homines agiles generans & bellico[sos] de Bruto propagatos qui de Troianis duxit originem*, 'a mountainous and marshy land producing agile and warlike men descended from Brutus who led [their] ancestors from the Trojans'.[29] Rather than a tool of power asserting direct supremacy, Matthew's map instead reflects the cosmopolitan mindset of his chronicle.[30]

What, then, was England to Matthew Paris, and how did its people fit into Europe? This brief chapter on CCCC 16 shows that Matthew sought neither to wall England off from the continent nor to claim it as the next empire through a typical *translatio imperii* narrative. Alternatively, though always writing a history focused on England, he gave precedence to the conception of the English as members of a Christian community stretching across Europe, a multilingual zone of cultural exchange. To this end, he purposefully increased the geographical scope of Roger's chronicle, which would be further magnified during the years solely under his control. His maps, marginal illustrations, and emendations echo these textual concerns, and would, I argue, have signalled them clearly to a reader of CCCC 16. This is somewhat unique, especially when comparing Matthew to the most famous English chroniclers of the twelfth century—this was, after all, a period where the English, or Anglo-Normans, were attempting to take over all of Britain while also defining themselves in contrast to the 'barbarous rudeness'[31] of other marginal peoples. This manuscript then, especially in the age of Brexit, can teach a modern audience much about what it means to be separate and yet also whole. By reading the manuscript as a holistic object itself—as an object which brings together text, glosses, illustrations, and maps—in a way that is reflective of Matthew's own world view, the 'rambling clutter' looks a bit less fragmentary and significantly more cohesive.

Furthermore, the full scope of Matthew's historical vision is best realized because of the digitization efforts of Parker on the Web. Though Parker on the Web has, in some ways, reinforced the scholarly separation of image and text discussed above (MS 16 is split online into two separate entries, one with the prefatory material and the other with the text), the nature of digital manuscript study immediately breaks down these divisions or, at least, allows for the opportunity to challenge traditional ways of reading. Only because of digitization can the manuscript be viewed simultaneously in multiple windows (or even on multiple screens, with an optimal computing set-up). One could, hypothetically, peruse the *Chronica* beside an image of Matthew's prefatory map (perhaps then his purported imperialist agenda might not be trumpeted so vigorously) or even the Veronica (as a reminder of the drama of the page). Likewise, for greater ease of reading, a digitized edition of the *Chronica* could be viewed alongside the manuscript in order to imagine how the illustrations and glosses combined with text to form a holistic object. The malleability of the digital object even allows for further annotation, collapsing the temporal divide between physical and digital object while giving the reader the opportunity to participate in the same kind of paratextual creation as Matthew himself in the thirteenth century. The argument of this chapter has been that scholars fail Matthew Paris unless the text of the *Chronica* is considered in its most immediate context: the manuscript page. How would that be possible for readers around the world if not for Parker on the Web? The digital surrogate makes accessible these necessary paratextual materials from a distance—indeed, I myself have never truly *seen* the manuscript. I cannot imagine a context for reproduction more appropriate (or powerful), given that this manuscript works so diligently to place England within the multilingual zone of cultural exchange that was Matthew's Christian Europe. The digitization efforts of Parker on the Web give anyone with Internet access an opportunity to examine Matthew's hand at work, and, indeed, what could be more flattering for a thirteenth-century monk than that?

Notes

1 For an overview, see V. H. Galbraith, 'Roger Wendover and Matthew Paris', in *Kings and Chroniclers: Essays in English Medieval History* (London: Hambledon Press, 1982), pp. 5–48; Richard Vaughan, *Matthew Paris* (Cambridge, Cambridge University Press, 1958), pp. 21–34.
2 Björn Weiler, 'How Unusual Was Matthew Paris? The Writing of Universal History in Angevin England', in *Universal Chronicles in the High Middle Ages*, ed. Michael Campopiano and Henry Bainton (York: York Medieval Press, 2017), pp. 199–222, at p. 210.
3 Vaughan has, more precisely, argued that CCCC 26 was produced under Matthew's supervision and that CCCC 16 and 14 are 'almost entirely autograph'. See Vaughan, *Matthew Paris*, p. 21. See also Vaughan, 'The Handwriting of Matthew Paris', *Transactions of the Cambridge Bibliographical Society* 5 (1953): 376–94, at pp. 390–1.
4 See Melvin Jefferson, 'The Conservation of Parker MSS 16 and 26, "The Chronica Majora"', in *Care and Conservation of Manuscripts 9: Proceedings of the Ninth International Seminar Held at the University of Copenhagen, 14th–15th April 2005*, ed. Gillian Fellows-Jensen and Peter Springborg (Copenhagen: Museum Tusculanum Press, 2006), pp. 69–81, at p. 72. Parker 'borrowed' the manuscripts from two (unfortunate) men (Edward Aglionby and Robert Talbot), likely at the prompting

of Matthias Flacius Illyricus, the German compiler of the Magdeburg Chronicles, who wrote to Parker in 1561 asking for Matthew Paris manuscripts.

5   Jefferson, 'The Conservation of Parker MSS 16 and 26', pp. 70, 74.

6   Jefferson, 'The Conservation of Parker MSS 16 and 26', p. 77.

7   Suzanne Lewis, *The Art of Matthew Paris in the Chronica Majora* (Berkeley: University of California Press, 1987), p. 56.

8   Weiler, 'How Unusual Was Matthew Paris?' writes, with regard to Matthew, 'In high medieval England, insularity denoted geographical, not intellectual isolation: just because chroniclers had to wait for news to cross the Channel, it neither followed that they had not heard of nor that they were not curious about the affairs of Christendom at large … There was never a time when England did not form part of a larger European whole', p. 201. See also Weiler, 'Matthew Paris on the Writing of History', *Journal of Medieval History* 35 (2009): 254–78.

9   See Weiler, 'How Unusual Was Matthew Paris?', pp. 204–205; 'Matthew Paris on the Writing of History', p. 277.

10 Matthew Paris, *Chronica majora*, ed. H. R. Luard, 7 vols. (London: Longman & Co., 1872–84), vol. 5, p. 196. Translation from Richard Vaughan, *Chronicles of Matthew Paris: Monastic Life in the Thirteenth Century* (New York: St. Martin's Press, 1984), p. 276.

11 Matthew Paris, *Chronica majora*, vol. 5, p. 61; Vaughan, *Chronicles of Matthew Paris*, p. 73.

12 Matthew Paris, *Chronica majora*, vol. 5, p. 63; Vaughan, *Chronicles of Matthew Paris*, p. 177. This was, reportedly, so that the bishop's head would be fouled by the beast's diarrhea (*alvi profluvium*).

13 Matthew Paris, *Chronica majora*, vol. 5, p. 63; Vaughan, *Chronicles of Matthew Paris*, p. 177.

14 Matthew Paris, *Chronica majora*, vol. 5, p. 64; Vaughan, *Chronicles of Matthew Paris*, p. 177.

15 Matthew Paris, *Chronica majora*, vol. 5, p. 65; Vaughan, *Chronicles of Matthew Paris*, p. 177.

16 See Vaughan, *Matthew Paris*, p. 119.

17 Matthew Paris, *Chronica majora*, vol. 5, pp. 7 and 50; Vaughan, *Chronicles of Matthew Paris*, pp. 134, 165.

18 Vaughan, *Matthew Paris*, p. 124.

19 Lewis, *The Art of Matthew Paris*, notes that these manuscripts 'constitute the first known medieval example of a historical text to have been provided with an extensive body of illustrations', p. 19.

20 Lewis, *The Art of Matthew Paris*, pp. 43–45.

21 Matthew Paris, *Chronica majora*, vol. 3, p. 7; translation from Lewis, *The Art of Matthew Paris*, p. 126.

22 Lewis, *The Art of Matthew Paris*, p. 127.

23 Matthew Paris, *Chronica majora*, vol. 3, p. 7; translation from Lewis, *The Art of Matthew Paris*, p. 126.

24 See Lewis, *The Art of Matthew Paris*, pp. 302–3. Weiler, 'How Unusual Was Matthew Paris?' has noted that a major purpose of the *Chronica* was to provide a record of good deeds to imitate and bad ones to avoid. For more on Matthew's apocalypticism, see Weiler, 'History, Prophecy, and the Apocalypse in the Chronicles of Matthew Paris', *English Historical Review* 133 (2018): 253–83.

25 See Björn Weiler, 'Historical Writing and the Experience of Europeanization: The View from St Albans', in '*The Making of Europe': Essays in Honour of Robert Bartlett*, ed. John Hudson and Sally Crumplin (Boston: Brill, 2016), pp. 203–43, at pp. 212–13, for further discussion.

26 See Björn Weiler, 'Matthew Paris in Norway', *Revue Bénédictine* 122 (2012): 153–81.

27 See Daniel K. Connolly, 'Imagined Pilgrimage in the Itinerary Maps of Matthew Paris', *The Art Bulletin* 81.4 (Dec. 1999): 598–622; Daniel K. Connolly, *The Maps of Matthew Paris: Medieval Journeys through Space, Time and Liturgy* (Woodbridge: The Boydell Press, 2009); Katherine Breen, 'Returning Home from Jerusalem: Matthew Paris's First Map of Britain and Its Manuscript Context', *Representations* 89 (2005): 59–93.

28 In fact, Breen, 'Returning Home from Jerusalem', argues that the return to England is also important, as the imagined journey could sacralize geographic movement in England (which can also be imagined as pilgrimage).

29 The one exception to this point is the map in London, British Library, Royal 14, which claims *Britannia nunc dicta Anglia ... que complectitur* [sic] *Scociam, Galeweiam et Walliam*, 'Britain is now called England, which encompasses Scotland, Galloway, and Wales'. Most scholars have assumed the Royal map was also made by Matthew and, naturally, must be an early sketch version gone horribly wrong. I, however, agree with Connolly's argument that the map was not produced by Matthew and instead created during the reign of Edward I for propaganda purposes (*The Maps of Matthew Paris*, pp. 174–91).

30 Granted, that is not to say there are not moments of critique of the Welsh in the *Chronica*. Matthew vacillates between Giraldian criticisms and praise at different points in his history.

31 R. R. Davies, *The First English Empire: Power and Identities in the British Isles: 1093–1343* (New York: Oxford University Press, 2000), pp. 113–41.

15 Cambridge, Corpus Christi College, 144 and 402

Mercian intellectual culture in pre-Conquest England (and beyond)

Lindy Brady

Cambridge, Corpus Christi College,[1] 144, the early ninth-century Corpus Glossary,[2] contains 8,712 entries, making it the largest alphabetical glossary from pre-Conquest England.[3] The bulk of this text is in Latin,[4] but over 2,000 words are glossed in Old English[5] in a Mercian dialect. Widespread belief about the Corpus Glossary's origins has held that it varied in only insignificant ways from its sources,[6] which had been produced at Canterbury under the auspices of Theodore and Hadrian.[7] Yet dialect and paleographical evidence indicate a Mercian origin for the Glossary.[8] As a famously 'lost kingdom',[9] Mercian literary culture has received less attention than the golden ages of Bede's Northumbria and Alfred's Wessex.[10] Here, I shall argue that the learned richness of the Corpus Glossary, newly accessible through Parker 2.0, shows a significant intellectual culture in Mercia during the gap between the known 'nodes' of literary activity in this region (Felix's *Vita Sancti Guthlaci* in the early eighth century and the importance of Mercian scholars to Alfred's translation programme in the late ninth),[11] broadening our appreciation of the range of literary activity that took place throughout the Anglo-Saxon period.[12] I will also argue that folios 1r–3v of CCCC 144 are a significantly original production, specifically, a Carolingian epitome. This enhances our understanding of the close intellectual connections between Mercia and the Carolingian world.[13] Evidence for an ongoing literary tradition in this region extends beyond the Norman Conquest in CCCC 402, a copy of *Ancrene Wisse* discussed by Carla Thomas in this volume. Texts like the Corpus Glossary are important windows into the intellectual lives of their producers and users, and CCCC 144 shows us that there was an innovative and deeply learned literary culture in Mercia in the early ninth century with connections to the Carolingian intellectual world.

This chapter does not discuss the technical details of Parker 2.0, though being able to access glosses through the digital medium is crucially important, because the functionality of the zoom tool allows us to hone in on often small or partially erased words and letters, and to be able to return frequently to check details, something not possible previously in the days of limited research travel. Rather than focusing on technology itself, my goal is to show the value of visual access to entire manuscripts even to those like me, historians and textual scholars not directly engaged in digital huma-nities projects, in opening up new ways of thinking about texts like the Corpus Glossary which would benefit from more attention. The complexity of the textual tradition surrounding early medieval glossaries has function-ally limited their study to philologists and a small group of specialists.[14] Working on these glossaries is a daunting task:[15] a dizzying amount of information is coupled with the necessity of painstakingly minute source work to recover the process through which they were compiled, combined, and rearranged.[16] The Corpus Glossary is well-studied by philologists, but it has not received much attention as a text in its own right.[17] In the fairly damning words of W. M. Lindsay:[18] 'the personality of the [Corpus Glos-sary's] compiler fades into insignificance. His rôle was hardly more than a book-binder's'.[19] This paper takes its cues from the work of Michael Lapidge[20] and Rosamond McKitterick,[21] who both stress the importance of early medieval glossaries as windows into the intellectual surroundings which produced and used them. McKitterick's term 'glossary chrestomathy' in particular offers a way forward: it 'denotes composite collections of glos-saries and re-focuses our attention on the contents of such books and their function, rather than their origin'.[22] This approach informs the current dis-cussion. What knowledge does the Corpus Glossary hold? What do its contents tell us about the interests and abilities of those who produced and used it?

To begin, I have been using 'Corpus Glossary' as shorthand for CCCC 144, but the manuscript actually contains three texts. The First Corpus Glossary runs from folios 1r–3v, and bears the incipit *Interpretatio nominum ebrai-corum et grecorum*. It contains a list of (mainly) Hebrew names from the Bible and Greek technical terms of grammar, metre, and rhetoric, with inter-pretations.[23] The second text is the Corpus Glossary proper, technically known as the Second Corpus Glossary, a large collection of glossed *lemmata* in a mixture of Latin, Old English, and (mostly) transliterated Greek, rear-ranged in AB order. This runs from folios 4r–64v and bears the incipit *Incipit glosa secundum ordinem elimentorum alphabeti*. As their *incipits* make clear, these texts were designed as a pair. Finally, following the Corpus Glossary is a bifolium containing a fragment of Priscian produced by an Irish scribe in the twelfth century,[24] folded inside out so that its leaves are now in reverse order, and sadly beyond the scope of this chapter. Taking my cue from McKitterick, I will focus on the contents and function of the Corpus Glossary, not the routes through which it compiled its sources. As Bradshaw long ago pointed out, the value of glossaries could not have been solely analogous to that of modern dictionaries, because there is no guarantee that a monastery would own copies of the texts from which a given glossary's *lemmata* were drawn.[25] In other words, these works must have had additional inherent value in the knowledge they contained.

In the case of CCCC 144, that value is immediately evident in the manu-script's layout. The First and Second Corpus Glossaries were planned in tandem: the layout of CCCC 144 shows that these texts were beautifully designed and spaced to complement one another. What, then, does their form tell us about their function? I will begin with the First Corpus Glossary, to consider the interpretation of this section of CCCC 144.[26] Compared to the Second, the First Corpus Glossary is much shorter, far more tightly focused, and infinitely easier to digest and navigate as an inclusive collection of material. As its *incipit* suggests, its focus is largely narrowed to a key subset of knowledge: Hebrew names and Greek terminology. The First Corpus Glossary contains 342 items, 237 (70%) of which are Hebrew and Greek proper nouns occurring in the Bible, subsequently given an interpretation in Jerome's *Liber interpretationis hebraicorum nominum*, Eucherius's *Instructiones* (which in part overlaps Jerome),[27] or Isidore's *Etymologiae* (which overlaps both).[28] The First Corpus Glossary is 'the largest collection of this kind in England'.[29] A further 52 items (15%) are transliterated Greek terms of grammar, metre, and rhetoric, and their explications, drawn from a known grammatical glossary.[30] Several entries are trilingual, in the *tres linguae sacrae* of Hebrew, Greek, and Latin.[31] Finally, as Filippa Alcamesi has recently demonstrated, the third significant category of items in the First Corpus Glossary—32 entries (9%) which are glossed in Old English—come from one or more class glossaries. As she writes, 'it is evident that they are representative of distinct semantic fields: seafaring, birds, plants, members of family and society, tools and common objects, as well as biblical terms'.[32] Of these entries, 'the majority of them are ultimately derived from Isidore's *Etymologiae*; there are also entries which go back to the Bible and to Hiberno-Latin sources, in particular the *Hisperica famina*'.[33]

I argue that the First Corpus Glossary was deliberately designed to be the more frequently consulted portion of this manuscript. The material it contains appears in the sources from which the Corpus Glossary as a whole drew its entries,[34] but was deliberately culled and pulled to the front in a narrowed, thematic section,[35] a phenomenon unique among the Corpus Glossary's contemporaries and antecedents. This has important implications for how we understand the intellectual background of the compilers and users of this manuscript. If Lapidge's observation that the organization of medieval libraries can be deduced from book-lists to be: 'in the sequence bibles, Church Fathers, theology, classical authors',[36] following this logic, biblical information, the bulk of the First Corpus Glossary, would have been pulled to the front of CCCC 144 as the most important, separating sacred from secular material and awarding the former the foremost place in the manuscript. Yet the presence of Greek grammatical terminology and Old English encyclopaedic information in the First Corpus Glossary suggests that this text was compiled and separated from the Second Corpus Glossary for more than purely theological reasons. I think it is an example of a well-known teaching tool, a Carolingian epitome: a condensed subset of information which was considered most important to know, yet with which a beginning student might not be familiar.[37]

Carolingian epitomes were designed for teaching. The texts central to a monastic education 'were often too unwieldy for novices early in their education and with only a limited grasp of Latin. The solution took the form of compilations of excerpts reworked into textbooks and simplified for the use of beginning students'.[38] The First Corpus Glossary is designed in precisely this way. It is a unique text: while the information it contains exists elsewhere, no other glossary isolates this material and combines it in this way. While separating biblical information by itself would be of obvious theological or practical value (for use in preaching), the grammatical and encyclopaedic material signals that the First Corpus Glossary likely had a dedicated schoolroom use. Explications of important biblical items would be some of the most important information a monastic pupil could learn, and the addition of transliterated Greek terminology on language suggests this text's teaching appeal: 'after a few general definitions there are batches on the noun and its parts, gender, declensions and cases, followed by glosses on prosody, syllables, feet, metres and caesurae'.[39] This is precisely the type of information that one would want to have at hand in a classroom, yet the terminology would be difficult to keep straight, and having readily accessible definitions seems desirable in a teaching situation.

The inclusion of the Isidorian and Hiberno-Latin encyclopaedic information glossed in Old English is fascinating, but it is more difficult to guess why the compiler included these items here. Perhaps these items, through their glossing in the vernacular, demonstrate a desire to link the intellectual community of Anglo-Saxon England with that of the classical and late antique worlds displayed in this source material through the intimate connection of having native terminology for even this most esoteric body of knowledge. The community that designed and used the First Corpus Glossary did so for an audience that studied Hebrew names, Greek grammatical terms, and Old English encyclopaedic information regularly enough that a focused reference guide (or, I have argued, a teaching tool) was deemed desirable. This, coupled with the text's format, tells us much about the intellectual life of the community that produced it. As McKitterick has shown, glossaries like CCCC 144 were a central part of Carolingian intellectual culture in the ninth century.[40] The First Corpus Glossary's form as a Carolingian epitome indicates that Mercia had a vested engagement in continental scholarship beyond the reign of Offa, underlining the importance of the 'hollow shape' that is Cenwulf's reign:[41] nothing direct, but lots of hints.[42]

The types of knowledge contained in both the First and Second Corpus Glossaries were valued by the community that produced CCCC 144, but these documents were used for different reasons. The Second Corpus Glossary contains almost 9,000 entries in a blend of Latin, Old English, and transliterated Greek (with one word preserved in the Greek alphabet) in AB alphabetical order. Here too, rather than discussing the complicated process by which this material was compiled, I will focus on the contents of the Second Corpus Glossary and what this tells us about the intellectual life of the community that compiled it. The Second glossary was designed for function-ality: its AB order and clear spacing and headwords for each section meant that it could function as a dictionary. Yet most entries were unlikely to have existed outside the texts from which they were originally culled, and we have no way of knowing whether or not whoever compiled it still held those texts. If one did not have a copy of Gildas's *De excidio et conquestu Britanniae* to hand, it is unlikely that the text's highly esoteric vocabulary would have been encountered elsewhere, and there would be no external need to look up the definitions of particular words. This suggests an inherent value in the infor-mation in its own right. The Corpus Glossary was treated not just as a dic-tionary, but also as an encyclopaedia that held knowledge valuable for its own sake.[43] We know that Anglo-Saxon readers sat down with books like the Corpus Glossary as a means of learning in this way because of Aldhelm. A relationship between the Corpus Glossary and Aldhelm's works had long been known,[44] but as Lindsay demonstrated, 'Aldhelm got the stranger part of his vocabulary from glossaries rather than from a wide reading of Latin authors ... [these are not] "Corpus borrowings from Aldhelm". They are Aldhelm's borrowings from the predecessors (or contemporary rivals) of Corpus'.[45] More recent scholarship has confirmed the extent to which, to quote Lapidge, 'it is well known that Aldhelm's Latin writings reveal a developed taste for glossary words'.[46]

For the Corpus Glossary, then, we must imagine a reader like Aldhelm, someone who looked to this manuscript not just when he did not know a word in another text he was reading, but also to study the material within it for its own sake. What type of knowledge would he have gained from this text? The Corpus Glossary incorporated material from a wide range of sources.[47] One category from which it drew *lemmata* and glosses is histor-ical works. These include glosses from Rufinus's Latin translation of Euse-bius's Greek *Church History*, Orosius's *Historiarum Adversus Paganos*, Jerome's *De viris illustribus*, the Bible, and Gildas's *De excidio et conquestu Britanniae*. From these sources, our reader would have drawn a broad vocabulary from these classical and late antique narratives of world and biblical history. A second category of source material encompasses other glossaries of a miscellaneous nature, namely the Abstrusa and Abolita Glossaries, two continental compilations from monastery teachers, from which our reader would gain exposure to classical vocabulary like that of Virgil.[48] Finally, the third category of knowledge represented in the Corpus Glossary comes from the Latin/Greek grammatical material contained in Phocas's Grammar, the *Hermeneumata*, and the Philoxenus Glossary. Phocas's short grammar contains both Latin and Greek.[49] The *Hermeneu-mata* is a class glossary derived ultimately from the *Hermeneumata pseudo-Dositheana*, a schoolbook which was continuously used throughout the Latin-speaking parts of the Roman Empire by pupils who wished to learn Greek,[50] and the Philoxenus Glossary is a Latin-Greek compilation from the grammarians Festus, Charisius, and others.[51] From these, our reader would have drawn Latin and Greek grammatical and rhetorical knowledge and vocabulary.[52] Even if the users of the Corpus Glossary did not have access to the complete texts from which these glossary entries were originally stripped, a reader of CCCC 144 would still encounter an enormous amount of learning, in Latin, Greek, Hebrew, and Old English, from the classical, late antique, and medieval worlds.

The First and Second Corpus Glossaries, then, demonstrate the presence of a vibrant intellectual culture in Mercia in the early ninth century, in the gap between the known literary activities of Felix and the Mercian scribes and translators at King Alfred's court. A comparable manuscript in some ways, CCCC 402 (a Latin and Middle English manuscript of the thirteenth-century anchoritic handbook *Ancrene Wisse*), bolsters my arguments for the continuity of Mercian literary culture, this time across the Norman Conquest.[53] As J. R. R. Tolkien first recognized, the *Ancrene Wisse* is part of a group of texts written in what he deemed 'AB language': a dialect of early Middle English from the West Midlands, near the Welsh border, the region that Mercia would become.[54] Just as Mercian intellectual culture in Anglo-Saxon England can be hard to glimpse when so few 'original' Mercian literary productions have survived, so too has it been difficult to appreciate the literary culture of the Welsh borderlands after the Norman Conquest when most scholarship has understood 'English' and 'Welsh' literary traditions as diametrically opposed to one another. Recent work on the literary culture of the March of Wales by Simon Meecham-Jones,[55] Joshua Byron Smith,[56] and Georgia Henley[57] has done much to rectify this oversight. Yet while it has long been known that *Ancrene Wisse* contains Welsh loanwords,[58] this text has never been fully studied as a product of the Welsh borderlands, a region that combined significant English and Welsh intellectual influence into something uniquely its own. The *Ancrene Wisse* was written in the early thirteenth century, before the Edwardian conquests of Wales in the late thirteenth century seemed like a foregone conclusion in English history. A sustained study of the *Ancrene Wisse* as a piece of Marcher literature would tell us a great deal about the continuity of intellectual tradition in this region throughout the centuries.

I hope this chapter has convinced readers that pushing on received wisdom about literary 'originality' in the medieval world with the help of tools like Parker on the Web 2.0 allows us to find evidence of intellectual activity even in so-called 'derivative' works. While it has long been recognized that medieval glossaries contain a wealth of knowledge, scholars have tended to treat only those locales which first compiled these texts as centres of learning, relegating the producers of subsequent copies to mere 'bookbinders'. Yet CCCC 144 reveals that the community which produced and used this manuscript had a wealth of knowledge on hand and thought carefully about how best to present and access it. The knowledge contained in CCCC 144 in early ninth-century Mercia provides a reasonable foundation for this kingdom's later reputation as a centre of continued Latin learning in King Alfred's day,[59] while its form reflects the

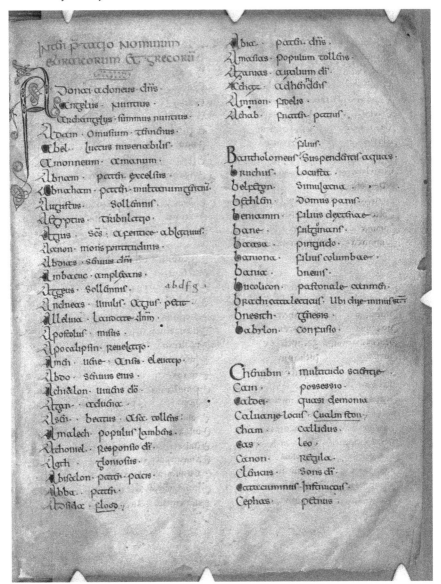

Figure 15.1 The Parker Library, Corpus Christi College, Cambridge, MS 144, f 1r.

continued intellectual influence of the Carolingian world even after the reign of Offa had come to an end, suggesting that Cenwulf extended Mercia's political power longer than has been believed. Placing the two unlikely manuscripts of CCCC 144 and 402 together also highlights the continuity of intellectual tradition in Mercia across the centuries. Finally, this case study reminds us of the continued importance of individual manuscripts in drawing broader conclusions. Even a manuscript like CCCC 144, relatively late within the tradition of Anglo-Saxon glossaries, can demonstrate significant innovation via its substantial translation of glosses to the vernacular, consistent use of AB alphabetical order, and creation of a separate, thematic, First Glossary in the format of a Carolingian epitome focused on largely Hebrew and Greek material. Such innovations demonstrate the ways in which individual scribes and compilers were invested in making the information contained within glossaries like those of CCCC 144 increasingly accessible to the members of their community. And now, the range of possibilities opened up by Parker on the Web 2.0 enables more scholars to understand these innovations than ever before.

Notes

1 I am grateful to Frederick M. Biggs, Marios Costambeys, David F. Johnson, and Andrew Rabin for invaluable suggestions at various stages of this project.

2 The Corpus Glossary has been edited by J. H. Hessels, ed., *An Eighth-Century Latin-Anglo-Saxon Glossary Preserved in the Library of Corpus Christi College, Cambridge (MS no. 144)* (Cambridge: Cambridge University Press, 1890) and W. M. Lindsay, ed., *The Corpus Glossary* (Cambridge: Cambridge University Press, 1921); and discussed most extensively by W. M. Lindsay, *The Corpus, Épinal, Erfurt and Leyden Glossaries* (London: Oxford University Press, 1921).

3 Hessels, *Eighth-Century Glossary*, p. xiv; and Patrizia Lendinara, *Anglo-Saxon Glosses and Glossaries* (Aldershot: Ashgate, 1999), p. 16.

4 See Michael Lapidge, 'The School of Theodore and Hadrian', *Anglo-Saxon England* 15 (1986): 45–72; and J. D. Pheifer, 'Early Anglo-Saxon Glossaries and the School of Canterbury', *Anglo-Saxon England* 16 (1987): 17–44.

5 See Bernhard Bischoff and M. B. Parkes, 'Paleographical Commentary', in *The Épinal, Erfurt, Werden, and Corpus Glossaries*, Early English Manuscripts in Facsimile 22, ed. Bernhard Bischoff, Mildred Budny, Geoffrey Harlow, M. B. Parkes, and J. D. Pheifer (Copenhagen: Rosenkilde and Bagger, 1988), pp. 22–5, at p. 25. Sherman M. Kuhn, 'The Dialect of the Corpus Glossary', *Publications of the Modern Language Association* 54 (1939): 1–19.

6 The Corpus Glossary copied material from the Épinal-Erfurt Glossary, alongside additional material discussed below, and rearranged it further into 'AB' alphabetical order (all 'Ab-' glosses, all 'Ac-' glosses, etc.). As it was doing so, the Corpus Glossary also recast many of the explications from the Épinal-Erfurt Glossary from Latin into Old English: see Lindsay, *The Corpus, Épinal, Erfurt and Leyden Glossaries*, pp. 88–94 for a full list of these items.

7 See Lapidge, 'The School of Theodore and Hadrian', and Pheifer, 'Early Anglo-Saxon Glossaries'. Yet the evidence for a Canterbury origin of the Corpus Glossary and its manuscript is not firm at all, as Michelle P. Brown notes in 'Mercian Manuscripts? The "Tiberius" Group and Its Historical Context', in *Mercia: An Anglo-Saxon Kingdom in Europe*, ed. Michelle P. Brown and Carol A. Farr (London: Leicester University Press, 2001), pp. 278–91, at p. 280.

8 See Bernhard Bischoff and M. B. Parkes, 'Paleographical Commentary', in *The Épinal, Erfurt, Werden, and Corpus Glossaries*, p. 25. See, more recently, Michelle P. Brown, 'Mercian Manuscripts? The "Tiberius" Group and Its Historical Context', in Brown and Farr, *Mercia: An Anglo-Saxon Kingdom in Europe*, pp. 278–91. Brown places CCCC 144 into a sub-category of 'Canterbury School' manuscripts within a Mercian Schriftprovinz.

9 Michelle P. Brown and Carol A. Farr, 'Introduction: Mercia, a Culture in Context', in Brown and Farr, *Mercia: An Anglo-Saxon Kingdom in Europe*, pp. 1–10, at p. 1.

10 On Mercia, see Ann Dornier, ed., *Mercian Studies* (Leicester: Leicester University Press, 1997); Michelle and Farr, eds., *Mercia: An Anglo-Saxon Kingdom in Europe*; and Lindy Brady, *Writing the Welsh Borderlands in Anglo-Saxon England* (Manchester: Manchester University Press, 2017). Because the corpus of surviving Mercian works is so slender, textual attention to Mercia's literary output has focused on palaeography, art history, and dialect. It is in this last respect which the Corpus Glossary has been treated as 'Mercian', and there only sparingly.

11 See Mechthild Gretsch, 'The Junius Psalter Gloss: Its Historical and Cultural Context', *Anglo-Saxon England* 29 (2000): 85–122, at p. 104.

12 This argument is of course indebted to that of Elaine Treharne, *Living through Conquest: The Politics of Early English, 1020–1220* (Oxford: Oxford University Press, 2012).

13 See Janet L. Nelson, 'Carolingian Contacts', in Brown and Farr, *Mercia: An Anglo-Saxon Kingdom in Europe*, pp. 126–43.

14 See *Anglo-Saxon Glossography: Papers Read at the International Conference held in the Koninklijke Academie voor Wetenschappen, Letteren en Schone Kunsten van België, Brussels, 8 and 9 September 1986*, ed. R. Derolez (Brussels: Paleis der Academiën, 1992); *Practice in Learning: The Transfer of Encyclopaedic Knowledge in the Early Middle Ages*, ed. R. H. Bremmer, Jr. and K. Dekker (Leuven: Peeters, 2010); and *Rethinking and Recontextualizing Glosses: New Perspectives in the Study of Late Anglo-Saxon Glossography*, ed. P. Lendinara, L. Lazzari, and C. Di Sciacca, Textes et études du moyen âge 54 (Porto: Fédération Internationale des Instituts d'Études Médiévales, 2011).

15 On the different ways in which glossing itself was used for learning, see Paul Russell, 'Teaching between the Lines: Grammar and *Grammatica* in the Classroom in Early Medieval Wales', in *Grammatica, Gramadach and Gramadeg: Vernacular Grammar and Grammarians in Medieval Ireland and Wales*, ed. Deborah Hayden and Paul Russell (Amsterdam: John Benjamins, 2016), pp. 133–48. Glossed words (*lemmata*) and their explications were stripped from their manuscript context and compiled into *glossae collectae*, which were copied first in batches by source text (glosses from Orosius, glosses from Gildas, etc.), as in the Leiden Glossary. The exemplar from which the Corpus Glossary is derived incorporated the material in the Épinal-Erfurt Glossary (which itself was copied from the Leiden Glossary) alongside that of additional *glossae collectae*. As J. D. Pheifer, *Old English Glosses in the Épinal-Erfurt Glossary* (Oxford: Clarendon Press, 1974), p. xxix, writes, 'Corpus thus provides what is virtually a third text of the Épinal-Erfurt Glossary, and one which derives from the archetype independently of the common exemplar of Épinal and Erfurt since it gives a more correct reading, not likely to be the result of scribal correction, in a significant number of cases where the latter share a common error.' As this (no longer extant) exemplar was copied by the scribe of our manuscript, Corpus 144, he both recast many of the Latin explications in his sources into Old English and rearranged all the entries into AB alphabetical order (that is, alphabetized by first and second letter) to produce the manuscript that remains today. On this process, see Lindsay, *The Corpus, Épinal, Erfurt and Leyden Glossaries*, pp. 1–16; 36–8; 44–53; and *passim*; see pp. 88–94 for a full list of glossary items known to be recast in Old English.

16 'To trace even one item is often to have a feeling of connections too various to follow, branching off like possible moves in a chess game or as through a labyrinth'; Alan K. Brown, 'Toward Unifying the Corpus of Old English Glossaries', in Derolez, *Anglo-Saxon Glossography*, pp. 99–114, at p. 111.

17 See David W. Porter, 'The Antwerp-London Glossaries and the First English School Text', in *Rethinking and Recontextualizing Glosses*, pp. 153–77, at pp. 168–70. Porter's excellent study nonetheless demonstrates the ways in which scholarship on glossaries has privileged the earliest manuscripts in an effort to reconstruct the curriculum of the Canterbury school, which he views as 'the birth of written English', p. 177.

18 In addition to the works already cited, see W. M. Lindsay, *Studies in Early Mediaeval Latin Glossaries*, ed. Michael Lapidge (Aldershot: Ashgate, 1996).

19 Lindsay, *The Corpus, Épinal, Erfurt and Leyden Glossaries*, pp. 1–2.

20 See here Michael Lapidge's comments on the 'selective editing' of multilingual glossaries containing Old English; Michael Lapidge, 'Old English Glossography: The Latin Context', in his *Anglo-Latin Literature 600–899* (London: Hambledon Press, 1996), pp. 169–81 at p. 171: 'Glosses and glossaries are the best evidence we have of the Anglo-Saxons' intellectual response to the texts they studied, but if we wish ultimately to understand their intellectual world, we must … turn our attention to the wider Latin context in which glosses occur and on which glossaries were based.'

21 Rosamond McKitterick, 'Glossaries and Other Innovations in Carolingian Book Production', in *Turning over a New Leaf: Change and Development in the Medieval Book*, ed. Erik Kwakkel, Rosamond McKitterick, and Rodney Thomson (Leiden: Leiden University Press, 2012), pp. 21–76.

22 Anna Dorofeeva, 'Strategies of Knowledge Organisation in Early Medieval Latin Glossary Miscellanies: The Example of Munich, Bayerische Staatsbibliothek, Clm 14388', in *Writing the Early Medieval West: Studies in Honour of Rosamond McKitterick*, ed. Elina Screen and Charles West (Cambridge: Cambridge University Press, 2018), pp. 161–83 at p. 63.

23 Lindsay, *The Corpus Glossary*, p. 188. For more on Hebrew in medieval manuscripts, see Carla María Thomas, Chapter 17 in this volume.

24 Bischoff and Parkes, 'Paleographical Commentary', p. 22 and n. 120. The leaves contain part of the section on patronymics from *Institutiones grammaticae* II (34–38I, pr. *Grammatici latini*, ed. H. Keil, II (Leipzig, 1855), pp. 64–74.

25 Bradshaw, 'Collected Papers', p. 462, cited in Lindsay, *The Corpus, Épinal, Erfurt and Leyden Glossaries*, p. 1.

26 Lendinara, *Anglo-Saxon Glosses and Glossaries*, 18, notes that 'the entries show a series of amusing mistakes which derive from a limited knowledge of Hebrew'.

27 See Kees Dekker, 'Eucherius of Lyons in Anglo-Saxon England: The Continental Connections', in Bremmer and Dekker, *Practice in Learning*, pp. 147–73.

28 Lendinara, *Anglo-Saxon Glosses and Glossaries*, p. 18, noting further, 'Not all the "Hebrew" entries go back to the *Liber interpretationis*: some are drawn from other works by Jerome, which suggests the possible circulation of lists of Hebrew nouns (and their interpretations) gathered from his various writings.' See also Dekker, 'Eucherius of Lyons in Anglo-Saxon England', pp. 160–2 for further discussion of the overlap.

29 Lendinara, *Anglo-Saxon Glosses and Glossaries*, p. 18.

30 Lendinara, *Anglo-Saxon Glosses and Glossaries*, p. 18. These Greek terms come from a known glossary: see Helmut Gneuss, 'A Grammarian's Greek-Latin Glossary in Anglo-Saxon England', in *From Anglo-Saxon to Early Middle English: Studies Presented to E.G. Stanley*, ed. Malcolm Godden, Douglas Gray, and Terry Hoad (Oxford: Oxford University Press, 1994), pp. 60–86.

31 Lendinara, *Anglo-Saxon Glosses and Glossaries*, p. 19.

32 Filippa Alcamesi, 'The Old English Entries in the First Corpus Glossary (CCCC 144, FF. 1R-3V)', in *Rethinking and Recontextualizing Glosses: New Perspectives in the Study of Late Anglo-Saxon Glossography* (Turnhout: Brepols, 2011), pp. 509–41 at p. 511.

33 Alcamesi, 'Old English Entries in the First Corpus Glossary', p. 539.

34 While the entries in the First Corpus Glossary stem ultimately from Jerome, Eucherius, and Isidore, they also appear throughout many of the glossaries upon which the Corpus Glossary drew; Lendinara, *Anglo-Saxon Glosses and Glossaries*, p. 18.

35 As Filippa Alcamesi points out in 'Old English Entries in the First Corpus Glossary', pp. 510–11.

36 Michael Lapidge, 'Surviving booklists from Anglo-Saxon England', in *Learning and Literature in Anglo-Saxon England: Studies Presented to Peter Clemoes on the Occasion of his Sixty-fifth Birthday*, ed. Michael Lapidge and Helmut Gneuss (Cambridge: Cambridge University Press, 1985), pp. 33–89 at p. 36.

37 See Michael M. Gorman, 'A Carolingian Epitome of St Augustine's *De Genesi ad Litteram*', *Revue d'Études Augustiniennes et Patristiques* 29 (1983): pp. 137–44 at p. 137; Clare Woods, 'A Contribution to the King's Library: Paul the Deacon's Epitome and its Carolingian Context', in *Verrius, Festus and Paul*, ed. Fay Glinister and Clare Woods (London: Institute of Classical Studies, 2007), pp. 109–35; and Rosamond McKitterick, *The Carolingians and the Written Word* (Cambridge: Cambridge University Press, 1989).

38 *The Disputatio puerorum: A Ninth-Century Monastic Instructional Text*, ed. Andrew Rabin and Liam Felsen, Toronto Medieval Latin Texts 34 (Toronto: The Pontifical Institute of Mediaeval Studies, 2017), p. 1; continuing, pp. 1–2: 'These primers distilled the essence of canonical texts into digestible units that made the teachings of the Church accessible while also highlighting those elements of Christian doctrine deemed most necessary for a novice monk to know.'

39 Lendinara, *Anglo-Saxon Glosses and Glossaries*, p. 18.

40 Rosamond McKitterick, 'Glossaries and Other Innovations in Carolingian Book Production', in Kwakkel *et al., Turning over a New Leaf*, pp. 21–76.

41 Simon Keynes, 'The Kingdom of the Mercians in the Eighth Century', in Hill and Worthington, *Æthelbald and Offa*, pp. 1–21, at p. 19; and see his comments on Cenwulf at p. 18.

42 For another such hint, see Rebecca Rushforth, 'Annotated Psalters and Psalm Study in Late Anglo-Saxon England: The Manuscript Evidence', in Lendinara, Lazzari, and Di Sciacca, *Rethinking and Recontextualizing Glosses*, pp. 39–66, at p. 56.

43 This point has been emphasized by McKitterick, 'Glossaries and Other Innovations', pp. 73–4.

44 Lindsay, *The Corpus, Épinal, Erfurt and Leyden Glossaries*, p. 97: 'That Aldhelm … was a source of the Corpus Glossary has been generally believed since Napier's paper, reported in the "Academy" of 1894, p. 398 (cf. his Old English Glosses, p. xii n.); and Goetz in the Thesaurus Glossarum (apparently at Schlutter's instigation) refers several items of EEi or of Erf. to Aldhelm passages.'

45 Lindsay, *The Corpus, Épinal, Erfurt and Leyden Glossaries*, p. 100; see pp. 97–105 for full argument.

46 Michael Lapidge, 'The Career of Aldhelm', *Anglo-Saxon England* 36 (2007): 15–69, at p. 40.

47 Lindsay, *The Corpus, Épinal, Erfurt and Leyden Glossaries, passim*.

48 Lindsay, *The Corpus Glossary*, p. v.

49 Lindsay, *The Corpus, Épinal, Erfurt and Leyden Glossaries*, pp. 2–7.

50 Lindsay, *The Corpus Glossary*, p. v, and *The Corpus, Épinal, Erfurt and Leyden Glossaries*, pp. 7–10.

51 Lindsay, *The Corpus Glossary*, pp. v–vi.

52 On transliterated Greek in Anglo-Saxon England, see Gneuss, 'A Grammarian's Greek–Latin Glossary in Anglo-Saxon England', pp. 60–86.

53 See Bella Millett, ed., *Ancrene Wisse: A Corrected Edition of the Text in Cambridge, Corpus Christi College, MS 402, with Variants from Other Manuscripts*, vol. 1 Early English Text Society os 325, 236 (Oxford: Oxford University Press, 2005 and 2006).

54 J. R. R. Tolkien, '*Ancrene Wisse* and *Hali Meiðhad*', *Essays and Studies* 4 (1929): 104–26.

55 Simon Meecham-Jones, 'Where was Wales? The Erasure of Wales in Medieval English Culture', in *Authority and Subjugation in Writing of Medieval Wales*, ed. Ruth Kennedy and Simon Meecham-Jones (New York: Palgrave Macmillan, 2008), pp. 27–55.

56 Joshua Byron Smith, *Walter Map and the Matter of Britain* (Philadelphia: University of Pennsylvania Press, 2017).

57 Georgia Henley, 'Monastic Manuscript Networks of the Anglo-Welsh March: A Study in Literary Transmission' (unpub. PhD dissertation, Harvard University, 2017).

58 Those loanwords, *cader* 'cradle' and *baban* 'baby', share an obvious thematic significance, and it does not require an enormous leap of faith to suggest that intermarriage between English and/or Norman men and Welsh women would be the most likely route of transmission.

59 See Simon Keynes, 'King Alfred and the Mercians', in *Kings, Currency and Alliances: History and Coinage of Southern England in the Ninth Century*, ed. Mark A. S. Blackburn and David N. Dumville (Woodbridge: The Boydell Press, 1998), pp. 1–45.

16 *Philologia* and philology
Allegory, multilingualism and the Corpus Martianus Capella

Elizabeth Boyle

Cambridge, Corpus Christi College, 153 is a late ninth- or early tenth-century copy of Martianus Capella, *De nuptiis Philologiae et Mercurii*, originally produced in Wales, but brought to England early in its history and supplemented there.[1] It has previously been studied in relation to its multilingual glosses (in Latin and Old Welsh), its palaeography (an early example of the use of Caroline minuscule in an Insular context), and its provenance. The purpose of this short contribution is twofold: first, to improve upon the inadequate manuscript description which I wrote in 2009 for the original Parker on the Web site; and second, to consider briefly a less studied aspect of the manuscript's importance, namely its value as a witness to the advanced study of allegorical literature in early medieval Wales. This takes us beyond the bounds of the digital, but my new work is facilitated by that medium suggests this manuscript has implications for the way that other forms of literature may have been read and understood in early medieval Wales.

My original manuscript description for CCCC 153 read as follows:

> This is a late ninth-century copy of Martianus Capella (fourth/fifth century), *De nuptiis Philologiae et Mercurii*, with glossary and tenth-century additions. The manuscript is Welsh, and includes many Old Welsh glosses, which were published by Whitley Stokes. The text is in a variety of hands, including an attractive Caroline minuscule—an early example of the use of this style in the British Isles—and thus attests to contacts between Francia and Wales in the ninth and tenth centuries. The manuscript seems to have been in England early in its history and was supplemented there.

This description has a number of flaws, including an over-emphasis on the vernacular Welsh glosses at the expense of the (far more numerous) Latin glosses; the potentially misleading use of the term 'glossary' to describe what might be more accurately termed *glossae collectae* on folios 69–86; and the overall wording, which fails to convey that the English additions to the manuscript consisted of two distinct stages. Scholars have argued for a first phase of augmentation during which the lacuna in Book III seems to have been filled (folios 19–28) and corrections made elsewhere to the text: this may have taken place in St Augustine's, Canterbury, in the 930s. The second stage comprised the addition of the aforementioned *glossae collectae*, which were added *c.* 950x975.[2] I therefore propose the following updated manuscript description:

> This is a late ninth- or early tenth-century copy of Martianus Capella (fourth/fifth century), *De nuptiis Philologiae et Mercurii*. The manuscript was produced in Wales and is extensively glossed in Latin and Old Welsh. The text is in a variety of hands, including an attractive Caroline min-uscule—an early example of the use of this script in an Insular context—which attests to contacts between Francia and Wales in the ninth and/or early tenth century. The manuscript was in England (perhaps St Augus-tine's, Canterbury) by the 930s, when the text was corrected in places and the lacuna in Book III filled (ff. 19–28). A few decades later, *glossae col-lectae* on *De nuptiis* were added to the end of the manuscript (ff. 69–86).

I have erased the reference to Whitley Stokes's nineteenth-century edition of the Old Welsh glosses, as his work has now largely been superseded by two MA theses produced in Utrecht: namely, Karianne Lemmen, 'The Old Welsh Glosses in Martianus Capella, Revised and Rearranged with Newly Found Glosses', unpublished MA thesis (Utrecht University, 2006) and, most recently, Lars Nooij, 'The Old Welsh Glosses on Martianus Capella Reconsidered: An Edition, Commentary and Analysis', unpublished MA thesis (Utrecht University, 2015). The Latin glosses have been edited in Sinéad O'Sullivan, ed., *Glossae aeui Car-olini in libros I-II Martiani Capellae De nuptiis Philologiae et Mercurii*, Corpus Christianorum Continuatio Mediaevalis 237 (Turnhout: Brepols, 2010). The Old Welsh glosses have tended to be studied for their lexicographical value, as early witnesses of Old Welsh, rather than their intellectual content, but in what remains here, I would like to offer a *prolegomenon* to the study of medieval Welsh engagement with Martianus's extraordinary text.

Our knowledge of ecclesiastical education in early medieval Wales is limited, and scholars are generally reliant on comparative evidence from Anglo-Saxon England and early medieval Ireland to flesh out the sparse testimony from the period before the introduction of reformed Continental monastic orders (most notably the Cis-tercians). Current scholarly knowledge suggests that the survival rate of manu-scripts from early medieval Wales is extremely poor. What little evidence we do have from Wales, however, suggests a serious scholarly engagement with Latin authors, ranging from the biblical verse epic of Juvencus (Cambridge, University Library, Ff. 4. 42) to the *Ars amatoria* of Ovid (Oxford, Bodleian Library, Auct. F. 4. 32).[3] Although these manuscripts do contain glosses which elucidate gramma-tical and syntactical points, they also contain considerable evidence for layered readings of the texts which go far beyond elementary comprehension. Further-more, these manuscripts contain evidence for multiple readings, with a 'cumulative gathering of comment' which accrued over time.[4] They should therefore not be regarded as isolated outliers, but rather can be considered reflective of an advanced stage of the pedagogical process in early medieval Welsh ecclesiastical schools.

Important, though later, supporting evidence is provided by the work of the family of Sulien of Llanbadarn, active *c.* 1100. An example of their scholarship can be found in the form of Cambridge, Corpus Christi College, 199, an elegant copy of Augustine's *De trinitate*, produced by Sulien's son Ieuan, probably in the last decade of the eleventh century.[5] Studies of the works of the family of Sulien suggest that collectively they may have been familiar with a range of Classical authors, including Virgil, Ovid, Lucan, Juvencus, Statius, Horace, and Juvenal.[6] This appears to reinforce what we have seen in the earlier manuscript evidence in terms of the range and nature of the authors whose works are represented, thus offering a tentative glimpse of the curriculum of the early medieval Welsh classroom.

The nature of the glosses on Cambridge, Corpus Christi College, 153 are such that they indicate an equally profound engagement with Martianus Capella's work. As Paul Russell has noted, the glossators of this manuscript are more concerned with 'explanation and exegesis than elementary language teaching'.[7] What influence might deep engagement with *De nuptiis* have on the way that literature was read and understood in early medieval Wales? First, we must note that *De nuptiis* was one of the most ambitious and extensive works of allegory composed in the late antique world. Martianus was North African (from modern-day Algeria) and is thought to have worked as a jurist, although from *De nuptiis* is clear that he was also trained in the Platonic tradition espoused by Plotinus. His description of *Philologia*, pale-faced from her study of the universe, gives some sense of the tone of his composition as well as of the full and subtle characterization of Philology herself as the young, female embodiment of scholarly knowledge:

> An vero quisquam est, qui Philologiae se asserat pervigilia laborata et lucubrationem perennium nescire pallorem? Quae autem noctibus universis coelum, freta, tartarumque discutere, ac deorum omnium sedes curiosae indaginis perscrutatione transire, quae textum mundi, circulorumque volumina vel orbiculata parallela, vel obliqua decussata polose, et limmata, axiumque vertigines, cum ipsorum puto siderum multitudine numerare, nisi haec Philologia gracilenta quadam affectione consuevit …

> Is there anyone who claims he does not know the wearisome vigils of Philology, the constant pallor that comes from her studies at night? For who is there who discusses the heavens, the seas, seething Tartarus, for whole nights at a time, and traverses in her careful research the homes of all the gods—who considers the constitution of the world, the girding circles, the parallels, the oblique circles and colures, the poles and climates and rotations, and the multitude of the stars themselves—unless it is this slender girl, who is devoted to these pursuits?[8]

Martianus's work is generally regarded as strange and its imagery as deliberately outlandish. Some of the metaphors which emerge from his humanizing of learning as the 'slender girl', Philology, are strikingly pertinent to the study of representations of textual materiality. Here, for example, learning is characterized as vomit:

At illa omni nisu magnaque vi quidquid intra pectus semper senserat evome-
bat. Tunc vero illa nausea ac vomitio laborata in omnigenum copias con-
vertitur literarum. Cernere erat, qui libri quantaque volumina, quot linguarum
opera ex ore virginis defluebant … Sed dum talia virgo undanter evomeret,
puellae quam plures, quarum Artes aliae, aliae dictae sunt Disciplinae, sub-
inde, quae virgo ex ore effuderat, colligebant, in suum unaquaeque illarum
necessarium usum facultatemque corripiens … Postquam igitur illam bib-
liothecalem copiam nixa imitatus virgo diffudit, exhausto pallore confecta
Athanasiae opem, quae tanti laboris conscia fuerat, postulavit.

The girl strained hard and with great effort vomited up the weight she
was carrying in her breast. Then that nausea and labored vomit turned
into a stream of writings of all kinds. One could see what books and what
great volumes and the works of how many languages flowed from the
mouth of the maiden … But while the maiden was bringing up such
matter in spasms, several young women, of whom some are called the
Arts and the others the Disciplines, were straightway collecting whatever
the maiden brought forth from her mouth, each one of them taking
material for her own essential use and her particular skill … After the
maiden had with travail brought forth from deep inside herself all that
store of literary reproduction, worn out and pale with exhaustion, she
asked help from Immortality, who had witnessed such a great effort.[9]

That this inventive and profoundly allegorical text on the liberal arts was read by at
least some scholars in early medieval Wales, as evidenced by Cambridge, Corpus
Christi College, 153, should perhaps have some implications for the way that we
read other genres of literature from early medieval Wales. Up until the late twentieth century, it was the scholarly norm to read and interpret medieval Welsh literature on a surface level, with the assumption that it largely reflected the late
recording of much earlier 'mythological' narratives: thus supernatural women
represented ancient pre-Christian goddesses who had lingered into the Christian
literature of the Middle Ages; stories of military campaigns and bloody warfare
reflected the 'heroic' warrior ethos of society, and so on.[10] Gradually, more
sophisticated literary (as opposed to mythological or folkloristic) interpretations
were offered, and individual compositions came to be regarded as being capable of
sustaining more complex or multivalent readings.[11] Modern scholarship on medieval Welsh narrative literature—particularly work by Helen Fulton and Catherine
McKenna—has highlighted readings which view the texts as political allegories,
commenting, for example, on encroaching Norman power and the diminution of
Welsh political autonomy through the medium of narratives set in a distant past.

However, whether the corpus of medieval Welsh narrative literature bears
sustained allegorical reading from a perspective which is not (or at least not
only) political is not, as far as I am aware, something which has yet been inves-
tigated. The implications for medieval Welsh literature of thinking about it
through the interpretative lens of Martianus's *De nuptiis*—or, to phrase the

problem more strongly, the critical implications of medieval Welsh authors thinking *like* Martianus—has not been explored. By contrast, to turn to one of Wales's near neighbours, there has been some study of the question of whether medieval Irish narrative literature can or should be read as allegory. In a 2016 article, I used three passages of explicitly allegorical literature in medieval Irish literature as case studies for exploring some of the methodological problems and intellectual issues around reading medieval Irish literature more broadly as allegorical, suggesting that some common images and motifs would perhaps have been immediately recognized by a learned audience as richly symbolic on a metaphorical level.[12] Learned authors and audiences in medieval Ireland, I suggest, could speak and understand a common figurative language, with recognizable 'vocabulary' in the form of particular motifs or character types. My contribution was part of a wider volume which explored grammatical education in medieval Ireland and Wales from a standpoint which understood *grammatica* in its medieval sense, a capacious framework which incorporated the reading and interpretation of narrative literature on the literal and figurative levels.[13]

Paul Russell's contribution to the same volume explored three case studies of glossed manuscripts from medieval Wales—Oxford, Bodleian Library, 572, folios 41v-47r (*De raris fabulis*) and the above-mentioned Ovid, *Ars amatoria* and Juvencus, *Evangeliarum libri quattuor*—which, he argued, trace the progressive classroom teaching of Latin from elementary study of vocabulary and morphology (in *De raris fabulis*) through the study of poetry (in the Ovid) to advanced textual commentary (in Juvencus).[14] The educational programme and its indebtedness to late antique grammatical authorities shows that classroom education in early medieval Wales must have been thoroughly comparable to that of its neighbours, both to the west and the east. Just as the vernacular literate culture of medieval Ireland has deep intellectual indebtedness to Latin grammarians such as Priscian and Donatus, so we should consider that the vernacular literary culture of medieval Wales might be similarly indebted.[15] Indeed, a further hint of the contribution of Latin grammatical writings to medieval Welsh vernacular texts can be seen in the fact that the name of the grammarian Donatus, *Dwned*, becomes a common noun in Welsh meaning any grammar book in general and then, by extension, 'talk' or 'gossip'.

Paul Russell has suggested that the fact that Ovid becomes associated almost entirely with love poetry (and, indeed, love more generally) in medieval Wales is a sign that his *Ars amatoria* was known in a way that his *Metamorphoses*, for example, was not. As Russell notes, there are many accounts of shapeshifting in medieval Welsh literature, and yet Ovid was not associated with physical transformation by Welsh authors.[16] We must therefore remain cautious and not overstate the influence that Classical and late antique authors had on medieval Welsh literature: it is vital that we begin with the texts that can be shown to have been read in Wales on the basis of surviving manuscript evidence or the citation of such works in medieval Welsh texts. The Corpus Martianus Capella is significant evidence in that regard. However, Russell has also warned of reading too much into learned references to authorities such as Ovid in later medieval Welsh poetry, noting that many such references may represent 'hazy recollections of the schoolroom' rather than reflecting deep engagement with Latin works. By contrast, our evidence from early medieval Wales—while more slight than the multiple references to authorities such as Ovid, Virgil, and Donatus in late medieval poetry—suggests more serious and profound scholarship within the field of *grammatica* and the Latin grammatical tradition (broadly conceived). It is into this context that Cambridge, Corpus Christi College, 153 fits.

If allegorical literature was a known and acceptable vehicle for the transmission of grammatical knowledge, as in Martianus's *De nuptiis*, then we should not be surprised if other learned genres operate on comparably sophisticated literary and symbolic levels. Robin Chapman Stacey has argued convincingly that this is the case in relation to the surviving legal texts from later medieval Wales. In her magnificent recent study of the imaginary of medieval Welsh law, Stacey has articulated the idea that medieval Welsh law texts possess a rich symbolic language, and writes, for example, of how 'treasure and landscape can mean more than themselves: the glittering world of a courtly past, the hope for a brilliant future to come and, most especially, the advent of a narrative with the potential to transcend the strictly literal'.[17] She argues that such symbolic reading of legal texts allows one to identify persistent strands of metaphoric thinking throughout the texts. In writing about the way that the medieval Welsh law-books move from the 'Laws of Court' to the 'Laws of Country', she writes that 'what we have here is a progression from culture to nature that is as marked and symbolically significant as any journey ever undertaken by the heroes of medieval Welsh literature'.[18] Indeed, she goes so far as to suggest that 'spatial metaphors arguably lie at the heart even of how important parts of the law itself were conceptualized', noting the use of architectural metaphors such as the notion of 'columns' of law.[19] Accepting Stacey's argument in relation to sustained metaphor in medieval Welsh legal texts must surely have implications for the way that we read literary narratives produced in the same *milieu*, and this brings us back to Martianus Capella—for allegory, of the sort produced by Martianus, is simply metaphor that is sustained for the duration of a narrative.

A minimalist reading of the significance of Cambridge, Corpus Christi College, 153 would be that a single Welsh centre had access in the late ninth or early tenth century to a Frankish copy of Martianus's *De nuptiis*, that the manuscript itself was taken within a few decades of its production to England and that Martianus's text had no subsequent influence on Welsh education or literature. However, as noted above, our slight manuscript evidence for the early Middle Ages, and our more abundant evidence for the later Middle Ages would suggest that the allegorical approach to *grammatica* articulated in *De nuptiis* was entirely consonant with, and potentially influential for, medieval Welsh narrative literature and other learned genres. The nature and extent of the influence of the allegorical mode on medieval Welsh written culture remains a subject ripe for investigation, and I hope that this short chapter has served as an invitation to further study.[20]

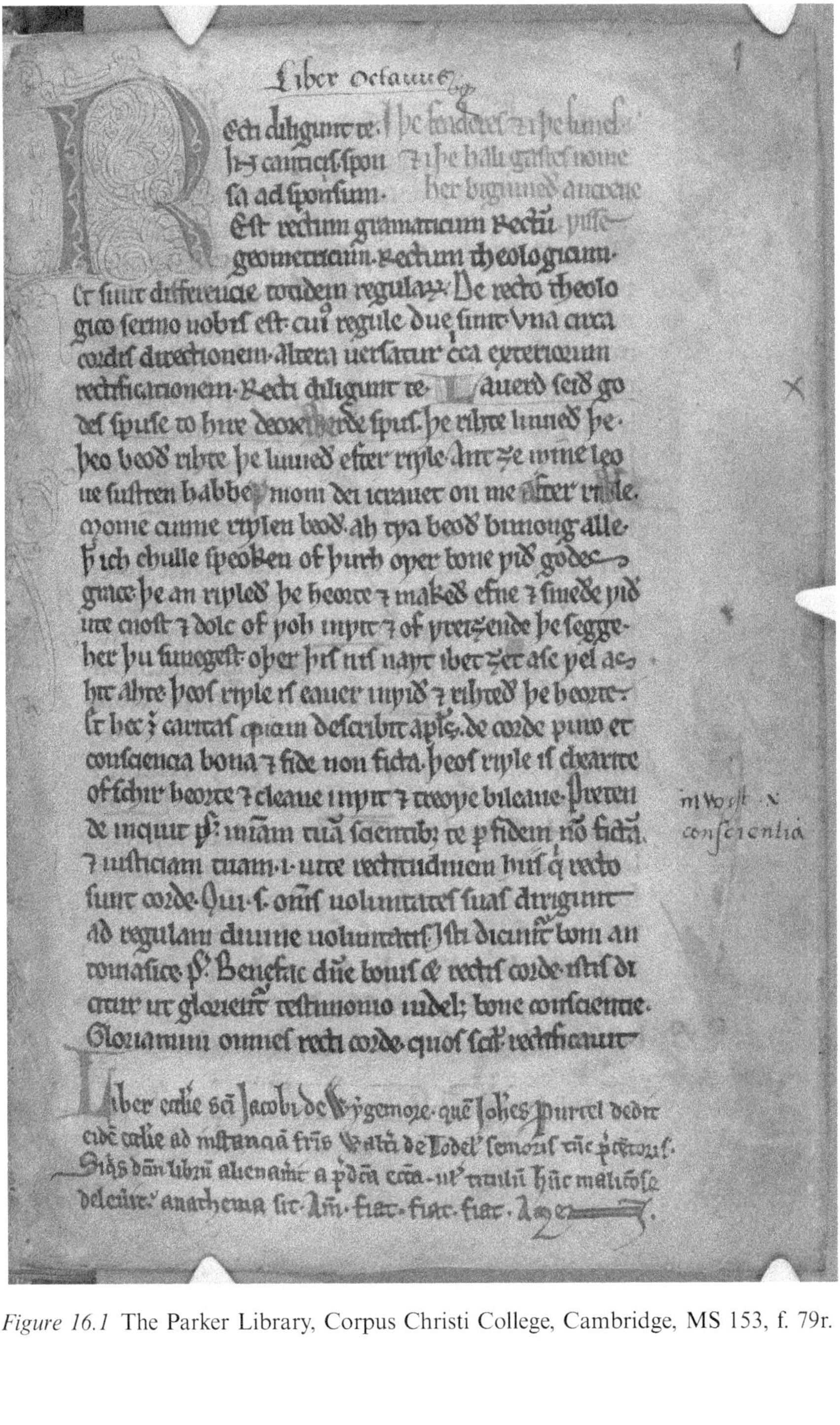
Liber octauus

Recti diligunt te.
In canticis spon-
sa ad sponsum.
Est rectum gramaticum. Rectum
geometricum. Rectum theologicum.
Et sunt differencie totidem regularum. De recto theolo-
gico sermo nobis est. cuius regule due sunt. Una circa
cordis directionem. altera uersatur circa exteriorum
rectificationem. Recti diligunt te. Lauerd seið godes spuse to hire deorewurðe spus. þe rihte luuieð þe.
þeo beoð rihte þe luuieð efter riwle. Ant ȝe mine leo-
ue sustren habbeð moni dei icrauet on me efter riwle.
monie cunne riwlen beoð. ah twa beoð bimong alle.
þ ich chulle speoken of þurh ower bone wið godes
grace. þe an riwleð þe heorte 7 makeð efne 7 smeðe wið-
ute cnost 7 dolc of woh inwit 7 of wreiȝende þe segge.
her þu sunegest. oþer þis nis nawt ibet ȝet ase wel as
hit ahte. þeos riwle is eauer inwið 7 rihteð þe heorte.
Et hec est caritas quam describit apostolus. de corde puro et
consciencia bona 7 fide non ficta. þeos riwle is chearite
of schir heorte 7 cleane inwit 7 treowe bileaue. Pretende inwit x
inquit psalmista misericordiam tuam scientibus te per fidem non fictam. conscientia
7 iusticiam tuam. id est uite rectitudinem. hiis qui recto
sunt corde. Qui scilicet omnes uoluntates suas dirigunt
ad regulam diuine uoluntatis. Isti dicuntur boni an-
tonomasice. psalmista Benefac domine bonis et rectis corde. Istis di-
citur ut glorientur testimonio uidelicet bone consciencie.
Gloriamini omnes recti corde. quos scilicet rectificauit

Liber ecclesie sancti Jacobi de Wygemore quem Johannes Purcel dedit
eidem ecclesie ad instanciam fratris Walteri de Lodel' senioris tunc precentoris.
Si quis dictum librum alienauerit a predicta ecclesia uel titulum hunc maliciose
deleuerit anathema sit. Amen. fiat. fiat. fiat. Amen.

Figure 16.1 The Parker Library, Corpus Christi College, Cambridge, MS 153, f. 79r.

Notes

1 Martianus Capella, *De Nuptiis Philologiae et Mercurii*, ed. Ulrich F. Kopp (Frankfurt: Franz Varrentrapp, 1836); William Harris Stahl, trans., *Martianus Capella and the Seven Liberal Arts, Volume II: The Marriage of Philology and Mercury* (New York: Columbia University Press, 1977).
2 Alison Peden, 'Science and Philosophy in Wales at the Time of the Norman Conquest: A Macrobius Manuscript from Llanbadarn', *Cambridge Medieval Celtic Studies* 2 (1981): 24–45; Sinéad O'Sullivan, 'The Corpus Martianus Capella: Continental Gloss Traditions on "De Nuptiis" in Wales and Anglo-Saxon England', *Cambrian Medieval Celtic Studies* 62 (2011): 33–56.
3 The fullest study to date of our extant medieval Welsh manuscripts will soon appear in the form of Daniel Huws, *A Repertory of Welsh Manuscripts and Scribes, c. 800–c. 1800* (Aberystwyth: National Library of Wales, 2020). The Cambridge Juvencus manuscript has been digitized at: http://cudl.lib.cam.ac.uk/view/MS-FF-00004-00042/1
4 Paul Russell, *Reading Ovid in Medieval Wales: Text and Context* (Columbus: Ohio State University Press, 2017), p. 76.
5 Digitized at: https://parker.stanford.edu/parker/catalog/sk095st1718
6 Russell, *Reading Ovid*, p. 215, citing the work of Michael Lapidge, David Howlett, and Sarah Zeiser.
7 Russell, *Reading Ovid*, p. 218.
8 *De Nuptiis Philologiae et Mercurii*, ed. Kopp, I.37, pp. 80–1; Stahl, trans., *Martianus Capella*, p. 19.
9 Martianus Capella, *De Nuptiis*, II.135–9, ed. Kopp, pp. 187–90; Stahl, trans., *Martianus Capella*, pp. 47–8.
10 For an influential example of this approach, see Proinsias Mac Cana, *The Mabinogi*, 2nd ed. (Cardiff: University of Wales Press, 1992). For a deconstruction of this approach, see, for example, Ronald Hutton, 'Medieval Welsh Literature and Pre-Christian Deities', *Cambrian Medieval Celtic Studies* 61 (2011): 57–85.
11 Some key works include Joan N. Radnor, 'Interpreting Irony in Medieval Celtic Narrative: The Case of *Culhwch ac Olwen*', *Cambridge Medieval Celtic Studies* 16 (1988): 41–59; Catherine McKenna, 'Revising Math: Kingship in the Fourth Branch of the *Mabinogi*', *Cambrian Medieval Celtic Studies* 46 (2003): 95–117; Catherine McKenna, 'The Colonization of Myth in *Branwen ferch Lŷr*', in *Myth in Celtic Literatures*, ed. J. Nagy, CSANA Yearbook 6 (Dublin: Four Courts Press, 2007), pp. 105–119. See also the review article by Paul Russell, 'Texts in Contexts: Recent Work on the *Mabinogi*', *Cambrian Medieval Celtic Studies* 45 (2003): 59–72.
12 Elizabeth Boyle, 'Allegory, the áes dána and the Liberal Arts in Medieval Irish Literature', in *Grammatica, Gramadach and Gramadeg: Vernacular Grammar and Grammarians in Medieval Ireland and Wales*, ed. D. Hayden and P. Russell (Amsterdam: John Benjamins, 2016), pp. 11–34.
13 The approach was indebted to Martin Irvine, *The Making of Textual Culture: 'Grammatica' and Literary Theory, 350–1100* (Cambridge: Cambridge University Press, 1994).
14 Paul Russell, 'Teaching between the Lines: Grammar and *Grammatica* in the Classroom in Early Medieval Wales', in Hayden and Russell, *Grammatica, Gramadach and Gramadeg*, pp. 133–48.
15 For a recent discussion of Irish evidence, see Deborah Hayden, 'A Medieval Irish Dialogue between Priscian and Donatus on the Categories of Questions', in *Dá dTrian Feasa Fiafraighidh: Essays on the Irish Grammatical and Metrical Tradition*, ed. G. Ó Riain (Dublin: Dublin Institute for Advanced Studies, 2017), pp. 67–93.
16 Russell, *Reading Ovid*, p. 221.

17 Robin Chapman Stacey, *Law and the Imagination in Medieval Wales* (Philadelphia: University of Pennsylvania Press, 2018), p. 55. The Parker collection, of course, contains the important Latin witness to medieval Welsh law; namely, Cambridge, Corpus Christi College, 454, which is digitized at: https://parker.stanford.edu/parker/catalog/nt577mx7842

18 Stacey, *Law and the Imagination*, p. 40.

19 Stacey, *Law and the Imagination*, pp. 30, 31.

20 At a late stage in the preparation of this piece (too late for the careful incorporation it deserves), a study by Paul Russell was published which adds an important new dimension to the consideration of metaphoric thinking in medieval Wales, primarily in relation to grammar but perhaps also to the architectural metaphors detected in the legal tracts by Chapman Stacey. See Paul Russell, 'Distinctions, Foundations and Steps: the Metaphors of the Grades of Comparison in Medieval Latin, Irish and Welsh Grammatical Texts', *Language and History* 63:1 (2020): 47–72.

17 Remediation and multilingualism in Corpus Christi College, 402

Carla María Thomas

Cambridge, Corpus Christi College, 402, which contains a copy of the *Ancrene Wisse*, invites the reader to think about the notion of remediation within the context of not only the digital humanities via reproduction and materiality but also multilingualism. As Parker on the Web presents it, the *Ancrene Wisse*, the only text in the manuscript, is a 'treatise on the religious life intended for anchoresses or nuns, written in the first half of the thirteenth century'.[1] It is not certain precisely where or when the work was created, but it comes from the West Midlands between 1200 and 1250. CCCC 402 is one of the earliest Middle English manuscripts to survive, then, and its dialect has been localized to northern Herefordshire or southern Shropshire.[2]

What makes the *Ancrene Wisse* particularly interesting is that it was translated not only into French but also into Latin. In the scholarship of post-Conquest England, many scholars tend to discuss translation and multilingualism as hierarchical with Latin and French at the top, and the English vernacular employed to reach a broader lay audience or to make political statements. In contrast, the transmission history of the *Ancrene Wisse* demonstrates how the work was translated into Latin in order to broaden the audience from the original intended readership of three sisters to include 'a wider audience of religious, including male and female regulars as well as recluses'.[3] Only one copy of the earlier French translation survives from about the beginning of the fourteenth century, and it was, according to Bella Millett, 'a close rendering of what appears to have been a good early text of the English version'.[4] However, later French translations also survive as compilations in three manuscripts, according to evidence in a table of contents preceding the *Vie de gent de religion*, which is 'based solely on *Ancrene Wisse*, using the Preface, Parts 2 and 3, and an extract from Part 4'.[5] As Millett discusses in her introduction, Nicholas Watson and Jocelyn Wogan-Browne have asserted that 'the "Compilation" was originally intended as "an expanded rewriting" of *Ancrene Wisse* as a whole, but was subsequently modified to accommodate more general pastoral aims' and only made use of the concluding sections of Parts 1 and 8.[6]

This 'rewriting' is significant because the 'Compilation' was meant for a more general audience even though the wording of the *Ancrene Wisse* itself was not necessarily altered to reflect this: the *Vie* was for 'all kinds of religious, of either sex', while the first two compilations targeted 'a general audience including both religious and laity'.[7] The *Ancrene Wisse* blurs our understanding of the literary and intellectual transference seen, analogously in a linguistic way, in the Latin-to-French-to-English translation history of the roughly contemporaneous *Brut* chronicle—first with Geoffrey of Monmouth, then Wace, and finally Laȝamon. Instead, this remediation demonstrates the messiness and inherent chaos of multilingualism: there is no one-way trajectory, but rather, an ongoing mutual exchange of knowledge. The language used in each textual manifestation of a given work is dictated by the needs of the intended audience, or as Bredehoft might put it, its 'local individuality'.[8] In this case, it was a matter of expanding not only to the Anglo-Norman laity but also to the religious literate in Latin, thus elevating a work in the English vernacular through an added layer of Latinity via translation. This is a characteristic of late Old English poetry, written in what Thornbury has dubbed the 'Southern mode', which extends to the West Midlands where both the *Ancrene Wisse* itself and this manuscript witness originated.[9]

However, the multilingualism of the *Ancrene Wisse* is not limited to this macro level of translation and transmission history, but also extends to the internal use of more than one language within the text itself. Aside from the Welsh borrowings of *cader* and *baban*, the languages employed—mostly Latin and some Hebrew—are even more interesting in the way that they are integrated or imbedded into the English vernacular. As Dorothy Kim notes in her forthcoming book *Jewish/Christian Entanglements:* Ancrene Wisse *and Its Material Worlds*, the *Ancrene Wisse* performs 'macaronic multilingualism'.[10] That is, the Latin is often translated very loosely or left to stand on its own, suggesting that its readers *could* comprehend it, which is ironic since the originally intended readers were women who, supposedly, could not read Latin.[11] Therefore, unlike other manuscripts in the Parker Library, such as Cambridge, Corpus Christi College, 144, which was used as a linguistic teaching tool in both dictionary and encyclopaedic form, the *Ancrene Wisse*'s audience would have needed to already know, or have some reading knowledge of, the languages with which it was presented. The macaronic multilingual text is akin to a multilingual person who can codeswitch between two or more languages, often 'extra or intra-sentential switching'—and it demands its reader be similarly multilingual.[12]

Kim is particularly interested in the kinds of translation that 'self-identify by utilizing the terms "eibresche" and "englisc"' in the *Ancrene Wisse* because of the way this form of translation

> ... strengthens the connection between Hebrew and English while problematizing the use of the intermediary language, Latin. It privileges the direct correlation between Hebrew and English by casting all of the most important Old Testament exemplars for the anchoritic reader in a Hebrew/English dialectic. Latin appears, on the other hand, in a series of anti-exemplars that diminish the importance of Latin in Hebrew name lists and that obfuscate the line that translating Hebrew to English generally followed.[13]

Here, then, the *Ancrene Wisse* is dismissing its Latin intermediary; it *seems* like mediation is not required between the Hebrew original and English translation. The macaronic multilingualism of the *Ancrene Wisse* thus brings me to remediation and hypermediacy by way of hyperreality. In his 2010 book, *Virtually Anglo-Saxon: Old Media, New Media, and Early Medieval Studies in the Late Age of Print*,[14] Martin Foys discusses digital facsimiles, specifically those of *mappae mundi*. Foys begins by invoking Jean Baudrillard's 'hyperreality', which he explains as that place 'where the sign of the real approaches the real itself, where the copy precedes the original and ultimately obscures it, and where reality is not reproduced but in fact produced by the signifying medium'.[15] In regards to the *language* of the *Ancrene Wisse*, I would consider the Hebrew-translated-into-English as the 'sign of the real'. For the post-Conquest English audience of the *Ancrene Wisse*, the original Hebrew is obscured, albeit mentioned briefly to ensure that it, like Latin, is also a sacred language. Thus, the English vernacular of the *Ancrene Wisse* may be seen to act as a copy that 'precedes the original', thereby manufacturing its own reality through 'the signifying medium'.

External to the content itself, the translations—the subsequent textual, material manifestations of the work—may be considered as a similar production rather than reproduction. Indeed, reconsidering the quotation above from Kim's book in which the work is dismissive of the intermediary Latin, what, then, do we make of Latin translations? Kim's interpretation would, essentially, render the vernacular work the opposite, with Latin violently insinuating itself into a content that does not seem to want it there—except for the several biblical and commentary excerpts scattered throughout the work. The moments in which the work refers to 'englisc', however, would not only be obscured by the productive signifying medium; indeed, English would be obliterated, completely erased. Granted, one would have to compare all the Latin translations with the English texts to prove this claim, which is beyond the scope of this chapter.

This notion of the hyperreal via multilingualism in content and transmission leads me to Jay David Bolter and Richard Grusin's notion of remediation and hypermediacy. They define 'remediation' as 'the formal logic by which new media refashion prior media forms'.[16] The immediate example would be digital images made available to us through digital archives, like Parker on the Web, which present us with new media that 'refashion' the 'prior media form' of the physical manuscript page. However, if we are thinking of 'media forms', then this logic should also extend, I think, to other 'forms' that we analyse in literary studies, such as verse. In fact, 'new media forms' should include languages as well—the transmission of the Latin and French translations of the vernacular English *Ancrene Wisse* should be seen as distinct forms from the latter, presented anew for different audiences in subsequent centuries that the author may never have even imagined when he set out to write down this rule for the sisters.

Remediation, however, is just 'one of the three traits of [Bolter and Grusin's] genealogy of new media', with the other two including 'hypermediacy' and '(transparent) immediacy'.[17] Hypermediacy is 'a style of visual representation whose goal is to remind the viewer of the medium', and it is considered a 'strategy of remediation'.[18] The third trait, and the second strategy of remediation, is (transparent) immediacy, which is 'a style of visual representation whose goal is to make the viewer forget the presence of the mechanism (canvas, photographic film, cinema, and so on) and believe that he is in the presence of the objects of representation'.[19] Similar to to-scale facsimiles in hardcopy before them, digital facsimiles often have one or more characteristics of immediacy, such as including the graphic of the turning page as we hit 'Next'. The sole purpose of such a visual is to further obscure the fact that the material artefact is not actually in our presence; we cannot hear the pages rustle, nor can we feel the suede-like or waxy texture of the membrane between our fingers, nor can we sneeze at the dust in nooks and crannies of cosy rare book archives. The illusion is entertaining, even aesthetically pleasing, but it adds nothing but obfuscation to one's experience of the digital reproduction of the 'real'. Instead, it produces something entirely different.

However, digital technologies can break us out of the linearity of reproduction if they can embrace the hyperreal and allow the reproduction to be something altogether new, to truly remediate the manuscript image in such a way that gives us access to knowledge that any medieval reader of a single manuscript never could have imagined while simultaneously and overtly acknowledging the manuscript's novelty and differences. Through the collaboration of Parker on the Web and Mirador, we have a glimpse of what else is possible. As Bredehoft reminds us, many digital editions still reinforce the linearity of reading a manuscript or printed text not only by our desire to read them textually but also by the very nature of coding, which requires linearity; Bredehoft refers to the 'remarkable and innovative' part of a digital text that is the 'invisibility or unseeability of its physical manifestations'.[20] However, with viewers like Mirador where we can import numerous manuscripts at once, the process necessarily breaks out of the linear—we are no longer necessarily reading the *text*, but maybe we are seeing the text. For example, such non-linearity would provide the opportunity to discover more easily deviations in subsequent reproductions of a work, like the different copies of the late twelfth-century *Poema Morale* or the way that language is deployed in the various copies and translations/ remediations of the *Ancrene Wisse*. The sort of seeing and reading made available in Mirador's digital space is radically different from the linearity of reading a simple printed edition or a digital one that replicates the ideologies and logic of the printed medium. And, perhaps, it brings viewers back to an experience more akin to reading a medieval manuscript, particularly those that contain decorated initials, miniatures, or other illuminations, which would encourage a non-linear engagement with the 'real'.

The newly developed digital tools that allow us to look at more than one digitized manuscript at a time and mark it up is a revolutionary way to do manuscript studies. On the level of multilingual studies, for example, the side-by-side comparison of the multilingual manuscripts of the *Ancrene Wisse* would better aid an endeavour to understand, sociolinguistically, what happens when an English text, which is also a macaronic multilingual text, suddenly switches its linguistic medium. The fact that the *Ancrene Wisse* is translated into French or Latin, not to mention in pieces rather than in its entirety, and compiled alongside other non-English devotional texts presents an extraordinary level of remediation. By comparing these disembodied or disassociated parts with the earlier English iterations in a fluid, flexible medium like Mirador, scholars could gain greater insight to the ways in which people in post-Conquest England navigated, understood, and lived with multilingualism. If the scribe of CCCC 402 felt no need to distinguish between the English vernacular and Latin in their writing of the *Ancrene Wisse*—supported by the fact that none of the non-English words and phrases is rubricated, as was the tradition of sermon collections in this period—then juxtaposing the English texts with later translations would help us understand the multilingual and multicultural milieu in which such a work was created and transmitted.

One of the first things Dorothy Kim mentions in the introduction of her book is the distinctly multilingual, multicultural, and multiracial environment of the Welsh Marches in which the *Ancrene Wisse* arose. Not only was there English, but there was also Irish, Welsh, Hebrew, Anglo-Norman, Latin, Flemish, and Breton. As her study persuasively demonstrates, the allosemitism of the author behind the *Ancrene Wisse*, which was likely not isolated simply to him but a symptom of his localized environment, is evidenced in his use of English and Hebrew as surreptitiously dismissive of Latin, and the work draws little to no influence from the Irish, Welsh, or French literary traditions and lexicon.[21] Qualitatively, Hebrew carried more significance for the author than Latin, even though the latter was more important *quantitatively* as the *lingua franca* and likely the language of most of the author's sources. Nevertheless, just as CCCC 402 is remediated in pixels and source code for anyone viewing the manuscript with Mirador, so too was the secular rule for the anchoresses, appearing, first, in vernacular English and then remediated into French and Latin.

Remediation, I believe, is an important concept for medieval manuscript studies, and not just in the ways I have shown. Even if one work is transmitted over the centuries in the same language, as O'Brien O'Keeffe and others have demonstrated, each particular manifestation of the work within an individual community is a slightly different production, not reproduction, of the real.[22] Additionally, most texts do not survive in single-text manuscripts, like CCCC 402, but rather with a variety of other texts alongside them. Each variation, addition, omission, splicing, and rearranging of works produces a wholly new literary text that is related to but distinct from the mystical *ur*-text. Then, consider the complexity of remediated texts via translation and different physical media—first through print, moving from parchment to paper, mass production of critical editions, early digital editions, and now manipulatable images of more than one manuscript at a time with developing viewers like Mirador with IIIF and the algorithms behind such platforms. Approaching manuscript studies in conjunction with the digital and multilingual through the lens of remediation, hyperreality, and immediacy is useful for tying all these threads together and to arrive at a clearer idea of a culture that is remediated endlessly.

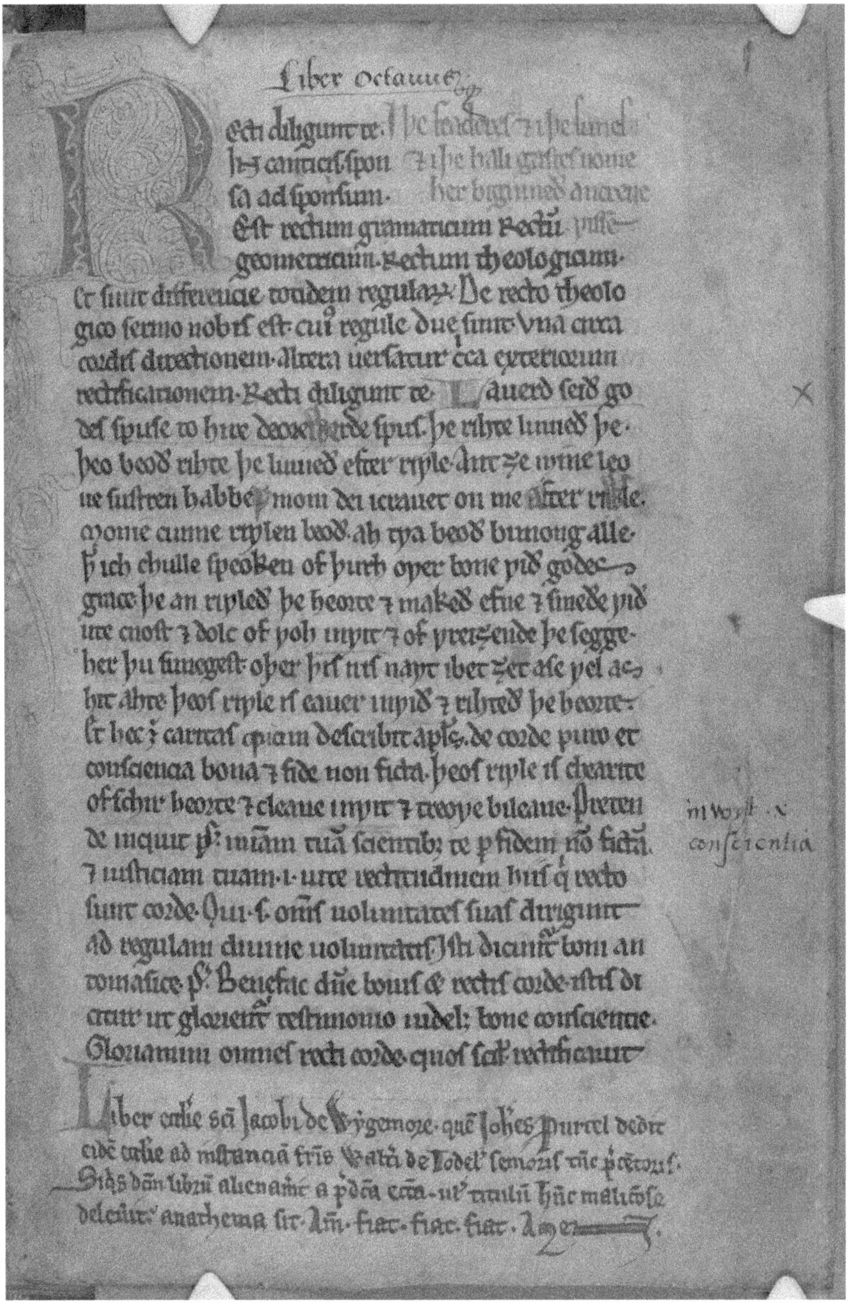

Liber Octauus

Figure 17.1 The Parker Library, Corpus Christi College, Cambridge, MS 402, f. 1r.

Notes

1 'Cambridge, Corpus Christi College, 402: *Ancrene Wisse*', Parker Library on the Web: https://parker.stanford.edu/parker/catalog/zh635rv2202 <accessed 23 March 2018>.

2 Bella Millett, *Ancrene Wisse, the Katherine Group, and the Wooing Group* (Cambridge: Cambridge University Press, 1996), p. 11, fn 7.

3 Bella Millett, ed., *Ancrene Wisse: A Corrected Edition of the Text in Cambridge, Corpus Christi College, MS 402 with Variants from Other Manuscripts*, Early English Text Society os 325 (Oxford: Oxford University Press, 2005), p. xviii.

4 Millett, *Ancrene Wisse: A Corrected Edition*, p. xv.

5 Millett, *Ancrene Wisse: A Corrected Edition*, p. xxiii.

6 Millett, *Ancrene Wisse: A Corrected Edition*. For Watson and Wogan-Brown's essay, see 'The French of England: The *Compileison, Ancrene Wisse*, and the Idea of Anglo-Norman', *Journal of Romance Studies* 4.3 (2004): 35–59.

7 Millett, *Ancrene Wisse: A Corrected Edition*, p. xxiii.

8 Thomas Bredehoft, *The Visible Text: Textual Production and Reproduction from Beowulf to Maus*, Oxford Textual Perspectives (Oxford: Oxford University Press, 2014), p. 67.

9 For more on the Southern mode, which did not rely upon translation *per se* so much as *seeming* like an Old English poem *could* have originated from a Latin source text, providing a sheen of Latinity to an otherwise vernacular product, see Emily V. Thornbury, *Becoming a Poet in Anglo-Saxon England* (Cambridge: Cambridge University Press, 2014), pp. 223–38.

10 Dorothy Kim, *Jewish/Christian Entanglements: Ancrene Wisse and Its Material Worlds* (Philadelphia University of Pennsylvania Press, forthcoming), p. 57.

11 Kim, *Jewish/Christian Entanglements*, p. 57.

12 Kim, *Jewish/Christian Entanglements*, n. 167.

13 Kim, *Jewish/Christian Entanglements*, p. 82.

14 Martin Foys, *Virtually Anglo-Saxon: Old Media, New Media, and Early Medieval Studies in the Late Age of Print* (Gainesville: University of Florida Press, 2010).

15 Foys, *Virtually Anglo-Saxon*, p. 14.

16 Jay David Bolter and Richard Grusin, *Remediation: Understanding New Media* (Cambridge, MA: MIT Press, 1999), p. 273.

17 Bolter and Grusin, *Remediation*, p. 273.

18 Bolter and Grusin, *Remediation*, p. 272.

19 Bolter and Grusin, *Remediation*, p. 272.

20 Bredehoft, *Visible Text*, p. 158.

21 Kim, *Jewish/Christian Entanglements*, p. 5.

22 See, for example, Katherine O'Brien O'Keeffe, *Visible Song: Transitional Literacy in Old English Verse*, Cambridge Studies in Anglo-Saxon England (Cambridge: Cambridge University Press, 1990).

Part 5

Forms of reading

18 Living with books in early medieval England

Solomon and Saturn, bibliophilia, and the globalist Red Book of Darley

Erica Weaver

> For Books are not absolutely dead things … I know they are as lively, and as vigorously productive, as those fabulous Dragons teeth; and being sown up and down, may chance to spring up armed men.
>
> John Milton[1]

How did tenth-century readers describe the experience of reading—or merely holding—books? The related early medieval experience of education has received much more attention, with an important new study by Irina Dumitrescu that illuminates the emotionally fraught and sometimes troubling relationships that subsisted between teachers and students.[2] In this chapter, I look to the Red Book of Darley (Cambridge, Corpus Christi College, 422) as a window into the broader book culture that subsumed them.[3] Rather than tracing the bonds shared by schoolmasters and pupils or patrons and poets, then, I trace the similarly intimate, if occasionally more private, affective entanglements of early medieval English readers and their manuscripts, as embodied by the images and poems in CCCC 422.

Interpersonal associations no doubt filtered into the reading habits of early medieval readers in important ways, but the individual, sometimes emotional experiences of readers who coveted books *even when they did not read them* has been much less studied. Indeed, even as we have examined our own sensual and affective responses to medieval manuscripts as haptic objects,[4] we have paid less attention to the abstract bibliophilia of their makers, who envisioned Bede reclining on pillows surrounded by books and revelled in images of themselves seated cross-legged amid tottering stacks of writing, as in Byrhtferth of Ramsey's *Enchiridion* and in *Solomon and Saturn II*, respectively—both images that I will return to at the end of this chapter.

Of course, William H. Sherman and others have helpfully examined readers' marks, from loopy signatures, pen trials, and marginal notes to scribal reworkings of texts and full-page self-portraits of medieval and early modern owners and copyists,[5] and early English manuscripts with known makers and owners such as Ælfwine's Prayerbook and the Eadwine Psalter have drawn plenty of attention.[6] Indeed, 1990 ushered in the broadened approach to codicology known as the New Philology, which stipulates that literary texts

exist within their material contexts, so that the physical layout of the book—
its illumination, script, marginal notes, and surrounding texts—constitutes the
text at hand.[7] So, just as scribal errors can reveal points of confusion, marginal additions can also testify to the way certain texts were received at various points in time.

Yet, manuscript studies has taken less stock of the kinds of entanglements
that have recently come to the fore in book history writ large, as exemplified
most notably by Leah Price's *How to Do Things with Books in Victorian
Britain*—that is, the study of 'bookish transactions' that do not necessarily
involve reading or writing at all, such as Victorian women matching their
vade mecums to their gowns.[8] Or, for that matter, late fifteenth-century
women, for whom beautiful books could serve as both fashionable accessories
and mother–daughter heirlooms, as in the 1496 will in which a Lincolnshire
father prescribed 'that my doughter lady ffitzhugh have a boke of gold,
enameled, that was my wiffes, whiche she was wounte to were'.[9]

To be sure, such literary accessorizing doesn't foreclose actual reading.
Moreover, we certainly have our own forms of not reading—most common
among them the tendency to live alongside aspirational bedside reading piles
or the desperate efforts put forth by many of us to read texts that continually
escape us, whether due to linguistic barriers, the lack of a modern edition, or
general inscrutability as in the famously unreadable Voynich manuscript with
its unique, perpetually beguiling alphabet.[10] As Amy Hungerford has
observed, our present-day experience of reading is predominantly one of
never being able to read 'it all'.[11]

But here, I do not mean failure or inability to read per se. Nor do I (or
Price) have in mind 'bookish transactions' in the form of the embodied traces
of reading that mark the pages of medieval manuscripts, such as the enlarged
illustrations of Christ's side wound, which have been almost rubbed away by
medieval devotees,[12] or the less glamorous but equally bodily testaments of
dirty and sometimes ragged corners, which record repeated skin-on-skin contact between sheets of parchment and their readers' thumbs and index fingers
in the turning of much-loved pages.

I am thinking instead of less readerly marks, which show books forming a part
of non-literary life: the incisions and burns that demonstrate that the Exeter
Book served as a cutting board, a kind of trivet for a hot poker, and a coaster as
well as a *mycel Englisc boc be gehwilcum þingum on leoðwisum geworht*, 'large
English book about diverse topics written in verse'.[13] Or the marginal note
recounting the ransoming of the Codex Aureus *mid clæne golde*, 'with pure gold',
and what it says about the trade value of gold-flecked parchment folded between
gem-encrusted boards.[14] And even the broader associations of the embodied
letters preserved in CCCC 422 and now widely consultable in Parker on the
Web—those moments of bookish encounters that move beyond 'merely reading',
to borrow a phrase from Kinohi Nishikawa.[15] Indeed, the aforementioned will is
notable in that it bequeaths a book that is distinguishable not by its contents or
subject matter, but by its *de luxe* cover and memorial significance.

In this chapter, I will thus read the so-called Red Book of Darley as a record of early medieval readerly experience as well as a record of the sometimes equally enthralling experience of not reading but of coming close, not necessarily to contact relics or to lavishly illuminated codices but merely to stacks of philosophical treatises and theological tractates—that is, the cosy comfort of being surrounded by books even if only imaginatively or aspirationally, which is, after all, also the experience of perusing Parker on the Web. As I will argue, CCCC 422 accordingly offers a case study for early medieval thinking about books themselves and the ways in which they could shape the lives of the people who lived alongside them—as well as a testament to the global investments of early medieval English bibliophiles, who imaginatively assembled *larcræft* ('knowledge') from far-flung libraries in Libya, Greece, and India, as in the Old English poems now known as *Solomon and Saturn I* and *II*, which form a part of CCCC 422's decidedly global entanglements. Indeed, I argue that CCCC 422 offers a fascinating lens into early medieval thinking about textuality, reading, attention, and book culture broadly conceived.

CCCC 422: Provenance and contents

Consisting today of two parts, CCCC 422 had been joined together by the twelfth century. The first section (pp. 1–26) was copied in the mid-tenth century and contains—to continue in the affective vein—one of the most delightful clusters of Old English texts: a series of dialogues, partially in poetry and partially in prose, between Solomon, the famously learned King of Israel, and the enthusiastic bookworm Saturn, a Chaldean prince. This is a fascinating early English innovation, which reshapes the long-enduring Solomon and Marcolf tradition for a North Atlantic audience.[16] In the sixteenth century, likely at the behest of Archbishop of Canterbury Matthew Parker, this portion was gathered together at the beginning of the manuscript, where it remains, but it initially served as a substantial set of flyleaves for what is today the second part of CCCC 422 (pp. 27–586) but may more accurately be thought of as the original core of the book: the missal and related texts, which give the manuscript its larger nickname as 'the Red Book of Darley', because of its later provenance at the church of St Helen, Darley Dale, in Derbyshire. A sixteenth-century addition on the last page records this moniker as 'the rede boke of darleye in peake in darbyshire', relating that 'This booke was sumtime had in such reverence in darbieshire that it was comonlie beleved that whosoever should sweare untruelie upon this booke should run madd'.[17] As Daniel Anlezark observes, this manuscript is thus 'exceptional among Anglo-Saxon books, in that it is known to have spent the later Middle Ages in a parish, apparently passing during the Reformation period into the custody of a parishioner, "Margaret Rollesleye widow"', who testifies to a mid-sixteenth-century female readership.[18] Still later, the manuscript was given to Matthew Parker, who bequeathed it to Corpus Christi College in 1575.

The manuscript's earlier provenance is less clear, although the two parts had been bound together by the twelfth century—and likely by the end of the tenth. It is uncertain where the Solomon and Saturn material was initially copied, although as John Mitchell Kemble observed, 'It consists of twenty-six pages, written in a close, beautiful, and, as it appears, female hand'.[19] For 'close' and 'beautiful', M. R. James substitutes 'small', 'round', and 'flat-topped', repeating that it is a 'hand which Kemble conjectured to be that of a woman'.[20] This speculation about the manuscript's 'female hand' is unsurprisingly unverifiable (and, presumably, unlikely), but it provides an important reminder that even the seemingly-detached eye of the palaeographer can be seduced by a 'close, beautiful' hand in ways that are now uncomfortably gendered.[21] More recently, Daniel Anlezark has persuasively argued that the texts that now appear at the beginning of CCCC 422 were originally composed in Glastonbury in the 930s, when the monastery was home to the circle of early Benedictine reformers, including Dunstan (the future Archbishop of Canterbury) and Æthelwold (the future Bishop of Winchester).[22] Indeed, Anlezark posits that the runes in CCCC 422 are 'likely to be a symptom of transmission in circles interested in alternative alphabetical systems'.[23]

Due to some references in the liturgical calendar, the missal portion may be securely ascribed to Sherborne *c*. 1061. It is possible that the conjoined manuscript may have made its way to Worcester by the late tenth or early eleventh century, which would let it cross paths with some of the Old English texts in CCCC 367, which Peter Stokes examines in greater detail in Chapter 7 of this volume. This bit of the manuscript's travels relies on similarities between an excommunication formula that was added into the margins of CCCC 422 and a contemporary Worcester manuscript, however, so it is suggestive but by no means certain.[24]

The manuscript's two sections have traditionally been viewed as an inappropriate pair, with scholars dismissing the Solomon and Saturn material as an unsuitably superstitious accompaniment to the liturgical material, but this unfairly maligns the highly learned and altogether utterly applicable poetry and prose—as well as the complex interplay of the manuscript's texts and images, which inform each other across the codex.[25] Moreover, the missal section contains a range of texts that may be productively read alongside *Solomon and Saturn I* and *II*, including computistical material, prognostics, a liturgical calendar, and Paschal tables in Old English and Latin, followed by the Order of the Mass, along with ornamental initials and two decidedly textual illustrations from the life of Christ: one depicting Christ enthroned among angels, holding an open book (p. 52), and the other at the Crucifixion (p. 53) as Figure 18.1.

Facing each other, these images introduce the Order of the Mass. The first forms a part of the Preface of the Mass, with the text fitted into and around the mandorla, and the second fits into the historiated initial 'T' that opens the Canon of the Mass and here serves as the cross on which Christ is crucified.

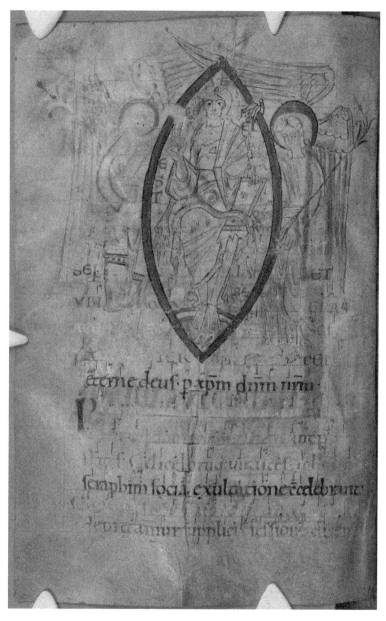

Figure 18.1a The Parker Library, Corpus Christi College, Cambridge, MS 422, p. 52.

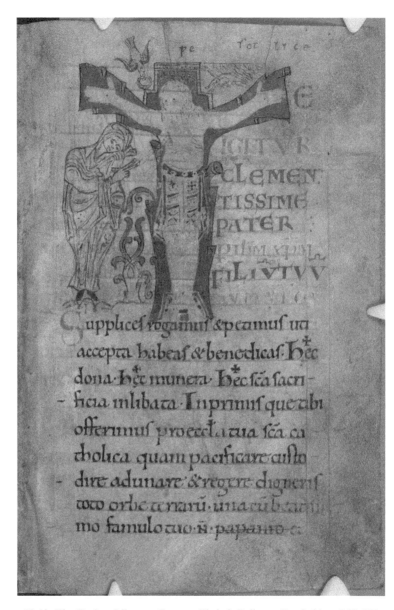

Figure 18.1b The Parker Library, Corpus Christi College, Cambridge, MS 422, p. 53.

As Catherine E. Karkov has observed,

> the way in which text and image are brought together in these two drawings is highly unusual, if not unprecedented … the opening lines of text function as a part of the images, an aspect of the manuscript that is every bit as unusual as its combination of texts or the iconography of its drawings.[26]

Together with the personified letters of the Lord's Prayer in *Solomon and Saturn I*, these illustrations are particularly helpful for thinking through textual embodiment and the experience of living with books in early medieval England.

Embodied letters

The idea of the word made flesh, which comes to dwell among its readers as an embodied presence, of course descends from the Gospel of John, with its opening declaration that *On frymðe wæs word, and þæt word wæs mid Gode, and þæt word wæs God*, 'In the beginning was the word, and the word was with God, and that word was God.'[27] Ælfric of Eynsham muses on this corporeal manifestation of the divine word, relating that the shepherds notified of the birth of Christ agreed among themselves, *Uton gefaran to Bethleem, and geseon þæt word þe geworden is, and God us geswutelode*, 'Let us go to Bethlehem, and see the word that has come to be, and that God has made known to us.'[28] With his wordplay on the *word* that is *geworden*, Ælfric emphasizes the overlap of language and embodiment, naming and incarnation.

This is precisely the duality that the Red Book of Darley Crucifixion enacts, with its conflation of text and image rendering the same lines of ink both the initial 't' of 'te igitur' and the cross itself. Here, the letter forms an essential part of both a living text and the holy rood at the centre of Christian salvation, embedding Christ's crucified body into literary experience and vice versa. And this conflation resounds throughout the manuscript as a whole, for the illustrations at the beginning of the Mass enact the same textual presence of the runes in *Solomon and Saturn I*, the first text in CCCC 422, which likewise models this phenomenon of the religious text that crystalizes as a physical image projected into the lives of its readers.[29] Indeed, in both instances, the conflation of text and image is crucial. Moreover, both the Crucifixion image and the runic letters of *Solomon and Saturn I* transform the practice of reading into a practice of summoning and encountering bodies.

The poem stages an extended dialogue on the powers of the *Pater Noster* or Lord's Prayer, which is presented as a text with talismanic protective properties that allow the runic letters of the Latin prayer's opening words to take shape as soldiers that beat demonic assailants back into Hell. As Solomon says, *þæt gepalmtwiguda Pater Noster … morðor gefilleð, / adwæsceð deofles fyr, Dryhtnes onæleð … heregeatowe wegeð* (lines 39–52b, 'That palm-twigged Pater

Noster ... fells murder, puts out the devil's fire, ignites the Lord's ... it bears battle-gear').[30] In addition, it restores the mind of its reciter, fascinatingly making the prayer-within-the-poem an antidote to the broader manuscript's later purported ability to make the foresworn 'run madd'.[31] Throughout, *Solomon and Saturn I* presents the *Pater Noster* as a physical, bookish presence. As Katherine O'Brien O'Keeffe has demonstrated, it must be read directly from the manuscript—rather than heard aloud—for the poem's runic letter forms to be legible, since they are embedded in the page but not the poem's metre.[32] Moreover, like a book, *Godes cwide* (line 63a, 'the word of God') is *gylden* (line 63a, 'golden'), *gimmum astæned* (line 63b, 'set with gems'), and *hafað sylfren leaf* (line 64a, 'has silver leaves'). It is the ultimate image of the word made flesh, taking shape not in the body of Christ as at the outset of the Mass but as a magnificent tome.

Even the opening letters of the prayer, which are given in both their runic and Roman forms, come to life as soldiers that resemble their inky forms. 'P' and its runic counterpart peorth, for instance, enter the fray bearing weapons that resemble the Roman letter form: *hafað guðmæcga gierde lange, / gyldene gade, ond a ðone grimman feond / swiðmod sweopað* (lines 90–92a, 'that warrior holds a long staff, a golden goad, and that strong-minded one eternally scourges the fierce enemy'). The letter P's long ascender thus becomes a long staff, and its rounded bow a goad.[33] Similarly embodied (and armed) paired letters follow suit, spelling out *pater noster qui es in caelis*, 'Our Father, who art in Heaven'—the opening words to the prayer. As the poem proceeds, then, the runic and Roman letters join the fray two by two, stabbing the demon, grabbing him by his feet, and firing arrows into his hair. *Solomon and Saturn I* thus becomes a fearsome sort of pop-up book, wherein the letters leap out from between the pages and wage war. While Milton may have meant 'not absolutely dead' playfully, then, his notion that books are 'as lively, and as vigorously productive, as those fabulous Dragons teeth' that, at least under Medea's direction, 'may chance to spring up armed men' is vividly enacted in *Solomon and Saturn I*.[34]

The Old English *Prose Pater Noster Dialogue*, which follows *Solomon and Saturn I* in CCCC 422, likewise gives the prayer bodily form, presenting another skirmish between shape-shifting demonic forces, the struggling reader, and the Lord's Prayer, which is again armed to the teeth.[35] In response to Saturn's opening question, *Ac hu moniges bleos bið ðæt deofol ond se Pater Noster ðonne hie betwih him gewinnað?* (lines 2–3, 'So, how many shapes will the devil and the Pater Noster take when they when they struggle against each other?'), Solomon confidently answers *þritiges bleos* (line 5, 'thirty shapes'), before describing each of them in elaborate detail. As Solomon notes, for instance, *Pater Noster hafað gylden heafod ond sylfren feax* (line 53, 'The Pater Noster has a golden head and silver hair'), echoing the golden coloring and silver pages of the bookishly embodied *Pater Noster* in *Solomon and Saturn I*. Rather than a gem-studded codex, however, the prayer is here imagined as an enormous head with long, luxuriantly thick hair, for, as

Solomon assures Saturn, *ðeah ðe ealle eorðan wæter sien gemenged wið ðam heofonlicum wætrum uppe on ane ædran, ond hit samlice rinan onginne eall middangerd, mid eallum his gesceaftum, he mæg under ðæs Pater Nosters feaxe anum locce drige gestandan* (lines 53–6, 'even if all of earth's waters were mingled with the heavenly waters on high in one channel, and it began to rain in unison, the whole world, with all its creatures, could stand dry under a single lock of the Pater Noster's hair'). This protective ability further ties the Solomon and Saturn material to the devotional images that initiate the Order of the Mass in CCCC 422. As Ælfric explains in *De auguriis* ('On Auguries'), the cross was similarly thought to be capable of banishing demons, with images of the Crucifixion offering protection to their viewers, so the *Pater Noster* reworkings and the illustrations could serve a similar purpose in projecting words—and words made flesh—into physical space so as to form a protective barrier for their viewers.[36]

Although the spiky combat letters may seem somewhat unsettling, these are thus ultimately texts about the comforting presence of books, whose use far surpasses acts of reading or not reading. Saturn hopes to be overwhelmed or daunted by the Lord's Prayer, describing his experiences with having *onlocen* (line 3a, 'unlocked') books from around the world as a preamble that has prepared him to encounter the prayer in a more bodily, immediate way (lines 1-3). This image of books locking and unlocking knowledge is a fitting tribute to the now freely available Parker on the Web, since both Solomon and Saturn poems are heavily invested in what we might think of as open-access textual circulation, but it is also a testament to the power of books and the texts they contain. Like *Solomon and Saturn II*, which I will discuss in the following section, they are texts of comfort and protection, for which the vivid imagery and violent scenes ultimately offered solace and safety.

As the Solomon and Saturn texts suggest, then, early medieval readers imbued their books with a powerful form of efficacy. Indeed, when beset by demons, early medieval saints would start reciting the *Psalms* and *poof!* The demons would immediately disperse.[37] *Solomon and Saturn I* provides a poetic analogue. As James Paz puts it, the poem explicitly 'uses the Pater Noster to show how literary knowledge can be made effective in the world'.[38] In this way, it resembles not only the texts of the liturgy but also the Old English metrical charms, which Paz argues were 'not simply meant to be pleasing on the ear but composed in order to enact a change in the world and, in many cases, to actively coerce nonhuman entities into a response'.[39] Indeed, as scholars such as Marie Nelson and Paz have shown, the charms provide a particularly rich analogue to the Solomon and Saturn poems, sometimes even requiring would-be healers to recite the Lord's Prayer or the names of the Seven Sleepers of Ephesus, mobilizing religious texts as healing incantations that were both physically and mentally restorative—the ultimate performatives in J. L. Austin's sense of the term.[40]

Encompassing charms for protection from a swarm of bees, charms for if your cattle fall ill, or if your land is barren, or your body wasted by illness, these remedies constitute the earliest surviving medical texts from northern Europe, preserving Byzantine, Greek, Roman, North African, and native British practices. Like the Solomon and Saturn texts, they feature lore drawn from across the Mediterranean from the third to the ninth centuries, weaving early medieval England into a broader culture of bookish scientific exchange. *Solomon and Saturn II* likewise promises far-flung knowledge, introducing Saturn as a world traveller, who has assembled what I like to think of as a kind of early medieval world literature anthology. In pursuit of books on books from across the globe, he:

> Land eall geondhwearf, /Indea mere, East Corsias, /Persea rice, Palestinion, /Niniven ceastre, ond Norð Predan, /Meda maððumselas, Marculfes eard, /Saulus rice, swa he suð ligeð /ymb Geador norð, /Filistina flet, fæsten Creta, /wudu Egipta, wæter Mathea, /cludas Coreffes, Caldea rice, /Creca cræftas, cynn Arabia, /lare Libia, lond Syria, /Pitðinia, Buðanasan, Pamhpilia, Pores gemære, /Macedonia, Mesopotamie, /Cappadocia, Cristes eðel /Hieryhco, Galilea, Hierusalem.

> travelled through all the lands: the Indian ocean; East Cossias; the Persians' kingdom; Palestine; the city Nineveh; and the North Parthians; the Medes' precious halls; Marcolf's land; Saul's kingdom, where it lies near Gilboa to the south and near Gadara to the north; the Philistines' home; the stronghold of the Cretans; the woods of the Egyptians; the waters of the Midians; Mount Horeb; the realm of the Chaldeans; the Greeks' skills; the people of Arabia; the learning of Libya; the land of Syria; Bythinia; Bashan; Pamphilia; the edge of Porus; Macedonia; Mesopotamia; Cappadocia; Christ's homeland, Jericho, Galilee, Jerusalem. (lines 7b–23)

Here, it is interesting to note that, testifying to a similarly expansive network of trade and travel, some of the herbs mentioned in the Old English charms were only available around the Mediterranean, with directions for the use of ingredients traded from distant areas, including frankincense, pepper, silk, ginger, and myrrh—much as the Saturn of *Solomon and Saturn I* boasts that he has read books from Libya, Greece, and India.

Yet, the charms relate not only to *Solomon and Saturn I* but also to the prognostics, which are preserved elsewhere in the Red Book of Darley and provide another intriguing point of overlap that suggests that CCCC 422 was assembled as a devotional miscellany combining scientific and literary learning—or, the general fruits of book culture—from around the world. While I do not wish to argue for any intentionality in their inclusion in CCCC 422, I thus argue that the Solomon and Saturn material is of a piece with the devotional practice embodied by the missal and the prognostics. Rather than superstitious texts that were at odds with the devotional material of the liturgical calendar and the Mass, the Solomon and Saturn triad, prognostics, and other texts were highly learned works, representing cutting-edge research brought to England from far beyond its borders. Here, I advocate for the globalism of the Old English Solomon and Saturn texts—and thus the globalism of the Red Book of Darley as a whole and the bibliophilia to which it testifies.[41]

Getting cosy

While these books are, of course, most helpful when they are actually read, *Solomon and Saturn II* also underscores the cheering prospect of a stack of manuscripts and the ways in which books give us pleasure even when we merely anticipate reading them. As I have argued above, the Red Book of Darley was a highly learned, worldly manuscript, but it is also a manuscript that is resolutely engaged with the comforts of staying home surrounded by books. Focusing on the affective benefits of books, Solomon declares, *Bec sindon breme, bodiað geneahhe / weotodne willan ðam ðe wiht hygeð, / gestrangað hie ond gestaðeliað staðolfæstne geðoht, / amyrgað modsefan manna gehwylces / of ðreamedlan ðisses lifes* (*SolSatII*, lines 60–64a, 'Books are glorious, they instantly make known a sure will to the one who attends [to them]. They strengthen and firm up unwavering thought, cheer the mind of each man against the anxieties of this life'). Books are restorative and strengthening. They act *geneahhe* ('instantly'). And, like the divine word made flesh, they make things known when they come to dwell among us.

Moreover, as the *Solomon and Saturn* poet relates and as Rossell Hope Robbins has argued, manuscripts are also sources of true mirth, encompassing alchemists' 'hocus-pocus' rolls, which were sometimes over 20 feet long and 3 feet wide; coaching in how 'to make a woman daunce naked'; and instructions for a number of practical jokes among a wide array of other topics.[42] Ultimately, books of all kinds offer *hælo hyðe, ðam ðe hie lufað* (*SolSatII*, line 68, 'the harbor of salvation to those who love them'). They are not only sources of protection—even, for early medieval believers, salvation—but also of humbler comfort and nearer harbours. As the later English poet John Skelton remarked, the sight of a particularly well-bound book 'would have made a man whole that had been right sickly'.[43]

There is something about their presence in our physical space that is, itself, a consolation, so in closing, I turn now to thinking about the affective dimensions of their digital surrogates. Whereas *Solomon and Saturn II* revels in stacks of books that cheer all those who live alongside them, *Solomon and Saturn I* and the illustrations of Christ in majesty and Christ crucified imagine texts themselves as physical presences, with a string of letters conjuring and themselves becoming a series of firmly embodied, anthropomorphized beings. CCCC 422 thus provides a number of particularly-striking analogues for the relationship between a material object and its surrogates, whether they take shape in our imaginations or on our screens. Indeed, *Solomon and Saturn I* imagines itself as a corporeal presence in the same way that we must remember that our flattened screens are stand-ins for sometimes-heavy, often unwieldy objects. The old continuum between orality and literacy, or between the page and the 'real' embodiment of the text in the lives of its readers, is here echoed in the new continuum between material codex and digital facsimile.

Because I have not yet had a chance to examine the codex in-person even though I have examined its edited texts many times, I had not realized just how badly damaged, battered, and generally worn the opening to *Solomon and Saturn I* is until zooming in on its ragged margins and battered opening page in the digital viewer. Here, our capacity to zoom and scroll through the Parker database brings its own joy—not in the physical act of actually touching the past, but in the pleasure of the highly technical, of the scientific and exact practice of looking closely, with better lighting and more intense magnification than we could easily secure in a reading room. And so, instead of close reading, here we have a kind of close looking that, in turn, reminds us not only of the text/image synthesis in CCCC 422 but also of all the earlier readers of the manuscript, who marked these poems not with any marginal notes or *signes-de-renvoi* but with their sweat and the smoke from their fires.

The digital simulacrum is thus somewhat paradoxically itself a reminder of the bookishness of the Red Book of Darley and of the ways in which it was stained and passed about by the readers whose use has all but erased the text. Indeed, the first folio is in M. R. James' terms 'very illegible', with the opening of *Solomon and Saturn I* usually recovered from Cambridge Corpus Christi College, 41, where the first 95 lines of the poem were added into the margins of the Old English *Bede*—two very different textual records that we don't get a sense of at all when reading the poem in a modern edition but which we can conveniently unite both in the reading room and on our screens.[44] Moreover, with Parker on the Web, we see James' catalogue description overlaid on the folio as a digital annotation that fuses text and paratext.

Even as Parker on the Web has helped to give me a better sense of the text as it actually circulated across hundreds of years, however, I still have no idea how large CCCC 422 is and certainly not how heavy it would be to hold it in my hands, or perhaps in my lap—something that I was reminded of when rereading *Solomon and Saturn II* with its manuscript context in mind. Towards the end of the poem, Saturn recalls witnessing earlier debates about fate and foreknowledge, remembering how *sægdon me geara / Filistina witan, ðonne we on geflitum sæton, / bocum tobræddon ond on bearm legdon, / meðelcwidas mengdon, moniges fengon* (lines 252b–55, 'they told me long ago, the wise men of the Philistines, when we sat in debate, piled up books and spread them in our laps, interposed our comments, took up many topics'). The intimacy of this moment, as they sit talking together beneath a pile of books exchanging ideas, perhaps roughly turning the pages or gesturing wildly in their excitement, is a poignant reminder of the lives of early medieval books as they were imagined in active use and circulation. It is also a

Cambridge, Corpus Christi College, MS 422: The Red Book of Darley.

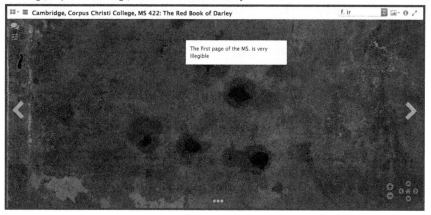

Figure 18.2 Screenshot of CCCC 422 and Parker annotations from M. R. James.

reminder of another bookish dream from the early Middle Ages: that of abundance—of books numerous enough to be stacked in piles and of books spread open and texts circulating widely and freely. In actuality, the typical early medieval 'library' could be contained in a single trunk, and Michael Lapidge has surmised that 'when an Anglo-Saxon scholar wished to consult a book', he didn't so much sequester himself in a wood-panelled room as 'he got down on his hands and knees and rummaged around in the chest until he came upon the book he required'.[45]

Whether in fantasy or in actuality, however, wise people come together around books. Similarly, Byrhtferth of Ramsey envisions Bede *fægere gebolstrod*, 'pleasantly propped up with pillows', and enjoins his students and readers, *We lætað þæt se getiddusta wer her sitte, nu we his gewritu smeagað*, 'Let's pretend that this most skilled person is sitting here, now that we are scrutinizing his writings.'[46] This imaginative intimacy enables Bede, like the runes in *Solomon and Saturn I*, to come forth from his books and sit among them, just as Byrhtferth's text itself ripples into our own world when we reread it—in part thanks to Byrhtferth's own signature admonitions. Throughout, he enjoins both us and his pupils: *Gemun þu, la rædere!* ('Remember, oh you Reader!', line 64). As Rachel Moss has observed,

> This kind of empathetic identification with people in the past can be discouraged as an unprofessional response for a professional historian, as if our vulnerable bodies are not a powerful means of connecting with a past that exists otherwise only in archives, in libraries, on paper; or on parchment, skin stripped of its vulnerability, flesh smoothed out of imperfect hairy life into something flat.[47]

Yet, it is a kind of identification that we need more of and one that CCCC 422 and the other manuscripts discussed in this volume can offer, particularly in their newly accessible second home, Parker on the Web.

Indeed, the ability for anyone with an Internet connection to relate to the early medieval past through books with globetrotting poems, vivid illustrations, and cheerful images of an international body of scholars in passionate debate is a means of disrupting other, darker kinds of identification with the past, and especially racist fantasies of a static, all-white early medieval England. Above all, the so-called 'Red Book of Darley' and Parker on the Web writ large enable viewers to trace a wider early medieval world and 'to draw lovingly out of fragmentary evidence what it might have meant to be a person in the past', as Moss beautifully describes the impulse of historical work.[48] It also gives us the freedom to relate to the books of the past in a way that we otherwise cannot: sitting cross-legged, with our laptops in our laps and these books on our screens. Like their earliest readers, we can now bring them to our own classroom debates and conferences as well as our private nooks. We can even read them in our pyjamas or leave them carelessly pulled up while we pour a drink or leave the room—a practice of casually living alongside our manuscripts that early medieval readers would have recognized.

Notes

1 John Milton, *Areopagitica*, ed. John W. Hales (Oxford: Clarendon Press, 1886), p. 5.
2 Irina Dumitrescu, *The Experience of Education in Anglo-Saxon Literature* (Cambridge: Cambridge University Press, 2018).
3 This manuscript is numbers 110 and 111 in Helmut Gneuss and Michael Lapidge, *Anglo-Saxon Manuscripts: A Bibliographical Handlist of Manuscripts and Manuscript Fragments Written or Owned in England up to 1100* (Toronto: Toronto University Press, 2014), pp. 118–19.
4 See, for instance, Rossell Hope Robbins, 'Mirth in Manuscripts', *Essays and Studies* 21 (1968): 1–28; Richard A. Dwyer, 'The Appreciation of Handmade Literature', *The Chaucer Review* 8.3 (1974): 221–40; Jennifer Borland, 'Unruly Reading: The Consuming Role of Touch in the Experience of a Medieval Manuscript', in *Scraped, Stroked, and Bound: Materially Engaged Readings of Medieval Manuscripts*, ed. Jonathan Wilcox (Turnhout: Brepols, 2013), pp. 97–114; and Christopher De Hamel, *Meetings with Remarkable Manuscripts* (London: Penguin Books, 2016).
5 William H. Sherman, *Used Books: Marking Readers in Renaissance England* (Philadelphia: University of Pennsylvania Press, 2008). On scribal interventions, see also Matthew Fisher, *Scribal Authorship and the Writing of History in Medieval England* (Columbus: Ohio State University Press, 2012).
6 Though initially one volume, Ælfwine's Prayerbook now survives in two manuscripts: London, British Library, Cotton Titus D. xxvi + xxvii. For further details, see Gneuss and Lapidge, *Anglo-Saxon Manuscripts*, no. 380, pp. 305–7. The Eadwine Psalter was copied in the mid-twelfth century and is now Cambridge, Trinity College, R. 17. 1.
7 For an overview of the special issue that coined the term, see Stephen G. Nichols, 'Introduction: Philology in a Manuscript Culture', *Speculum* 65 (1990): 1–10.

8 Leah Price, *How to Do Things with Books in Victorian Britain* (Princeton, NJ: Princeton University Press, 2012).

9 The will of Sir Thomas Borough, National Archives, Records of the Prerogative Court of Canterbury, 11/10; Image Reference 553/374. Margaret Roos, his wife, had died in 1488. For more on late medieval women accessorizing with golden books, see Susan E. James, *The Feminine Dynamic in English Art, 1485–1603: Women as Consumers, Patrons and Painters* (New York: Ashgate, 2009), pp. 82–6.

10 For further discussion, see Raymond Clemens and Deborah E. Harkness, *The Voynich Manuscript* (New Haven: Beinecke Rare Book & Manuscript Library, 2016). For an example of the kinds of attention Voynich attracts, see Lawrence Goldstone and Nancy Bazelon Goldstone, *The Friar and the Cipher: Roger Bacon and the Unsolved Mystery of the Most Unusual Manuscript in the World* (New York: Doubleday, 2005).

11 Amy Hungerford, 'On Not Reading', *The Chronicle of Higher Education*, 11 September 2016: https://www.chronicle.com/article/On-Refusing-to-Read/237717

12 For an overview of the latter practice, see Michelle M. Sauer, 'Touching Jesus: Christ's Side Wound & Medieval Manuscript Tradition', *Women's Literary Culture and the Medieval Canon*, 5 January 2016: blogs.surrey.ac.uk/medievalwomen/2016/01/05/touching-jesus-christs-side-wound-medieval-manuscript-tradition/; Nancy Thebaut, 'Bleeding Pages, Bleeding Bodies: A Gendered Reading of British Library MS Egerton 1821', *Medieval Feminist Forum: A Journal of Gender and Sexuality* 45.2 (2009): 175–200.

13 This entry forms a part of Leofric's donation list, which is currently bound at the start of the Exeter Book manuscript (folios 1–2); see Richard Gameson, 'The Origin of the Exeter Book of Old English Poetry', *Anglo-Saxon England* 25 (1996): 135–85, at p. 135.

14 Max Adams, 'The Ransom of the Golden Gospel: On the Trail of the Codex Aureus', Royal Literary Fund, 16 June 2017: https://www.rlf.org.uk/showcase/the-ransom-of-the-golden-gospel/

15 Kinohi Nishikawa, 'Merely Reading', *Publications of the Modern Language Association* 130 (2015): 697–703.

16 For an overview of the Solomon and Marcolf tradition, see Jan M. Ziolkowski, *Solomon and Marcolf*, Harvard Studies in Medieval Latin 1 (Cambridge, MA: Dept. of the Classics, Harvard University; distributed by Harvard University Press, 2008).

17 M. R. James, *A Descriptive Catalogue of the Manuscripts in the Library of Corpus Christi College Cambridge*, 2 vols. (Cambridge: Cambridge University Press, 1912), vol. 2, p. 315. For further background, see Gneuss and Lapidge, *Anglo-Saxon Manuscripts*, no. 111, pp. 118–19.

18 Daniel Anlezark, *The Old English Dialogues of Solomon and Saturn*, Anglo-Saxon Texts 7 (Woodbridge: D.S. Brewer, 2009), p. 4, n. 20. M. R. James transcribes the signature, which was added to the bottom margins of pp. 130 and 131, as 'Margaret Rollysleye wydowe' (*Descriptive Catalogue*, p. 320).

19 John Mitchell Kemble, *The Dialogue of Salomon and Saturnus: With an Historical Introduction* (London: Printed for the Aelfric Society, 1848), p. 132.

20 M. R. James, *Descriptive Catalogue*, vol. 2, p. 315.

21 I have not been able to find a study of this phenomenon in particular (that is, the palaeographical assignation of a manuscript to a female scribe based on its supposedly delicate script), but it appears to work in the reverse way as well (that is, manuscripts known to have been copied by women take on a delicate cast in palaeographical descriptions). As Alison I. Beach helpfully summarizes, 'Female hands have been described variously as delicate, irregular, nervous, and light— judgments based on attitudes toward women rather than on sound paleographical evidence. Women at a particular scribal center may have been trained to write a

highly distinctive book hand, but only its demonstrated use by female copyists marks that hand as feminine.' Alison I. Beach, *Women as Scribes: Book Production and Monastic Reform in Twelfth-Century Bavaria* (Cambridge: Cambridge University Press, 2004), p. 5.

22 Anlezark, *The Old English Dialogues of Solomon and Saturn*, pp. 50–7. Charles D. Wright has similarly suggested the court of Athelstan, where the young Dunstan and Æthelwold both spent time, as a possible point of origin, although he also mentions the court of Alfred as a possibility—a supposition that has received support from Patrick P. O'Neill and Erik Wade. I find the Alfredian context unconvincing, however. Wright, *The Irish Tradition in Old English Literature*, Cambridge Studies in Anglo-Saxon England (New York: Cambridge University Press, 1993), pp. 267–69; Patrick P. O'Neill, 'On the Date, Provenance and Relationship of the "Solomon and Saturn" Dialogues', *Anglo-Saxon England* 26 (1997): 142–52; Erik Wade, 'Language, Letters, and Augustinian Origins in the Old English Poetic *Solomon and Saturn I*', *Journal of English and Germanic Philology* 117 (2018): 160–84.

23 Anlezark, *Old English Dialogues of Solomon and Saturn*, pp. 28–9. On alternative alphabets and *Solomon and Saturn I*, see also E. J. Christie, 'By Means of a Secret Alphabet: Dangerous Letters and the Semantics of *Gebregdstafas* (*Solomon and Saturn I*, Line 2b)', *Modern Philology* 109 (2011): 145–70.

24 Anlezark, *Old English Dialogues of Solomon and Saturn*, p. 4. For further discussion, Anlezark directs readers to Mary Swan, 'Mobile Libraries: Old English Manuscript Production in Worcester and the West Midlands, 1090–1215', in *Essays in Manuscript Geography: Vernacular Manuscripts of the English West Midlands from the Conquest to the Seventeenth Century*, ed. Wendy Scase (Turnhout: Brepols, 2007), pp. 29–42, at p. 39.

25 On the latter, see especially Catherine E. Karkov, 'Text and Image in the Red Book of Darley', in *Text, Image, Interpretation: Studies in Anglo-Saxon Literature and its Insular Context in Honour of Éamonn Ó Carragáin*, ed. Alastair Minnis and Jane Roberts (Turnhout: Brepols, 2007), pp. 135–48.

26 Karkov, 'Text and Image', pp. 136–7.

27 John 1:1, quoted in Old English by Ælfric of Eynsham in his 'Nativitas Domini' ('Sermon on the Nativity of our Lord'), ll. 166-67, ed. Peter Clemoes, *Ælfric's Catholic Homilies: The First Series*, EETS s.s. 17 (Oxford: Oxford Univ. Press, 1997), pp. 190–97.

28 Luke 2:15. Ælfric, 'Nativitas Domini', ll. 163–65, ed. Clemoes, *Ælfric's Catholic Homilies*.

29 I thank Catherine Karkov for encouraging me to think more about how the illustrations in CCCC 422 relate to what I am describing in *Solomon and Saturn I*. Tiffany Beechy has traced a similar phenomenon in CCCC 41, which contains a fragment of *Solomon and Saturn I* and which, she argues, likewise explores connections between incarnational language, the divine word, and manuscript compilation. Beechy, 'The Wisdom Tradition and Irish Learning in CCCC 41', paper presented at the 53rd International Congress on Medieval Studies at Kalamazoo, May 12, 2018. See, too, her 'The "Palmtwigede" Pater Noster Revisited: An Associative Network in Old English', *Neophilologus* 99 (2015): 301–13.

30 All citations of the Solomon and Saturn texts are from Anlezark, *Old English Dialogues of Solomon and Saturn*, and will be cited in-text by line number.

31 James, *Descriptive Catalogue*, vol. 2, p. 315.

32 Katherine O'Brien O'Keeffe, *Visible Song: Transitional Literacy in Old English Verse* (Cambridge: Cambridge University Press, 1990), p. 58.

33 Interestingly, 'P', which *Solomon and Saturn I* describes as 'the fierce first letter' (lines 88b–89a, *ierne… prologa prima*) is also given a full-page ornamental initial just before the two facing illustrations from the life of Christ. CCCC 422, p. 51.

34 Milton, *Complete Prose Works*, vol. 2, p. 492. See the epigraph to this chapter for the full quotation.

35 Heide Estes has argued that this prose text should be read together with the poems that bracket it as one unified work in 'Constructing the Old English Solomon and Saturn Dialogues', *English Studies* 95.5 (2014): 483–99.

36 Ælfric of Eynsham, *De auguriis* ('On Auguries') lines 97–101, ed. and trans. Mary Clayton and Juliet Mullins, *Old English Lives of Saints*, Dumbarton Oaks Medieval Library 59 (Cambridge, MA: Harvard University Press: 2019), vol. 2, pp. 118–39, at 128. On roughly contemporaneous beliefs about the cross' defensive qualities, see Helen Foxhall Forbes, 'Sealed by the Cross: Protecting the Body in Anglo-Saxon England', in *Embodied Knowledge: Historical Perspectives on Belief and Technology*, ed. Marie Louise Stig Sørensen and Katharina Rebay-Salisbury (Oxford: Oxbow Books, 2012), pp. 52–66.

37 See, for instance, B.'s *Vita Dunstani*, ed. Michael Winterbottom and Michael Lapidge, *The Early Lives of St Dunstan* (Oxford: Clarendon Press, 2012).

38 James Paz, 'Magic That Works: Performing *Scientia* in the Old English Metrical Charms and Poetic Dialogues of Solomon and Saturn', *Journal of Medieval and Early Modern Studies* 45.2 (May 2015): 219–43, at p. 235.

39 Paz, 'Magic that Works', p. 225.

40 For their alternative treatments, see M. Nelson, 'King Solomon's Magic', *Oral Tradition* 5.1 (1990): 20–36, and Paz, 'Magic that Works'. J. L. Austin, *How to Do Things with Words* (Cambridge, MA: Harvard University Press, 1962).

41 In highlighting the globalism of CCCC 422, I am in no way rehearsing a rejected "Eastern" origin for *Solomon and Saturn* and am mindful of Kathryn Powell, 'Orientalist Fantasy in the Poetic Dialogues of Solomon and Saturn', *Anglo-Saxon England* 34 (2005): 117–43; and Tristan Major, 'Saturn's First Riddle in *Solomon and Saturn II*: An Orientalist Conflation', *Neophilologus* 96.2 (2012): 301–13 ; as well as the generative synthesis of Tiffany Beechy, 'Wisdom and the Poetics of Laughter in the Old English Dialogues of Solomon and Saturn', *Journal of English and Germanic Philology* 116.2 (2017): 131–55.

42 Robbins, 'Mirth in Manuscripts'. For examples of each of these things, Robbins directs curious readers to Cambridge, Fitzwilliam Museum, 276, a sixteenth-century paper roll that provides instructions for preparing the Philosopher's Stone; Oxford, Bodleian Library, Ashmole 1378, Part III (SC 7798), p. 73; and Oxford, Bodleian Library, Douce 257 (SC 21831).

43 Philip Henderson, ed., *The Complete Poems of John Skelton, Laureate* (London: J. M. Dent, 1964), p. 385.

44 James, *Descriptive Catalogue*, vol. 2, p. 316.

45 Michael Lapidge, *The Anglo-Saxon Library* (Oxford: Oxford University Press, 2006), p. 62.

46 Byrhtferth of Ramsey, *Enchiridion*, ed. Peter S. Baker and Michael Lapidge, *Byrhtferth's Enchiridion*, Early English Text Society ss 15 (Oxford: Oxford University Press, 1995), p. 66.

47 Rachel Moss, 'The Vulnerable Academic Body', *Avidly: A Channel of the Los Angeles Review of Books*, 21 June 2018: http://avidly.lareviewofbooks.org/2018/06/21/the-vulnerable-academic-body/. Here, I am reminded, too, of Carolyn Dinshaw's model of queer historiography, in which a reader 'desires an affective, even tactile relation to the past' in her *Getting Medieval: Sexualties and Communities Pre- and Postmodern* (Durham: Duke University Press, 1999), p. 142; and as she develops these desirous touches further in *How Soon is Now? Medieval Texts, Amateur Readers, and the Queerness of Time* (Durham: Duke University Press, 2012).

48 Moss, 'The Vulnerable Academic Body'. For helping me think through the force—and modes—of intimacy we can cultivate with old (and particularly with Old English) texts and manuscripts, I thank my co-editor and co-author, Daniel C. Remein, as well as our contributors in *Dating Beowulf: Studies in Intimacy*, ed. Remein and Weaver (Manchester: Manchester University Press, 2020).

19 Severed heads and sutured skins

Catherine E. Karkov

I came to Parker on the Web 2.0 with very limited experience of Parker on the Web 1.0, having had access to it only during a month I spent at Stanford in the spring of 2015. Parker on the Web 2.0 was thus a new experience for me. The access to the manuscripts it allows and the quality of the digitization are phenomenal, as one would expect. What I want to focus in in this chapter, however, is not the quality of the images but the accompanying information and annotation that Parker on the Web 2.0 provides, and the way its presence or absence made me think and feel differently about the manuscripts upon which I focus, Cambridge, Corpus Christi College, 23 and 4.[1] I ended up spending more time with CCCC 4 than I did with CCCC 23, in part because I know CCCC 23 a lot better having been to the Parker to read it in the flesh on several occasions, but also because the annotations to CCCC 4 really got me thinking about the larger project of digitization and the information Parker on the Web 2.0 makes available on manuscripts, as well as thinking about the nature of and unexpected connections between the two manuscripts with which I am concerned. It is worth noting at the outset that the annotations available on the site are the page level details from the M. R. James catalogue of the Library's manuscripts rather than information provided specifically for the Parker on the Web project.

CCCC 23 is a composite manuscript, the first part a fragmentary late tenth- to eleventh-century copy of Prudentius's *Psychomachia* and *Peristephanon*, with one surviving page of the *Libri contra Symmachum*. The first text is illuminated; the rest of the manuscript is not, although there are marginal doodles made by the artist of the *Psychomachia* and at least one later artist throughout. Part 2 is a twelfth-century copy of Orosius's *Seven Books of History against the Pagans* ornamented only with decorative initials and marginal doodles. The Prudentius manuscript is the work of three scribes and one artist working somewhere in the south of England, most likely Canterbury or Malmesbury, while the Orosius was copied by six scribes working in Dover in the second quarter of the twelfth century. This connects it with the CCCC 4 manuscript, the Dover Bible, Volume II, written and illustrated at Christ Church, Canterbury, of which Dover was a dependency. The Bible was at Dover by 1389 and is the work of multiple artists and an uncertain number of scribes, all writing in the remarkably homogeneous style developed at Christ Church in the mid-twelfth century. It too is a composite manuscript, its first quire consisting of a fifteenth-century copy of part of the Book of Job.

I will begin with the earlier of the two, CCCC 23. The Orosius text that comprises part 2 is rarely discussed alongside the Prudentius, although the Parker on the Web title of the manuscript (taken from the M. R. James catalogue of the library)[2] does make it more integral than have many catalogues in the past simply by titling it 'Anglo-Saxon illustrated Prudentius. Orosius',[3] and the description of the Orosius tells us, 'The second volume is a copy of Orosius; *Historia adversus paganos* of 417–18, written by six scribes working in Dover in the second quarter of the twelfth century. One of these scribes is also found in CCCC MS 462. The two manuscripts were probably bound together by Parker'.[4] Reading this made me want to go look at CCCC 462, but I will resist. (The fact that it would so easily be possible for me to do so, however, is one of the most obvious advantages of the digital project). In checking the bibliography for CCCC 23 I find very little attention devoted to the Orosius in comparison to that on the Prudentius texts, and most of the latter is focused on the *Psychomachia*, the illuminated section of the manuscript. This is, as the description tells us, a 'famous' illustrated manuscript. The linked record in the James catalogue reveals that it is famous because of its 89 drawings, but detailed information on the individual drawings is lacking. I know what they depict because I have worked with this manuscript, the original, physical manuscript, many times before. It is an old favourite, and I am delighted to be able to zoom in on details of the drawings and the way they relate physically to the text. However, were I a student or someone coming to the manuscript for the first time, I might be a bit lost. There are advantages to being lost; for example, it motivates the investigator to read more about a manuscript so that they can orientate themselves. On the other hand, some basic information about what I am looking at would be helpful. If the scholar can read the Latin titles or their Old English gloss, they will know that the upper drawing on folio 16v (Figure 19.1) depicts Humility offering the severed head of Superbia to Hope, but where does the horse come into it? Annotations to the images, similar to those we find in CCCC 26,[5] a fifteenth-century copy of Matthew of Paris's *Chronica maiora*, Part 1, would be helpful. Again, this is a problem with page-level annotations being linked to the James catalogue in which the *Chronica maiora* is given detailed annotations while the reader is directed elsewhere for information on the Prudentius. The result is that there is absolutely no annotation to the drawings in CCCC 23, although we are told rather a lot about the manuscript's opening decorated initial on folio 2r. (The drawing on the folio is of Lot, his companions and herds taken captive.) Modern users want and need more, especially art historians who might wish to

consult the manuscript. There is an opportunity here for scholars to provide enriched annotations that could be included in future. Looking
through the *Psychomachia* drawings, however, it is evident to anyone that
the violent battle between the Virtues and the Vices, and the death and
often the dismemberment of the latter, are the primary subjects depicted.

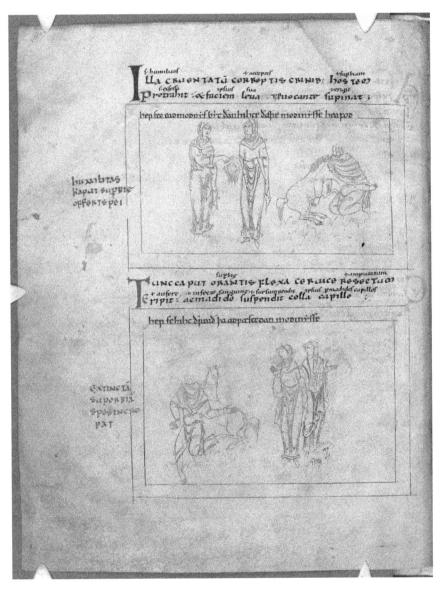

Figure 19.1 Humility and Hope with the severed head of Superbia. CCCC MS 23,
f. 16v.

Clicking through the two manuscripts and clicking back and forth between them has interested me not only in what is depicted and described within individual manuscripts, but also in the themes and differences that emerge between manuscripts. I turn to CCCC 4, the Dover Bible. The two volumes of the Dover Bible together make a huge manuscript, which I clicked through. Digital resources encourage clicking, and I have found this one of the unexpected advantages of Parker 2.0. Clicking back and forth, I noticed things I might never have noticed reading through each manuscript slowly page by page—or at least I would never have noticed them so quickly. Again, I become interested in the choices that James made about what and how to annotate and the impact of those choices on what is available to the modern user. Major decorated and historiated initials (that is, those at the beginnings of the biblical books) are annotated, but not others, for example the initial on folio 109r, even though the artists clearly considered them worthy of elaboration and spent a lot of time planning and decorating them. And why is there no annotation for the historiated initial on folio 115v of CCCC 3 with the story of David and Goliath? This is a pretty spectacular initial. And here I am confused. Parker 2.0 tells me this is folio 115v, but Kauffmann's catalogue of Romanesque manuscripts illuminated in the British Isles lists it as folio 117v.[6] Going back to the manuscript description, I see that the old foliation, and presumably this is the one Kauffmann was using, was incorrect. Oddly, what seems to be the annotation for this initial turns up on folio 114v. The annotation has to be for the initial on folio 115v, as it is the only depiction of Goliath in the manuscript. As I later learned, it has simply been placed on the wrong page by accident and will hopefully be in the right place by the time this account is published.

To turn to volume 2: first, there is a problem with the description, which says that this volume contains Psalms through to the end of the New Testament. It does not; it begins with Job, but Job up to folio 10r is in a fifteenth-century hand. Why has Job been cut off, so to speak, in the description? It is annotated, but the annotations tell me nothing about these fifteenth-century initials, which are beautifully ornamented with pen flourishes. The *Beatus Vir* initial to Psalm 1 also gets no description (Figure 19.2). Now, some of the annotation to volume 2 is very complete, for example, the seated writer in the initial 'O' of Ecclesiasticus on folio 66v (Kauffmann's folio 64v). I become drawn to the images of authors and writers. The initial on folio 169v is not just an 'initial with Matthew', as the annotation describes it; it is also an Evangelist portrait and should be identified as such.

I know I have belaboured the point about problems with the annotation of these manuscripts, and I realize that these are omissions or errors that can easily be added or corrected by scholars in future (although this also raises the issue of the increasing demands for free scholarly time and labour). I should also admit that when I first started clicking through the Dover Bible, I found the annotations intrusive, but then when I turned to CCCC 23 I missed them. Only then did I begin to focus on what they did or

nouo. & abduxi mulierin deduxi suris ex eorū genere filiorū istī septuaginta milia vnos. De tribu aūtem leui dicentē octoginta octo vnos. ex q̄ꝫ quattuor principes prȳ esse cantuonibꝫ mstra irr. & saph. ēman. gethan. & idichun. Usꝗ eorū diuidens sepcua ginta duos vnos. sub clamauit laudem cantio nū dn̄o. Et un quidē eos feriebat cymbalū. alius cychara. & alt̄ tuba cornea exaltant. Sn medio aūt eorū stabat dauid. tenens ipse psalcerū. Arca aūt antecedebat septem chori. & sacrificiū intuliss. Popstea autem unius sequebat̄ p̄ arca. Sic q̄ oms̄ psalmi dd̄ numero. el. quoy omniū quidē nouem feert ipse dd̄xxxi. n̄ t̄ sup̄ sepē. Lxxx. in dauid xii. in asaph, xi. midabun, vm. hilscbore. imū moysi. duo m̄stolomoné. u. maggei & zachariam feert iraꝗ oms̄ psalmi dd̄ numero. el. Dia psalmē nume ro Lxv. Cantici graduū numero quindecim. Psal mus prim̄ nusti adsignat̄ est qm̄ omniū est. dein quisati̅ intelligit̅ inspino. nisi p̄mogenit. ut. me ipso inscripto non fuerit necessaria. Dein q̄ ipse psalm̄ xpi memmoné facit & aduersus. xpm uti. Expendendo psona in scribendi. causam omnino n̄ bit ordinem hystorie mmutari. Legim̄ & inu tut psalmoni. si psalm̄ n̄ sedm̄ hystoria si sedm̄ pphiam tegunt. ita ordinem psalmorum turba re n̄ potest ordo tituloni. Psalm̄ oms̄ qm̄ scribun tur ipsi dauid. ad xp̄i ponent sacramenti. quia dauid dicit̅ est xp̄o.

Prefacio ieronimi presbiteri.

Psalterium Rome dudum positus emendara: iuxta Lxx. interp̄t̅ licet cursim magna illud ex parte corrxera. qd̄ quia rursū uiderss o pausa & eustochni scriptori uitio dep̄ uatū. plusꝗ ānteqqu̅ errore qm̄ noua emdatione nateret. cogris f̅r ut eori q̄dam uoua sessiss. iam artuū exercean. & obliquis sulsi renascentis spinad eradicem. equi̅ esse dicenter. ut qd̄ crebro male putulat. crebri̅ succidat̅. Unde consuera pfanod cōmotio camuos. qbs̄ forte laborisrie desudar. qm̄ q̄ exemplaria ubinīsmodi habere uoluerint. ut que diligent̄ emendata cum cura & diligen tia transcribane. Horū sibi ūnīꝗsꝗ: ut iaceuse li neam. ut signa radientia. idest uel obelus est uel astericos. Er ubicūꝗ uidir̅ uirgula p̄cedentem.

abea usꝗ ad duo puncta. que impressū. sciar in Lxx. trīslatori p̄ haberi. Ubi autem stelle simileni dinem pspexerit. de hebreu uoluminibꝫ auditū nouerit. Eꝗue usꝗ ad duo puncta iuxta theodo cionis dum taxat editionem q̄ simplicitate ser monis. a Lxx. mīsabu̅ n̄ discordar. hec q̄ nob & stu diose auꝗ: fecisse me sciens. non ambigo multos fo re. quia t̄ muidia t̄ supatuo malene contemnere. uidere p̄clara qm̄ discere. & turbulento magis rino qm̄ depurissim̄ fonte potare.

In consilio impiorū: q̄ et in uia pecca torū non stetit. et in cathedra pestilentie non sedit. Sed in lege d̄ni uoluntas eī: & in lege eī meditabitur die ac nocte. Et erit tamquā lignum quod plantatū est secus decursus aquarum: quod fruc tum suū dabit intempore suo. Et foliū eī non defluet: & omnia quecūꝗ: faciet p̄spabuntur. Consilio iustorum. Non sic impii non sic: sed tamqꝫ puluis quē picit uent̄ a facie terre. Sꝫ eatorss in do n̄ resurgunt impii in iudicio: neqꝫ pec Qui nouit d̄ni uiā iustoy: & iter impioru̅ peri bit. Psalmus dauid.

Figure 19.2 Initial to Psalm 1 (*Beatus vir*). CCCC MS 4, f. 14r.

did not reveal. The annotations are important not only because they are a feature of Parker on the Web 2.0 that one does not get when reading the original manuscript but also because the making of a digital facsimile is an extension of the making of the original manuscript. There are also issues of responsibility and transparency in the making of any digital archive, and we should know who is doing what and why when it comes to their making. Who makes the decisions, and who executes them? Who is responsible for the information we provide to, in this case, a potentially unlimited public with varying degrees of historical knowledge and an increasing interest in and appropriation or misappropriation of the Middle Ages and its afterlives?[7] But the names and roles of those who produce the digital surrogates are also part of the life and biography of the manuscripts, members of the scribal genealogy of manuscripts about which Cassiodorus wrote.[8] Moreover, the initials of the Dover Bible articulate the manuscript, so I think it is important that they are, in turn, articulated correctly. This is particularly important because so many of the initials, especially in CCCC 4 (Dover Bible, Volume II), are about the process of manuscript production. Amongst art historians, the manuscript is arguably most famous for the initial on folio 242r, which shows the artist (or an artist) at work. At left, the artist is busy painting *this* initial, while at right his assistant grinds the pigments necessary to his work. If we go back to the *Beatus Vir* initial of Psalm 1 (Figure 19.2), we find David not only composing the Psalms but composing them with representations of the primary animals from which medieval manuscripts were made: the cow, the sheep, and the goat in front of him. In the initial 'Q' of the *incipit* to Luke's Gospel on folio 193v (Figure 19.3), Luke grasps both stylus and calf as if he is about to sacrifice the calf with it, writing his Gospel with the calf's skin and blood, just as salvation history is itself written with the body and blood of Christ stretched, according to Augustine, like a manuscript skin across the heavens.[9] Luke appears again in the opening initial to the Acts of the Apostles on folio 221v, this time holding a stylus and tablet. The two books were traditionally paired, as the 'former treatise' referred to here in the Acts is generally taken to be the earlier Gospel, and in this manuscript the initials of the two books help to make that point.

Manuscript production involves violence, the severing of skin from body, and violence unites CCCC 4 with CCCC 23—the implicit violence done to the animal in the illumination made explicit through the skin of the manuscript in the former, and the visual and textual violence enacted in the drawings and text on the skin of the animal in the latter. In these manuscripts, the death and dismemberment of the animal is intimately connected to the death and dismemberment of the human, with the aim of their several, or severed (or sutured, to borrow a word from Sarah Kay)[10] parts providing lessons for the reader in proper Christian conduct.

Opening CCCC 23, we are introduced to the manuscript by a severed body part, a foot now attached to the inside cover (CCCC 23, 'Front inside binding

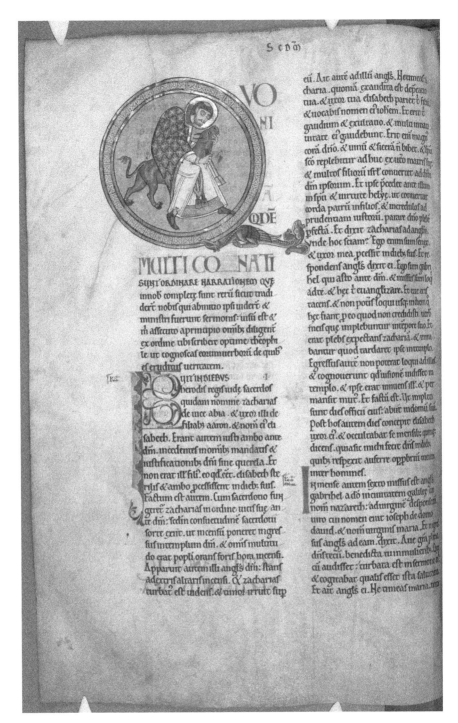

Figure 19.3 Incipit to the Gospel of Luke. CCCC MS 4, f. 193v.

FLD A)' but formerly pasted over folio 1r, and prior to that, part of a completely separate manuscript. The script here is fifteenth century, so the foot has to date to some time prior to its transcription. There is another drawing of a bodiless torso looking astonished, or perhaps simply deep in thought, on the otherwise blank folio 1r. Mildred Budny suggests that it and several of the other marginal drawings in the Prudentius part of the manuscript are either by the original artist or were added in the eleventh century.[11] The lamb on the right side of the image is showing through the parchment from the drawing of the Sacrifice of Isaac on folio 1v, neatly, if entirely fortuitously, illustrating the connection between the animal and the human. In the story of the Sacrifice, the skin and life of the ram will be offered instead of Isaac's. In fact, severed heads and clothing (a form of outer skin) appear in a number of places throughout the manuscript.[12] These were all added in the eleventh to the thirteenth centuries, according to Budny.[13] Severed body parts has become a running theme, helping to unite this manuscript's two sutured-together parts, as we shall see below.

The *Psychomachia*, or 'battle for the human soul', is a text all about skin, flesh, dismemberment, and what is written in or on the body. It externalizes the sins of the flesh so that the reader can internalize the warnings written in and on the severed body parts of the Vices. After the prologue, with its story of Abraham and Isaac, the battle between the Virtues and the Vices is framed by the defeat of Worship of the Old Gods (*Veterum cultura deorum*) at the beginning (folio 4v) and Discord/Heresy (*Discordia/Heresis*) at the end (folios 334–35r; see also Figure 19.4). The wounding and tearing of the manuscript skin at the opening of the battle (folio 4rv) calls attention to the manuscript's fleshy existence. The numerous blank spaces left for drawings that were never completed do the same. Curiously, it is the digital images that have made me much more aware of these damaged and empty surfaces. Clicking back and forth between manuscripts has also made me think about the different skins of manuscripts 4 and 23. The parchment used for CCCC 23 is of a lower quality, dirty, brown, torn, and stained in comparison to the Dover Bible's lighter and more evenly toned surfaces, although it too has suffered wear and damage. Again, this is appropriate, uncannily so, as the *Psychomachia* is all about the death and dismemberment of the Vices whose skins are stained with the sins of the flesh. I have written about them in terms of the silencing of their voices, the gendering of their bodies, and the relationship between body, book, and voice, and I do not want to repeat myself, so I am going to focus here on skin.[14] The blank spaces left for illustrations on folio 5r would have been for the depiction of Faith's victory over Worship of the Old Gods, whom, according to the text, she tramples beneath her feet. Interestingly, in the drawing on folio 4v, the eleventh-century artist seems to have reversed the way in which the two are depicted from the descriptions in Prudentius's text. In the text, Faith has dishevelled hair and bare shoulders and arms, but she is unarmed, and it is Worship of the Old Gods with her fillet-decked head who strikes first. The artist has to have reversed the depictions of the two, because

Faith appears dressed elegantly again in the next completed miniature on folio 5v, in which she crowns the Virtues and directs them to clothe themselves in purple.

The remaining Vices meet a variety of gruesome fates: Lust is beheaded; Wrath impales herself on her own sword; Pride falls into a pit, is trampled by her own horse, and beheaded, her severed head, as we have seen, held

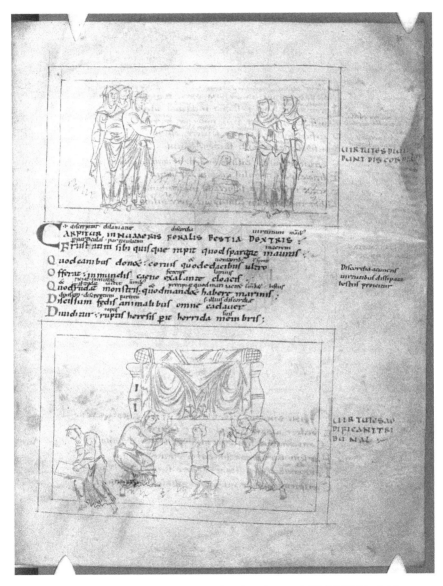

Figure 19.4 Discord/Heresy dismembered by the Virtues. CCCC MS 23, f. 35r

up in triumph by Hope and Humility (Figure 19.1); Luxuria is thrown from her chariot, mangled beneath its wheels, and finally crushed by a rock dropped on her by Sobriety; Avarice is strangled and stabbed by Good Works; Discord/Heresy is stabbed in the mouth and then torn to pieces by the collective Virtues (Figure 19.4). This final death is a reminder of the relationship between the tongue as a fleshy organ and one that is within, though not confined to, the body, and a tongue meaning language, whether spoken or written.[15]

The *Psychomachia* is a battle that takes place for, but also within the human soul and the human skin, and in it human and animal skin again meet. The Vices are like animals—Wrath, for example, gnashes her teeth and foams at the mouth—because, as the text tells us over and over again, they are devoted to the sins of the flesh, the appetites contained within our fallen human skins. The martyrs of the *Peristephanon* are exactly the opposite; their bodies, like their souls, are virtuous, and this is demonstrated by their overcoming of their earthly skin and flesh, which is repeatedly torn and wounded. Book 1, the martyrdom of Emeterius and Chalidonius, makes the relationship between the written book and the skins of the martyrs clear, opening with the words *Scripta sunt caelo duorum martyrum vocabula, aureis quae Christus illic adnotavit litteris sanguinis notis eadem scripta terris tradidit*, 'The names of the two martyrs are written in heaven, Christ has recorded them there in letters of gold, while on earth he has written them in letters of blood.'[16] Lawrence is stretched and roasted like a calf or sheep, taunting his torturer to eat his flesh. Eulalia's flesh is cut and the name of the Lord written into it in blood. Vincent's body is stretched, torn apart, roasted, salted, and basted with fat. Cassian, a teacher of reading and writing, is punctured, or punctur(ate)ed to death by the pens of his pupils. Hippolytus is dragged by horses, his body torn apart and scattered across the landscape, its parts gathered up by his followers, just as it is gathered and assembled in Prudentius's text. Romanus, whose story comes first in Anglo-Saxon copies of the *Peristephanon*,[17] has his body stretched, his face and body cut with long lines, every wound becoming 'a mouth uttering praise' (*tot ecce laudant ora quot sunt vulnera*, line 570), and his tongue, which Romanus himself says, 'plays the part of a nimble quill' (*lingua plectrum mobile*, line 935), cut out.[18] Even then he will not stop talking until his neck is finally broken. His death and that of the infant Barulus, who is martyred with him, result in the production of two books, the first composed of the governor's papyrus scrolls, which disintegrate and are destroyed by time, and the second a heavenly book written by an angel.

An angel standing in the presence of God took down all that the martyr said and all he bore, and not only recorded the words of his discourse but with his own pen drew exact pictures of the wounds on his sides and cheeks and breast and throat. The measure of blood from each was noted, and how in each case the gash ploughed out the wound, whether deep or wide or on the surface, long or short, the violence of the pain, the extent of the cut; no drop of blood did he let go for nought.[19]

Irina Dumitrescu has recently explored the relationship between tongue as both flesh and language in the *Peristephanon*, and Prudentius's authoring of a 'self' through the stories he writes, the writing on the animal skin here forming a human sense of embodied self.[20] Vice and Virtue are inscribed in human skin in these stories written on animal skin, and this is a point of intersection, encounter, or perhaps 'suture' would again be the more appropriate word, between the skins of those who made and read the manuscripts and the page. Skin is also what aligns the two books of nature and scripture for Augustine. In his *Confessions* XIII.15.16, he wrote:

> Who but you, our God, made for us that firmament of authority to be over us in your divine scripture. For the heaven will be folded up like a book and is now stretched out over us like a skin. Your divine scripture has more sublime authority since the death of those mortals who dispensed it to us. And you know, Lord, you know how you clothed human beings with skins as soon as they became mortal through sin. And so you have stretched out the firmament of your book like a skin, your words assuredly in concord, which you spread over us through the ministry of mortals. For by their very death the solid firmament of authority in your words as authored by them is stretched out sublimely over all beneath, which, while they were alive on earth was not so sublimely stretched out over us. You had not yet spread out that heaven like a skin, you had not yet made known everywhere the fame of their deaths.[21]

As Kay notes, in this passage 'Augustine holds out the hope of redemption towards which each individual should strive by means of an act of reading which will envelope him in a new skin in exchange for his old one'.[22] The allegory of the *Psychomachia* and the hagiography of the *Peristephanon* in CCCC 23 materialize this idea through merging the skin of the book with the skin of the Virtues and Vices in the former and the skin of the martyrs in the latter.

CCCC 23 as it comes down to us is not just the tenth- to eleventh-century Prudentius manuscript, it is also the twelfth-century Orosius. The allegorical battle that takes place within the human soul that we see in the *Psychomachia* is both historicized and individualized in the martyrdom of saints in the *Peristephanon* and is then extended to universal secular history from a Christian perspective in the *Seven Books of History against the Pagans*. This may have been one of the reasons Matthew Parker bound the two manuscripts together, this and/or the fact that they both preserve texts by fourth- to fifth-century Spanish authors, but there are many connections that can be made between the contents of these different texts, especially with regard to their references to reading, books, and dead bodies or severed body parts.

Orosius addresses the *History* to Augustine, whom he claims commissioned the work from him. While we cannot be certain that this was in fact the case, Augustine did write of Orosius that he sought to refute the 'false and pernicious doctrines through which the souls of men in Spain have suffered much more grievous wounds than have been inflicted on their bodies by the sword of barbarians'.[23] The souls, temporarily housed within our human skins represented in the *Psychomachia*, and freed from those skins in the *Peristephanon*, remain the ultimate focus of this part of the manuscript. The *History* is written in seven books, reflecting the seven days over which God, the author of all things,[24] authored his Creation as well as the prominence of the number seven in biblical, eschatological, and allegorical thinking in general including, perhaps, the seven Virtues and Vices. Seven, Orosius writes, is the number 'by which all things are judged',[25] and all the evils about which he writes are either the manifestation of sin, beginning with original sin, or God's punishment of sin.[26] A home in the kingdom of heaven is that towards which each Christian strives, and it is to be found by remaining on the path of the Virtues and not being deflected by the temptation of the Vices.[27]

In the *History*, there is the battle between good and evil, vice and virtue, but there is also the battle between a pagan past and a Christian present that begins with the fall of Adam and Eve, the moment at which, according to Augustine, human beings were clothed with their mortal skins. The human and the animal are both warriors in and victims of these battles. In the preface to Book 1, Orosius describes himself as a dog, disciplined, obedient, and always ready to fight in the cause of his master, God. The sinful nature of human beings, however, also brings with it the punishment and destruction of animals and the earth itself: 'because of man's sin, the world is implicated in his crimes, and in order to bring our excesses to heel, the very earth on which we live is punished with all other animals dwindling away and its fields becoming barren'.[28] That earth is again and again saturated with blood and covered with the dead and their dismembered bodies. The episodes of slaughter, murder, cannibalism, and other such horrors are too numerous to explore here,[29] suffice it to say that in the *History* the sins of humanity are written in blood on the earth in contrast to the heavenly canopy of divine scripture written with the body and blood of Christ. Orosius himself wrote from the authority and information of other books, from all that he could discover in 'the records of the histories and annals that are to be had at this present time',[30] but books too are as fragile as human or animal skin, and just as easily destroyed by sin or ignorance. The Library in Rome, for example, was destroyed by God as a punishment for the depravities of the emperor Commodus.[31]

The final book details the sack of Rome by the Goths, and the warfare amongst the barbarian nations of Spain that has spilled much blood on both sides. Orosius ends with a summary that turns the reader's attention back to Augustine and reminds us of why and for whom this book was written.

I have set down with Christ's aid, the lusts and punishment of sinful men, the conflicts of our age, and the judgments of God from the beginning of the world to the present day, that is over 5618 years. I have done this as briefly and as clearly as possible, separating the years which through the nearer presence of Christ's grace are Christian ones from the previous chaos of disbelief. So now I am secure in the enjoyment of the one thing for which I ought to long—the fruit of my obedience. As for the quality of my little works, you, who commissioned them, must see to that—if you publish them, they must be approved of by you, but if you destroy them, you will have disapproved of them.[32]

Author and reader/patron here become co-producers of the book, but more importantly, the life of this book and the skins on which it was originally written rest in the hands of its reader.

The *History* is a book about the improvement of the world since its conversion to Christianity, and to convert is to be baptized, to shed one's old skin and acquire a new one, just as in Augustine's model of reading. Perhaps ironically, working with the virtual skin of the Parker on the Web 2.0 manuscripts has made me more aware of all the different skins of the original manuscripts, especially of the animal skin of the manuscripts and its relation to specific images and texts, than I may well have been in working with the physical manuscripts and their literal skins. It has made me more aware of what is lost in the digital, and hence the very different materialities of manuscript and digital skins. Only in working with each does what is lost in not working with the other become apparent.

Notes

1 CCCC 23: https://parker.stanford.edu/parker/catalog?utf8=Ł&exhibit_id=parker&search_field=manuscript_number&q=023 CCCC 4: https://parker.stanford.edu/parker/catalog?utf8=Ł&exhibit_id=parker&search_field=manuscript_number&q=004

2 Montague Rhodes James, *A Descriptive Catalogue of the Manuscripts in the Library of Corpus Christi College Cambridge*, 2 vols. (Cambridge: Cambridge University Press, 1909, 1912).

3 For example, Elżbieta Temple, *Anglo-Saxon Manuscripts 900–1066, A Survey of Manuscripts Illuminated in the British Isles* (London: Harvey Miller, 1976), vol. 2, no. 48 describes it as 'Prudentius, Psychomachia and other Poems'. Mildred Budny, *Insular, Anglo-Saxon, and Early Anglo-Norman Manuscript Art at Corpus Christi College, Cambridge, an Illustrated Catalogue*, 2 vols. (Kalamazoo, MI: Medieval Institute Publications, 1997), vol. 1, no. 24, catalogues and describes only 'MS 23, Part I. The Corpus Prudentius', although 'Part II. [The Dover Orosius]' is listed in the index of manuscripts and mentioned in the description of the manuscript (pp. 275, 287, 290). Admittedly, as the titles of both catalogues suggest, they are concerned only with the pre-Conquest portion of the manuscript, but in cataloguing only one portion of its contents, they give a misleading suggestion of what any visitor to the library would find, and suggest that a manuscript's life stops with only that portion of the volume in which a given scholar might be interested.

4 https://parker.stanford.edu/parker/catalog/nz663nv2057

5 See, for example, the annotations to folio 1r: https://parker.stanford.edu/parker/ca talog/rf352tc5448

6 C. M. Kaufmann, *A Survey of Manuscripts Illuminated in the British Isles*, vol. 3: *Romanesque Manuscripts 1066–1190* (London: Harvey Miller, 1975).

7 See, for example, Paul B. Sturtevant: https://www.publicmedievalist.com/schro dinger/; Sierra Lomuto: www.inthemedievalmiddle.com/2016/12/white-nationalism -and-ethics-of.html; Andrew Elliott: https://www.publicmedievalist.com/vile-love-a ffair/; James M. Harland: https://www.publicmedievalist.com/race-in-the-trenches/; Helen Young: www.inthemedievalmiddle.com/2017/08/white-supremacists-love-m iddle-ages.html?m=1

8 See L. W. Jones, ed. and trans., *An Introduction to Divine and Human Readings by Cassiodorus Senator* (New York: Columbia University Press, 1946), p. 109.

9 See below n. 21.

10 Sarah Kay, 'Legible Skins: Sheep, Wolves, and the Ethics of Reading in the Middle Ages', *postmedieval: a journal of medieval cultural studies* 2 (2011): 13–32; Kay, *Animal Skins and the Reading Self in Medieval Latin and French Bestiaries* (Chicago: University of Chicago Press, 2017).

11 Budny, *Insular, Anglo-Saxon, and Early Anglo-Norman Manuscript Art at Corpus Christi College, Cambridge*, pp. 280, 292, 322.

12 See folios FLDA, 1r, 7v, 103v, 123r.

13 Budny, *Insular, Anglo-Saxon, and Early Anglo-Norman Manuscript Art at Corpus Christi College, Cambridge*, p. 437.

14 C. E. Karkov, 'Broken Bodies and Singing Tongues: Gender and Voice in the Cambridge, Corpus Christi College 23 *Psychomachia*', *Anglo-Saxon England* 30 (2001): 115–36.

15 See further C. Mazzio, 'Sins of the Tongue in Early Modern England', *Modern Language Studies* 28.3/4 (1998): 93–124, esp. pp. 93–7.

16 *Prudentius*, trans. H. J. Thomson, 2 vols. (Cambridge, MA: Harvard University Press, 2014), vol. 1, p. 98.

17 It is actually Book X, though it seems never to appear in its numerical order. All translations are my own unless otherwise stated.

18 *Prudentius*, trans. H. J. Thomson, pp. 266, 290.

19 *Prudentius*, trans. H. J. Thomson, pp. 302–3 (lines 1121–30). Translation Thompson's.

20 Irina Dumitrescu, 'The Martyred Tongue: The Legendaries of Prudentius and Theresa Hak kyung Cha', *postmedieval: a journal of medieval cultural studies* 8 (2017): 334–51.

21 Augustine, *Confessions*, vol. 2, *Books IX–XIII*, ed. and trans. Carolyn J. B. Hammond (Cambridge, MA: Harvard University Press, 2014), pp. 402, 404.

22 Kay, *Animal Skins and the Reading Self*, p. 24.

23 Paulus Orosius, *Seven Books of History against the Pagans*, trans. Irving W. Raymond (New York: Columbia University Press, 1936), p. 6.

24 Orosius, *Seven Books of History against the Pagans*, trans. A. T. Fear (Liverpool: Liverpool University Press, 2010). (Book 6.1.3).

25 Orosius, *Seven Books of History against the Pagans*, trans. p. 323 (Book 7.2.9).

26 Orosius, *Seven Books of History against the Pagans*, trans. A. Fear, p. 35 (Book 1.1.12).

27 'The mind, enlightened by its guide, reason, sees, in the midst of the virtues by which it rises up through an innate disposition, though it is turned from its path by the vices, the knowledge of God as its citadel.' Orosius, *Seven Books of History against the Pagans*, trans. Fear, p. 261 (Book 6.1.1).

28 Orosius, *Seven Books of History against the Pagans*, trans. Fear, p. 73 (Book 2.1.1).

29 See e.g. Books 1.4.2, 1.4.6, 2.7.6, 2.9.10, 2.14.1, 4.4.7, 5.23.18, 7.16.3.

30 Orosius, *Seven Books of History against the Pagans*, trans. Fear, p. 109 (Preface to Book 3).
31 Orosius, *Seven Books of History against the Pagans*, trans. Fear, p. 348 (Book 7.16.3).
32 Orosius, *Seven Books of History against the Pagans*, trans. Fear, p. 414 (Book 7.43.19–20).

20 Books consumed, books multiplied

Martianus Capella, Ælfric's *Homilies*, and the International Image Interoperability Framework

Alexandra Bolintineanu

This chapter brings into conversation two manuscripts in the Parker collection. The first is Cambridge, Corpus Christi College, 162, an early eleventh-century south English collection of Old English homilies, mostly by Ælfric. The second manuscript is Cambridge, Corpus Christi College, 153, a late ninth-century Welsh copy of Martianus Capella's fifth-century encyclopaedic allegorical work, *De nuptiis Philologiae et Mercurii* (The Wedding of Philology and Mercury).[1] The books are part of the historic Parker Library at Corpus Christi College, Cambridge; their digital avatars are accessible through Parker on the Web.[2] I want to bring these two books in conversation with their digital platform, Parker on the Web, around the themes of wonder, text technologies, and the gathering and multiplication of books through time. Specifically, I want to focus on what Alan Liu calls 'media encounters': narratives, present in 162, 153, and Parker on the Web itself, about encounters with text technologies. All three resources vividly imagine encounters with text technologies and the physical book, encounters that are linked to themes of wonder, consumption, and community. In each of these resources, books in their material forms evoke wonder: they are linked to eating and nourishment; they increase and multiply and sustain communities of reading. These vignettes of encounters with books—not abstracted texts or knowledge, but physical artefacts—not only reflect two influential medieval authors' conceptualizations of knowledge and its transmission but also allow us to trace how digital scholarship platforms such as Parker on the Web refract medieval ways of thinking about the sustainable production and transmission of knowledge. My focus will be on Cambridge, Corpus Christi College, 162 (henceforth CCCC 162), and within it, Ælfric's Mid-Lent Homily (CH I.12). But I shall begin with a moment in Martianus Capella that brings these themes together.

Martianus Capella's *Wedding of Philology and Mercury* uses the allegory of a courtship and marriage between Philology (learning) and Mercury (eloquence) to depict the intellectual landscape of the liberal arts curriculum. I want to focus on one specific moment in the allegory: when Philology, entering the 'bond of celestial matrimony', is about to drink the cup of immortality and ascend among the gods. But first, Philology must vomit up the 'inner fullness' weighing her down. So Philology throws up 'a stream of writing of all kinds' in a great multiplicity of material forms, intellectual subjects, and disciplinary visual languages.[3]

Tiffany Beechy frames this moment as a manifestation of a thematic motif that she explores within Indo-European textual traditions—an unusual thematic cluster of 'consumption, purgation, poetry, divinity, sweetness'. This thematic cluster imagines poetry 'as a joint product of the human and the divine' and is 'ultimately related to the canonical figure at the very center of Christian doctrine, the word made flesh, whose ingestion into the body forms the rite of Eucharistic communion'.[4] In Martianus Capella, Philology must be purged of a multiplicity of books before she can drink the sweet drink of immortality, marry Divine Eloquence, and take her place among the gods. 'Learning', Beechy argues, 'becomes immortal only by its marriage with eloquence. Eloquence is not a mere tool for conveying knowledge—it is the very key to its apotheosis'.[5] What strikes me here is that the knowledge that Philology vomits out is not abstracted. On the contrary, knowledge is allegorized as a multiplicity of specific physical forms, made insistently concrete through vivid sensory imagery: the books' mediums range from papyrus and linen to parchment to linden bark to stone; their visual languages include musical notation, geometrical figures, natural science illustrations, and sacred hieroglyphs; even their haptic and olfactory aspects make themselves felt through the reference to the 'smeared ... cedar oil' and the muses gathering 'countless volumes into their laps'. As Philology produces learned knowledge on her way to apotheosis, she does so in a variety of vividly imagined text technologies.[6]

This engagement with text technologies runs through the three vignettes I bring into conversation in this chapter. The first vignette, discussed above, is Martianus Capella's description of Philology vomiting a stream of vividly concrete books. The second is Ælfric's exegesis of Christ's miracle of the loaves and fishes, interpreted as the multiplication of Christian theological tradition across generations, consumed by, and nourishing, communities of faith. The third vignette is Parker on the Web itself, an exemplary manifestation of IIIF: a digital framework for understanding medieval books both as material objects (simultaneously text and image) and as digital avatars, consumed by a variety of technologies and nourishing a variety of forms of scholarship.

CCCC 162 is an early eleventh-century collection of homilies, mostly by Ælfric. D. G. Scragg describes it as 'a carefully constructed *temporale*'[7] with an emphasis on Lenten material. Based on the book's physical characteristics—relatively few abbreviations, clear punctuation, consistent capitalization, generous spacing, and heavy weight—Elaine Treharne argues the book was designed for public reading 'upon some kind of lectern'. (406–7) Based on readerly annotations, as Treharne, Kathryn Powell, and Kathryn Lowe have demonstrated, this manuscript was carefully read and thoughtfully annotated from the early eleventh to the thirteenth centuries.[8]

Within this book and its learned readers' interventions, I want to focus on one Ælfrician homily that meditates on wonders, books, and the role of text technologies in pointing the way to God. This is the Mid-Lent Sunday (CH I.12) from the *Catholic Homilies, First Series.*[9] Its pericope is John 6:1–14, where Christ feeds the multitude with loaves and fishes. Godden points out that Ælfric draws chiefly on Augustine's 24th Tractate on St John's Gospel as well as on Bede, Haymo, and possibly Alcuin.[10] However, in the passages on which I focus, Ælfric draws very closely on Augustine above all other sources.

Following Augustine, Ælfric first retells the episode of the loaves and fishes (lines 1–25). Then he proceeds to interpret each element of the story allegorically, *æfter gastlicum andgite* (lines 26–39, 'according to the spiritual sense'). When he reaches the miracle itself, the narrator turns from this particular miracle (*tacen*, 'sign or miracle') to *wundra* more broadly (a word that, in Old English, encompasses both marvels and miracles) and places this particular miracle of Christ in the wider framework of divine operation in the world:

> Fela wundra worhte god. & dæghwamlice wyrhð: Ac ða wundra sind swiðe awacode. on manna gesihðe: for ðan þe hi sind swiðe gewunelice. Mare wundor is þæt god ælmihti. ælce dæig fet ealne middaneard. & gewissað þa godan. þonne þæt wundor wære þæt he ða gefylde fif þusend manna mid fif hlafum: Ac þæs wundrodon men na for ði þæt hit mare wundor wære. ac for ði þæt hit wæs ungewunelic. Hwa sylð nu wæstm urum æcerum: & gemænigfylt þæt gerip of feawum cornum. buton se ðe þa gemænigfylde þa fif hlafas. Seo miht wæs þa on cristes handum & þa fif hlafas wæron swilce hit sæd wære: Na on eorðan besawen. ac gemæ-nifyld fram þam þe eorðan geworhte (ll. 54–63).

> God has worked, and daily works, many wonders; but those miracles are much weakened in the sight of human beings, because they are very usual. A greater wonder it is that God Almighty every day feeds all the world, and directs what is good, than that wonder was, that he filled five thousand men with five loaves: but human beings wondered at that, not because it was a greater miracle, but because it was unusual. Who now gives fruit to our fields, and multiplies the harvest from a few grains of corn, but he who multiplied the five loaves? The might was there in Christ's hands, and the five loaves were, as it were, seed, not sown in the earth, but multiplied by him who created the earth.

Godden surveys Ælfric's attitude towards wonders, noting that Ælfric tends to be cautious around *wundra* ('wonders' or 'miracles'). As Godden notes, Ælfric privileges spiritual wonders, such as the sacrament of baptism, faithful prayers, or good works, over spectacular physical miracles. Godden cites this particular passage of CH I.12 as an example of Ælfric's attitude that 'physical miracles are of dubious value and origin',[11] I read the passage differently. Ælfric, following Augustine, is arguing a fortiori: if this one miracle of the loaves and fishes evokes wonder and awe, how much more wonder should the daily workings of creation draw forth? Far from diminishing the miracle of the loaves and fishes, the passage frames this particular miracle as a metonymy of divine operation in the world. The language of the passage is thick with repetition. It emphasizes the wonder of creation through insistent, repeated mentions of wonder and plenitude (*fela wundra / mare wundor / wundor / wundredon / mare wundor*), of nourishment and multiplication (*gefylde / gemenigfylt / gemaenigfylde / gemenigfyld*). The passage evokes a capacious, generous, nourishing creation.

A marginal annotation in CCCC 162, transcribed below and italicized, supports my interpretation. This annotation amplifies the wonder, widening Creation's scope to *ealle gesceafta*. Through verbal adornment, it further emphasizes the moment, as word pairs prescribe a devotional response to this wonder: *inlice 7 eadmodlice* ('inwardly and humbly'); *his miltse 7 are* ('his mildness and mercy'):

> Seo miht wæs þa on cristes handum & þa fif hlafas wæron swilce hit sæd wære: Na on eorðan besawen. ac gemænifyld fram þam þe eorðan geworhte *7 ealle gesceafta. Uton for þi inlice 7 eadmodlice on hyne gelyfan 7 his miltse 7 are geornlice biddan.*[12]

> The might was there in Christ's hands, and the five loaves were, as it were, seed, not sown in the earth, but multiplied by him who created the earth a*nd all creatures. Therefore we ought to inwardly and humbly believe in him and earnestly pray for his mildness and mercy.*

After contextualizing the miracle of the loaves and fishes within divine creation, Ælfric returns to the present episode, and again emphasizes its significance:

> Ðis wundor is swiðe micel & deop on getacnungum. Oft gehwa gesihð fægere stafas awritene. þonne heraðhe ðone writere & þa stafas & nat hwæt hi mænað.
> Se ðe cann þæra stafa gescead. he heraðheora fægernysse. & ræt þa stafas. & understent hwæt hi gemænað. On oðre wisan we scawiað metinge. & on oðre wisan stafas. ne gæð na mare to metinge buton þæt ðu hit geseo. & herige. Nis na genoh þæt ðu stafas scawie. buton þu hi eac ræde. & þæt andgit understande.
> Swa is eac on ðam wundre þe god worhte mid þam fif hlafum. ne bið na genoh þæt we ðæs tacnes wundrian. oððe þurh þæt god herian buton we eac þæt gastlice andgit understandon (ll. 64–68).

> This miracle is very great, and deep in meaning. Often someone sees beautiful letters written; then he praises the writer and the characters, and does not know what they mean. He who understands the meaning of the letters praises their beauty, and reads the letters, and understands what

they mean. In one way we look at a picture, and in another at letters. Nothing more is necessary for a picture than that you see and praise it: but it is not enough to wonder at letters without, at the same time, reading them, and understanding their meaning. So also it is about the miracle which God worked with the five loaves: it is not enough that we wonder at the miracle, or praise God on account of it, without also understanding its spiritual sense.

The Augustinian pairing of *wundor* ('wonder') and *tacnung* ('sign') is characteristic of Ælfric's work: wonder is not only the extraordinary, the thing or occurrence that evokes shock and awe, terror and delight; it is the extraordinary, as Carolyn Walker Bynum notes, charged with significance.[13] Wonders are signs. The pairing of *wundor* and *tacen* and their cognates occurs throughout the Ælfrician corpus. Of the approximately 90 proximate co-occurrences of *wunder* and *tacen* in the *Dictionary of Old English* corpus, almost half, 45, belong to Ælfric's writings. (By comparison, the next-biggest contributors of this pairing are the Psalms, with 10 occurrences, and Bede, with 3).[14] In Ælfric, as in Augustine, wonder demands engagement with, and understanding of, its deep significance. Turning to this particular passage, Godden argues that 'wonder at miracles is associated by analogy with the illiterate' and even notes a 'disparaging tone in which Ælfric refers to mere wonder at miracle stories'.[15] But I think Ælfric's treatment of wonder is more nuanced than that. Ælfric does not disparage the wonder response itself—he urges his audience to combine this wonder response with understanding of 'the wonder's spiritual sense'. Within the Augustinian metaphor of the *faegere stafas*, the 'beautiful letters', Ælfric does not suggest that a good reader should treat letters instrumentally, as mere utilitarian carriers of meaning. Rather, the good reader 'praises their beauty, and reads the letters, and understands what they mean'. This response to metaphorical beautiful letters would have been amplified by the physical form of CCCC 162. Decorated initials mark the beginning of each homily. Moreover, as Treharne points out, the manuscript is 'expertly made with relatively good parchment', and beautifully readable, with clear punctuation, consistent capitalization, and generous spacing. Treharne argues it is designed as a public reading book—one that not only invites admiration of beautiful letters, but supports the task of reading the letters and understanding what they mean.[16]

Finally, Ælfric compresses and slightly reworks Augustine's passage. That is, he omits Augustine's depiction of miracles as divine spoken language, 'tongue of their own', and makes the analogy entirely visual and textual, about 'beautifully written letters'. This has the effect of emphasizing textuality over speech. Following Augustine and Bede, textuality becomes—alongside food and feeding—the homily's overarching metaphor of the transmission of Christian teaching through the Old Testament, to Christ Himself, to the apostles, and the learned theologians of the Church. Breaking the loaves,

Christ causes them to multiply and grow in his hands: so Christian teaching grows, and its books multiply, with the fertility Ælfric ascribes to Creation itself, through the expounding of wise teachers. Multiplying loaves become multiplying books, become multiple wonders, become the divine operating in the world.

The homily closes by returning to wonders and miracles, their necessary transmutation into written, heard, and spoken words—words created, words consumed, words recreated:

> þæt folc geseah ða þæt wundor 7 hi ðæs swiðe wundrodon: þæt wundor is awriten 7 we hit gehyrdon. þæt ðe on him heora eagan gedydon: þæt deð ure geleafa on us. Hi hit gesawon. 7 we his gelyfað þe hit ne gesawon: 7 we sind for ði beteran getealde: swa swa se hælend be us on oðre stowe cwæð. Eadige beoð þa ðe me ne geseoð. 7 hi hwæðre gelyfað on me. & mine wundra mærsiað.[17]

> Those people saw the wonder and greatly wondered about it. That wonder is written, and we have heard it. What their eyes did for them, that does our faith for us. They saw it, and we believe it who did not see it; and we are therefore accounted as better, just as the Savior says of us elsewhere, 'Blessed are they who did not see me, and who nevertheless believe in me, and praise my wonders',

Ælfric's insistent transmutation of wonders into words and understanding is especially striking because it is not typical of Old English religious writing, either in religious verse or in homiletic prose. Both in religious poetry and in homilies, the divine is not transubstantiated into words. Quite the opposite: it is heralded by declarations of unknowing and inexpressibility, asserting that no one exists among human beings who can encompass the divine in words or understanding.[18] Having surveyed elsewhere a more extensive catalogue of declarations of unknowing,[19] I will limit myself to one example here:

> For þan we habbað micle nydþearfe, þa hwile þe we her syndon on þys lænan life & on þyssum gewitendlicum, þæt we þonne on þære toweardan worulde mægen 7 moton becuman to life þæs heofoncundan rices 7 to þam wundre þære ecean eadignesse, þær we moton siððan orsorglice lybban 7 rixian butan ælcre onwendednesse mid him, emne swa ure dryhten hælende Crist, 7 mid eallum his halgum, gif we hit gearnian willað mid urum godum dædum. Nis þonne næniges mannes gemet þæt he mæge asecgan þara goda & þara yðnessa þe God hafað geearwod eallum þam þe hine lufiað & his <bebodu> healdan willað 7 gelæstan.[20]

> For we have great need of this, that while we are in this temporary and transitory life, that we afterwards may come to the life of the heavenly kingdom and to the wonder of eternal blessedness, where we will be allowed to live without care and reign without any changefulness with Him, even our Lord Saviour Christ, and with all His saints, if we will

earn this with our good deeds. It is therefore not within any human being's measure to express the good things and the advantages that God has prepared for all those who love Him and who want to keep and perform His commandments.

Like Ælfric, the anonymous homilist invokes divine wonder, the wonder of eternal blessedness in Heaven. Yet the response to the wonder is not to call for understanding or for wise teachers to expound the wonder in written words. Quite the opposite: the wonder's magnitude is invoked through a statement that such translation is beyond the measure of any human being.

In contrast to the anonymous homilist's declaration of unknowing, Ælfric follows Augustine in depicting wonders not just as susceptible to, but as demanding of, human words and human comprehension. Far from rendering divine wonders as beyond the reach of human language, Ælfric renders them as *faegere stafas* ('beautiful letters'), written human language that demands a response both as image and as carrier of meaning. This textualization of divine wonders gives Ælfric's audiences, be they preachers or monks or laypersons, a model of affective and cognitive response to the wondrous and the divine. It teaches the congregation to wonder and to praise, but also to interpret wonders for spiritual significance. It invites the congregation into the Christian textual tradition, in which words and written books multiply like loaves and fishes across generations of learned speech and teaching, consuming and transmitting the divine.

Subsequent generations take up the homilist's invitation: well before CCCC 162 enters the collection of sixteenth-century Archbishop Matthew Parker,[21] the book shows extensive user experience. At the beginning of the eleventh century, the book is carefully compiled around Lenten themes, with a view to public reading.[22] As early as 1000–12, an annotator may have been 'revising homilies in this manuscript for preaching'—by referencing the Viking attacks of his day, and so adapting the homilies to England's political and devotional climate.[23] Subsequently, readers from the eleventh to the thirteenth centuries gloss, annotate, correct, expand, or compress Ælfric's text. These annotators testify to learned, careful, thoughtful involvement with Ælfric's homilies; to the gathering of 'the profundity of the doctrine' that Ælfric enjoins upon teachers and theologians; and to the reproduction, across communities, of Ælfric's own theological teaching.[24]

In the twenty-first century, in Parker on the Web 2.0, CCCC 162 appears before new communities of readers through its digital avatar. In web design and vocabulary, Parker on the Web continues the thematic cluster that associates the encounter with material books with wonder, consumption, and community. Parker on the Web presents itself as a 'digital exhibit' of the Parker Library's 'treasure trove of rare medieval and Renaissance manuscripts, as well as early printed books', a formulation that foregrounds both the wonder of the collection and the site's engagement with material books. Among the site's curated features, 'Worlds Real and Imagined' scatters its narrative with expressions of wonder, whether by describing the books' bodies (such as Matthew Paris' 'magnificent and memorable' *Chronica maiora* in CCCC 16i) or by referring to marvels evoked by the texts themselves (such as the magician Merlin's building of Stonehenge in CCCC 154).[25] The second curated feature, 'The History of the Book', recalls Philology's vomit: it sets forth examples of books in a variety of formats and media, from immense genealogical scrolls to papyrus fragments, from manuscript codices to woodblock prints and incunabula.[26] In Parker on the Web's catalogue itself, the focus on the material book continues just as vividly. This theme surfaces in the catalogue itself, where Parker on the Web implements the viewer Mirador, enabling readers to navigate the books' digital avatars both as text and as image, and continuing the duality suggested by Ælfric and Augustine. Turning to Ælfric's *Catholic Homily* I.12 (CCCC 162, p. 267) as an example, readers are enabled to interact with the *faegere stafas* of the homily both as text and as pictures: the bubble icon, at the top left of the viewer, displays text annotations of the manuscript; the slider icon, just below, allows any user (including those who might not be able to read the text) to change the image, rotating it, adjusting its brightness, even inverting its colours. The IIIF manifest, the data that determines how Mirador displays the book, continues the engagement with the physical book: it acts as a kind of binding, determining the order in which pages become visible in the digital book-object. Nor is the theme of the reading community absent: if the reader follows the IIIF icon below the Mirador screen, the first layer of documentation she encounters describes 'the researchers, students and the public at large' whose interaction with digital images the framework is designed to facilitate, as well as the 'many of the world's great cultural institutions' who have adopted the framework. On the IIIF website itself, 'community focused' is the very first phrase below the banner of the site. The theme of consumption and nourishment surfaces later: as the IIIF documentation puts it—in wording I trace back to a 2014 article—IIIF enables the implementation of 'many different styles of viewer … that **consume** the information to enable a rich and dynamic user experience, **consuming** content from across collections and hosting institutions'.[27] Within IIIF, the book appears as images; behind these images, further structured text, the manifest, binds together the text-bearing images of the manuscript and our own annotations; together, these data create the digital book-object to be 'consumed' by viewers and reading communities.

   Here they are, side by side, these three moments of reflection on technologies of text. Martianus Capella depicts the profusion of material books vomited by Philology on her way towards the gods. Ælfric, following Augustine, imagines the miracle of the loaves and fishes as beautiful letters, praised for their beauty, understood for their meaning. And in our own moment, the IIIF framework models and imagines the relationship of text, image, and physical books, consumed by digital platforms and nourishing scholarly communities. In each of these moments, the work of words is anchored in the material: in the human body, through images of nourishment or purgation; and in the book, through references to the books' materiality, visuality, and interaction with reader communities. And the work of words is capacious and generative as my examples have shown. IIIF's description of its data model continues the thematic of consumption, multiplication, and regeneration of knowledge in the form of material written texts and their digital avatars. Each of these vignettes above is what Beechy calls 'attempts at cultural curatorship in the face of change'. Martianus Capella, she notes, 'writing at the end of the Classical era in the time of Augustine, compiles the curriculum of the liberal arts under the auspices of pagan allegory'.[28] Ælfric fits within Beechy's paradigm: he writes at the turn of the first millennium, in the shadow of Viking attacks (even the marginal annotations of CCCC 162 bear witness to this clear and present danger) and in the deeper shadow of an imminent Last Judgment.

A millennium after CCCC 162's compilation, we are fellow inhabitants of troubled times, and our own field of digital humanities bears witness to the imperative of 'cultural curatorship in the face of change'.[29] In a 2014 keynote, Bethany Nowviskie reflects on anthropogenic climate change and biodiversity loss on a global scale. Against the backdrop of wildlife extinction, 'an ending of things, a barring of doors, not seen since the colossal dying that closed the Mesozoic Era, 66 million years ago', Nowviskie considers digital humanities' work of archiving, reconstruction, and sustainability, 'the digital recovery of texts, objects, and traces of human experience thought long since lost to time'. She ends, not unlike Ælfric, by emphasizing communities of practice, bound together by whispered translations.[30] The concern with recovery and reconstruction is similarly evident within medieval studies. In *Speculum*'s 2017 'Digital Middle Ages Supplement', the term 'reconstruction' and its cognates appear 13 times in the overview of medieval digital humanities alone, describing one or more projects in every single category of digital medieval studies.[31] And within the medievalist IIIF community, projects such as *Fragmentarium* or *John Stow's Books* use IIIF's affordances for digital reconstructions of broken books or dispersed libraries.[32] Like Martianus Capella's vision of Philology vomiting a wild variety of books before consuming immortality, like Ælfric's image of the loaves and fishes miracle as *faegere stafas* ('beautiful letters') multiplying and nourishing across generations, Parker on the Web confronts the problem of cultural curatorship, of transmitting knowledge and warding off its loss. Its technologies are new, but its ways of imagining knowledge are continuous with its medieval past. It offers an abundance of books to be consumed by, and to nourish, a multitude of readers; beautiful letters and images, travelling together across time.[33]

Notes

1 The editions consulted for these two texts are: for CCCC 153, William Harris Stahl and Richard Johnson, *Martianus Capella and the Seven Liberal Arts: The Marriage of Philology and Mercury* (New York: Columbia University Press, 1971), vol. 2; for CCCC 162, Peter Clemoes, ed., *Ælfric's Catholic Homilies. The First Series*, Early English Text Society, ss 17 (Oxford: Oxford University Press, 1997). For Martianus Capella, I cite Stahl and Johnson's translation; for Old English texts, translations are my own. The facsimiles consulted for these two texts: 'Cambridge, Corpus Christi College, MS 153: The Corpus Martianus Capella', Parker on the Web: https://parker.stanford.edu/parker/catalog/wb769ft6889 <accessed 25 July 2018>; and 'Cambridge, Corpus Christi College, MS 162: Old English Homilies', Parker on the Web: https://parker.stanford.edu/parker/catalog/ft757ht3699 <accessed 25 July 2018>.

2 Dot Porter comprehensively discusses terms naming digitized manuscripts, in 'Is This Your Book? What We Call Digitized Manuscripts and Why it Matters', Dot Porter Digital, accessed 1 May 2020: www.dotporterdigital.org/is-this-your-book-what-digitization-does-to-manuscripts-and-what-we-can-do-about-it/. See also Abigail G. Robertson, 'A note on technology and functionality in digital manuscript studies,' in this volume, 33–37.

3 See, for further discussion of this passage, Elizabeth Boyle, Chapter 16 in this volume.

4 Tiffany Beechy, 'Consumption, Purgation, Poetry, Divinity: Incarnational Poetics and the Indo-European Tradition', *Modern Philology* 114 (2016): 149–69, at pp. 150–1.

5 Beechy, 'Consumption, Purgation, Poetry, Divinity', p. 157.

6 Martin Foys points out not only the 'careful detailing of the multiple physical forms of Philologia's textual vomit', a diversity of physical media matching a diversity of ideas and disciplines, but also 'the notion that language meaningfully joins human and textual physicality'. See Martin K. Foys, 'A Sensual Philology for Anglo-Saxon England', *postmedieval: a journal of medieval cultural studies* 5 (2014): 456–72, and especially 458–9. For a discussion of the diversity of media in Philology's vomit, see also M. Eisner, 'The Return to Philology and the Future of Literary Criticism: Reading the Temporality of Literature in Auerbach, Benjamin, and Dante', *California Italian Studies* 2.1 (2011): https://escholarship.org/uc/item/4gq644zp, cited by Foys, 'A Sensual Philology for Anglo-Saxon England', p. 458.

7 D. G. Scragg, 'Cambridge Corpus Christi College 162', in *Anglo-Saxon Manuscripts and Their Heritage*, ed. P. Pulsiano and E. Treharne (Aldershot: Ashgate, 1998), pp. 71–83, at p. 80.

8 K. Powell, 'Viking Invasions and Marginal Annotations in Cambridge, Corpus Christi College 162', *Anglo-Saxon England* 37 (2009): 151–71: doi:10.1017/S0263675109990184; Kathryn A. Lowe, 'Filling the Silence: Shared Content in Four Related Manuscripts of Ælfric's *Catholic Homilies*', *Digital Philology: A Journal of Medieval Cultures* 4 (2015): 190–224: https://muse.jhu.edu/ <accessed 25 June 2018> ; E. Treharne, 'Making their Presence Felt: Readers of Ælfric, *c*. 1050–1350', in *A Companion to Ælfric*, ed. Hugh Magennis and Mary Swan, Brill's Companions to the Christian Tradition, 18 (Leiden and Boston: Brill, 2011), pp. 399–422.

9 Peter Clemoes, ed., *Ælfric's Catholic Homilies*, pp. 275–80. Translations from the Old English are my own.

10 Malcolm Godden, ed., *Ælfric's Catholic Homilies: Introduction, Commentary, and Glossary*, Early English Text Society (Oxford: Oxford University Press, 2000), pp. 94–101.

11 Godden, *Catholic Homilies: Commentary*, p. 85; M. Godden, 'Ælfric's Saints' Lives and the Problem of Miracles', in *Old English Prose: Basic Readings*, ed. P. E. Szarmach and Deborah A. Oosterhouse (New York: Garland, 2000), pp. 287–310; and F. M. Biggs, *Sources of Anglo-Saxon Literary Culture: The Apocrypha*. Instrumenta Anglistica Mediaevalia 1 (Kalamazoo, MI: Medieval Institute Publications, 2007).

12 Clemoes, *Ælfric's Catholic Homilies*, pp. 275–80. Italics my own.

13 Caroline Walker Bynum, 'Wonder', *American Historical Review* 102 (1997): 1–26. doi: 10.1086/ahr/102.1.1; http://resolver.scholarsportal.info/resolve/00028762/v102i0001/1_w.

14 *Dictionary of Old English Web Corpus*, ed. Antonette diPaolo Healey, John Price Wilkin, and Xin Xiang (Toronto: University of Toronto, 2009): http://tapor.library. utoronto.ca/doecorpus/ <accessed 30 June 2018>.

15 Godden, *Catholic Homilies: Commentary*, pp. 93–94.

16 Treharne, 'Making their Presence Felt'.

17 Lines 135–40.

18 Alexandra Bolintineanu, 'Beyond the Sun's Setting: Webs of Unknowing in Old English', *Digital Philology: A Journal of Medieval Cultures* 4 (2015): 160–89: https://muse.jhu.edu/ <accessed 25 July 2018>.

19 Bolintineanu, 'Beyond the Sun's Setting'.

20 Donald G. Scragg, ed., *The Vercelli Homilies and Related Texts*, Early English Text Society os 300 (Oxford: Oxford University Press, 1992), p. 178.

21 For discussions of Matthew Parker's use of Ælfric's theology, see Aaron J. Kleist, 'Monks, Marriage, and Manuscripts: Matthew Parker's Manipulation (?) of Ælfric of Eynsham', *Journal of English and Germanic Philology* 105 (2006): 312–27. See also N. B. Bjorklund, 'Parker's Purpose for His Manuscripts: Matthew Parker in the Context of His Early Career and Sixteenth-Century Church Reform', in *Old English Literature in Its Manuscript Context*, ed. J. T. Lionarons, Medieval European Studies 5 (Morgantown: West Virginia University Press, 2004), pp. 217–41.

22 For the book's compilation, see Scragg, 'Cambridge Corpus Christi College 162', p. 80; and Lowe, 'Filling the Silence'. For an analysis of the book's function in public reading, and for an in-depth analysis of the readers' visible interactions with the manuscript, see especially Treharne, 'Making their Presence Felt', pp. 409–10. Godden, *Catholic Homilies Commentary*, pp. 94–101.

23 Powell, 'Viking Invasions and Marginal Annotations', p. 151.

24 Treharne, 'Making their Presence Felt'.

25 'Worlds Real and Imagined', Parker Library on the Web, https://parker.stanford.edu/ parker/feature/previous-exhibition-worlds-real-and-imagined accessed 1 May 2020>.

26 'The History of the Book', Parker Library on the Web, https://parker.stanford.edu/ parker/feature/previous-exhibition-the-history-of-the-book, accessed 1 May 2020>.

27 R. Sanderson, B. Albritton, R. Schwemmer, and H. Van de Sompel, 'Shared Canvas: A Collaborative Model for Digital Facsimiles', *International Journal on Digital Libraries* 13 (2012): 3–16. See also: https://iiif.io/api/presentation/2.1/. For a useful problematization of 'consumers' and its cognate terms in DH, see Andrew Prescott, 'Consumers, Creators or Commentators?: Problems of Audience and Mission in the Digital Humanities,' *Arts and Humanities in Higher Education* 11: 1–2 (February 2012): 61–75: doi:10.1177/1474022211428215.

28 Beechy, 'Consumption, Purgation, Poetry, Divinity', p. 68.

29 Bethany Nowviskie, 'Digital Humanities in the Anthropocene', DH2014 Keynote Lecture: http://nowviskie.org/2014/anthropocene/ <accessed 21 February 2018> ; Eira Tansey, 'When the Unbearable Becomes Inevitable: Archives and Climate Change': http://eiratansey.com/2017/05/16/fierce-urgencies-2017/

30 Bethany Nowviskie, 'Digital Humanities in the Anthropocene'.

31 D. J. Birnbaum, S. Bonde, and M. Kestemont, 'The Digital Middle Ages: An Introduction', *Speculum* 92. S1 (2017): S1–S38.

32 *Fragmentarium*: https://fragmentarium.ms/<accessed 31 July 2018>; Alexandra Gillespie *et al.*, *John Stow's Books*: https://oldbooksnewscience.library.utoronto.ca/ <accessed 31 July 2018>.

33 I am deeply grateful to Benjamin Albritton, Georgia Henley, and Elaine Treharne for their creativity, generosity, and labour, both in organizing the Collegium that brought about this volume, and in editing the volume itself.

21 Making a home for manuscripts on the Internet

Michelle R. Warren

Home page is a comforting metaphor. It suggests familiarity and welcome. It is among the many ingenious metaphors that domesticated the Internet by making strange new digital things feel like recognizable old things. When I first came to Parker Library on the Web 2.0, I felt as if someone had rearranged the furniture while I was out on a brief errand. I was disorientated. I couldn't even find my favourite book. But then I started to look around, trying out the new views opened by the new arrangements. The more I looked, the more clearly I perceived the conceptual work that a home page does in shaping our experience of historical documents and of the libraries that safeguard them. As such, they are one of the research tools that are partly responsible for how we interpret the past.

Parker Library on the Web first launched in 2009. In its time, Parker 1.0 was a remarkable innovation that adapted a combination of manuscript, print, and digital norms to conjoin cataloguing with images of the items catalogued. The home page, however, minimizes the site's novelty by drawing on familiar frameworks established through four hundred years of cataloguing. Parker 1.0 cannily reconnects with Archbishop Matthew Parker's bequest by featuring his name in the largest letters on the page, just as his name is italicized in larger letters on the first page of the indenture that set out the legal terms for operating the library and caring for the books (CCCC 575, page 1a). Some form of Parker's name was used in the titles of subsequent catalogues—until M. R. James, Parker 1.0's immediate predecessor and primary source.[1] And so the Internet address 'parkerweb.stanford.edu' returns to the library's foundation even as it marks several ruptures—most notably the displacement from Corpus Christi College, Cambridge to Stanford University.

Countering the newness of 'web', the three manuscript images at the centre of the home page deepen the site's historical lineage. In the middle sits St Dunstan (909–988CE), Archbishop of Canterbury—Parker's ancient and most prestigious predecessor (CCCC 181, folio 1r). Dunstan is flanked by a decorated initial from the life of the even more ancient St Guthlac (674–715) (CCCC 389, folio 22v) and by a snippet of a Middle English motet (CCCC 8, folio Ar). Collectively, these images reference Parker's animating vision of

English vernacular Christianity. They thus loop back to the library's origins in Reformation politics.

The images evoke the materiality of the historical collection, further signalled by the surrounding images of vellum, handwriting, and border decoration. The featured images also show the materiality of digital representation: the descriptions, shelfmarks, and folios appear to 'pop up' as overlays when scrolled over. This effect is created by colour shifts in the screen pixels, giving the illusion of a transparent layer. For brief moments, the uniquely historical and the uniquely digital collocate. Similarly, the typeface 'MS Trebuchet Sans Serif' fuses medieval technology with print forms encoded into pixels: it is defined as a 'humanist' typeface named after a medieval siege engine designed specifically for the Internet (https://en. wikipedia.org/wiki/Trebuchet_MS). In all of these ways, the visual message of the Parker 1.0 home page bridges the collection's long history with the latest digital affordances.

The site's textual description echoes Parker's original conditions of access, which required the library to be open during certain hours: 'WELCOME. Corpus Christi College and the Stanford University Libraries welcome you to Parker on the Web—an interactive, web-based workspace designed to support use and study of the manuscripts in the historic Parker Library at Corpus Christi College, Cambridge'. The repeated 'welcome' emphasizes openness, conditioned on institutional cooperation. The online workspace is presented as an extension

Figure 21.1 Parker 1.0 Home page, screen capture from archived page
https://swap.stanford.edu/20170124002144/https://parker.stanford.edu/parker/actions/page.do?forward=home

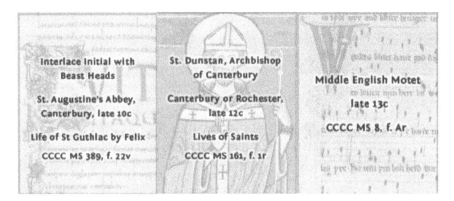

Figure 21.2 Home page image identifications, screen captures from archived page
https://web.archive.org/web/20100621231457/http://parkerweb.stanford.
edu/parker/actions/page.do?forward=home

of the reading room in Cambridge. The surrounding hyperlinked text is equally welcoming, with a multiplicity of access points across the top and bottom of the page that provide flexibility for both newcomers and experts. The whole is bound by a thin lined frame, leaving a wide margin of white space to fill the rest of the screen. This framing device, used throughout the site's pages, echoes the table forms found in print catalogues. All in all, the Parker 1.0 home page fuses the aesthetics of manuscript, print, and digital forms.

Several aspects of the site navigation substantiate the home page's 'welcomes'. On the top line, the 'About' link brings up extensive documentation explaining the history of the library, the catalogues, the production of the site itself, the institutional partners, and (as of Release 1.2) the role of conservation in digital reproduction. Here, the complexity of the project comes into view. It was an international partnership between Cambridge, Corpus Christi College; Cambridge University Library; Stanford University Libraries; the Andrew W. Mellon Foundation; and the Gladys Krieble Delmas Foundation. The names of the many individuals who worked on the project 2004–09 are listed as well as the technical specifications of the photography and the website itself. Next to the 'About' link, the 'Tutorials' link opens to a page with five introductory videos on how to use the site. Although the videos, made with QuickTime, no longer function, they were wisely accompanied by text transcriptions: this 'best practice' for sensory processing accessibility is also a best practice for archival sustainability.

Further welcomes populate the footer. The 'Links' page lists 'Comparable Sites', where users could find more digital resources for manuscript study. A second tab opens a page with an extensive list of 'Tools & Resources': bibliography, textual databases, dictionaries, biographies, and musical resources. This list gathers a snapshot of the digital tools of scholarship *c.* 2010. The 'Glossary' addresses the needs of anyone not familiar with manuscripts and technical terminology: it is a revised version of the British Library online glossary, based on Michelle Brown's *Understanding Illuminated Manuscripts*.[2] And just in case the home page doesn't provide enough guidance and one gets lost, the 'Site Map' lists all the site's pages on one screen. Finally, 'Contact Us' invites interaction with the real people who maintained both the site and the manuscripts, inviting questions and feedback. Parker 1.0 is thus a comprehensive portal for manuscript studies—a catalogue, a handbook, an institutional history, and an Internet tutorial all in one.

All of these welcoming factors reflect the governing vision of Christopher De Hamel, who brought a spirit of openness to the library as a whole. The digital catalogue and the reproduction of manuscript images extend what he saw as the library's founding identity:

> In theory, it has been open to readers since 1574, but for several centuries it was almost impossible to gain admission. These days we are glad to welcome scholars of all nationalities to see and study the treasures of the Parker Library. Corpus Christi College is delighted that the new Parker Library on the Web facility now allows even more people access to these breathtaking manuscripts, which are truly the heritage of the world.[3]

All through the planning phases of the project, the website was described as a free resource.[4] The commitment to represent the whole collection—the 'unloved' manuscripts alongside the 'treasures', in the words of Suzanne Paul—also removed some of the filters of selection that would otherwise predetermine accessibility.[5]

Digital publishing, however, requires infrastructure that brings new forms of restriction. The home page thus also includes links to legal information that communicate the terms of intellectual property. The 'Copyright' notice invokes the legal codes of both the United Kingdom and the United States. It also addresses how users' data will be handled as digital property, with more details outlined under the 'Privacy Policy'. Both pages are written in a gentle, informative tone even as they expose the fact that using an Internet site is anything but private. These transparent notices protect users as well as the library, though it might have been a new concept that studying medieval manuscripts would involve the UK Data Protection Act of 1988.

Most jarring for the welcome spirit of home, however, is the invitation to 'Click here for information about site subscriptions'. The link connected to the German publisher Harrassowitz, where it was explained that access to the site's full features—high resolution images, bibliography, and search—came with a hefty price tag marketed to institutions: $9,500 purchase with annual maintenance fee of $480 or annual subscription of $3,500, with discounts for consortia of subscribers. The purpose was clearly stated: 'to generate income to ensure that the resource can be maintained, enhanced, and forward-migrated as necessary'.[6] Stanford served as the licensor and the License Agreement spelled out user rights and promised product stability through migration; licensees were also offered a 'local copy' for offline use—for free if 'the Product' were discontinued. The Harrassowitz FAQ describes in detail the maintenance expenses that the fees will cover—and specifies that a sustainable business model was a condition of the grants that paid for the four-year project to photograph the manuscripts and build the site: 'such support was contingent on the development and execution of a business plan to secure support from users to offset the substantial expense of ongoing operations'.[7] Parker 1.0 was thus a subscription offered by Stanford Libraries through Harrassowitz with the laudable goal of maintaining a durable resource.

The high price of access was widely criticized for creating a new barrier to scholarship. The subscription, like other commercial knowledge resources, divided the scholarly community into those with institutional access and those without. The effects of this model on scholarship in general are deep and enduring. They are of course not new to digital publishing but continuous with the market forces that characterize print, as Siân Echard has shown for British Library projects.[8] And the commercial model is one version of responsible stewardship. The project explicitly recognized the digital files as a new physical asset that would require conservation measures akin to the manuscripts themselves: 'The project is of major importance for creating and preserving quality images of unique materials. All images and metadata have been placed in a managed digital preservation repository.'[9] Digital reproduction thus increased the amount and type of material that needed preservation, thereby increasing costs. Ironically, De Hamel had originally envisioned digitization as a source of revenue for making the library self-sustaining.[10] In practice, the projected costs of digital curation outstripped potential revenue.

While the 'open' ethos of the Internet shifted expectations for ease of access, archival access at Parker Library (and everywhere) is always contingent on a number of factors that create overlapping exclusions—whether by curatorial whim (as De Hamel intimated), the ability to climb the stairs, or the financial means to travel. The digital catalogue reconfigured forms of access and exclusion that already existed. Its effects were similar to those of Early English Books Online, neatly summarized by Bonnie Mak:

> Those without access to EEBO must nevertheless locate their studies with respect to the work of those who benefit from an institutional subscription to the database. Through this phenomenon, EEBO will be established as a canonical resource in the lives of those for whom legitimate access to it is precluded. The significance of such a lacuna for 'have not' scholars and for scholarship more broadly has yet to be fully grasped.[11]

While EEBO remains the commercial product that it has always been—since Eugene Power started microfilming at the British Library in the 1930s—the commercial phase of Parker on the Web had a more limited run, 2009 to 2018. Its effects will be working their way through scholarship for some time but they are already yielding to new ones.

One of the most touted—and welcome—new features of Parker 2.0 is its open access. The termination of subscriptions has been widely praised as aligning the resource with current norms for public knowledge systems. Free, however, doesn't mean without constraint. Every resource—digital or other-wise—has structures that make some things highly visible and other things difficult or impossible to see. Our task as users is to understand how those structures interface with our research questions so that we can remain alive to how those questions themselves emerge from within the constraints of infra-structure. In this way, we can also keep open the possibility of imagining questions that push beyond a given constraint to seek answers elsewhere. In my initial confusion over the Parker 2.0 home page, I became very conscious of how my habits of thought had acculturated to the Parker 1.0 design. In navigating the new dissonance, I saw the workings of Internet technology with new clarity.

The home page for Parker 2.0 displays a succinct mix of continuities and ruptures with Parker 1.0. The top line identifies 'Stanford Libraries' by name and logo, indicating that the site is part of a larger repository. The site title remains the same—although 'on the web' is now the same font size on the same line, no longer a diminutive addition. A new subtitle clarifies the scope for new comers who may not already know about Parker Library: 'Manu-scripts in the Parker Library at Corpus Christi College, Cambridge'. The featured image reiterates the library's identity—depicting the Wilkins Reading Room (1827), with a portrait of Parker in the distance and an overlay image with the college's name and logo (a pelican). This photo represents the physical space where James would have prepared his catalogue in the early twentieth century and where Parker 1.0 started. The page as a whole, how-ever, performs the break that website design has made with the printed page: it no longer fits on my laptop screen as a single image but requires scrolling to access all of its features. This adaptation responds to hardware changes, in which screens come in a great variety of sizes and web software is increasingly designed to adapt to multiple viewing environments.

The descriptive text remains welcoming, with two additional sentences that condense the essential 'About' information from Parker 1.0:

> Corpus Christi College and the Stanford University Libraries welcome you to Parker Library on the Web, a digital exhibit designed to support use and study of the manuscripts in the historic Parker Library at Corpus Christi College, Cambridge. The Parker Library is a treasure trove of rare medieval and Renaissance manuscripts, as well as early printed books. Almost all manuscripts in the Parker Library collection have been fully

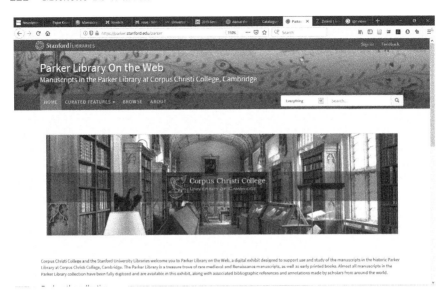

Figure 21.3 Parker 1.0, screen capture of featured image and navigation.

digitised and are available in this exhibit, along with associated bibliographic references and annotations made by scholars from around the
world.

Instead of a 'workspace', however, the site is identified as an 'exhibit'. This
change in terminology reflects the change from a cataloguing model (1.0 as a
digital edition of James) to a repository model (2.0 as an image database).
Indeed, Parker 2.0 has a second URL that locates the site within the broader
collection of Stanford Libraries' digital exhibits (https://exhibits.stanford.
edu/parker). Here, it becomes clear that Parker 2.0 adapts a shared template
designed for curated exhibits of all kinds that draw from the Stanford Digital
Repository   (https://library.stanford.edu/research/spotlight/technology).   In
these exhibits, images are 'served' from the repository using the syntax of the
International Image Interoperability Framework (IIIF), probably the most
significant technical innovation developed since the conception of Parker 1.0
almost 20 years ago. IIIF defines a standard for hosting images that enables
them to be used in any networked environment that recognizes the standard.
It thus enables automated online aggregation of images that share the standard syntax. This interoperability makes Parker 2.0 part of a larger interactive digital ecosystem rather than (only) a dedicated destination for images
of Parker manuscripts.

The navigation options above and below the Wilkins Room image reinforce
the spirit of 'welcome'. The top line mostly replicates the options from Parker
1.0, which are common components of web page design: Home, Browse,

Search, About (which replicates most of the 1.0 text). Navigation also includes a new option that reinforces the site's identity as an exhibit: 'Curated Features'. Most of these pages draw the site closer to Parker Library in Cambridge, as the Wilkins Room photo has already signalled: the pages include information about where manuscripts have been loaned as well as digital exhibits that derive from analogue exhibits curated in the Wilkins Room. These exhibits provide some of the newcomer orientation that was previously part of the Glossary on Parker 1.0, although in a narrative rather than dictionary form. Combined with the featured photo, these exhibits reground the site in Cambridge even as IIIF multiplies the potential locations of the manuscript images.

Scrolling down below the featured image and welcome text, two rows of images define navigation for two types of 'exploration', duplicating some of the top line functions. 'Explore the collection' includes three parts: Manuscripts, Page-level Details (Annotations), and Bibliography. 'Explore special topics' takes the place of Parker 1.0s Tutorials, with three 'Hints and Tips': The Basics for Parker 2.0, Bibliography, and The Manuscript Viewing Window (Mirador Viewer, https://projectmirador.org/). Relative to Parker 1.0, Bibliography is a more prominent resource, as it wasn't previously part of the home page navigation. The site as a whole is obviously more welcoming in the absence of subscription and with Contact Us duplicated as a 'Feedback' form; the names and emails of the three managing librarians are highlighted in the left navigation panel on the About page (Anne McLaughlin, Alex Devine, Benjamin Albritton). The absence of Privacy information is curious, given the expansion of data protection measures over the past decade. With a little digging through https://exhibits.stanford.edu/parker, though, you can find your way to the page for 'opt out analytics' (https://library.stanford.edu/opt-out). The treatment of Copyright is both more open and more discrete. Rather than a home page announcement, rights are defined in the More Details of the manuscript descriptions and in the Viewing Window's Information tab. Creative Commons for non-commercial use provides flexibility for born-digital image use, while established print Copyright remains in place for publishing. These navigation features largely replicate functions available on Parker 1.0 but reconfigure the emphasis: Bibliography has the same status as the Manuscripts; Rights are attached to the images more than to the site itself.

The use of images as navigation 'links' showcases illustration as a prized feature of both manuscripts and IIIF—the syntax that defines where and how to display an image on a web page. Each image visually echoes the navigation text: a figure reading a book for the Manuscripts, figures with writing materials for the Bibliography, and a figure pointing to his eye for the Viewing Window. The Wheel of Fortune humorously (?) illustrates 'Page-level Details', where the details are not systematic and may or may not be helpful. Similarly, two friendly (?) beasts beckon viewers into the site navigation tutorial. Even the static header is self-referential (a border for a border). Redundant messaging—through text and image, or colour and text—is one recommended strategy for accessible web design. Unlike the images featured on Parker 1.0, these images function referentially even if one knows nothing more about their source or content. Clicking on them doesn't reveal their identity but rather opens a page with the advertised function.

The image sources are identified in the page's source code. No longer on the surface, 'popping up' for the average user, the shelfmarks and folios can be found with a modest understanding of advanced web browser functions and Hyper Text Markup Language (HTML). Browsers include menus with titles like 'developer tools' or 'web developer' that show the HTML code that defines how a page looks and works. Here, the IIIF syntax is readable by both machines and humans. It draws the image extracts from the digital repository by defining how much of a targeted file to display and where. By reading through the page source code, I could recognize the shelfmarks and folios— and then navigate to them through the Search box. The Description for each manuscript provided overall context for each item's history and significance. The Descriptions, crucially, were formerly subscription-protected Summaries on Parker 1.0, written variously by Suzanne Paul, Nigel Morgan, Neil Coates, Rebecca Rushforth, and Elizabeth Boyle. Described by Paul as something of an 'afterthought', the Descriptions are now the main point of entry for learning about an unfamiliar manuscript.[12] For more detail, I clicked on 'More Details'—where I found a link to a digital scan from James's catalogue, which usually described the specific image I was trying to identify. I found it easier, however, to locate descriptive details by returning to Parker

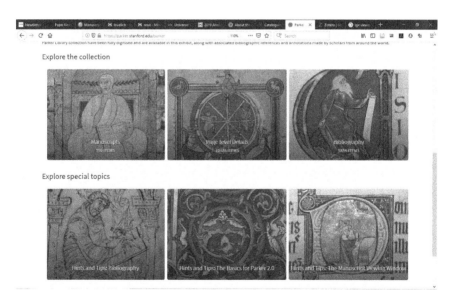

Figure 21.4 Parker 2.0, screen capture of navigation.

1.0, with its neatly formatted, annotated, and corrected edition of James's entries. On the image of the specific folios, the Page-level Details tended not to describe the images but rather to transcribe incipits and rubrics. My experience identifying unknown images in unknown sources made clear that Parker 2.0 was no longer a digital edition but instead a born-digital tool with a complex relationship to pre-digital histories. Relative to Parker 1.0, its mechanisms are both more transparent and more mystifying.

In one case, the source code pointed to a static JPEG file and did not include a shelfmark in its syntax. I turned to the Feedback form to ask about the source, receiving almost immediately a detailed and informative email reply from Benjamin Albritton (September 20, 2019). He explained that Bibliography required a different approach to image display because the bibliography resource on Zotero.org doesn't have images. The navigation images are rendered by a piece of code—a 'widget'—that uses the results of a saved search for the image file in the repository. Since a search for Bibliography doesn't return any images, a file was created—and the syntax for retrieving it thus lacks the usual identifiers. This situation shows how the standard architecture of the home page had to be 'hacked' in order to generate a consistent visual effect. The home page, moreover, embeds the same IIIF syntax that structures the manuscript images themselves—indeed, it draws (with one exception) from the very same files that are also drawn into the Viewing Window. At the level of code, then, navigation and content converge. Such is the purpose of IIIF—to enable digital image files to be re-used and re-configured in dynamic online environments. With the right syntax, you can 'take' the images to another viewer or application, arranging them according to your own specifications. Parker 2.0 thus marks a new moment in digital manuscript studies where users can also become makers.

And so, after much research, it becomes apparent that the navigation images combine iconographic messaging with historical significance. The Manuscripts are presented by Luke, from the Gospels of St. Augustine (CCCC 286, folio 129v). This is the collection's oldest book and of paramount significance to Archbishop Parker as it was associated with the ancient origins of Christianity in Britain and at Canterbury in particular. The Page-level Details derive from a copy of the *Historia Anglorum* (CCCC 66, p. 66), an English history that signals Parker's nationalist interests. Isaiah from the Bury Bible (CCCC 2II, folio 220v) guides us to Bibliography—a small snippet from a very large book, also among the library's most famous. The 'Hints and Tips' for Bibliography come from a famous writer—St Jerome, depicted composing the Life of St. Paul (CCCC 389, folio 1v). This book also came from Canterbury—and provided the image of St Guthlac for Parker 1.0. The friendly beasts for 'The Basics of 2.0' come from the beginning of the Bury Bible (CCCC 2I, folio 1v). Finally, King David points us to the 'Viewing Window' from within a gilded 'D' in the lavishly illustrated Peterborough Psalter (CCCC 53, folio 38v). One further image to mention—the first identified in the source code—is the floral

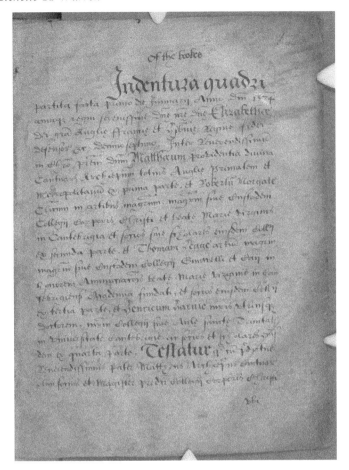

Figure 21.5 The Parker Library, Corpus Christi College, Cambridge, MS 575, p. 1a.

border at the top of the page: it is symbolically in the 'English' style and from the 'first' book in the catalogue, containing copies of works by Gregory the Great (CCCC 1, folio 31r). Collectively, these manuscripts represent some of the library's most famous as well as some of the issues of greatest concern to Parker. In this sense, the home page continues the strategies of Parker 1.0, albeit less overtly. Their more prominent role is to convey the functions of the site itself as a tool.

It's been almost two years since the opening of Parker 2.0. I have settled in to the new arrangements at home. But I would like us all to remember the old ones too. Parker 1.0 is not only evidence of an important historical moment in the practice of medieval studies and library science, it reveals the current arrangements to be *arrangements*—not natural, inevitable, or neutral, but the product of a complex interaction of protocols, communities, machines, and capital. All of these components are integral to the way we arrive at historical interpretation—not obstacles to overcome but infrastructures to understand. The consequences of that understanding are in turn essential to manuscript studies and information management in the current digital century.[13]

Notes

1 M. R. James, *A Descriptive Catalogue of the Manuscripts in the Library of Corpus Christi College, Cambridge*, 2 vols. (Cambridge: Cambridge University Press, 1909–12); Parker 1.0 'About' page: https://swap.stanford.edu/20170124002144/https://parker.stanford.edu/parker/actions/page.do?forward=home.

2 Michelle P. Brown, *Understanding Illuminated Manuscripts: A Guide to Technical Terms* (Malibu, CA: J. Paul Getty Museum, 1994): https://www.bl.uk/catalogues/illuminatedmanuscripts/glossary.asp.

3 'Parker Library on the Web' (Harrassowitz Verlag, 2009): https://web.archive.org/web/20090414101321/http:/www.harrassowitz.de/Parker_on_the_Web.html.

4 *The Parker Library Appeal: An Appeal for Funds for the New Parker Library*, Corpus Christi College (Cambridge: Cambridge University Press, 2000); Christopher De Hamel, *The Parker Chronicle: Friends of the Parker Library Newsletter*, vols. 1–4 (2005–8).

5 Suzanne Paul, 'Function', lecture presented at Celebrating Parker 2.0 at Stanford University: Stanford Text Technologies Fourth Annual Collegium (25 March 2018).

6 'Parker Library in the Web', Harrassowitz Verlag.

7 'Parker Library in the Web', Harrassowitz Verlag.

8 Siân Echard, *Printing the Middle Ages* (Philadelphia: University of Pennsylvania Press, 2008), pp. 208–9.

9 Parker 1.0, 'About'.

10 Christopher De Hamel, interview in *The Pelican* 19 (2010): 8–11, at p. 10.

11 Bonnie Mak, 'Archeology of Digitization', *Journal of the Association for Information Science and Technology* 65 (2014): 1515–26, at p. 1521.

12 Paul, 'Function'.

13 My sincerest thanks to Suzanne Paul, for sharing her unpublished work and for generous feedback on a draft of this chapter, and to Benjamin Albritton, for responding so quickly and thoughtfully to my technical queries.

Index

Aberystwyth, National Library of Wales 49–50
Abolita Glossary 146
Abstrusa Glossary 146
Accessibility to manuscript repositories 2, 4, 33, 36, 39, 67, 84, 100, 107, 116, 139, 142, 149, 186, 218, 219
Ælfric, Abbot 50, 65, 179, 181, 187, 188, 205–215
Æthelred II, King 77
Ælfwine, Abbot 173, 186
Æðelbert, King of Kent 122–24, 126
Albritton, Benjamin 223
Aldfrith, King 103
Aldhelm 105, 146
Alfred, King 147, 188
Ancrene Wisse 5, 8, 142, 147, 163–67
Andrew W. Mellon Foundation 10, 218
Anlezark, Daniel 175, 176
annotation 2, 11, 35, 47–49, 50, 95, 97, 116–18, 123, 125, 133–35, 139, 184, 185, 190–93, 195, 206, 208, 211, 212, 213, 222, 225
Aquinas, Thomas 26
Asser, Bishop 42, 112
Augustine, Saint 5, 40, 41, 45, 93–97, 106, 116, 119, 120, 122–24, 155, 156, 195, 200–202, 207–9, 211–13, 225
Austin, J. L. 181

Backhouse, Janet 37
Barbier, Jean 78
Barlow, Frank 125–26
Barrington, Candace 5
Batman, Stephen 85
Baudrillard, Jean 30, 165
Baydawi, Abd Allah 44
Beach, Alison 187

Bede 41, 65, 93, 96, 97, 103–5, 121–26, 142, 173, 184, 185, 207, 209
Beechy, Tiffany 188, 206, 213
Benjamin, Walter 38, 41
Berger, John 38, 39
bibliophilia 173, 183
Biblissima 12
binding 26, 33, 68–69, 71, 76, 78, 195, 212
biography of manuscripts 70, 72, 195
Biscop, Benedict 103
Bodleian Library 25, 49, 74, 78
Bolter, Jay David 165
Book of Benefactors (St Albans Abbey) 46
Book of Kells 40
Boyle, Elizabeth 7, 8, 224
bracketing 35
Bradshaw, Henry 143
Bredehoft, Thomas 164, 166
Breen, Katherine 137
Bremmer, Rolf 102
British Library 1, 25, 26, 37, 44, 46, 50, 219–21
Broken Books 30
Brown, Bill 126
Brown, Michelle 149, 219
Budny, Mildred 71, 114, 115, 121, 197, 202
Bury St Edmunds 119, 225; Bury Bible 225
Bynum, Caroline Walker 30, 209
Byrhtferth of Ramsey 173, 185

Campagnolo, Alberto 14, 67
Cannell, Gill 113
Canterbury 28, 102–7, 116, 121, 123, 142, 155, 190, 225; commentaries 102, 104–7; Canterbury School 100–107, 151

Canterbury Tales (Chaucer) 5, 51
Capella, Martianus 7, 8, 154, 155, 158, 159, 205, 206, 212, 213
capitalization 5, 35, 45, 48, 206, 209
Cardinal Reiner, 133
Caroline minuscule 154, 155
Cassiodorus 25, 195
Center for Spatial and Textual Analysis 1
Chaucer, Geoffrey 4–5, 6, 58–9, 82, 86, 88
Chronica Maiora 46, 53, 131–37, 139–41, 191, 212
Clark, James 40, 47, 52, 53
Clark, Kenneth 40, 47, 52, 53
Cnut 77, 125
Coates, Neil 224
codex 6, 18–22, 34, 40–42, 76, 78, 79, 85, 93, 94, 96–98, 100, 103, 132, 174–76, 181, 184, 212
Codex Amiatinus 40
codicology 6, 57, 64–72, 75, 114, 173
Colgrave, Bertram 123
Connolly, Daniel 137, 141
Connolly, Margaret 83
copyright 9, 17, 219, 223
Corpus Glossary 142–47, 150, 152
Cotton, Robert 39, 42–44
Cotton Library 42, 44; fire of 1731 44, 125
Crostini, Barbara 35
crusades 27, 47, 48, 133
cursive script 58, 59, 61, 65

Dag, Thomas (or Day) 44
Dale, Darley 175
David, King 225
Davies, Richard (Bishop of St Davids) 45, 49, 50, 53, 54, 141
De Diceto, Ralph (Dean of St Paul's) 46
De Hamel, Christopher 9, 39–41, 43, 219, 220
Dekker, Kees 100–103, 105, 109
Denning Fund 1
Deshman, Robert 126
Despenser, Bishop Henry 47–48
Devine, Alex 223
DigiPal 3, 12, 114
digital interface 85
digital preservation 23–24
digital surrogates 33, 35, 40, 78, 82, 107, 112, 113, 139, 183, 195
digital and analogue user experience 75, 97, 211–212

digitization effects 1, 4–5, 11, 38–40, 46, 51, 64, 74, 85, 97, 138, 139, 190; as revenue 220; as 'translation' 120–26; as process 17–23; as re-creation 25–31
Donatus 158, 159
Dover Bible 190, 193, 195, 197
Doyle, Kathleen 25
Dumitrescu, Irina 173, 200
Dunstan, Saint 26, 176, 188, 216
Durham University 49

Early English Books Online (EEBO) 220, 221
Echard, Siân 6, 220
e-codices 11
Endres, Bill 26
Exeter Book 5, 38, 51, 174

facsimiles 3, 33, 35, 39, 68, 82–85, 87, 97, 98, 107, 165, 166, 184, 195
Fafinski, Mateusz 5–7, 120, 123
Fastolf, Sir John 57
Federal Agencies Digital Guidelines Initiative (FADGI) 19
Florentius of Valeranica 26
Flores Historiarum 131, 133
Flower, Robin 49, 50, 53, 54
Ford, A. J. 123
Forkbeard, Svein 125
Fox, Deb 21
Foys, Martin 165, 214
Frampton, Richard 47, 53
Franton, Edward 83–85
From the Page 12
Fulton, Helen 157

Galway, Margaret 87
Gambier, Yves 93
Gameson, Richard 114
Geoffrey of Monmouth 138, 164
Geraldus Cambriensis (Gerald of Wales) 50
Geza, Theodore 45
Gildas 146, 150
Gill, Eric 86
Gladys Krieble Delmas Foundation 10, 218
Global Currents 1, 12
glossing 3, 6, 7, 33, 35, 95, 97, 102, 114–16, 119, 138, 139, 142–46, 149–51, 154–56, 158, 191, 211
Gneuss, Helmut 121
Go, Michaela 21
Gobbitt, Thom 75, 77

Goble, Warwick 86
Godden, Malcolm 207, 209
GoldenThread 19
Goldthwaite, R.A. 30
Goobi 21, 22
Google 31
Grafton, Anthony 42, 52, 53
Graham, Tim 126
Grant, Raymond 121
Greenblatt, Stephen 26
Gregory, Pope 6, 106, 112, 115–17,
    119, 226
Grusin, Richard 165
Guthlac, Saint 216, 225

Hardiman, Emma 26
Hardman, Phillipa 86
Harrassowitz 219, 220
Harvey, Barbara 47, 53, 60, 63, 202, 203
Hector, L. C. 47, 53
Heigemeir, Ray 21
Henley, Georgia 147
Henry of Huntingdon 138
Higden, Ranulph *(Polychronicon)* 47
Historia Anglorum 225
Hitchcock, James 44
Hsy, Jonathan 5
Html 224
Hungerford, Amy 174
Huntingfield Psalter 29
hypermediacy 165

illumination 82, 94–95, 166, 174, 195
Image Science Associates 19
incunabula 212
Ine of Wessex 77
ink 25, 27, 28, 47, 65, 85, 104, 179
Innocent, Pope 135
International Image Interoperability
    Framework (IIIF) 8, 9, 11, 13, 23, 30,
    48–50, 57, 72, 167, 206, 212, 213,
    222–25
Intranda 21
Isfahani, Mahmud 44
Item Driven Image Fidelity (IDIF) 18
Iverson, Gunilla 35

Jakobson, Roman 93
James, M.R. 10, 64, 67, 72, 83–85, 176,
    184, 190, 191, 193, 216, 221, 222,
    224, 225
James, Thomas 71
Japan 2, 43, 53
Jefferson, Melvin 132

Jensen, Brian M. 35
Jerome, Saint 104, 144, 146, 152, 225
John of Gaunt 48
John of Malvern 47–48
Joscelyn, John 121
Jullien, François 93, 120

Karkov, Catherine 3, 8, 176
Kay, Sarah 195, 200
Keller, Michael 10
Kemble, John Mitchell 176
Ker, Neil 65–67, 71, 114, 115, 118, 119,
    121, 125
Keynes, Simon 102, 103, 105
Kiernan, Kevin 38
Kim, Dorothy 3, 164, 165, 167
Koran 44
Kurzweil, Ray 31
Kwakkel, Erik 63, 77

Laȝamon 164
Lähnemann, Henrike 25
Lapidge, Michael 104, 115–17, 119, 143,
    144, 146, 185
Larratt Keefer, Sarah 124, 127, 128
Leiden Glossae Collectae 100, 104
Leiden Glossary 101, 102, 105–7, 150
Leofric, Bishop 121, 124–26
Leofric Missal 124, 126
Lewis, Suzanne 132, 135
Lindsay, W. M. 143, 146
Liu, Alan 205
Lloyd, L. J. 125
loanwords 147, 153
Louvre 39
Lovett, Patricia 25
Lowe, Kathryn A. 206
Luard, Henry 46
Lumby, J. R. 47

Mabillon, Jean 74, 75, 80
Mak, Bonnie 220
manuscript heft 2, 6
Manuscripts of the West Midlands 3
Manuscripts
    Aberystwyth, National Library of
        Wales
        3024C (Gerald of Wales) 50
    Cambridge, Corpus Christi College
        (CCCC)
        1 (Gregory the Great) 142, 226
        2i (Bury Bible) 225
        2ii 225
        3 193

4 (Dover Bible) 8, 190, 193–96
7 (St Albans Book of Benefactors) 46
8 216
14 132
16 (Annals) 7, 46, 131–41, 143, 145, 147, 149, 151
16i (*Chronica maiora*) 212
23 (Prudentius) 190–93, 195, 197–98, 200, 202, 203
26 57, 58, 60, 132, 135, 137, 139, 191
41 (Old English Bede) 93, 94, 96, 97,120–26, 188
53 225
61 6, 58, 82, 84–88
66 (Historia Anglorum) 225
76 46
81 (Homer) 44
97 41
98 41, 82, 87, 82, 88
98a 41
122 41
140 (Old English Gospels) 125
144 (Corpus Glossary) 7, 142–45, 147–49, 151, 164
153 (Martianus Capella) 7, 154, 156, 157, 159, 205, 214
154 212
161 (Saints Lives) 112, 115–17, 119
162 (homilies) 8, 205, 206, 208, 209, 211–14
181 216
183 (Gospel book) 100, 105, 108
197A (Chronicle) 47, 53
199 (Augustine *De Trinitate*)156
210 6, 57–61, 63
249 (Koran) 44
286 (Gospels of St Augustine) 5–7, 93–97, 120, 121, 123, 125, 225
320 6, 101, 103–8
322 6, 112–19
367 6, 64–73, 115, 176
383 (Lawcodes) 6, 74–81, 127
384 (Arabic translation of John's Epistle I) 44
389 216, 225
391 114, 124
401 (*Tawali' al-Anwar min Matali' al-Anzar*) 44, 45
402 (*Ancrene Wisse*) 5, 142, 147, 163, 165, 167
422 (Red Book of Darley) 173–89
454 (Laws of Hywel Dda) 50

462 191
478 (Armenian Psalter) 45
480 (Greek Psalter) 45
545 52
546 52
575 216
580A 52
583 52
Cambridge, Trinity College
   R. 17. 1 (Eadwine's Psalterium triplex) 28, 186
Cambridge University Library
   Dd. 1. 1 60
   Ff. 4. 42 (Juvencus) 155
   Ii. 1. 33 65
Exeter Cathedral Library 3501 (The Exeter Book) 51
Hildesheim Dombibliothek
   Hildesheim MS J27 25
Leiden, Bibliotheek der Rijksuniversiteit
   Vos. Lat. Q.69 (The Leiden Glossary) 102
London, British Library
   Additional 18160 50
   Cotton Claudius B. iv (The Old English Hexateuch) 44, 125
   Cotton Domitian A. i (Geraldus *Journey through Wales*) 50
   Cotton Galba A. ix and A. x 44
   Cotton Julius A. ii 103
   Cotton Nero D. vii 46
   Cotton Otho C. i, Part 2 113–16
   Cotton Tiberius A. i (Koran) 44
   Cotton Tiberius A. iii 103
   Cotton Titus C. xiv (Abd al-Wahhab al-Sha'rani) 44
   Cotton Titus D. xvii 44 (print volume)
   Cotton Titus D. xxvi+xxvii (Ælfwine's Prayerbook) 186
   Cotton Vespasian B. vi 100, 108
   Cotton Vespasian F. xvii (Merchant's Account Book) 43, 53
   Royal 2 B. v 108
   Royal 10 A. xiii 26
   Royal 13 B. xii 50
   Royal 14 C. vii 132, 141
   Royal 20 D. i (*Roman de Troie*) 86

New York, Pierpont Morgan Library
  M. 43 (Huntingfield Psalter) 29
Oxford, Bodleian Library
  Auctuarium F. 4. 32 (Ovid *Ars armatoria*) 156
  Bodley 340 (Old English Homiliary) 125
  Bodley 579 (Leofric Missal) 126
  Hatton 113 107
  Hatton 76 114–15
  Junius 11 (Old English Junius Book of Poetry) 125
  Tanner 3 114
Paris, Bibliothèque National de France
  Latin MS 1196 86
  Latin MS 2825 108
Philadelphia, Museum of Art
  Ms 1945–65–1 86

marginalia 2, 7, 41, 43, 46–48, 53, 65, 66, 76, 83, 85, 95, 107, 121, 124, 125, 127, 128, 131, 132, 134, 135, 138, 173, 174, 184, 190, 197, 208, 213–15, 218
Marks, Richard 85
Martianus Capella 7, 8, 154–59, 205, 206, 212, 213
Mascagni, Pietro 21
McCarty, Willard 28
McKenna, Catherine 157
McKitterick, David 42
McKitterick, Rosamond 143, 145
McLaughlin, Anne 72, 223
Medingen Psalter 25
Meecham-Jones, Simon 147
Mercia 7, 103, 142, 145, 147, 148, 150
metadata 2, 4, 10, 17, 19, 34, 35, 61, 94, 96, 97, 220
metatextuality 35
microfiche 107
microfilm 4, 221
Millett, Bella 163
Mirador 8, 23, 38, 48, 57, 113, 121, 166, 167, 212
mise-en-page 7, 28
Morgan, Hollie 118
Morgan, Nigel 224
Musk, Elon 31
Muybridge, Eadweard 21
Mynors, R. A. B. 123

Nadin, Mihai 28
National Archives (Kew) 60
National Library of Wales, Aberystwyth 14, 49, 50, 53, 54, 161

Nevill, Anne 83
New Philology 173
Nishikawa, Kinohi 174
Northumbria 142
Nowell, Laurence 49, 54
Nowviskie, Bethany 213

Orosius, Paulus 86, 150, 190, 191, 200, 201
Ovid 155, 156, 158, 159
O'Keeffe, Katherine O'Brien 180

palaeography 3, 6, 23, 72, 75, 114, 150, 154,
Paris, Matthew, *Chronica Maiora* 46; 7, 9, 13, 52, 53, 57, 71, 80, 82, 88, 94, 95, 121, 131–37, 139–41, 175, 186, 191, 193, 200, 211, 212, 215, 216
Parker, Matthew, Archbishop 9, 13, 52, 53, 71, 82, 121, 175, 200, 211, 215, 216
Parker Library 1, 6, 34, 37–39, 41–43, 45, 46, 49–51, 72, 82, 87, 93, 113, 114, 164, 205, 211, 216, 217, 219–21, 223
Parker on the Web 1, 2, 7–13, 57, 60, 61, 64, 67, 72, 75–77, 80, 85, 98, 112, 113, 120, 121, 127, 138, 139, 147, 149, 154, 163, 165, 166, 174, 175, 181, 184, 186, 190, 191, 195, 202, 205, 206, 211–14, 216, 217, 221, 227; Parker 1.0 11, 216–26, 223; Parker 2.0 1, 7, 9–13, 37–49, 51, 85–88, 100, 106, 107, 112–17, 142, 193, 221–26
Parkes, Malcolm B. 28, 59, 82, 83, 85
Patten, William 45, 49, 53
Paul, Suzanne 219, 224
Pearson, John 22
Pennell, Dorote 84, 85
Peter I (Cyprus) 48
Petrucci, Armando 59
Pfaff, Richard 124
Philoxenus Glossary 146
Phocas 146
Pierpont Morgan Library 1, 32
Piers Plowman (Langland) 4, 51
pocketbooks 77–79
Porter, Dot 3, 67, 151
Powell, Kathryn 206
Power, Eugene 221
Prescott, Andrew 4, 5
Price, Leah 174
Prudentius 190, 191, 197, 199, 200, 202

Quartodecimanism 101, 102, 109
quills 3, 26, 199

Raguso, Benedetto Cotrugni 59
Ralph of Diceto 46, 135
Rambaran-Olm, Mary 5
Red Book of Darley 173, 175, 179,
  182–84, 186
remediation 7, 8, 38, 106, 163–67
Robert of Jumièges 124
Robinson, Pamela 60
Roman de la Rose 11
rubrication 35, 75, 103, 104,
  106, 116, 119, 125, 134,
  167, 225
Rufinus 101, 146
Rushforth, Rebecca 224
Russell, Paul 150, 156, 158
Russian Primary Chronicle 43

Salesbury, William 45, 49, 50,
  53, 54
Salter, Elizabeth 82
Sawyer, Daniel 78, 81
scanners 19
Schoenberg Centre for Manuscript
  Studies 1, 68
Scott, Kathleen 86
Scragg, Donald G. 206, 207
scribes 96, 121–22, 147, 149,
  190–91
Sherman, William H. 173
Shirley, John 84, 85
Siferth 97
size of manuscripts 2, 6, 34, 58, 64,
  75–80, 87, 88
Smith, Joshua Byron 147
Smith, Thomas 44
Smithfield Decretals 27
Smithsonian Digitization Program
  Labs 18
Solomon, King 8, 110, 121, 173, 175,
  176, 179–85, 188
Space X 31
Spinola Hours 41
Stacey, Robin Chapman 159
St Albans 46–47
Stanford 1–3, 9–11, 17, 18, 21, 23, 38,
  48, 190, 217, 218, 220–22
Stanford Ordinary People Extraordinary
  Stories project (SOPES) 2
Stanford Text Technologies 1, 3
Stanley, William 71
Stafford, Ralph 48

Steinhart, Eric 31
Stokes, Peter 3, 114, 115, 121, 176
Stokes, Whitley 155
St Paul's Cathedral 46, 75
Strayler, Alan 46, 47
Stubbs, Estelle 3, 13, 14, 47, 53
Svein Forkbeard 125

TEI (Text Encoding Initiative) 10
Theodore, Archbishop of Tarsus 44, 45,
  96, 101–6, 109, 142, 149
Thiel, Peter, and Tesla 31
Thomas, Carla M. 5, 8, 142
Thompson, Andrew 10
Thrift, Nigel 121
Titivillus 27, 28
Tolkien, J. R. R. 147
Treharne, Elaine 65, 115, 119,
  126, 209
Tremulous Hand of Worcester 106, 107,
  113, 114, 118
Trinity College, Cambridge 1
Troilus and Criseyde (by Chaucer) 58,
  82–84, 88

underlining 35, 145

Vanderkuil, Wayne 20
Vatican Library 49
Vines, Amy 83
Virgil 146, 156, 159
VisColl 6, 67, 68, 70, 72

Wærferth 112–114
Wace 164
Wade, Erik 188
Wakelin, Daniel 58, 60, 63
Walbers, Birte 100
Wales 45, 49, 50, 141, 133, 138, 147,
  154–59, 164, 167, 205
Walsingham, Thomas 46, 48
Walter, Archbishop Hubert 46
Walters Art Gallery 1
Wanley, Humfrey 74
Watson, Nicholas 163
Weiler, Bjorn 131, 133
Wendover, Roger 131
Wessex 77, 142
Westminster Abbey 47
Westminster Chronicle 47, 48, 53
Wheloc, Abraham 121
Wilkins Reading Room 221–23
William of Malmesbury 138
Williams, Don 19

Wintershill, William 46
Wogan-Browne, Jocelyn 163
Worcester 57–60, 112–19, 176
Worcester, William 57–60, 113
Wordsworth, William 122

Wormald, Francis 94
Wormald, C. Patrick 77
Wytlum, William 46

Zotero.org 225